D1730057

Avgouleas/Marjosola (Eds.)
Digital Finance in Europe: Law, Regulation, and Governance
ECFR Special Volume 5

European Company and Financial Law Review

Ondernemingsrecht
RdS
Rev. prat. soc.
Rev. Sociétés
Riv. Società
SZW
ZGR

———

Edited by
Pierre-Henri Conac, Holger Fleischer, Jesper Lau Hansen, Maarten J. Kroeze, Hanno Merkt, Andres Recalde Castells, Edmund Schuster, Christoph Teichmann, Marco Ventoruzzo, Marieke Wyckaert

Special Volume 5

Digital Finance in Europe: Law, Regulation, and Governance

Edited by
Emilios Avgouleas and Heikki Marjosola

DE GRUYTER

Volume Editors:
Professor *Emilios Avgouleas*, Chair in International Banking Law and Finance, University of Edinburgh
Dr. *Heikki Marjosola*, University of Helsinki

ISBN 978-3-11-074941-0
e-ISBN (PDF) 978-3-11-074947-2
e-ISBN (EPUB) 978-3-11-074951-9
DOI https://doi.org/10.1515/9783110749472

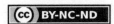

This work is licensed under the Creative Commons Attribution-NonCommercial-NoDerivatives 4.0 International License. For details go to https://creativecommons.org/licenses/by-nc-nd/4.0/.

Library of Congress Control Number: 2021946984

Bibliographic information published by the Deutsche Nationalbibliothek
The Deutsche Nationalbibliothek lists this publication in the Deutsche Nationalbibliografie; detailed bibliographic data are available on the Internet at http://dnb.dnb.de.

© 2022 with the authors, editing © 2022 Heikki Marjosola and Emilios Avgouleas, published by Walter de Gruyter GmbH, Berlin/Boston
The book is published open access at www.degruyter.com.

Printing and binding: CPI books GmbH, Leck

www.degruyter.com

Editorial

Global finance is in the middle of a radical transformation fuelled by innovative financial technologies exploiting big data, cryptography, artificial intelligence (AI) and machine learning, as well as new data sharing and distribution models. The transformation is affecting the entire financial value chain from capital raising and credit creation to payments and supply of financial services. Aided by an unusual macroeconomic environment manifested in ever-rising asset prices, unprecedented fiscal measures, and floor-breaking interest rates, the adoption of new technologies has gathered pace in the course of the Covid-19 pandemic. For example, just in a single week at the beginning of the pandemic the use of financial applications in Europe increased by more than 70%.[1] While it is too early to tell whether the rallying cryptocurrency markets or meme stock debacles represent extreme signs of hubris or more fundamental structural changes in financial markets, some signs are clear. The emerging generation of digitally savvy retail investors is not only freer of home-country bias – the classic predicament of the European „single financial market" – but are also less likely to accumulate their savings on sticky bank accounts. Beyond retail markets, institutional interest and adoption of digital assets is also growing and more crypto firms and infrastructures are being licensed to offer financial services, which further blurs the boundaries between the crypto economy and traditional finance.

The post-Brexit EU, deprived of its global financial centre, cannot afford to ignore the rising tide of digital finance. The Union is struggling to keep pace with global innovation hubs, particularly when it comes to experimenting with new digital forms of capital raising.[2] There is emerging consensus that the digital transformation of the EU single financial market requires brave and radical action that goes beyond isolated measures such as the 2nd Payment Services Directive[3] that heralded the era of Open Banking and the 4th Anti-Money Laundering Directive.[4] Moreover, following a decade of centralisation and building of a single rulebook for the EU financial markets, the Member States have little other choice than to wait for the Commission's initiative.

---

1 European Commission, Factsheet: A digital finance strategy for Europe, September 2020
2 *PWC*, 6thICO / STO Report, A Strategic Perspective, Spring 2020 edition (PWC Report).
3 Directive (EU) 2015/2366 of 25 November 2015 on payment services.
4 Directive 2018/843 of the European Parliament and Council of 30 May 2018 amending the Anti-Money Laundering Directive (EU) 2015/849.

ə OpenAccess. © 2022 Emilios Avgouleas and Heikki Marjosola, published by De Gruyter.
(cc) BY-NC-ND This work is licensed under the Creative Commons Attribution-NonCommercial-NoDerivatives 4.0 International License. https://doi.org/10.1515/9783110749472-001

The EU's strategic response has taken shape gradually alongside the EU's New Industrial Strategy,[5] which places digital finance at the centre of the mix of initiatives and policies aiming to achieve a more sustainable and competitive European economy. Finally, in September 2020 the Commission released a Digital Finance Package, which includes legislative proposals for a comprehensive legal framework for crypto-assets and market infrastructures based on distributed ledger technology (DLT). The proposals were joined with a revised Capital Markets Union strategy[6] and a new Digital Finance Strategy.[7]

The more advanced elements of the digitalization of finance such as the DLT, AI, and quantum computing technology as well as the rise of decentralised finance (DeFI) are setting the stage for a global battle of business models and philosophies, the outcome and consequences of which are unpredictable. Calibrating the EU digital finance strategy is therefore a balancing act that requires a deep understanding of the factors driving the transformation, be they legal, cultural, political or economic. This is challenging because the drivers are neither coherent nor do they all point to the same direction; some drivers promote decentralisation and increase competition, while others indicate that the future of finance might belong to few powerful firms and platforms. Similarly, while the transition to digital online finance may empower retail investors at a global scale and facilitate access to financial services, it also makes it more difficult to protect consumers and investors who are exposed to new channels of fraudulent or abusive conduct and risks that few understand. The same FinTech inventions that use AI, machine learning and big data to facilitate access to credit may also erect invisible barriers that further gender, social, racial and religious exclusion. The way such actors source, use and record data also presents countless data protection concerns.[8]

The joint organisers and co-editors of this special issue have collected a mix of established and promising law and finance scholars to scrutinise the challenges of digital finance from multiple public policy perspectives. First presented and discussed at a web-based conference 'Digital Capital Markets in Europe: The

---

5 Communication from the Commission, A New Industrial Strategy for Europe, 10 March 2020, COM/2020/102 final.

6 Communication from the Commission, A Capital Markets Union for people and businesses-new action plan, Brussels, 24.9.2020 COM(2020) 590 final

7 Communication from the Commission, a Digital Finance Strategy for EU, 24 September 2020, COM(2020) 591

8 European Commission, White Paper on Artificial Intelligence – A European approach to excellence and trust, COM(2020) 65 final; Communication from the Commission, Shaping Europe's Digital Future, COM(2020) 67 final.

Challenge of EU Market Integration' organised by the University of Helsinki Faculty of Law and the Edinburgh Law School in September 2020, the articles provide constructive and solutions-oriented analysis based on solid and up-to-date research.

The first three articles deal with the challenges of FinTech-enabled market transformation for the EU capital markets law, identifying several weaknesses in the existing as well as proposed legislation. The article by *Avgouleas* and *Seretakis* assesses the disruption of the financial services digital value chain by two radically opposing forces: oligopolistic market concentration based on platform finance operated by dominant global financial institutions and BigTech, on one hand; and the radical democratisation of investment markets brought about by open source DeFi protocols, on the other. Welcoming the Commission's digital finance package as a necessary first step, they argue that the package nevertheless reinforces the first trend while it underestimates the potential benefits of the latter. Therefore, Avgouleas and Seretakis suggest that the proposed DLT pilot regime should be widened to include also DeFi platforms, which are currently incompatible with the MiFiD II's complex web of rules. They offer a number of possible solutions to the integration of DeFi under the umbrella of EU EU financial services law. The article by *Macchiavello* and *Sciarrone Alibrandi* investigates marketplace lending, a more established but dynamically evolving market segment which raises important challenges. Based on careful unpacking of the dominant business models they argue that these platforms involve novel technological and other features which should be addressed by tailor-made legislation. At the same time, they identify a number of failures in the recently completed EU Regulation on European Crowdfunding Services Providers (ECSP). While effectively enhancing the protection of unsophisticated investors, they note that the Regulation failed to introduce flexible and functional rules for Europe's evolving crowdfunding ecosystem. Instead, they argue that the ECSP Regulation, and the extensive level 2 technical rules that followed it, establish an unnecessarily detailed and rigid regulatory framework that only applies to a limited number of services and products. As a result, the ECSP regulation could have a suffocating effect on this nascent financial industry in Europe, possibly transforming the lending/investment platforms from relatively neutral tech platforms into more traditional investment firms. The third article by *Giudici* and *Ferrarini* presents a critical view on the proposed Regulation on Markets in Crypto-Assets (MiCA). They argue that the proposal simply mirrors existing regulatory philosophy by imposing mandatory disclosure requirements on all issuers of crypto-assets, while ignoring alternative mechanisms based on market discipline and private enforcement. To facilitate new forms of capital raising and to avoid suffocating market innovation, they call for a more experimental regime that would offer a categorical exemption from EU disclosure rules to blockchain startups.

The regulation of new technologies in capital markets is not easy and interventions are often dictated by a crisis-induced precaution and haste. As *Gerner-Beuerle's* article shows, such efforts may turn out to be ineffective and have unintended consequences. The article shows that current regulations targeted at algorithmic and high-frequency trading stand on a particularly weak theoretical and empirical ground. The paper undertakes a comprehensive and critical review of the current regulatory tools concerning algorithmic and high frequency trading, arguing that there is little empirical support for most measures (especially so-called circuit-breakers). Gerner-Beuerle suggests that EU securities regulation should be better informed by market microstructure theory, e. g., as regards the mechanics of price formation, and tread with caution in areas where regulatory understanding remains incomplete.

The next two articles adopt a broader public policy perspective considering issues such as fairness and sustainability in the provision of digital financial services. Read together they offer a thorough exposition of the trade-offs and often intractable dilemmas raised by digital finance. The article by *Langenbucher* and *Corcoran* assesses how FinTech companies that embrace alternative credit scoring models based on AI fit into existing consumer lending, data protection and anti-discrimination regulations in the U.S. and EU and how these regulations need to be adjusted. The article adopts a case study approach, focusing particularly on a U.S. company Upstart.com and its AI-based credit scoring model as well as the no-action letter granted to the company by the U.S. Consumer Financial Protection Bureau. Identifying a number of risks and problems, the article demonstrates with clarity how machine learning algorithms deriving complex correlations from large data pools might give rise to indirect and hard-to-detect discriminatory practices. *Chiu's* contribution investigates the existing and missing links between sustainable and digital finance. She argues that the present policy initiatives are under-ambitious and incomplete particularly when it comes to the retail market. Sustainability criteria should be better integrated into the suitability assessments conducted under the MiFID II's investment advice regime. Looking further afield, she suggests adjusting the investment advice regime with a view to co-opting digital platforms and robo-advice channels to marketize indexes comprising sustainably-labelled financial products.

The final two articles by *Kulms* and *Marjosola* investigate the private law dimension of the EU digital capital markets from different angles. Kulms' article offers a broad perspective on the dynamic interface between FinTech regulation and private law using as test cases the law and regulation of five market segments: payment services, outsourcing of business models, crowdlending, robo-advice, and blockchain applications. Kulms posits that the Commission's digital finance strategy presents a tacit appeal to Member States to develop gap-filling private law remedies and thus trigger competition between national private legal orders. Highlighting several shortcomings of this approach, particularly in the areas of legal liability and data protection law, the article anticipates more centralised regulatory solutions. Finally, Kulms assesses the potential of regulatory sandboxes to operate as early warning mechanisms in identifying areas where the relationship between financial regulation, commodification of data and private law needs to be recalibrated. Marjosola's article assesses the EU Digital Finance Package from the perspective of token holders' proprietary rights and EU securities law. Marjosola welcomes the innovative and decentralised sandbox approach of the DLT Pilot Regime, which aims to encourage experimentation within the single financial market. Nonetheless, the article argues that the complete lack of private law harmonisation would magnify the unresolved legal risks of intermediated securities and further fragment the private law underpinnings of the EU capital market. The onset of security tokens and DTL-based holding systems necessitate a rethink of the scope of the EU's stagnated securities law harmonisation project. The new harmonisation agenda should, according to Marjosola, focus more clearly on transparent or disintermediated holding systems, which have been largely ignored, but also re-examine the current conflict of laws *acquis* regarding intermediated securities.

Table of Contents

Emilios Avgouleas and Alexandros Seretakis
Governing the Digital Finance Value-Chain in the EU: MIFID II, the Digital Package, and the Large Gaps between!

Abstract: The emergence of the complete digitization of the financial services value chain has gathered pace due to the advent of the Covid-19 pandemic. It is mainly premised on automation of the investment process through the use of algorithmic tools and remote delivery of services via integrated platforms and apps. During the same period, we have witnessed the emergence of decentralised finance, cryptocurrencies aside, and the increased use of blockchain technology. Together these developments promise radical changes in market structure and microstructure. The digitization of the finance value chain could cause respectively more market concentration or conversely radical democratisation of investment markets. For this reason, the choices of policy-makers will be of cardinal importance. At the same time, digitisation is the best opportunity so far to create a fully integrated EU market for new listings and secondary trading in securities, and to further SME access to finance, thus making reality the vision of an EU Capital Markets Union. While these developments raise critical challenges for EU policy-makers in the post-Brexit era, the regulatory landscape in the EU is still dominated by the older MIFID II approach to market regulation. Reform attempts seem over-cautious and unwilling to unleash the powerful forces of technology and innovation to avoid upsetting settled industry practices (and incumbent oligopolies). EU Regulation has to become more proactive fostering regulatory experimentation in tandem with technological one to make sure that consumers interests are safeguarded, competition is furthered, and essential finance infrastructure is not dominated by a tight rent-seeking oligopoly. Therefore, the EU Digital Finance package in its present form is a welcome yet timid step forward. A number of further reforms are required to accelerate the pace of regulatory adaptation to the challenges and opportunities of the new digital era for European markets strengthening post-Covid 19 economic recovery.

Emilios Avgouleas, Chair in International Banking Law and Finance, University of Edinburgh; Vis. Professor, School of European Political Economy, Luiss Guido Carli.
Alexandros Seretakis, LL.M (UCL, NYU), Assistant Professor of Law (Capital Markets/Financial Services), Trinity College Dublin. We are very grateful for constructive comments to Dr Heikki Marjosola, the co-editor of this special issue, and the participants of the joint Edinburgh-Helsinki webinar on Digital Finance in Europe.

∂ OpenAccess. © 2022 Emilios Avgouleas and Alexandros Seretakis, published by De Gruyter. (cc) BY-NC-ND This work is licensed under the Creative Commons Attribution-NonCommercial-NoDerivatives 4.0 International License. https://doi.org/10.1515/9783110749472-002

Keywords: MiFID II, Decentralised Finance, Platform Finance, MiCA, EU Digital package, Robo-advisors

Table of Contents

1 Introduction

For some time now the value chain[1] in financial services is being disrupted and reconfigured due to outside developments such as restrictive regulation, the evolution of information communications technology (ICT) and financial innovation in the form of development of new products.[2] Moreover, ICT and tolerant regulators have allowed financial services firms to disaggregate the financial services value chain into front, middle, and back offices. Back-office functions ranging from client on-boarding to transaction processing/verification and storage of cli-

---

1 Value chain analysis is a business management concept which was first coined by Michael Porter in his famous 1985 book *Competitive Advantage*. It is a process view of business organisations and is used to explain the organizations as a system comprising different sub-systems each with inputs, transformation processes, and outputs involved in the acquisition and consumption of resources (money, labour, raw or processed materials, stock of capital assets such as land and building) business management and administration. Value chain theory has had a profound influence on the management of the modern corporation, since it explains how the different types of relationships or 'linkages' within or outside a firm can be managed, leveraged, or commodified to create value to make a firm more competitive/profitable than its peers. See *Michael E. Porter*, Competitive Advantage: Creating and Sustaining Superior Performance, 1985.
2 PWC, Financial Services Technology 2020 and Beyond: Embracing disruption https://www.pwc.com/gx/en/financial-services/assets/pdf/technology2020-and-beyond.pdf (last accessed 29 January 2021).

ent data are often outsourced on the basis of contract to maximise savings through the use of highly specialised firms that offer infrastructure services.

This was more or less the model of internal business and industry-wide organisation in the global financial services sector for the past 30 years. But with the widespread use of technologies supporting automation such as Artificial Intelligence (AI) and Machine Learning, the infinite expansion of cloud storage, and the emerging popularity of Distributed Ledger technology (DLT), the finance value chain is now increasingly and irreversibly disrupted. Furthermore, the period post-covid 19 is the first that product development, market infrastructure, service supply and trade execution is moving towards a complete digital value chain.

There are five areas where financial technology has already had or is bound to have an appreciable impact: retail banking infrastructure, payments, capital markets infrastructure, investment advice and asset management. As regards retail banking and payments, both outside the scope of this article, transformation has come through the advent of open banking (data sharing to facilitate banking transactions)[3] and in payments where, cryptocurrencies aside, we see a plethora of new instruments under development. Similarly, the field of investment advice and, to some extent, asset management have undergone radical transformation mostly via the development of algorithmic devices that can ascertain customer's investment preferences including risk tolerance and return goals and accordingly recommend specific investment or generalized asset allocation strategies.

It is, thus, not surprising that the transformation of the marketplace and of the finance value chain is manifested today through two radically opposing models of financial services infrastructure integration. The first, is represented by the increasing domination of the financial services infrastructure by very large institutions like the American investment Black Rock that operates the infrastructure service Aladdin[4] and the Chinese powerhouse Ant Financial[5]. Furthermore, the

---

3 Directive (EU) 2015/2366/EU on payment services in the internal market (PSD II). Open banking refers to a banking system where third-party financial service providers are given secure access to financial data through APIs. This enables the networking of accounts and data between banks and non-bank financial institutions. Essentially, it allows new types of products and services within the traditional financial system. DeFi, however, proposes a new financial system that is independent of the current infrastructure. DeFi is sometimes also referred to as open finance.
4 See https://www.blackrock.com/aladdin
5 Ant Financial is an affiliate of Alibaba Group and before the recent pulling off of its floatation it was widely lauded as the world's biggest IPO. As early as 2018 Ant exceed in terms of valuation that of Goldman Sachs by 50 % ($150 billion, compared to Goldman Sachs' $99 billion). The key to Ant's growth lies in its platform business model which starts with payments, the Alipay service, and ends with offerings of money market funds. Ryan McMorrow, Nian Liu and Sherry

widely expected entry into the market for wholesale and retail financial services of Google, Facebook and other big technology companies, so-called Big Tech, will lead to further centralization of financial markets infrastructure due to network effect,[6] since the new technology sector shows a tendency to foster the domination of the market by a very small number of large firms.[7]

The second is represented by the strong emergence of DeFi even if for now it is operating in the alternative finance space and is mostly fueled by peer-to-peer lending or financial contracting that uses cryptocurrencies as collateral.[8] Besides, trade finance and other business and commercial banking activities (e. g., payments processing) are increasingly moving to a decentralised model that is, in fact, championed by big financial institutions.[9] The weak profitability of fintech start-ups may act as an accelerator for the adoption of the DeFI model. For example, it is only a matter of time for fintech firms that operate on very thin margins and are threatened with extinction once they have burn their seed cash to forge cooperate and compete relationships marketing and selling their products on decentralized platforms.[10] Moreover, the emergence of Decentralised Finance (DeFi) employing blockchain protocols is the first step towards a market infrastructure leap that will merge financial contract trading and trade settlement and possibly at a later stage investment advice and order execution which are today independent market functions/services.

Each of these developments in the financial services digital value chain presents a distinct challenge for financial regulation. The centerpiece of European

---

Fei Ju, "The Transformation of Ant Financial", FT.com, 26 August 2020, https://www.ft.com/content/c636a22e-dd3f-403e-a72d-c3ffb375459c (last accessed 30 January 2021). For more detailed analysis of the Ant Financial business model see section II.

6 The FT reports on Biden Administration's new SEC chairman: "That background will make him even more useful as a regulator at a time when the largest tech platform companies – from Google and Facebook to Amazon and Apple – are moving into the financial industry." Rana Foroohar, "Wall Street's Sheriff is on a Mission", FT.com 17 Jan. 2021, https://www.ft.com/content/7884afc4-6e8c-4b2f-910e-adff489f12b6 (last accessed 29 January 2021).

7 See *Eleanor Fox/Harry First*, "We Need Rules to Rein in Big Tech", NYU Law and Economics Research Paper No. 20–46 2020, 2–3.

8 Consensys, "Q3 Ethereum DeFi Report", available at https://consensys.net/insights/q3-defi-report/ (last accessed 29 January 2021).

9 M. Huillet, "HSBC: Blockchain Platform Will Keep Trade Finance Smooth Despite Coronavirus", 5 March 2020, CoinTelegraph.com, https://cointelegraph.com/news/was-2020-a-defi-year-and-what-is-expected-from-the-sector-in-2021-experts-answer (last accessed 29 January 2021).

10 See *Emilos Avgouleas/Aggelos Kiayias*, "The Architecture of Decentralized Finance Platforms: A New Open Finance Paradigm", Edinburgh School of Law Research Paper No. 2020/16, 2020.

legislation dealing with financial markets is the so-called MiFID II regime.[11] MiFID II, which replaced the original MiFID regime adopted in 2004 came into effect in the aftermath of the financial crisis.[12] MiFID II seeks to enhance investor protection and promote efficiency and transparency in financial markets. MiFID II focuses on both the micro-and-macro level.[13] On the micro-level, MiFID II at aims to reduce transaction costs reducing transaction costs and promote the liquidity of markets. On the macro-level, it seeks to tackle systemic risk and allow regulators to better monitor and supervise financial markets. But it is a complex piece of legislation that is not fit for the new digital era. Moreover, automation is already expanding into compliance with the regulatory framework through a number of applications, so-called RegTech,[14] that can be used from monitoring and tracing of illicit money flows to detection of "fake" information.

As the way value chain activities are carried out (e.g., manually or automated) determines costs and impacts on profits, the different paths of digitization of the finance value chain have profound implications both for market structure, namely the number of players competing in the market and their market share and market microstructure. The latter refers to market mechanics, including the process and outcomes of exchanging assets under explicit trading rules.[15]

A good example of the size of the challenge is presented by BlackRock/Aladdin type of infrastructure providers. While each of the services they supply is probably distinctly regulated and subject to different contractual arrangements between the supplier and the user firms, it is hard to understand in terms of internal systems' set up and configuration where the unbundling starts or ends. They are, in practice, one stop-shop platforms cosmetically divided in terms of internal systems configuration and business organisation in different segments in order to appear compliant with financial services regulation. An even bigger issue is what happens to all the data that goes through the system. Even with the highest data filters and controls in place the fact remains that colossal

---

11 The MiFID II regime comprises of Directive 2014/65/EU on Markets in Financial Instruments (MiFID II) and the Regulation (EU) No 600/2014 on Markets in Financial Instruments.

12 See generally, *Danny Busch/Guido Ferrarini* (ed.), Regulation of the EU Financial Markets: MIFID II and MIFIR, 2017.

13 *Guido Ferrarini/Paolo Saguato*, "Reforming Securities and Derivatives Trading in the EU: from EMIR to MIFIR", Journal of Corporate Law Studies 2013, 324–325.

14 *Eva Micheler/Anna Whaley*, "Regulatory Technology: Replacing Law with Computer Code", European Business Organization Law Review 2020, 349.

15 Thus, market microstructure studies, a branch of finance theory, concentrate on "how specific trading mechanisms [such as the order book, continuous auctions, the dealer market impact on market conditions, e.g., liquidity and] affect the price formation process." *Maureen O'Hara*, Market Microstructure Theory, 1995.

amounts of financial data are daily concentrated into the privately operated systems of one infrastructure provider.

None of this is a new problem. Broker-dealers faced in the past the issue of controls of information flows between human agents and management of conflicts of interest within the same business, first, with regards to client advice and portfolio management and the impact on it of own corporate finance advisory function and related transactions, and, secondly, with regards to interactions between client order execution and management of the proprietary order book. These concerns informed the prohibition of front-running in the first EU Market Abuse Directive, now expanded in its successor regime introduced by the Market Abuse Regulation (MAR).[16] The same applies to the expansion of the Conduct of Business (COB) and conflict of interests regime of MiFID I.[17] The few general principles contained in Investment Services Directive (ISD)[18] for the purpose of regulating investment conduct[19] were replaced with a detailed rulebook, which was further expanded in MiFID II and extended to include rules on product governance[20] to broaden customer protection. But today as data circulation processing is automated it can prove futile to just suggest ever more detailed and complex regulation when technology itself might, in fact, provide the desirable checks, controls, and remedies.

DeFi platforms also present challenges for the existing regulatory framework. It is hard to see how the different functions of such platforms can be disaggregated to be regulated as distinct investment services. For example, mining a new token via the platform, storing it in an individual digital wallet and using the wallet to trade on the platform, entrusting platform apps with asset alloca-

---

16 Regulation (EU) No 596/2014 on market abuse (market abuse regulation) OJ L 173/2014, 1–61, Art. 7(1). Articles 21 to 30 MiFID II as well as Article 24 MiFIR also apply to front running behaviour. They include the obligation for investment firms to act honestly, fairly and professionally and in a manner that promotes the integrity of the market (Article 24 of MiFIR), to act in accordance with the best interests of their clients (Article 24 MiFID II), to execute orders on terms most favourable to the clients (Article 27 MiFID II the client order handling rules (Article 28 MiFID II) and the obligation to identify and prevent or manage conflicts of interest (Article 23 MiFID II).

17 Directive 2004/39/EC on markets in financial instruments (MiFID I), Ch. II (Operating Conditions for Investment Firms).

18 Directive 93/22/EEC on investment services in the securities field OJ L 141/1993, 27–46, Art. 11.

19 The high-level approach was leaving very serious gaps for rule conflict in the internal market and led to an increase rather than decrease in transaction costs. See *Emilios Avgouleas*, "The Harmonisation of Rules of Conduct in EU Financial Markets: Economic Analysis, Subsidiarity and Investor Protection" 6 European Law Journal 72–92 (2000).

20 Articles 16(3) and 24(2) MiFID II.

tion advice and carrying execution function can create a real conundrum for the regulatory framework given also the fact that all the above activities might take place real time in an automated mode. How to unbundle a token that incorporates the service and the investment at the same time? Is the platform collectively a provider of financial services? Is a counterparty that is active in the in the platform on a regular basis a professional (albeit unregulated) investor? Or if the trade is continuous, is the counterparty a provider of an (unregulated) investment service in the same way that broker-dealers might act as MiFID II regulated systematic internalisers?[21]

Of course, most of today's DeFi activity is outside the regulatory perimeter (see Section II below), but this is a situation that is no longer tenable. Thus, the EU commission has recently proposed a digital finance package that aims to foster Europe's competitiveness and innovation in the financial sector.[22] The package includes a Digital Finance strategy, a Retail Payments Strategy, legislative proposals on crypto-assets and digital operational resilience and a pilot regime for market infrastructures powered by distributed ledger technology.[23] But the Digital Package that is still under consideration is only the beginning. EU financial services regulation will soon require a wholesale overhaul in order to keep pace with the digital transformation of the financial value chain both within the EU and globally.

This article will provide a critical evaluation of the EU financial services regime focusing on MiFID II and the EU Commission's Digital Finance Package. It highlights the gaps that have emerged in the oversight and regulation of the digital value chain in financial services. It will also explain the opportunities DeFi presents for achieving the key goals of the Capital Markets Union blueprint[24] such as EU retail market integration, SMEs access to finance, and democratization of investment markets, provided that key parts of DeFi are brought under the regulatory umbrella. For that to happen EU financial regulation must strike the right balance between the idiosyncrasies of DeFi and a rigid financial services

---

21 Article 4(1)(20) of MiFID II.

22 European Commission Press Release, Digital Finance Package: Commission sets out new, ambitious approach to encourage responsible innovation to benefit consumers and businesses, Brussels 24 September 2020.

23 Proposal for a Regulation on a pilot regime for market infrastructures based on distributed ledger technology. Distributed ledger Technology (DLT) is a secure database or ledger that is replicated across multiple sites, countries, or institutions with no centralized controller. The shared ledger keeps track of asset ownership and any recent iterations, automating asset transfers and storage on the chain and attendant records.

24 For the revamped blueprint of September 2020 see EU Commission Communication, A Capital Markets Union for people and businesses – new action plan COM/2020/590 final.

regime which, in its pursuit of a high level of investor protection, has also enabled incumbent operators to reap substantial rents through oligopolistic structures which have been solidified by regulation. And in this respect the proposed Digital Finance package is open to criticism. It ignores important aspects of the DeFi business model such as automated trading and execution through smart contracts that eliminates the need for intermediaries in the custodial chain. Then, it shows a total unwillingness to consider regulatory models that could integrate the most challenging aspects of DeFi such as permissionless access to trading and anonymous transacting (see Section II.2).

The article is organized in four sections with the present introduction. Section II offers an analytical view of the change digitization brings to the financial services value chain and the opportunities and risks that it poses. In this context it discusses in depth the platform-based business model in financial services and how this has created two entirely opposite trends, on the one hand, centralization / clusterisation of market/business functions and customer and data networks and, on the other, the largely unregulated model of decentralization. Section III explains the how these changes challenge MiFID II as the centerpiece of EU financial services legislation. It also considers the impact of the EU Commission proposals for a digital finance package. Section IV offers a few directions for reform including the widening of the EU pilot regime and brings the different stands of the present discussion to a comprehensive conclusion.

2 The Digitization of the Financial Services Value-Chain: Opportunities and Risks

When analyzing the effectiveness of a value chain model, Michael Porter introduced 10 cost drivers that help identify areas for improvement.[25] According to Porter risk management, research and development, human resources and

---

25 These are: (1) *Economies of Scale* identified via cost analysis for the size of the demand, (2) *Learning*, which refers to activities that change the environment for efficiency or improvement, (3) *Capacity Utilization*, which refers to procedures that keep capacity at efficient levels to prevent under-utilization or the addition of unnecessary capacity, (4) *Linkages among Activities*, which involves identification of areas of cross-functional improvement through coordination and optimization, (5) *Interrelationships among Business Units*, which refers to opportunities to share information and resources, (6) *Degree of Vertical Integration*, (7) *Timing of Market Entry* which may be riven by economic or world conditions and competitive position in the marketplace, (8) *Firm Policy of Cost or Differentiation*, (9) *Geographic Location*, and (10) *Institutional Factors* such as taxes, unions, and regulations. *Porter* (fn. 1), Ch. 1.

firm infrastructure are among the key components of a firm's value chain. This is entirely true in the case of financial services providers and all these areas are disrupted or transformed by the advent of the complete digitization of the financial value chain. However, the form a business is organised itself to extract the highest efficiencies from its value chain to fulfil its business objectives is equally very important. The paragraphs below examine the two opposing forms of the platform model that in itself drives the digitization of the finance value chain, namely the centralised and the decentralised platform model. Arguably, each form of platform organisation can have profound implications for the MiFID II regulatory paradigm.

2.1 The Centralised Platform Model and Network Effects

The platform-based model is used to mean a business model[26] that creates and harnesses value by facilitating exchanges between two or more interdependent groups which lead the creation of large and scalable networks of users and resources that can be accessed on demand.[27] For instance, businesses like Facebook, Uber, or Alibaba claim that exchange facilitation and user matching – ownership of the means of connection – is their only business and they don't directly create and control inventory via a supply chain the way linear businesses do, namely, they do not own the means of production. Arguably, these businesses are today much more than that as they are the monopolistic providers of the new products they have created, with the market for Internet search listings and market advertising[28] being the principal example. Therefore, the platform-based business model in finance should be understood as an integrated model of busi-

---

26 Inter alia, *Karl Taeuscher/Sven M. Laudien*, "Understanding platform business models: A mixed methods study of marketplaces", European Management Journal 2018, 319 – 329.
27 In simpler terms it means a digital locus or a fixed digital meeting point, which users access to interact, share interests, and multiply their networks substituting in the process older markets or creating new ones whose success, in turn, depends on the length and density of the network (network economies of scale).
28 The United States Justice Department filed a lawsuit against Google on 20 October2020 accusing the company of abusing its position to maintain an illegal monopoly over search and search advertising. In specific, Google has been accused of locking up deals with giant partners like Apple to fend off competition through exclusive business contracts and agreements to make its search engine the default option for users. Such agreements accounted for most of its dominant market share in Internet search (a figure that the US Justice Department put at over 60 percent. See Complaint, U.S. Department of Justice v Goggle LLC, https://www.justice.gov/opa/press-release/file/1328941/download (last accessed on 31/01/2021).

ness organization and management of customers that repackages and commoditizes for commercial purpose both platform generated user activity and relationships and data generated in this process.

It would be anachronistic for today's policymakers to adhere to older understandings of platform based business models and not recognize two undisputable market realities. The first relates to the domination of relevant distribution channels/networks by specific platforms as is, for example, the case with Ant Financial. Ant operates a platform business model that combines the very popular service Alipay[29] with lending, insurance and investing with its linear micro-lending and micro-investing. Ant's hybrid approach has created a financial services ecosystem of unparalleled breadth. Ant claims that through Ant Fortune which offers a platform to China's 116 mutual fund managers and reaches 180 million users it has democratized asset management and retirement planning. In reality, the platform's algorithm recommends funds based on each user's financial profile and goals, thereby closing financial literacy gaps that in the past may have prevented many users from investing. Also, given its very large pool of users, financial service providers can't resist joining its network. In addition, Ant has leveraged the network to introduce new financial (and proprietary) products, like the very popular money market fund Yue Bao. [30] An account with Yue Bao can be opened for as little as 1 yuan ($0.15).[31]

The second relates to the ability of applications connected to the platform to harness through data searching tools vast amounts of information about user so-

---

29 Similar to Paypal, Alipay processes payments between any two users, whether they're shoppers and small businesses, roommates, or street performers and commuters. Alipay has over 700M active users and completed over $8 trillion in transactions in 2017 – that's equivalent to 65% of China's GDP. Tero Ojanpera, "5 Steps- How Ant Financial Built a 200 billion platform business", 19 August 2020, https://intelligentplatforms.ai/5-steps-how-ant-financial-built-a-200-billion-platform-business/ (last accessed on 31/01/2021).

30 Emilie Valentova, "Yu'E Bao turned 185M e-commerce customers into financial investors", Harvard Business School Blog, 19 October 2015, https://digital.hbs.edu/platform-digit/sub mission/yue-bao-turned-185m-e-commerce-customers-into-financial-investors/ (last accessed on 31/01/2021).

31 It should be noted that in a supreme example of the risks that lie ahead if the centralised platform model is allowed to dominate the market for digital financial services Yue Bao was able to use Alipay data to identify users who left a positive balance in their Alipay digital wallet. Any users with a balance would be contacted, educated on the benefits on a money market fund, and invited to open an account. In a market starved for consumer financial products, Ant's investment platforms were an instant hit. Ant Group, "How Alipay changed the way China invests and helped a fund grow 400+ times over", 2 April 2019, https://medium.com/ali pay-and-the-world/how-alipay-changed-the-way-china-invests-and-helped-a-fund-grow-400-times-over-9c13f77af4b6 (last accessed on 31/01/2021).

cial interests and socio-economic preferences, spending habits and spending power, political leniencies, conjectured disposable income, and so on. Thus, it is hard to believe that the Big Tech firms like Google and Facebook plan to enter the market for financial services markets without intending to exploit the aforementioned data tools, which alongside the existing user network would offer them a distinct advantage over other financial services providers. On the contrary, it is quite common to attribute the domination of Big Tech over their markets due to the size of the network and misuse of client data. [32] Accordingly, regulators will have a Herculean task in their hands to prevent Big Tech dominating the financial services infrastructure.

At the same time, the risks of manipulating users' understanding and preferences is ever present, especially in retail markets. Similar to all other markets the power of framing in dictating consumer choices in financial services remains undiminished. The same applies to other cognitive limitations of individual investors and lay financial services users due to bounded rationality and other cognitive biases.[33] Deep learning neural networks[34] steeped in a wealth of informa-

---

32 The network effects of Big Tech platforms are so great (everyone wants their friends on the same platform, suppliers want their buyers on the same platform, etc.) "that barriers to entry are very high, and even the most promising prospective entrants have trouble finding the critical mass of users necessary to enter. There are periods of competition for the market; thereafter the market may tip to one dominant firm. A critical element of this new platform economy is data. The platforms vacuum up huge amounts of data from users of the platforms, and use the data not only for efficiencies but also for exploitations and exclusions . . . The platforms take much more data than they need to service the platform's users. Often, they take data without asking . . . The platforms take and combine." *Fox/First* (fn. 9) 2–3.

33 See for analysis Emilios Avgouleas, "Cognitive Biases and Investor Protection Regulation an Evolutionary Approach", Working Paper 2016, https://papers.ssrn.com/sol3/papers.cfm?abstract_id=1133214 (last accessed 29 January 2021).

34 Deep Learning Neural Networks (DLNN) are a subset of AI science and are the backbone of learning algorithms. In specific, the Artificial Neural Networks (ANNs) are the basis for deep learning. ANNs mimic the human brain through a set of algorithms which at a basic level comprise four main components: inputs, weights, a bias or threshold, and an output. Due to the fact that they are programmed to act on a continuum they do not, however, possess important capabilities of human brain such as the power to pause and reflect between a number of possible options. At the same time, DLNNs are used to allow information systems to train themselves to process and learn from data, namely, unlike older generation ANNs, DLN systems are self-teaching, learning as they go by filtering information through multiple hidden layers, in a similar way to a human agent. Thus, they are very effective in identifying hidden synapses and meanings due to their ability to use atypical logic that does not search for causal outcomes. For full analysis see *Charu C. Aggarwal*, Neural Networks and Deep Learning – A Textbook, 2018, p. 4–20.

tion about users can easily detect what makes consumers "tick". Subsequently consumer choice can be manipulated through the use of the right algorithms.[35]

The automation of retail investment management (asset allocation) via so-called robo-advisors presents the biggest risk in this context. It is often said that the rise of robo-advisors relates to the fact that these systems bring the benefits of expert investing to the retail markets at very affordable rates.[36] While this assertion is very accurate three other developments that have made possible the rise of robo-advisors should not be overlooked. The first relates to the robot's ability to perceive, understand, plan and navigate in the real world. Better cognitive ability means robots can work autonomously in diverse, dynamic and complex environments.

Relating to the first breakthrough is also the increased ability of robots to exercise precise control and dexterity in understanding the environment and manipulating objects. Technological improvements in this area allow robots to discharge tasks of greater diversity of tasks and be employed in a greater number of use cases. Finally, via natural language processing programmes robots' ability to learn from and collaborate with humans is greatly enhanced and even goes beyond verbal communications. Namely, the enhanced ability of robots to engage in verbal and non-verbal communication makes robots increasingly capable of working alongside human agents.

In the future, it will be very difficult to detect if the machine learning algorithm that powers the robo-advisor has not identified areas where human choice can be "legally" manipulated, by, for instance, restricting the number of recommended investments. Unless operating in a decentralized environment where this data could be stored in a cryptographic hash and be easily traced afterwards, *the ex post* use of explainability[37] techniques may not suffice to detect ir-

---

35 Natural language processing (NLP) is a branch of AI that helps computers understand, interpret and manipulate human language. NLP draws from many disciplines, including computer science and computational linguistics, in its pursuit to fill the gap between human communication and computer understanding. See Dr. Dataman, "Looking into Natural Language Processing (NLP)", 1 Nov. 2018, https://towardsdatascience.com/natural-language-processing-nlp-for-electronic-health-record-ehr-part-i-4cb1d4c2f24b (last accessed 29 January 2021).

36 *Benjamin P. Edwards*, "The Rise of Automated Investment Advice: Can Robo-Advisors Rescue the Retail Market?", Chicago-Kent Law Review 97 (2018), 106 – 108.

37 The OECD AI principles provide that AI actors must provide meaningful information, appropriate to the context, and consistent with the state of art: to foster a general understanding of AI systems . . . to enable those affected by an AI system to understand the outcome, and, to enable those adversely affected by an AI system to challenge its outcome based on plain and easy-to-understand information on the factors, and the logic that served as the basis for the prediction, recommendation or decision. OECD, "Recommendation of the Council on Artificial Intelligence"

regular and ad hoc instances of manipulation of user decisions via restricted choice as opposed to systematic algorithmic bias.[38] Auditing the entire robo-output at all times for sporadic bias is a task that goes beyond the capabilities of even advanced techniques used to interpret black-box behaviour.

2.2 Decentralised Finance: Can It Unbundle the Network Effect?

DeFi refers to an ecosystem of financial applications that are built on top of blockchain networks. As this is a generic definition, the term will be used in this article to specifically mean the movement that aims to create an open-source and transparent financial service ecosystem that operates without any central authority. DeFi platforms may be permission-based or permissionless with the latter being much more popular than the former. The users maintain full control over their assets and interact with this ecosystem through peer-to-peer (P2P), decentralized applications (Dapps). DeFi applications do not need any intermediaries or arbitrators. The code specifies the resolution of disputes that can be predicted in advance. Essentially, the Code is law among users and thus in the context of blockchain platforms it has been given the name *Lex Cryptographia*.[39]

2019, https://legalinstruments.oecd.org/en/instruments/OECD-LEGAL-0449 (last accessed 29 January 2021). Also, G20 Ministerial Statement on Trade and Digital Economy, https://g20trade-digital.go.jp/dl/Ministerial_Statement_on_Trade_and_Digital_Economy.pdf (last accessed 29 January 2021). A similar principle has been proposed by the EU High Level Group on AI. "AI systems and their decisions should be explained in a manner adapted to the stakeholder concerned. Humans need to be aware that they are interacting with an AI system, and must be informed of the system's capabilities and limitations". See EU high Level Group on AI, "Ethics Guidelines for Trustworthy AI" 2019, https://ec.europa.eu/digital-single- market/en/news/ethics-guidelines-trustworthy-ai (last accessed 29 January 2021).

38 There are broadly speaking two different groups of explainable AI techniques in development: AI methods that are inherently interpretable, "meaning the complexity or design of the system is restricted in order to allow a human user to understand how it works" and methods that deal with the more complex and challenging issue of how the 'black box' system works. The latter may involve a re-run of the initial model with some inputs changed to provide information about the importance of different input features. See Royal Society, "Explainable AI", Policy Briefing, November 2019, p. 11, https://royalsociety.org/-/media/policy/projects/explainable-ai/AI-and-interpretability-policy-briefing.pdf (last accessed 29 January 2021).

39 See generally *Primavera De Filippi/Aron Wright*, Blockchain and the Law – The Rule of Code, 2018 and *Georgios Dimitropoulos*, "The Law of Blockchain", Washington Law Review 111 (2020).

Whereas the mainstream financial system runs on centralized infrastructures managed by regulated, in the main, institutions, and intermediaries, decentralized finance is powered by code, runs on the decentralized infrastructure of the Ethereum blockchain or other blockchain models, where users are free to deploy immutable smart contracts. In addition, as the modular framework on which DeFi is built upon interoperable DeFi applications on public blockchains, users are able to design and operate entirely new financial markets, products, and services.[40] The configuration of DeFi inevitably leads to paradigm shifts in financial infrastructure and in the investment value chain. Simply put DeFi distributes risk, trust, and opportunity in an entirely different way, given the nearly total absence of intermediaries. But this does not mean elimination of all risk. On the contrary, in some cases risk becomes greater and risk distribution less predictable than in mainstream finance markets.

Since the eruption of the Covid-19 pandemic DeFi has experienced explosive growth that was more due to the fact that a new speculation avenue has opened up and less to the explosion of the price of key cryptocurrencies such as bitcoin and Ethereum.[41] Nonetheless, this explosion of speculative activity is also leading to a constant upgrade of the DeFi infrastructure.[42] It is reasonable to expect that DeFi platforms will soon emerge as a clear alternative to the centralised platform model.

Big financial institutions are already pioneering decentralised trade finance platforms where activity is taking place in a permissioned environment and within the framework of regulated institutions.[43] It is suggested that large financial

---

40 Because DeFi financial services and products are deployed on top of blockchains, single points of failure are eliminated. The data is recorded on the blockchain and spread across thousands of nodes, making fraud, censorship, or the potential shutdown of a service a complicated venture.

41 "DeFi's monumental rise in total value locked – starting this summer and surpassing $16 billion this month – has undoubtedly made the sector one of the most discussed topics of 2020". Max Yakubowski, "Was 2020 a 'DeFi year,' and what is expected from the sector in 2021? Experts answer", 23 Dec. 2020, CoinTelegraph.com, https://cointelegraph.com/news/was-2020-a-defi-year-and-what-is-expected-from-the-sector-in-2021-experts-answer (last accessed 29 January 2021).

42 "The DeFi ecosystem has launched an expansive network of integrated protocols and financial instruments. Now with over $13 billion worth of value locked in Ethereum smart contracts, decentralized finance has emerged as the most active sector in the blockchain space, with a wide range of use cases for individuals, developers, and institutions." Consensys (fn. 8).

43 The use of blockchain in trade finance by larger financial institutions, in a permissioned yet decentralised environment, is now an accepted and well tested use case. The first venture was the platform eTradeConnect launched in 2018 in Hong Kong and was backed by HSBC, BNP Paribas, Standard Chartered and nine other banks. This venture has now been replicated by consor-

institutions have an interest in being involved with DeFi in order to assume a leadership role in the forthcoming transformation of the finance business modus operandi and the ways financial services will be accessed and delivered in the future.[44]

Moreover, given the current popularity of DeFi platforms and the natural pull they present for start-up firms who wish to operate in an innovation intensive environment reaching a younger generation of investors who are more receptive to innovative and ethical investment offerings, and their structural advantages,[45] these platforms will inevitably prove an opportunity too great to be missed by struggling start-up fintech firms. These are, in any case, so flexible as to already operate on decentralized business models or adapt one to their needs. Therefore, it is not far into the future that we will see financial infrastructures, whether centralized or decentralized, that will integrate previously distinct investment service functionalities such as automated advice, portfolio management, underwriting, execution, reconciliation and settlement within a single platform.[46]

The move of DeFi into mainstream markets will represent in the view of many the replacement of regulation by (smart) contracting, so-called Lex Cryptographia. Nonetheless, to the extent that existing DeFi models will gradually crop up the mainstream finance space this view is false. In practice, regulation

---

tia of other big global financial institutions such as Deutche Bank, Santander, Rabobank etc which have collaborated with the Hyperledger Fabric-powered IBM blockchain to complete live operations. See Huillet, (fn. 11).

44 "Legacy behemoths such as JP Morgan and Goldman Sachs are notable proponents of DeFi, with a number of banks and financial institutions in financial verticals consortia testing decentralized systems to improve, inter alia, processing times for payments, trade finance, and interbank transfers. For these legacy financial institutions, embracing DeFi is as much as testing the new technologies for streamlining and enhancing their current processes as it is about being part of a potentially transformative movement that recognizes their leadership role and includes them." *Leon Perlman*, "Regulation of the Financial Components of the Crypto-Economy", Columbia School of International and Public Affairs Entrepreneurship and Policy Working Paper Series 2019, p. 21.

45 The structural benefits are, inter alia, low transaction costs, generation of distributed trust, and interoperable, borderless, and transparent business loci, and the broadening of financial inclusion via decentralized financial services which strongly appeal to younger entrepreneurs. Clearly, "[the] new area of financial technology [and] decentralized finance may reshape the structure of modern finance and create a new landscape for entrepreneurship and innovation, showcasing the promises and challenges of decentralized business models." See Yan Chen and Cristiano Bellavitis, "Blockchain Disruption and Decentralized Finance: The Rise of Decentralized Business Models", Journal of Business Venturing Insights 2020.

46 See *Avgouleas/Kiayias* (fn. 10).

of DeFI marketplaces and financial products would be a key factor in product evolution. Investor protection needs to point towards simplified regulatory rulebooks that will direct in a top-down approach the modalities of contract trading and transaction execution in the "smart contract's" code. Naturally, the said regulatory approach ought to take into account market practice, technological advantage, and participant preferences. This is a point of particular importance with respect to the way COB rules will develop in decentralised finance networks.

As already mentioned, DeFi is not without its risks and the only reason that its explosive growth has so far gone virtually unnoticed by regulators is the fact it is still only a tiny fraction of the overall volume of transactions conducted by global finance on a daily basis. Permissionless systems create incentives to the underworld to use them to transfer, invest or launder money that are either the proceeds of crime or tax evasion or can be used to finance terrorism. On the other hand, key crypto-operators claim that while permissionless DeFi platforms do not police and monitor identities and individual accounts they still operate effective systems to police the integrity of the market by monitoring activity. namely that they have transitioned from Know Your Customer (KYC) systems to Know Your Transaction (KYT) as a more effective way to detect suspicious transactions.[47] It is, however, a claim that has not been subjected to any outside scrutiny. In any case, given the threats the integrity of the financial system faces from many sources, KYT might have merit as a supplement of existing KYC and Anti-Money Laundering laws but not as a substitute.[48] Therefore, we do not regard mandating compliance of DeFI with KYC and money laundering checks as a significant barrier in any regulatory attempts to reap DeFi's most distinct advantages, summarised below, especially in the context of creating and integrated EU market for retail financial services.

DeFi infrastructures can, first, offer *flexibility and transparency in contract design* as well as a high level of *record security.* These stem from the fact that

---

47 "[K]now-your-transaction (KYT) . . . is privacy-preserving by evaluating behaviors of participating addresses rather than the identity of the participants. By providing KYT monitoring designed for blockchain-based assets with the highest quality on-chain data [KYT] provides AML checks to ensure transactions can remain anonymous while complying with regulations." Press release, "ConsenSys Launches Codefi Compliance", 8 June 2020, https://consensys.net/blog/press-release/consensys-launches-codefi-compliance/ (last accessed 31 January 2021).

48 In any case the view expressed here increasingly gains traction among crypto-exchanges as well, e. g., the Dutch Bitstamp traders cryptoexchange. We expect KYC to become the norm if not for accessing DApps and DEFexs at the very least in the context of taking funds out of them. Osato Avan-Nomayo, "Dutch crypto exchange users bemoan additional KYC requirements" 26 January 2021, CoinTelegraph.com

blockchain inherent properties of record immutability facilitate fraud-proof data coordination across the distributed ledger that is operated by decentralised platforms. The easy programmability of Ethereum blockchain allows the design and employment of highly programmable smart contracts with automated execution to create new financial instruments and digital assets.

Unlike earlier blockchain protocols Ethereum's composable software stack ensures that DeFi protocols and applications are built to integrate and complement one another. As a result, DeFi infrastructures enjoy a high level of *interoperability* offering developers and product teams the flexibility they need to build on top of existing protocols, customize interfaces, and integrate third-party applications.[49] In addition, DeFi platforms boost *market and trade transparency*. On the public Ethereum blockchain, every transaction is broadcast to and verified by other users on the network, although Ethereum addresses are encrypted keys that are pseudo-anonymous, which can still preserve trader privacy. Namely, network activity is visible to all users. This level of transparency around transaction data allows for uninhibited data analysis making orders and transactions highly auditable. Finally, substantial gains come from the elimination of the custodial chain, since DeFi platforms allow digital wallets to interact with other DApps and protocols while, market participants always keep custody of their assets and control of their personal data.

2.3 Market Microstructure, DeFI, and EU Financial Market Integration

Revamped permission-based and regulated DeFi platforms could offer distinct market channels for the implementation of EU plans with respect to the creation of liquid pan-European retail capital markets and market integration, widening access of SMEs and start-ups to capital markets finance, and fostering capital market innovation. These goals are some of the pillars of the revamped EU Commission strategy for the attainment of an EU Capital Markets Union, including a single EU brand for primary market listings.[50]

Simply put, EU regulators should closely scrutinize the aforementioned characteristics of DeFi platforms such as their ability to operate an open finance

---

49 For this reason DeFi protocols are called "money legos".
50 On the advantages of creating a single EU brand for securities listings see Emilios Avgouleas, Guido Ferrarini, "The Future of ESMA and a Single Listing Authority and Securities Regulator for the CMU: Costs, Benefits and Legal Impediments" In Busch, Avgouleas, Ferrarini (eds), Capital Markets Union in Europe (OUP, 2018), Ch. 4.

system on the basis of distributed trust enabled by cryptographic integration,[51] increased transparency, and amelioration of transactions costs.[52] If the DeFi properties are eventually verified, then market decentralization for, especially, smaller cap issuers should be embraced. In specific, tokenisation[53], which is one of the key properties of DeFi, and the ability of decentralised exchanges on blockchain to boost liquidity through pre-committed asset pools that act as market-makers could offer credible market solutions to many of the market microstructure obstacles that have prevented the EU from creating an integrated market for small cap (low capitalisation) stocks.

On the one hand, tokenization fuels tradability and thus it boosts liquidity due to positive network externalities. On the other hand, tokens, which are designed to be secure and instantly transferable, can also be programmed to carry as in-built properties a range of other functionalities. Thus, tokenization could help liquid markets to emerge for previously illiquid assets as, for example, a market for social market stakes or stakes in green economy SMEs.[54] This way not only access to market funding is broadened but also access to new types of investments and instruments that serve better sustainability objectives and the impact economy might emerge.[55]

Decentralized exchanges (DEXes)[56] seem to operate in a stable and unproblematic mode in a series of market contexts. Setting aside market interest that comes from the underworld, in taking a more fundamental view of DeFi it is very hard to see why what works for permissionless unregulated networks could not work for permissioned regulated networks operating decentralised markets where information discovery and investment education is also the responsibility of the user. And with every user building up a higher level of understanding of investments and investment expertise as well as expertise in information acquisition the higher the level of efficiency on which a decentralised

---

51 *Avgouleas/Kiayias* (fn. 10).

52 For arguments about the integrative properties of DLT markets in the context of the National Market System in the USA see *David C. Donald/Mahdi H. Miraz*, "Multilateral Transparency for Securities Markets through DLT" The Chinese University of Hong Kong Faculty of Law Research Paper No. 2019–05, 2019.

53 Simply speaking, a token is a digital asset that is created, issued, and managed on a blockchain. Tokenization represents a cornerstone of decentralized finance and a native functionality of the Ethereum blockchain.

54 See for further analysis *Avgouleas/Kiayias* (fn. 10).

55 Ibid. where this possibility was first suggested.

56 A DEX is defined here as a platform that allow users to trade digital assets directly between user wallets with the help of smart contracts and without the need for a trusted intermediary (the exchange) to hold their funds.

market operates.[57] This is of course an argument in favour of simpler or standardised investment instruments like stocks or bonds. For those instruments that require a higher level of investment sophistication and expertise or high information acquisition costs it is natural for centralised exchanges to dominate, especially if they are popular with investment intermediaries.[58] Furthermore, regulators could allow market players to carry experiments with respect to the operation of permissionless platforms where anonymity walls could be breached ex post at the behest of regulators. Arguably, what makes DeFi attractive to a large number of traders is the anonymity of permissionless platforms. Conversely, it is unknown whether there will be appreciable liquidity falls in the case of permissionless platforms with ex post controls.

Infrastructure services offered by DEXes tend to be cheaper in terms of trading and "listing" fees than centralized exchanges. This means that decentralised exchanges can be employed for the development of an EU listing brand for SMEs and start-ups. The existence of mechanisms that can offer automated market-making and other liquidity solutions is a very strong argument in favour of the above assertion.

On the other hand, issues of market microstructure like willingness of big institutions to make a market in the stock of smaller companies and the low levels of liquidity in relevant markets and consequently the appearance of higher mark-ups and bigger bid-ask spreads as well as higher volatility[59] can serve as a serious barrier to the entry of retail investors in these markets. As DEXes do not provide trading through an order book, liquidity problems could easily be exacerbated compared to centralised exchanges. However, the device automated market-markets (AMMs), which has recently been tried in DEXes, may offer an effective solution to the liquidity problem. AMMs trade from a pool of market players' pre-committed assets. They make a price algorithmically and stand ready to trade with interested buyers and sellers in the decentralised network resolving liquidity shortages.

---

57 *Vincent Glode/Christian Opp*, "Can Decentralized Markets Be More Efficient?", Jacobs Levy Equity Management Center for Quantitative Financial Research Paper, 2016.
58 Ibid.
59 On the liquidity premium see *Yakov Amihud*, "Illiquidity and stock returns: Cross-section and time series effects" (2002) 5 Journal of Financial Markets 31–56; *Yakov Amihud/Haim Mendelson/Lasse Heje Pedersen* "Liquidity and Asset Prices" (2005) Foundations and Trends in Finance 269–364; *Emilios Avgouleas/Stavros Degiannakis*, "Trade Transparency and Trading Volume: The Possible Impact of the Financial Instruments Markets Directive on the Trading Volume of EU Equity Markets" (2009) 1 International Journal of Financial Markets 96–123.

The AMMs may have two drawbacks. As a DEX does not provide an order book the price offered may not be a full reflection of supply and demand. On the other hand, with algorithms fixed on blockchain to monitor relevant trades the AMM can easily be fully informed of the trading volume that is going through the DEX or other markets and make uninformed predictions about incoming volumes based on past record. The second is that the AMM has to protect itself from aggressive arbitrageurs. In return for placing their assets with the AMM, liquidity providers are typically entitled to a pro-rata share of the transaction fees paid by traders for exchanging assets on the AMM. Returns in the form of transaction fees is the main incentive for agents to act as liquidity providers. These fees can be gradually adjusted by AMMs to make arbitrage costly and unprofitable.[60] Conversely it should be noted that since the expressions of interest to trade arrive sequentially in a DEX, the algorithmic system powering an uninformed AMM can adjust its prices and fees to what the overall market picture is. This replaces the price equalization function of centralised exchange's order book. In this case the AMM will just adjust its quotes in the same way operating more or less an extension of the application of the Glosten and Milgrom model.[61]

Enhanced transparency, the need to validate transactions using nodes, automated market-making and liquidity provision mechanisms in decentralised markets can protect these less than mature markets from the risk of illiquidity or from excessive insider dealing and market manipulation activity that is always evident in centralised markets on which SME and start-up issuers are traded. Finally, the elimination of clearing and settlement costs for tokenised stocks and bonds traded in DEXes and the streamlining of the stock-lending process and the ability to integrate stock collateral with corporate lending makes these markets ideal especially for the paper of smaller issuers and for those investing in them.

The inherent inability of DLT infrastructures to handle High Frequency Trading (HFT) will make the market more stable avoiding any wild price swings due to excessive speculation and volatility without losing in terms of market and in-

---

60 See *Vijay Mohan*, "Automated Market Makers and Decentralized Exchanges: A DeFi Primer, 30 October 2020.
61 See *Lawrence R. Glosten/Paul .R. Milgrom*, Bid, Ask and Transaction Prices in a Specialist Market with Heterogeneously Informed Traders. *Journal of Financial Economics*, 14:71–100, 1985; *Sanmay Das*, "A Learning Market-Maker in the Glosten-Milgrom Model" (2005) 5 *Quant. Finance* 169–180. See also *Yakov Amihud and Haim Mendelson*. Dealership Market: Market-Making with Inventory. Journal of Financial Economics, 8:31–53, 1980.

formation efficiency, since short selling[62] will, presumably, still be allowed. Absence of HFT will also reduce the possibility of algorithmic collusion in a very transparent market environment with robust trade validation mechanisms in place absent HFT. Moreover, HFT and algorithmic trade techniques that might end up distorting or event manipulating the market prices, as is for example, spoofing[63] are inherently impossible in decentralised markets. Any orders entering the system are self-executable limiting the possibility of cluttering the network with "spoofing" orders meant to mislead the market.

The selling of order flow by commission-free brokers like the Robinhood platform, recently implicated in the GameStop controversy, to new HFT market making intermediaries such as Citadel Securities[64] who run state of the art algorithms, makes an interesting example of the perils of continued intermediation in the liquidity space. While such intermediation in times of low volume low volatility may show the value of specialization in the value chain, it can be a source of major risks in the event of volume and volatility surges as it happened in the recent case of GameStop. DeFi platforms disrupting these practices can add a further stabilization mechanism in the market discouraging highly speculative HFT activity that also takes advantage of relatively long T+2 or longer settlement cycles.[65] Therefore, the shortening of the settlement cycles to T+0 in DLT markets would have market stabilization consequences dampening volatility and boosting user confidence in the marketplace.

---

62 On the possible efficiency benefits of short selling but also of the risks see *Emilios Avgouleas*, "A New Framework for the Global Regulation of Short Sales: Why Prohibition is Inefficient and Disclosure Insufficient" 376 Stanford Journal of Law, Business, and Finance (2010).

63 On how investors can strategically "spoof" the stock market see *Kyong Shik Eom/Kyung Suh-Park*. "Microstructure-based manipulation: Strategic Behavior and Performance of Spoofing Traders", Journal of Financial Markets 2013, 227–252. On trade-based manipulation see Emilios Avgouleas, The Mechanics and Regulation of Market Abuse: A Legal and Economic Analysis, 2005, Ch. 5.

64 On the tangled web of commission-free broker apps and liquidity brokers like Citadel see Nikhilesh De, "What Really Happened When Robinhood Suspended GameStop Trading", Coin-Desk.com, 16 February 2021, available at https://www.coindesk.com/what-really-happened-when-robinhood-suspended-gamestop-trading (last accessed on 27 March 2021).

65 We are indebted to Dr Heikki Marjosola for pointing out this possibility. See also *Michael McClain*, "Why Shortening the Settlement Cycle Will Benefit the Industry & Investors", 4 February 2021, DTCC.com Mr Mcclain is Managing Director and General Manager of Equity Clearing and DTC Settlement Services of Depository Trust and Clearing Corporation (DTCC), one of the biggest FMI providers in the world. Available at https://www.dtcc.com/dtcc-connection/ar ticles/2021/february/04/why-shortening-the-settlement-cycle-will-benefit-the-industry-and-in vestors (last accessed on 27 March 2021).

Potential advantages including substantial transaction cost savings can come from the operation of decentralized derivatives markets.[66] Ethereum-based smart contracts enable the creation of tokenized derivatives whose value is derived from the performance of an underlying asset and in which counterparty agreements are hardwired in code. DeFi derivatives can represent real-world assets such as fiat currencies, bonds, and commodities, as well as cryptocurrencies. Given the problem created by post-2008 regulations of over-the-counter derivatives markets (OTC) whereby large quantities of systemic risk are concentrated within central counterparties (CCP). DLT platforms can offer an alternative decentralized model for OTC derivatives trading and settlement with multiple points of failure, which can alleviate the pressure on CCPs and market derivatives markets more accessible and more efficient.[67]

Thus, it is incumbent on proactive regulators to run regulatory experiments and learn lessons from such experiments within DeFi in the secure environment of a sandbox. This would enable them to harvest the benefits of DeFi and curb its risks. The implementation of the Digital Finance package should be seen as being only the beginning in this process of EU market and regulatory transformation.

3 The Digital Value-Chain in Finance and MiFID II

MiFID II governs the provision of investment services in financial instruments.[68] MiFID II does not directly regulate platforms, but the different functionalities offered by platforms do fall under the ambit of MiFID II. For instance, both robo-advice services and trading venues are regulated by MiFID II. Furthermore, MiFID II imposes a series of product governance requirements on firms manufacturing or distributing financial instruments.[69] We undertake below a review of the existing regime to identify potential gaps that have already arisen through

---

66 *Emilios Avgouleasi/Aggelos Kiayias,* "The Promise of Blockchain Technology for Global Securities and Derivatives Markets: The New Financial Ecosystem and the 'Holy Grail' of Systemic Risk Containment" European Business Organization Law Review 2019, 81–110.
67 *Ibid.*
68 The definition of investment services and activities encompasses a wide range of activities, including the reception and transmission of orders, execution of orders, investment advice, dealing on own account, portfolio management, underwriting and the operation of trading venues that are multilateral trading facilities and organized trading facilities.
69 Articles 16(3) and 24(2) MiFID II, Articles 9 and 10 MiFID II Delegated Directive; ESMA Guidelines on MiFID II product governance requirements (ESMA35–43–620/5.02.2018).

the digitization of the finance value chain and the regulatory dilemmas that will arise in the future, especially in the context of DeFi platforms.

3.1 The Ambit of the MiFID II Regime for Robo-Advisors

The definition of investment services under MiFID II encompasses investment advice and portfolio management irrespective of whether they are automated or not. [70] Depending on the services provided by robo-advisors, their investment services could amount to investment advice or portfolio management. In case of a robo-advisor which solely provides advice with the client subsequently making the investment decision, the robo-advisor is offering investment advice pursuant MiFID II, defined as the provision of personal recommendations to a client.[71] If the robo-advisor also manages financial instruments on behalf of the client, then its service will fall within the definition of portfolio management. Portfolio management involves managing portfolios in accordance with mandates given by clients on a discretionary client-by-client basis where such portfolios include one or more financial instruments.[72] Robo-advisors offering investment advice or portfolio management must be authorized as investment firms.

An interesting twist here is the fact that under article 3, Member States may choose not to apply MiFID II to firms, which do not hold client funds and are not allowed to provide any investment service except the reception and transmission of orders in transferable securities or units of collective investment undertakings and/or the provision of investment advice in relation to such financial instruments.[73] As a result, robo-advisors that fulfil these conditions can remain outside the scope of MiFID II and be subject to the respective national regulatory regime. It should be noted that pursuant to article 3, the national regulatory regime must impose conditions for authorization and supervision and conduct of business obligations, but firms so regulated do not enjoy the MiFID II passport.

MiFID II introduces stringent authorization and conduct of business rules for robo-advisors, which qualify as investment firms. Apart from obtaining an authorization from competent authorities, the Directive requires investment firms to comply with strict capital requirements.[74] Furthermore, the Directive imposes

---

70 *George Ringe/Christopher Ruof*, "A Regulatory Sandbox for Robo Advice", European Banking Institute Working Paper Series 2018 no. 26, p. 29.
71 Art. 4(1)(4) MiFID II.
72 Art. 4(1)(8) MiFID II.
73 Art. 3 MiFID II.
74 Art. 15 MiFID II.

on regulated firms an overreaching duty to act honestly, fairly and professionally in accordance with the best interests of the clients.[75] Investment firms must manage and avoid conflict of interests between the different activities of the firms and the interests of clients.[76]

MiFID II introduces substantial and prescriptive disclosure requirements and establishes an overreaching duty to provide fair, clear and not misleading information to clients or potential clients.[77]. A cornerstone of MIFID's conduct of business regime is the requirement for investment firms, which provide portfolio management or investment services, to conduct a suitability assessment.[78] Firms must provide suitable recommendations for investment services and financial instruments based on relevant client information. To comply with these requirements robo-advisors ask clients to complete questionnaires and take other steps to explain their investment goals and risk appetite. Still, an interesting question arises in this context vis-à-vis robo-advisors that offer automatic rebalancing of client portfolios after the initial questionnaire and assessment. Are the investments comprising the rebalanced portfolio also suitable and appropriate?

3.2 MIFID II and Trading Venues

As far as trading venues are concerned MiFID II has imposed new regulations and introduced a new category of platforms, the so-called organized trading facilities. Pursuant to MiFID II, there are three categories of platforms, regulated markets, multilateral trading facilities (MTF) and organized trading facilities (OTF). In addition, MiFID II imposes regulatory requirements on systematic internalizers (SI). Regulated markets and MTFs are multilateral systems, which bring together or facilitate the bringing together of multiple third-party buying and selling interests in financial instruments in accordance with their non-discretionary rules.[79] An OTF is a multilateral system which is not a regulated market or an MTF and in which multiple third-party buying and selling interests in non-equity instruments, such as bonds, structured finance products, emission allowances or derivatives are able to interact in the system.[80] Furthermore, OTFs carry out execution on a discretionary basis. Instead of routing client orders to an RM,

---

75 Art. 24(1) MiFID II.
76 Art. 23 MiFID II.
77 Art. 24(3) MiFID II.
78 Art. 25(2) MiFID II.
79 Art. 4(1)(21) and (22) and Art. 19(1) MiFID II.
80 Art. 4(1)(23) MiFID II.

MTF or OTF firms may execute orders internally by acting on one side of the transaction on their own account. SIs are firms, which operate a bilateral system and deal on their own account when executing client orders outside a regulated market, an MTF or an OTF.[81]

Depending on the instruments traded and the mode of execution of orders, decentralized platforms may fall under the category of regulated markets, MTFs or OTFs. Since integrated platforms neither operate on a bilateral basis nor deal on their own account, they cannot take the form of SIs. On the other hand, it is possible that in the event that DeFi platforms offer trading services in MiFID II financial instruments, as is the provision under the proposed DLT pilot regime, then the aforementioned AMMs may be regarded as SIs. But this would place serious limitations to the function of AMMs on DeFi platforms. Therefore, the hope is that the present SI regime will not apply to automated market makers if they are dealing with low cap stocks and it can be shown that the AMM is offering prices through objective market learning algorithms to facilitate liquidity for a fee and not to leverage a proprietary book for profit, if the pre-committed pool of assets that AMMs operate can be paralleled to a proprietary trading book.

Furthermore, MTFs and OTFs exhibit certain important differences.[82] Most notably, while OTFs may only trade non-equity instruments, MTFs can trade both equity and non-equity ones. Moreover, OTFs carry execution on a discretionary basis. In contrast, MTFs apply non-discretionary rules when it comes to order execution. Fintech platforms and apps, which offer customers trading on a wide range of instruments, are more likely to be organized as MTFs deploying multilateral systems and carrying execution based on non-discretionary rules. Similarly, DeFi platforms are very unlikely to act as OTFs offering discretionary services. At the same time, the EU pilot regime makes room for the operation of DLT MTFs. Clearly, permissioned DeFi platforms could qualify as DLT MTFs under the pilot regime, discussed in section 5 below.

Another issue that might arise here is in connection with primary market listings. Regulated markets are subject to more prescriptive rules regarding the admission of financial instruments for trading.[83] Furthermore, issuers of financial instruments on regulated markets must comply with initial, ongoing ad-hoc disclosure obligations.[84] Overall, the operation of a regulated market entails considerable costs for a Fintech platform.

---

81 Art. 4(1)(20) MiFID II.
82 See generally *Danny Busch*, "MIFID II and MIFIR: Stricter Rules for the EU Financial Markets", Law and Financial Markets Law Review 2017, 126–128.
83 Art. 51 MiFID II.
84 Art. 51(3) MiFID II.

The operation of a MTF or an OTF is considered to be investment activity and therefore the operator is considered an investment firm and subject to transparency and organizational requirements.[85] Apart from the general organisational requirements applicable to all investment firms, such as the management of conflicts of interest, MTFs and OTFs are subject to additional specific organisational requirements. For instance, MTFs must establish non-discretionary rules for execution.[86] Moreover, they are prohibited from trading for their own account.[87] Furthermore, MTFs are not subject to client-facing rules, such as best-execution requirements.[88] In contrast, OTFs have discretion at execution and order level but are subject to client-facing rules, such as best-execution requirement.[89] What is more, they are allowed to trade for their own account in certain circumstances.[90]

As far as RMs are concerned, the operation of an RM is not considered to be investment activity under MiFID II.[91] Instead, the operator must be licensed as a regulated market and subject to a different set of rules, which even though bear similarity with the rules applicable to RMs, they are not identical. For example, the proportionality approach, which is adopted for investment firms, does not apply to RMs.[92] It is unlikely, however, that a DEX trading MiFID II financial instruments will ever seek such authorization. The principal advantage of RMs apart from the prestige and seal of approval that their listings convey is the depth of their order book. However, as DEXes do not operate on the basis of a trading book they do not have any incentive to ever seek authorization as RMs.

3.3 Fintech Platforms and the MIFID II Product Governance Regime

Integrated one-stop-shop fintech platforms may also become distributors, when offering or recommending an investment product, or even manufacturers of financial products, when creating, developing, issuing or designing their own investment products. In this scenario, the platform will also be subject to MiFID II

---

85 Art. 4(1), Art. 4(2) and Annex I, Section A MiFID II.
86 Art. 19(1) MiFID II.
87 Art. 19(5) MiFID II.
88 Art. 19(4) MiFID II.
89 Art. 20(6) MiFID II.
90 Art. 20(3) MiFID II.
91 Art. 44 MiFID II.
92 See Art. 16(4) MiFID II.

rules regarding product governance. The Directive imposes a wide range of strict product governance rules on investment firms distributing or manufacturing financial instruments. Product manufacturers are required to have in place a product approval process, which includes the identification of a potential target market for the product and assessment of all relevant risks to such target market.[93]

Furthermore, MiFID II subjects product manufacturers to product governance arrangements, which address conflicts of interest, threats of market integrity and financial stability.[94] Moreover, firms are required to conduct periodical review of the products they manufacture.[95] Pursuant to MiFID II, distributor firms must identify the actual market for the investment product.[96] What is more, they must ensure that adequate product governance arrangements are in place so that the products and services they offer or recommend are compatible with the needs, characteristics, and objectives of the target market.[97] In case the distributor is not the manufacturer of the product, it must obtain from the manufacturer all relevant information regarding the product and the product approval process.[98] Distributors must also regularly review their product governance arrangements and the products they offer or recommend.[99]

Clearly if DeFi platforms started acting as "distributors" of MiFID II financial instruments they would find it hard to comply with the product governance regime and both platform members and regulators would have to show willingness to evolve the regime without diluting investor protection. We suggest that one way to do that is if DeFi platforms have an onboarding process for new financial products who are approved and validated only if it can be shown that the "manufacturer" of the product and the "distributor" have already complied with the MiFID II requirements. In any case this is a wider problem that will have to be resolved at some point if DeFi products are to come under the MiFID II regulatory umbrella, since some of these products may not even have an identifiable "manufacturer".

---

93 Art. 16(3) and Art. 24(2) MiFID II, art. 16(3)&24(2).
94 Art. 16(3) MiFID II.
95 *Ibid.*
96 Art. 16(3) and Art. 24(2) MiFID II.
97 *Ibid.*
98 Art. 16(3) MiFID II.
99 *Ibid.*

3.4 Evaluation of MiFID II

Overall, integrated fintech platforms and their different functionalities are subject to a host of MiFID II rules. Platforms are required to comply with MiFID II as firms offering robo-advisory services, operating trading venues and manufacturing and/or distributing investment products. As a result, they are caught by a complex web of conduct and client protection rules. The rules differ depending on the category to which the client belongs and the type of investment service. Overall, fintech platforms are subject to different licenses and rules depending on the type of trading platform they are operating.

On the other hand, the hurdles are much higher for decentralized Fintech platforms. We have already noted the matter of AMMs and the SI regime and the challenge of bringing a DeFi platform under the product governance regime. Another major challenge is compliance with COB rules on a DeFi platform. For example, there is the question of who discharges COB duties under the MiFID II regime if neither the platform nor the counterparty is authorized as an investment firm.[100] Therefore, ingenuous solutions must be found to allow the aforementioned advantages of DeFi platforms to materialize without sacrificing consumer/investor welfare or vice versa.

For instance, decentralized integrated platforms provide direct access to retail investors willing to trade in the platform. However, trading venues do not offer direct access to investors. Instead, investors obtain access via financial intermediaries. Trading venues accept as members or participants only investment firms, credit institutions and other institutions, which possess an adequate level of trading ability and sufficient organizational standards and resources. Moreover, MiFID II was adopted before the rise of digital finance and does not account for the problems posed by new technological developments. As a result, its rules are unable to deal with the new conduct, operational and financial stability issues posed by integrated decentralized platforms, such as aggravated conflicts of interests caused by the integration of functions and operational and cyber-security risks.

4 DLT Platforms and the New EU Pilot Regime

The proposed EU pilot regime on DLT seeks to facilitate the use of distributed ledger technologies in the issuance, trading and settlement of a narrow set of

---

100 See for further discussion *Avgouleas/Kiayias* (fn. 10).

MiFID financial instruments: "transferable securities".[101] It removes, on the one hand, regulatory obstacles and, on the other, it closes regulatory gaps especially with respect to market integrity, transparency and investor protection.[102] Thus, the pilot regime allows DLT market infrastructures to obtain temporary exemptions from constraining requirements imposed by EU financial services legislation. At the same times, it purports to bolster financial stability and investor protection by targeting specific risks posed by DLT platforms.

The Commission's proposal creates an EU-wide regulatory sandbox for DLT market infrastructures. It should be noted that the regime introduced by the Proposal is optional and time limited. The permission to operate under the pilot regime and the exemptions are granted for a period of up to six years from the date of the specific permission.[103] Furthermore, after a five-year period from the entry into application of the Regulation, ESMA and the Commission would be required to make an assessment of the pilot regime, including the costs and benefits of extending the regime for another period of time, making the regime permanent with or without modifications or terminating it.[104]

The pilot regime introduces two new categories of DLT market infrastructures, the DLT Multilateral Trading Facility (DLT MTF) and the DLT Securities Settlement System (DLT SSS).[105] Market participants, which are authorized as an investment firm or a market operator under MiFID II or as a Central Securities Depository (CSD) under CSDR[106] can apply for permission to operate a DLT MTF or a DLT SSS under the pilot regime and obtain specific permission to be-

---

101 Art. 3 Proposal for a Regulation on a Pilot Regime.

102 For a discussion on regulatory obstacles to the widespread adoption of DLT see *Alexandros L. Seretakis*, Blockchain, Securities Markets and Central Banking in: Philipp Hacker, Ioannis Lianos, Georgios Dimitropoulos and Stefan Eich (ed.), Regulating Blockchain. Techno-Social and Legal Challenges, 2019.

103 Art. 7(4) and Art. 8(5) Proposal for a Regulation on a Pilot Regime.

104 Art. 10 Proposal for a Regulation on a Pilot Regime.

105 According to article 2(4) of the Proposal 'DLT multilateral trading facility' or 'DLT MTF' means a multilateral trading facility , operated by an investment firm or a market operator, that only admits to trading DLT transferable securities and that may be permitted, on the basis of transparent, non-discretionary, uniform rules and procedures, to: (a) ensure the initial recording of DLT transferable securities; (b) settle transactions in DLT transferable securities against payment; and (c) provide safekeeping services in relation to DLT transferable securities, or where applicable, to related payments and collateral, provided using the DLT MTF. Article 2(5) defines a DLT securities settlement system as a securities settlement system, operated by a 'central securities depository', that settles transactions in DLT transferable securities against payment.

106 Regulation (EU) No 909/2014 on improving securities settlement in the European Union and on central securities depositories (CSDR).

come temporarily exempt from certain rules. In order to strike a balance between the need to safeguard financial stability and the need to promote innovation and experimentation, the Proposal places limits on the type of transferable securities that can be admitted to trading on a DLT MTF or recorded in a CSD operating a DLT SSS.[107]

Recognizing that the current regulatory regime is unfit for tackling some the risks that may be posed by DLT technology, the Proposal includes strict safeguards aimed at protecting investors, consumers and the financial system.[108] Operators of DLT infrastructures are required to establish a detailed business plan including a description of the technical aspects and use of DLT technology. In addition, the rules under which the DLT market infrastructure operates, including the legal rights, obligations, liabilities of the operators, members, participants, issuers and clients, must be in writing and publicly available. Moreover, the operators must establish rules governing risk management, access to the infrastructure, the participation of validating nodes, the management of conflicts of interest. The operators of DLT market infrastructures shall also ensure that they have in place adequate IT and cyber arrangements. Furthermore, operators must safeguard the integrity, security and confidentiality of any data stored. In addition, the Proposal subjects operators to strict rules regarding the safekeeping of funds, collateral and DLT transferable securities. Finally, the operator of a DLT market infrastructure shall establish a publicly available strategy for transitioning out of or winding down a particular DLT market infrastructure.

The national competent authorities are responsible for administering the pilot regime and granting specific permission to operate under the pilot regime. Applicants must furnish competent authorities a variety of information, including the business plan, the overall IT and cyber security arrangements, the exemptions requested and the justification.[109] The authorities can refuse to grant permission to operate under the pilot regime if they consider that there are risks to investor protection, market integrity or financial stability or there is

---

107 Only shares and certain categories of bonds are eligible for trading on a DLT MTF or DLT SSS. In the case of shares, the market capitalization or the tentative market capitalization of the issuer must be less than EUR 200 million while in the case of convertible bonds, covered bonds, corporate bonds or public bonds (other than sovereign bonds), the issuance size must be less than EUR 500 million. Sovereign bonds cannot be admitted to trading on a DLT market infrastructure. Furthermore, the total value of securities recorded on a DLT infrastructure cannot exceed EUR 2.5 billion. Art. 3 Proposal for a Regulation on a Pilot Regime.
108 Art. 6 Proposal for a Regulation on a Pilot Regime.
109 Art. 7(2) and Art 8(2) Proposal for a Regulation on a Pilot Regime.

the danger of regulatory arbitrage.[110] The permission to operate under the pilot regime shall be valid throughout the European Union.[111]

DLT market infrastructures can request exemptions from certain rules that are incompatible with the use of DLT in the trading and post-trading of securities. DLT infrastructures requesting such exemptions will have to comply with specific conditions attached to each exemption and any additional conditions that may be imposed by national competent authorities. Accordingly, while Regulation (EU) No 909/2014 requires intermediation by a CSD as regards the recording of a transferable security and the settlement of related transactions, this could potentially take place on a distributed ledger as part of the same activity. To avoid replication of the recording on both the distributed ledger and the CSD, which would impose a functionally redundant overlay to the trade lifecycle of a financial instrument handled by DLT market infrastructures, a DLT MTF should be able to request an exemption of the book-entry requirement and the recording with a CSD set by Regulation (EU) No 909/2014. This applies when the DLT MTF complies with equivalent requirements to those applying to a CSD. In particular, a DLT MTF may request exemptions to perform activities that are currently performed by intermediaries, such as a CSD. Pursuant to article 4(2) of the Proposal, a DLT MTF may be permitted to admit to trading DLT transferable securities that are not recorded in a CSD but are instead recorded on the DLT MTF's distributed ledger. A similar exemption is introduced for DLT SSS, which are also subject to an intermediation obligation. [112]

Moreover, the pilot regime allows applicants to seek exemption from MiFID rules, which require traditional trading venues to give access to retail investors through financial intermediaries such as investment firms or credit institutions.[113] These rules are incompatible with DLT systems, whose business model is premised on peer-to-peer trading. Similarly, article 40 of CSDR provides for the settlement of payments in central bank money, if available and practicable, or otherwise in commercial bank money.[114] Cutting off DLT platforms within the sandbox from decentralised forms of payment used in DLT ecosystems that would bolster the number of market participants may prove counter-productive and a different approach should be considered in this context, including connec-

---

110 Art. 7(4) and Art. 8(4) Proposal for a Regulation on a Pilot Regime.
111 Art. 7(5) and Art. 8(5) Proposal for a Regulation on a Pilot Regime.
112 Art. 5(4) Proposal for a Regulation on a Pilot Regime.
113 Art. 4(1) Proposal for a Regulation on a Pilot Regime.
114 The Proposal will allow, however, a DLT SSS to request an exemption allowing thus the settlement of payments in commercial bank in a token-based form, or in the form of a e-money token. Art. 5(5) Proposal for a Regulation on a Pilot Regime.

tivity with permissionless platforms whose anonymity could be breached ex post. [115] Furthermore, a DLT SSS may also be exempted from certain other requirements applicable to traditional settlement systems that are incompatible with DLT systems, such as requirements with respect to dematerialized form of securities, securities accounts, recording of securities, segregation of assets, extension and outsourcing of activities and services and standard link access between CSDs and to other market infrastructures.[116]

5 Conclusions and Recommendations

The advent of digitization means that the value chain of global finance is irreversibly transformed. This transformation is so far manifested in the context of two radically opposing trends. The first trend is that of total vertical integration and industry concentration both with respect to wholesale and retail markets. The other trend is represented by DeFi infrastructure. The common characteristic of both market organization models is integration of the supply of financial services into one-shop platforms. Already key financial markets are dominated by platforms like Blackrock's Aladdin (offered to large western asset managers) and Ant Financial (geared towards the Chinese retail markets). DeFi platforms powered by DL technology could also offer an integration of functionalities such as automated advice, portfolio management, underwriting, execution, conciliation and settlement within a single platform in the model offered by Avgouleas and Kiayias.[117]

Both types of one-shop customer-driven multi-asset platforms could combine full connectivity between asset markets with easy access. Users will be able to access automated investment advice at any asset market. Robo-advisory services and the platforms where trading happens will be combined. Robo-advisors will decide on the direction of trades while also being part of the underlying platform where trade happens. At the extreme, the platform can become the advisor, distributor and manufacturer of products. The combination of robo-advisory services, settlement, custody and trading within a single platform poses a challenge to the current paradigm, which is premised upon a silo-based approach to the regulation of financial markets and participants.

---

115 Ibid.
116 Art. 5(2) and (6) Proposal for a Regulation on a Pilot Regime.
117 See (fn. 10).

While DeFi today is inextricably linked with cryptocurrencies of dubious value and risky lending as well as ad hoc transactions in the permission-less crypto-space, the promise of its infrastructure may not be discounted. Especially for financial regulators there are distinct benefits in the form of system resilience due to multiple points of failure, transaction auditability, market transparency, and ability to augment automated compliance and improve oversight.

Any lingering doubts about the resilience, functionality, scalability, and connectivity of this technology have been ameliorated by the massive explosion of DeFi activity without any reports about critical disruptions or system failures. The volume of uninterrupted transactions on DeFi platforms after the outbreak of Covid-19 – albeit of the kind discussed above – is in itself proof of the functionality and resilience of DeFi infrastructure. Therefore, there is a degree of justification in any regulatory attempts to try to co-opt the advantages of this technology and attendant business in the framework of mainstream finance and its regulation.

If brought within the regulatory perimeter under a flexible regime that understands the advantages and perils of automation and increasingly automated compliance, permissioned DeFi platforms powered by DLT can accelerate EU market integration and the realisation of the vision for an EU Capital Markets Union. DeFi infrastructures would, first, help to widen access to finance for SMEs and bigger firms, reducing the dependence of the EU economies from bank-funding. Secondly, they would undercut the rents of the big institutions relaxing the grip that BigTech can easily develop on retail markets. In addition, DeFi infrastructures would offer a higher level of protection to investors/consumers by enabling the operation of efficient (low-cost/high transparency) and reasonably liquid EU-wide markets for small cap stocks which could help the development of a *made in the EU* global brand for SME listings. Finally, it could help align consumer investment preferences and investment horizons with the composition of their portfolios due to the enhanced control they offer to end users.

EU financial regulation wrapped in the MiFID II concepts of investment services firms that hold a single point of entry license and distinct centralized trading and settlement venues is in need of a rethink, including from a model of a single firm authorization to authorization of multi-firm collaborative platforms. This is the only way to counter the eminent threat of control of EU financial market infrastructure (FMI) by dominant one-shop platforms owned by Big Tech or Big Finance. But it would place a considerable challenge to MiFID's approach and innovative solutions will have to be found including substantial automation of compliance.

However, the reconfiguration of EU financial regulation to meet the challenges in the mode of delivery of financial services in the EU and the transformation of FMI is poised to face formidable obstacles. First, incumbent firms may wish to maintain the status quo in order to preserve market shares and rents. Secondly, regulators will have to perform a hard balancing act since any reform that is not incremental is bound to have profound implications for the current EU model for the regulation of FMI.

Reform will have to weigh, on the one hand, the welfare benefits that furthering digital transformation may bring – given the fact that market digitization has become the official EU industrial policy – and, on the other, the fact that segments within the government and industry will present vertical integration and the transformation of the value chain as an opportunity to build European champions. Allegedly, these would be able to compete with US and Chinese financial services giants such as Blackrock and Ant financial services.

This is a false promise. As the EU financial services and data protection framework is much more restrictive than that under which US or Chinese big institutions operate, centralized finance platforms may lead to structural changes making the EU financial markets even more oligopolistic. Therefore, a policy favouring "EU champions" would boost rent-seeking, thus increasing rather than decreasing market cartelization.

In practical terms, EU policy-makers will have to reconsider the proposed DLT pilot regime. In particular, they will have to consider the widening of the proposed DLT pilot regime to include DeFi platforms which would not hold an authorization as a MiFID investment firm. This would place a considerable challenge to MiFID's approach and innovative solutions, such as substantial automation of compliance, will have to be found.

While a major step forward, the EU pilot regime in its present form is also a step backwards. As it is also argued by other authors in this volume (Giudici and Ferrarini, Marjosola), the pilot regime is informed by the expectation that new market trends centered around the new technology could fit into the existing disclosure and licensing based regulatory paradigm for EU financial markets. This is, however, an unfounded expectation reinforced by incumbent industry interests who wish to avoid a wholesale disruption of existing industry practices and the tight-knit oligopoly built on the back of a very complex and cumbersome rulebook. It looks towards the past and ignores the future both in terms of challenges for investor protection and market development and internal market opportunities.

DeFi poses in itself considerable challenges for regulators. It is, nonetheless, a route worth experimenting with and sanctioning as EU markets are being rebuilt in the post-Brexit era. DeFi platforms have the potential to provide the missing part in the EU Capital Markets Union jigsaw. Widening the proposed DLT pilot regime is also the best way to foster further digitization of the finance value chain in the EU and the materialization of attendant efficiencies without the undesirable consequences of market domination by large centralised fintech platforms. Conversely, properly regulated DeFi infrastructures can become a safe passage to the democratization and further integration of EU capital markets under the open finance paradigm.

Eugenia Macchiavello and Antonella Sciarrone Alibrandi
Marketplace Lending as a New Means of Raising Capital in the Internal Market: True Disintermediation or Reintermediation?

Abstract: Marketplace lending, enabled by technological innovation, represents a new opportunity for raising capital. It is regarded by the EU as having the potential to expand the financing options of SMEs and improve the integration of the Internal Capital Market. However, applying traditional legal categories and existing laws to marketplace lending and to other examples of the new "platform economy" is not simple. Member States have adopted very different regulatory responses towards marketplace lending, with negative effects on the internal market. The essence of the regulatory dilemma consists in determining whether marketplace lending represents – as it has been depicted by platforms themselves, particularly in contractual agreements through disclaimers – a true disintermediated method of raising capital, an innovative form of intermediation, or a traditional kind of intermediation disguised in new and fashionable clothing. The answer to this question has relevant consequences for the regulatory treatment of marketplace lending and it requires a uniform response in the EU, at least with respect to the largest cross-border platforms. After briefly describing marketplace lending in Europe and the various current trends in regulating it, the paper discusses the main regulatory issues from the perspective of the above-mentioned issues. It analyzes the recently adopted Regulation on European Crowdfunding Services Providers in order to verify whether the regulatory choices that it has made are effective, both for the further development of marketplace lending and for addressing the associated risks.

Eugenia Macchiavello, Assistant Professor of Financial Regulation, Department of Law, University of Genoa, Jean Monnet Centre of Excellence on Sustainable Finance and Law (EUSFiL). Although this paper is the result of the common efforts of the authors, §§ 2, 3, and 4 (including all sub-paragraphs) should be attributed to Eugenia Macchiavello, and § 5 to both authors.
Antonella Sciarrone Alibrandi, Full Professor of Banking Law and Financial Markets Law, School of Banking, Finance and Insurance Sciences, Università Cattolica del Sacro Cuore. Although this paper is the result of the common efforts of the authors, § 1 should be attributed to Antonella Sciarrone Alibrandi, and § 5 to both authors. The present paper is part of the research project funded by the Italian Ministry of Research 'PRIN 2017 Fintech: the influence of enabling technologies on the future of the financial markets'.

∂ OpenAccess. © 2022 Eugenia Macchiavello and Antonella Sciarrone Alibrandi, published by De Gruyter. (cc) BY-NC-ND This work is licensed under the Creative Commons Attribution-NonCommercial-NoDerivatives 4.0 International License. https://doi.org/10.1515/9783110749472-003

Table of Contents

1 Lending-Based Crowdfunding in the Framework of the Capital Markets Union and FinTech Action Plans: The "Platform Dilemma"

Marketplace lending (also called P2P lending or lending-based crowdfunding) consists of the provision of loans to consumers or businesses by a multitude of individuals or entities (a "crowd"), each supplying only a small portion of the amount requested, generally through an online platform. Together with equity crowdfunding, marketplace lending took root in the context of the last financial crisis and, since then, has experienced continuous growth, so that it has come to represent the largest segment of European alternative finance. In particular, the consumer-based segment comprises 41 percent of the European alternative finance market, while the business-lending segment represents 14 percent.[1]

---

1 Other relevant shares of the alternative market are equity-based crowdfunding at 6 percent,

In both these segments, the UK is the most significant contributor, followed by Germany, France, while the fourth biggest market is Poland, in the first segment, and the Netherlands, in the second one.[2]

Marketplace lending appears to contribute to the promotion of innovation[3] and expanding financial inclusion,[4] thanks to cost minimization[5] and the speed of the underwriting process. Business lending through crowdfunding platforms is growing rapidly: in 2018, British P2P business lending accounted for 11.59 percent of the annual estimated volume of total new loans to small and me-

---

real estate crowdfunding at 8 percent, and other types of securities at 5 percent. Other minor marketplace lending segments are balance sheet lending (in which the platform provides a loan from its balance sheet) for business (3 percent) and for consumers (0.1 percent). *Tania Ziegler et al.*, 'Shifting Paradigms – The 4th European Alternative Finance Benchmarking Report', (2019), p. 31–33, <https://www.jbs.cam.ac.uk/fileadmin/user_upload/research/centres/alternati ve-finance/downloads/2019-04-4th-european-alternative-finance-benchmarking-industry-report-shifting-paradigms.pdf> (last access for all electronic sources if not otherwise indicated: 11 August 2020). Last update to the text and sources: 7 February 2021.

2 See *Tania Ziegler et al.*, 'The Global Alternative Finance Market Benchmarking Report' (2020), p. 81–82, <https://www.jbs.cam.ac.uk/fileadmin/user_upload/research/centres/alternative-finan ce/downloads/2020–04–22-ccaf-global-alternative-finance-market-benchmarking-report.pdf>.

This and the following paragraphs draw from our previous contributions: *Eugenia Macchiavello*, 'Peer-to-peer Lending and the "Democratization" of Credit Markets: Another Financial Innovation Puzzling Regulators', Columbia Journal of European Law (2015) 21(3) 521, 540–42; *Id.*, 'Financial-Return Crowdfunding and Regulatory Approaches in the Shadow Banking, Fintech and Collaborative Finance Era', European Company and Financial Law Review 14(4) (2017) 662; *Guido Ferrarini/Eugenia Macchiavello*, 'FinTech and Alternative Finance in the CMU: The Regulation of Marketplace Investing, in: Emilios Avgouleas/Danny Busch/Guido Ferrarini (eds.), Capital Markets Union in Europe, 2018, p. 208 et seqq.; *Antonella Sciarrone Alibrandi et al.*, 'Marketplace lending. Verso nuove forme di intermediazione finanziaria?', Consob Quaderno Fintech No. 5/2019, <http://www. consob.it/documents/46180/46181/FinTech_5.pdf/a92a97f0-7d0e-43de-9fcd-4acfd97199f2>; *Eugenia Macchiavello*, 'What to Expect When You Are Expecting' a European Crowdfunding Regulation: The Current "Bermuda Triangle" and Future Scenarios for Marketplace Lending and Investing in Europe' (August 20, 2019), European Banking Institute Working Paper Series – No. 55/2019, <https://ssrn.com/abstract=3493688>.

3 About the tendency of nonbank lenders to finance more innovative projects than banks for reasons related to differences in funding costs and types, see *Jason Roderick Donaldson/Giorgia Piacentino/Anjan Thakor*, 'Intermediation Variety', (June 2019) NBER Working Paper No. 25946, <https://www.nber.org/papers/w25946>.

4 For the data about the percentage of unbanked or underbanked persons in certain EU countries, see *Ziegler et al*, (fn. 2), p. 94.

5 Platform operating costs are minimized through the use of technology (e.g. automated systems) and off-balance-sheet loans, the absence of transformation and maturity risk, and by the ability to avoid banking regulations: *Carlos Serrano-Cinca/Bego Gutierrez-Nieto/Luz López-Palacios*, 'Determinants of Default in P2P Lending', PLoS One 10(10) (2015), 1, p. 3.

dium-sized enterprises (SMEs), which represented a 25% growth rate over the previous year.[6] Furthermore, P2P consumer lending platforms appear to serve areas that may be underserved by traditional banks (because these areas have fewer branches or are economically depressed) and borrowers who are generally categorized by banks as subprime but able to sustain a loan.[7] It is also an interesting investment opportunity in terms of diversification (because it is an alternative and therefore more resilient market) and because of the possibility of both financial and nonfinancial/altruistic returns, while also improving competition, diversification, and innovation in the financial markets.[8]

Just as the financial crisis of 2007–2008 led to the initial explosion in crowdfunding, the pandemic and the global economic crisis that we have just gone through may potentially offer an opportunity for the phenomenon's further development. Since crowdfunding (and marketplace lending in particular) has proven in recent years to be an important alternative form of finance for consumers, start-ups, and SMEs, it could, in the wake of the pandemic, make a significant contribution to the fight against the negative economic effects of COVID-19.[9] Dur-

---

6 *Ziegler et al.* (fn. 2), p. 85.

7 *Julapa Jagtiani/Catharine Lemieux*, 'Do Fintech Lenders Penetrate Areas That Are Underserved By Traditional Banks?, Journal of Economics and Business 100 (2018) 43; *Id.*, 'Fintech Lending: Financial Inclusion, Risk Pricing, and Alternative Information', (26 December 2017), Federal Reserve of Philadelphia Working Paper No. 17/2017, available at <https://ssrn.com/abstract= 3096098>; *Julapa Jagtiani/Lauren Lambie-Hanson/Timothy Lambie-Hanson*, 'Fintech Lending and Mortgage Credit Access', Federal Reserve Bank of Philadelphia Working Paper No. 19–47, (November 2019), <https://www.philadelphiafed.org/-/media/research-and-data/publications/ working-papers/2019/wp19–47.pdf>; *Calebe De Roure/Loriana Pelizzon/Anjar V. Thakor*, 'P2P Lenders Versus Banks: Creak Skimming or Bottom Fishing?', SAFE Working Paper No. 206/ 2019, <http://hdl.handle.net/10419/203316> (as regards the German consumer credit market, P2P lenders target riskier borrowers and the risk-adjusted interest rates are lower than those offered by banks). About business lending (but more generally referring to lending platforms that are managed by Big Tech instead of crowdfunding platforms), see *Harald Hau et al.*, 'Fintech Credit, Financial Inclusion and Entrepreneurial Growth', (2018) Working Paper, abstract available at <https://editorialexpress.com/cgi-bin/conference/download.cgi?db_name=EEAESEM2018 &paper_id=598>; *Harald Hau et al.*, 'How FinTech Enters China's Credit Market', (2019), AEA Papers and Proceedings, 109, 60, <https://pubs.aeaweb.org/doi/pdfplus/10.1257/pandp.20191012> (observing that FinTech credit companies provide more credit to borrowers with lower credit scores).

8 Among other sources, see *European Commission*, 'Unleashing the Potential of Crowdfunding in the European Union', (Communication), COM(2014) 172 final 2, at 5, <http://ec.europa.eu/internal_market/finances/docs/crowdfunding/140327-communication_en.pdf>.

9 *Ratna Sahay et al.*, 'The Promise of Fintech Financial Inclusion in the Post COVID-19 Era', (2020), 16 et seqq., https://www.imf.org/en/Publications/Departmental-Papers-Policy-Papers/Is sues/2020/06/29/The-Promise-of-Fintech-Financial-Inclusion-in-the-Post-COVID-19-Era-48623.

ing 2020, however, the growth of marketplace lending was not as pronounced as it could have been,[10] probably in view of the fact that an adequate regulatory framework for the phenomenon had not yet been established in Europe, and, in the absence of an effective EU regime, governments did not offered targeted support to the activities of the platforms.

Yet, already in the earliest stages of the Capital Markets Union[11] and FinTech Action Plans,[12] the European Commission included crowdfunding service providers in the scope of action. More specifically, the Commission advanced in March 2018 a Proposal[13] for a Regulation on European Crowdfunding Service Providers for Business (hereinafter ECSP Regulation), in consideration of its potential for expanding SME financing options and for improving the integration of the Internal Capital Market. After a lengthy legislative process, during which the original

---

See also *European Commission*, 'Consultation on a New Digital Finance Strategy for Europe/FinTech Action Plan', (3 April 2020), <https://ec.europa.eu/info/sites/info/files/business_economy_euro/banking_and_finance/documents/2020-digital-finance-strategy-consultation-document_en.pdf>.

10 Preliminary data (April 2020) show a significant negative impact of the pandemic on marketplace lending, both as respects capital inflow (new investments) from investors and deal flow (the number of new projects registered on platforms) – in both cases, representing more than a 50 percent decline. There has only been a small impact thus far (in terms of payment delays and cash flow problems) on existing projects. The survey also reports on a lack of support for platforms from governments and certain measures taken by platforms to help crowd-borrowers (waiver of late repayment fees, delayed capital repayment on loans, operational support in the preparation of contingency plans, and provision of information on government subsidies): *European Crowdfunding Network (ECN)*, 'Early Impact of CoVid19 on the European Crowdfunding Sector' (April 2020), <https://eurocrowd.org/wp-content/blogs.dir/sites/85/2020/04/ECN_CoVid19_Survey_20200414.pdf>. A recent study (January 2021) shows improvements in the European mechanisms for raising capital (e.g., equity-based crowdfunding, including donation-based crowdfunding, which reported exceptional growth during the pandemic aimed at supporting hospitals, etc.), while a decrease in overall marketplace lending in terms of volume (-3 percent) and the number of transactions (-2 percent), despite an increase in the number of borrowers (which has grown by 8 percent), in particular new ones (+28 percent): Tania Ziegler et al., 'The Global Covid-19 FinTech. Market Rapid Assessment Study', (December 2020), 87–88, <https://www.jbs.cam.ac.uk/wp-content/uploads/2020/12/2020-ccaf-global-covid-fintech-market-rapid-assessment-study.pdf>.

11 *European Commission*, 'Action Plan on Building a Capital Markets Union' (Communication) COM/2015/0468 final (30 September 2015); *Id.*, 'Mid-Term Review of the Capital Markets Union Action Plan', COM(2017) 292 final (8 June 2017).

12 *European Commission*, 'FinTech Action Plan: For a More Competitive and Innovative European Financial Sector', (Communication) COM/2018/0109 final (8 March 2020).

13 *European Commission*, 'Proposal for a Regulation of the European Parliament and of the Council on European Crowdfunding Service Providers (ECSP) for Business', (8 March 2018) COM(2018)113.

proposal was subject to several modifications, the final text[14] was adopted by the Council only on 20 July 2020 and by the European Parliament on 7 October 2020; it was published in the Official Journal on 20 October 2020.[15] Significantly, this is the first regulation adopted in the FinTech sector at the EU level and, with regard to the basic choices contained therein, it therefore constitutes an important point of reference for further regulations that will be issued in the coming months.

The need for a European regulation focused on crowdfunding service providers can also be explained by the fact that this type of marketplace, although part of the more general phenomenon called the "platform economy",[16] often associated with the "sharing economy," but more recently re-defined as "crowd-based capitalism" because of its profit-driven character and concentrated power,[17] responds to financial needs and therefore poses particular issues. An online platform is generally identified as 'a digital service that facilitates interactions between two or more distinct but interdependent sets of users (whether firms or individuals) who interact through the service via the Internet ("multi-sided platforms").'[18] They tend to be characterized by a fragmentation of the traditional value chain and the provision of services by other users (not by the platform) who might simultaneously be both consumers and producers ("prosumers").

---

14 *Council of the European Union*, 'Position of the Council at first reading with a view to the adoption of a Regulation [...] on European crowdfunding service providers for business, and amending Regulation (EU) 2017/1129 and Directive (EU) 2019/1937', <https://data.consilium.eu ropa.eu/doc/document/ST-6800-2020-INIT/en/pdf≥.

15 Regulation (EU) 2020/1503 [...] of 7 October 2020 on European Crowdfunding Service Providers for Business. The Regulation will then enter into force the 20th day after the publication but will be applied from 10 November 2021, saved for differentiated dates of application for certain rules/cases. For a detailed analysis of the ECSP Regulation, please see: *Eugenia Macchiavello*, 'The European Crowdfunding Service Providers Regulation and the Future of Marketplace Lending and Investing in Europe: The 'Crowdfunding Nature' Dilemma', European Business Law Review 2021, 32(3) 557; *Id.*, 'Marketplace Lending and Investing in Europe and the EC Proposal for a Regulation on European Crowdfunding Service Providers for Businesses', in Elisabetta Bani/ Edyta Rutkowska-Tomaszewska/Beata Pachuca-Smulska (eds.), Public Law and the Challenges of New Technologies and Digital Markets, Volume II, 2020, p. 119; see also *Id.*, 'Disintermediation in Fund-raising: Marketplace Investing Platforms and EU Financial Regulation', in Iris H. Chiu/ Gudula Deipenbrock (eds.), Routledge Handbook on FinTech and Law, 2021, p. 291 et seqq.

16 *Orly Lobel*, 'The Law of the Platform', Minnesota Law Review 2016, 101(1), 87; *FSB*, 'Decentralised Financial Technologies. Report on Financial Stability, Regulatory and Governance Implications', (6 June 2019), <https://www.fsb.org/wp-content/uploads/P060619.pdf>.

17 See *Arun Sundararajan*, The Sharing Economy: The End of Employment and the Rise of Crowd-Based Capitalism, 2016.

18 *OECD*, An Introduction to Online Platforms and Their Role in the Digital Transformation, 2019, <https://www.oecd.org/innovation/an-introduction-to-online-platforms-and-their-role-in-the-digital-transformation-53e5f593-en.htm>.

This results in a complex nexus of multiple contracts governing the relationships among the users and between the platform and the users, and in the creation of peer-to-peer (P2P) marketplaces, in which platforms connect parties (often through algorithms) and provide standard contracts and rating systems to cope with the absence of a trusted party, with all participants benefiting from global network effects and broad accessibility.[19] As interpreted in light of the traditional systems of raising capital, this entails the replacement of traditional financial intermediaries, including underwriters, analysts, distributors, etc., with "P2P-marketplaces" (in both the primary and secondary markets).

In light of such a platform-based structure, it is not easy to apply traditional legal categories (such as those relating to financial instruments, markets, issuers, underwriters, etc.) to marketplace lending or to subject it to existing laws in various sectors (banking law, investment and markets regulation, AML/CT law, business law, consumer protection, etc.). This difficulty is enhanced by the variety of business models used in marketplace lending. None of the very different sets of rules adopted by several Member States to deal with the phenomenon have resulted in an effective regulatory response from an internal market point of view. Different levels of investor protection among countries and distorted competition are in fact detrimental to the goal of a high level of harmonization in financial regulation and to the postcrisis trend towards greater integration.

It is therefore to be welcomed that European authorities have chosen to issue a regulation aimed at clarifying, specifically with respect to ECSPs, the basic "platform dilemma". The crucial question relates, in fact, to whether marketplace lending represents – as originally described by actors in the sector, especially in contractual agreements by means of disclaimers – a true disintermediated method of raising capital, a mere informational and technical service,[20] an innovative form of financial intermediation, or a traditional type of financial intermediation disguised in new and fashionable clothing.

The answer to this question has relevant consequences for regulatory treatment of marketplace lending as well as its resulting market structure, and, at the same time, must be uniform in the EU, at least as regards the biggest and cross-border platforms.[21] The European Court of Justice (ECJ) has so far responded to

---

19 *OECD* (fn. 18), p. 11 et seqq.; *Linar Einav/Chiara Farronato/Jonathan Levin*, 'Peer-to-peer markets', NBER Working Paper No. 21496/2015, <http://www.nber.org/papers/w21496>.
20 Exempted under Art. 2(a) e-commerce Directive (No. 2000/31 [2000]); Art. 2(2)(d) Services in the Internal Market Directive (2006/123/CE), Art. 56 TFEU.
21 With respect to online platforms, see also Regulation (EU) 2019/1150 on promoting fairness and transparency for business users of online intermediation services and the proposals present-

such issues in the context of other economic sectors on a case-by-case (and "service-by-service") basis. For instance, in the transportation field, the ECJ has viewed Uber as a direct provider of transportation services (requiring a national license), under the theory that it created a new market ("non-professional transportation") and that its services (in principle, information society services) are an integral part of the new transportation market it has created, and the Uber exercises a decisive influence over the conditions under which drivers operate (e.g., the organization of the labour force, price-setting, control over quality, liability for damages, etc.).[22] On the other hand, in the accommodations sector, the ECJ has seen Airbnb as constituting a mere service of the information society and therefore exempted "sellers" from the need to procure national licenses as real estate agents because of the presence of a pre-existing market (for short-term accommodations, although only offered by professionals) and the lack of their decisive influence on the product (the platform does not set the rental price nor select the hosts or accommodations).[23] The Court has also been asked whether a P2P lending platform can be considered a "creditor" under Article 3(b) of the Consumer Credit Directive (2008/48/EC) where it has only facilitated P2P loans, but it did not issue a preliminary ruling due to the sudden default of the concerned platform.[24]

In the following sections, after describing the main business models of marketplace lending in Europe and each model's related risks, as well as various trends in the regulation of these models at the national level, we will analyze the recent ECSP Regulation to evaluate the choices made in the regulation with respect to the highlighted risks and, more generally, with respect to the platform dilemma, taking into account the possible effect of this regulatory approach on the market structure of European marketplace lending.

ed by the Commission in December 2020 (while this contribution was already under review) concerning a Single Market For Digital Services (COM(2020) 825 final) and concerning Digital Markets (COM(2020) 842 final).

22 Case C-434/15 *Asociación Profesional Élite Taxi v Uber Systems Spain SL* [2018] OJ C-72/2; case C-320/16 *Uber France Sas* (GC, 10 April 2018).
23 Case C-390/18 *Airbnb Ireland* (GC, 19 December 2019). See *Liesbet Van Acker, C-390/18 – The CJEU Finally Clears the Air(bnb) Regarding Information Society Services*, EuCML 2 (2020) 77.
24 Case C-311/15 *TrustBuddy AB v Lauri Pihlajaniemi* [2016] OJ C-38/46 and [2015] OJ C-294/38.

2 Marketplace Lending in Europe: Main Business Models and Related Risks

One of the main drivers adding complexity to the platform dilemma is the wide variety of business models that exist in the market today and that are available to both borrowers and lenders. Under the basic and (so far) most widespread model of marketplace lending (called a "client-segregated account"),[25] loans are disbursed by crowd-lenders (each providing small sums) at their own risk through contracts with crowd-borrowers, with the platform only facilitating transactions through the provision of various services, for which the platform is remunerated on a fee basis. For instance, the platform generally performs the pre-screening of applicants (e. g., based on credit scores and/or algorithms) and publishes the details of the project on its website, thereby putting crowd-borrowers and crowd-lenders in contact. Platforms also tend to set up communication and feedback systems,[26] provide boilerplate contracts, handle the contractual relationships that are formed (including credit collection) and, when a separate payment service provider is not used, money transfers. However, significant variations in the models exist and some solutions are aimed at reducing the typical information asymmetry in credit markets and at and aligning the interests of the platforms and the investors but at the same time the same enhance the role of the platforms. For instance, some platforms let crowd-lenders decide which loans to finance based on the objective characteristics of the loan (maturity, interest rate, risk category, collateral, size, reimbursement options, etc.) used as search filters and based on the available information (also 'soft' information, pitches, backers' support, etc.) about the crowd-borrower (e. g. sex, age, job, residence, purpose of the financing, etc.) but often suggest or impose a certain level of diversification on the crowd-investors. Some platforms feature lending groups that have a leader who co-invests and conducts due diligence in order to reduce information

---

25 *Committee on the Global Financial System (CGFS)/Financial Stability Board (FSB),* 'FinTech Credit. Market Structure, Business Models and Financial Stability Implications', 2017, p. 11 et seqq.; *Tania Ziegler/Rotem Shneor,* 'Lending Crowdfunding: Principles and Market Development', in: Roten Shneor/Liang Zhao/Bjørn-Tore Flåten (eds) Advances in Crowdfunding, 2020, 63, p. 68–70.
26 About reputational mechanisms in online credit markets that are useful for reducing information asymmetry and moral hazard by improving credit risk analysis and creating incentives not to default (so as to avoid social stigma), see *Xin, Yi,* 'Asymmetric Information, Reputation, and Welfare in Online Credit Markets' (August 1, 2020), <https://ssrn.com/abstract=3580468>; *Ruyi Ge et al.,* 'Predicting and Deterring Default with Social Media Information in Peer-to-Peer Lending', Journal of Management Information Systems 34(2) (2017) 401.

asymmetries. Some set up guarantee funds to cover crowd-borrower defaults but the characteristics of the same might differ significantly in terms of conditions to receive the compensation (e. g. based on the discretion of the platforms or, instead, on objective and predetermined criteria), order of satisfaction, amount of reimbursement (partial, total, which percentage of the capital invested).[27] The price of loans might depend on competitive bids or, more frequently, on the platform's rating of the crowd-borrowers.[28] Creditworthiness assessments are often based on innovative and technology-led systems that take into account not only traditional "hard" financial information (e. g., financial statements and credit scores) but also "soft" financial (e. g., payment history, including utility bills, and buying habits) and nonfinancial (e. g. social media likes or followers) information.[29] The platforms are remunerated in the form of fees, which are generally dependent on the volume of loans disbursed and/or the performance of the loans.[30]

Some platforms, following an increasingly popular business model, have set up algorithmic or "auto-bid" systems that automatically assign crowd-lenders' funds to crowd-borrowers based on their risk profiles and characteristics (expect-

---

27 *CGFS-FSB* (fn. 25) p. 8, 12 – 13; *Financial Conduct Authority (FCA)*, 'FCA, 'Loan-based ('peer-to-peer') and Investment-Based Crowdfunding Platforms: Feedback on Our Post-Implementation Review and Proposed Changes to the Regulatory Framework', (July 2018), CP 18/20, p. 18, 20, 30 – 31, <https://www.fca.org.uk/publication/consultation/cp18-20.pdf>.

28 For evidence of a better credit allocation when prices are set by platforms instead of an auction mechanism, see *Talal Rahimy*, 'Can Online Platforms Improve Resource Allocation by Controlling Prices?', (May 2020), <https://www.researchgate.net/publication/342200397_Can_Online_Platforms_Improve_Resource_Allocation_by_Controlling_Prices>.

29 On the ability of such systems to predict creditworthiness better than traditional credit scores, see *Julapa Jagtiani/Catharine Lemieux*, 'The Roles of Alternative Data and Machine Learning in Fintech Lending: Evidence from the LendingClub consumer platform', Financial Management 48 (2019) 1009; *Nikita Aggarwal*, 'Machine Learning, Big Data and the Regulation of Consumer Credit Markets: The Case of Algorithmic Credit Scoring' in: Nikita Aggarwal et al (eds) Autonomous Systems and the Law, 2019; *J. Yan/W. Yu/J. L. Zhao*, 'How Signaling and Search Costs Affect Information Asymmetry in P2P Lending: The Economics of Big Data', Financial Innovation 1(1) (2015) 19. See also *Cummins et al.* (fn. 30), p. 20 et seqq.; *Tobias Berg et al.*, 'On the Rise of FinTechs – Credit Scoring Using Digital Footprints', (July 15, 2019), Michael J. Brennan Irish Finance Working Paper Series Research Paper No. 18 – 12, <https://ssrn.com/abstract=3163781>.

30 These fees include origination fees (from the borrower), repayment fees (from the lender), late payment fees, trading fees, servicing fees, and others. See *Stijn Claessens et al.*, 'Fintech Credit Markets Around the World: Size, Drivers and Policy Issues', BIS Quarterly Review (23 September 2018), 29, p. 32, <https://www.bis.org/publ/qtrpdf/r_qt1809e.pdf>; *Mark Cummins et al.*, 'Addressing Information Asymmetries in Online Peer-to-Peer Lending', in: Theo Lynn et al. (eds), Disrupting Finance. FinTech and Strategy in the 21st Century, 2019, 15, p. 18.

ed return, interest rate, maturity, etc.),[31] also with an eye toward ensuring investment diversification. Some other platforms engage in co-lending; that is, the platform participates in each loan on the platform together with the crowd-lenders in a (generally) limited percentage of the total loan amount.

In another model, called the "notary" business model, which is common in Germany and the US, the platform prescreens borrowers, publishes the projects online, and collects the funds, but a bank originates the loans and immediately resells them to a Special Purpose Vehicles (SPV) created by the platform, which subsequently issues notes to crowd-lenders representing their portion of the credit and remains the only counterparty of the crowd-lenders. A variation of this model entails securitization of loans, which are disbursed by a bank, assigned to the SPV and then repackaged, with the SPV's notes sold to the crowd.

Another model (the "balance sheet" model), which is common in Australia, Canada, and the US, involves the platform collecting the funds from the crowd through bonds or equity and providing the loans on its account or buying the loans provided in the first place by a bank. Like the notary model, crowd-lenders have recourse only against the platform, but under the balance sheet model the platform assumes the risk of borrower defaults.

Finally, under the "guaranteed return" model, a variation of the balance sheet model, the platform ensures a certain return to crowd-lenders investing in loan portfolios having a composition that is decided by the platform. This

---

31 In 2017, a large number of European platforms offered auto-bid or auto-selection functions for P2P consumer lending (82 percent) and P2P property lending (67 percent), while the percentage was lower for P2P business lending (25 percent). See Ziegler et al., 'Shifting', (fn. 1), p. 40–41. Recent studies seem to evidence a better performance of algorithms in predicting defaults in China – which favours the use of auto-bid mechanisms – but also shows that the algorithms contain gender and race-based biases: *Runshan Fu/Yan Huang/Param Vir Singh*, 'Crowds, Lending, Machine, and Bias', June 24, 2020, <https://papers.ssrn.com/sol3/papers.cfm?abstract_id=3206027>. Better results in terms of welfare for lenders, borrowers, and platforms (Pareto efficiency) seem to be associated with passive models (in which platforms perform the information research) or bank-like models (in which platforms bear liquidity risks: e.g., the Bandora "Go and Grow" product). See *Fabio Braggion et al.*, 'The Value of "New" and "Old" Intermediation in Online Debt Crowdfunding', CEPR Discussion Paper No. 14740/2020, <https://cepr.org/active/publications/discussion_papers/dp.php?dpno=14740#>. Partially *contra* to these conclusions and challenging the ability of the automatic systems used by some British platforms to reach information efficiency, see *Julian R. Franks/Nicolas Andre Benigno Serrano-Velarde/Oren Sussman*, 'Marketplace Lending, Information Aggregation, and Liquidity' (March 16, 2020), European Corporate Governance Institute–Finance Working Paper No. 678/2020, Review of Financial Studies (Forthcoming), p. 3, <https://ssrn.com/abstract=2869945>.

model is widespread in China and growing also in the US and UK.[32] Compared with the auto-bid system, the platform management component of this model is more evident and a certain return is promised, but the difference can be nuanced by different levels of investor power, automation, and guaranteed returns.

The sector is constantly developing, with the regular appearance of new and interesting subsegments like invoice trading.[33] Invoice trading consists of a platform's facilitation of the sale of an enterprise's business receivables at a discount to investors so that the enterprise can gain liquidity, but this phenomenon will not be analysed here, as it deserves a separate discussion.

From a regulatory point of view, it is important to identify the risks inherent in marketplace lending and for regulators to be aware that each business model entails its own risks.[34] The most important of these risks pertain to crowd-lender/

---

32 About the different models, see *Eleanor Kirby/Shane Worner*, 'Crowdfunding: An Infant Industry Growing Fast', OICV-IOSCO Staff Working Paper 3/2014, <http://www.iosco.org/research/pdf/swp/Crowd-funding-An-Infant-Industry-Growing-Fast.pdf>; *CGFS/FSB* (fn. 25); *Claessens et al.* (fn. 30), p. 30 et seqq.

33 In 2017, invoice trading represented, at a volume of € 535.84 million, 15.9 percent of the European alternative finance market. It was the second-biggest subsector of this market after P2P consumer lending. See *Ziegler et al.*, 'Shifting' (fn. 1) p. 31. In 2018, it was the fourth-biggest, at a volume of €803 million. *Ziegler*, 'Global' (fn. 2) 78 – 79. Concerning the challenges in regulating invoice trading in Italy, *see Eugenia Macchiavello*, 'La Regolazione del FinTech tra Innovazione, Esigenze di Tutela e Level-Playing Field: L'inesplorato Caso dell'Invoice Trading', Banca, impresa e società 3 (2019) 497 (in Italian only, with English abstract). Art. 45(2)(d) of the ECSP Regulation considers extending its scope to this segment of the alternative finance market.

34 More extensively about the characteristics, business models, benefits, and risks of Financial Return Crowdfunding (FRC) and for references, see *Eugenia Macchiavello*, 'Peer-to-peer Lending' (fn. 2) p. 540 – 42; *Id.*, 'Financial-Return Crowdfunding' (fn. 2); *Guido Ferrarini/Eugenia Macchiavello*, 'Investment-based Crowdfunding: Is MiFID II Enough?', in: Danny Busch/Guido Ferrarini (eds.), Regulation of EU Financial Markets: MiFID II, 2017, p. 668 et seqq.; *Id.*, 'FinTech and Alternative Finance' (fn. 2); *John Armour/Luca Enriques*, 'The Promise and Perils of Crowdfunding: Between Corporate Finance and Consumer Contracts', The Modern Law Review 81(1) (2018) 51; *Antonella Sciarrone Alibrandi et al.* (fn. 2); *Mark Fenwick/Joseph A. McCahery/Erik P.M. Vermeulen*, 'Fintech and the Financing of Entrepreneurs: From Crowdfunding to Marketplace Lending' In: Douglas Cumming/Lars Hornuf (eds), The Economics of Crowdfunding, 2018; *FCA*, 'The FCA's Regulatory Approach to Crowdfunding and Similar Activities', (2013) CP13/13; *European Commission Financial Services User Group*, 'Crowdfunding from an Investor Perspective, (EU 2015), 25; *Mark Carney*, 'The Promise of FinTech – Something New Under the Sun?', speech at Deutsche Bundesbank G20 conference 'Digitalising Finance, Financial Inclusion and Financial Literacy', (Wiesbaden, 25 January 2017), <www.bankofengland.co.uk/-/media/boe/files/speech/2017/the-promise-of-fintech-something-new-under-the-sun.pdf?la=en&hash=0C2E1BBF1AA5-CE510BD5DF40EB5D1711E4DC560F>; *FSB*, 'Financial Stability Implications from FinTech. Super-

investor protection, and there are some variations in this risk depending on the business model under discussion.

Under the basic model, crowd-lenders face the risk of losing the capital invested, both because of the possibility of borrower default or, in the absence of an effective contingent plan and new servicing, the platform's default. They might also be harmed by misleading or insufficient information, herding,[35] lax pre-screening or other agency problems, and conflicts of interest with the platform; for example, with respect to the latter, where remuneration schemes are based on the volume and number of loans intermediated and only crowd-lenders bear the credit risk. Considering that investors contribute only a limited sum to each loan, a collective action problem is also present unless the platform assumes the role of the lenders'/investors' agent and has not itself defaulted.

When algorithms or even portfolio management systems are deployed, risk management, liability, and the parties against whom legal recourse is available become central issues.[36] Notary models entail the usual issues of "originate-to-distribute" models (in terms of incentives and legal recourse available only against the SPV) and (systemic) risks related to the closer interconnection with the banking sector. Balance sheet models are less innovative and therefore raise fewer foundational issues; they are closer to the structure of investment banks and investment funds.

Illiquidity represents an additional relevant risk on the investor side. To improve liquidity, some platforms offer crowd-lenders the opportunity to resell

---

visory and Regulatory Issues that Merit Authorities' Attention', (27 June 2017), <www.fsb.org/wp-content/uploads/R270617.pdf>; *CGFS/FSB* (fn. 25); *EBA*, 'Opinion on Lending-based Crowdfunding', EBA/Op/2015/03'; *ESMA*, 'Opinion on Investment-based Crowdfunding', ESMA/2014/1378; *Claessens et al* (fn. 30).

35 Studies attest to the fact that crowd-lenders seem subject to herding, but based on rational factors ("rational herding"), relying, correctly, on soft information and signals from more informed investors. See *Rajkamal Iyer et al.*, 'Screening Peers Softly: Inferring the Quality of Small Borrowers', Management Science 62(6) (2016) 1554; *A. Mohammadi/K. Shafi*, 'How Wise Are Crowd? A Comparative Study of Crowd and Institutions', (2019) Paper presented at DRUID19 Conference, Frederiksberg, Denmark, <https://conference.druid.dk/acc_papers/0j8pnrgwc9fqajb5ylj6ew9fuoh3ul.pdf> (most successful borrowers have a good online reputation and track record). Nonetheless, on the risk of investor biases and mispricing, see *Laura Gonzalez/Yuliya Komarova Loureiro*, 'When Can a Photo Increase Credit? The Impact of Lender and Borrower Profiles on Online Peer-to-Peer Loans, Journal of Behavioral and Experimental Finance 2 (2014) 44; *Saman Adhami/Gianfranco Gianfrate/Sofia A. Johan,* 'Risks and Returns in Crowdlending', March 3, 2019, <https://ssrn.com/abstract=3345874>; for a review of the relevant literature, see *Cummins et al.* (fn. 30), 20 et seqq.; *Alexander Bachmann et al.*, 'Online Peer-to-Peer Lending – A Literature Review', Journal of Internet Banking and Commerce 16(2) (2011) 1.

36 About marketplace lending and AI, see also the paper by Reiner in this Special Issue.

their rights on the platform (e.g., early reimbursement) or on P2P marketplaces ("bulletin boards").[37]

Recently, the sector has been characterized by a growing number of institutional and professional investors participating in the marketplace as lenders.[38] This raises issues about how to take advantage of institutional investors' ability to reduce information asymmetry (through, for example, the use of proprietary algorithms) while limiting the risk of cherry picking by these investors at the expense of retail investors.[39] It should be kept in mind that it has been in reaction to such "institutionalization" (as well as to liquidity problems) that many platforms in the US, China, and UK have recently moved away from the original "direct" and auction-based models to automatic investment and portfolio management models (while at the same reducing the information available on the platform); this has been done in order to decrease the resource disparity between retail and sophisticated investors.[40]

---

37 In 2014, 29 percent of lending-based platforms featured some form of secondary market for their products (versus only 9.5 percent of European equity-based platforms). See *Giuliana Borello et al.*, 'The Funding Gap and The Role of Financial Return Crowdfunding: Some Evidence From European Platforms', JIBC 20(1) (2015) 1, p. 13, 16.

38 Fifty-five percent of P2P business lending platforms and 38 percent of P2P property lending platforms have disclosed that in 2018 more than one-third of their volumes (versus only 10 percent of P2P consumer lending platforms) were funded by institutional investors. The level of "institutionalization" is different across countries, with high percentages in Benelux, Italy, and Germany (respectively, 90 percent, 88 percent, and 64 percent, but irrespective of the business model, and therefore including invoice trading, which is characterized by the dominance of institutional investors) and low percentages in the Commonwealth of Independent States, Eastern Europe, Central Europe, and the Baltics (respectively, 2 percent, 4 percent, 5 percent, and 5 percent). See *Ziegler et al.* (fn. 2), p. 86 – 88.

39 There is evidence that sophisticated investors – including retail investors using robo-advisors – outperform unsophisticated investors; for this reason, some platforms have decided to intensify prescreening while reducing information available to investors in order to level the playing field. See *Boris Vallée/Yao Zeng*, 'Marketplace Lending: A New Banking Paradigm?', The Review of Financial Studies 32(5) (2019) 1939; *Mohammadi/Shafi* (fn. 35) (institutional investors outperform retail investors in predicting borrower default, especially in the cases of riskier and smaller loans).

40 *Tetyana Balyuk/Sergei A. Davydenko*, 'Reintermediation in FinTech: Evidence from Online Lending', (August 8, 2019), Michael J. Brennan Irish Finance Working Paper Series Research Paper No. 18 – 17, 31st Australasian Finance and Banking Conference 2018, <https://ssrn.com/abstract=3189236> (theorizing a shift towards reintermediation in P2P lending markets because of improved screening by platforms, done in order to attract unsophisticated investors with their more passive attitude of reliance on the platform's efforts; however, the sample – and prediction – is limited to the US market, with some reference to the UK market); *Vallée/Zeng* (fn. 39),

Crowd-borrowers, on the other hand, might face collective action issues in debt restructuring, discrimination in selection,[41] abusive contractual terms, and negative consequences from the publication of unprotected corporate information.

Finally, the financial system might have to deal with the consequences of the inadequate management of platforms' operational risk with respect to fraud, cybersecurity, money laundering, and the financing of terrorism. Systemic risk remains low at present, but this may change in light of the sector's growth rate and increased interconnections with the mainstream financing sector. Some of these risks have begun to materialize with the first platform defaults in Europe, which have increased regulators' attention and concerns.[42]

3 Regulatory Trends and Main Policy Issues in Various European Countries

Member States' regulatory responses to marketplace lending, as mentioned above, have been extremely varied.[43] Marketplace lending platforms, for in-

---

p. 1946. With respect to the UK P2P market and the move towards auto-bid and institutional investments as a response to liquidity shocks, see *Franks et al.* (fn. 31).

41 About the risk of discrimination against certain minorities when using algorithms in credit markets, see *Andreas Fuster et al.*, 'Predictably Unequal? The Effects of Machine Learning on Credit Markets' (March 11, 2020), <https://ssrn.com/abstract=3072038>.

42 The Swedish platform TrustBuddy went into administration in October 2015 and has been investigated for "serious misconduct" by its management, while the British platform Lendy entered into administration in May 2019: <http://www.p2pfinancenews.co.uk/2019/05/29/p2p-administrations-a-timeline/>. See also fn. 24.

43 For a comparative analysis of the main European systems and related discussion, please refer to the contributions indicated in footnote 2 and to: *European Commission*, 'Crowdfunding in the EU Capital Markets Union', Commission Staff Working Document, SWD(2016) 154 final, <https://ec.europa.eu/info/system/files/crowdfunding-report-03052016_en.pdf>; *Matthias Klaes et al.*, 'Identifying Market and Regulatory Obstacles to Crossborder Development of Crowdfunding in the EU', (2017), <https://ec.europa.eu/info/sites/info/files/171216-crowdfunding-report_en.pdf>; *CrowdfundingHub*, 'Crowdfunding Crossing Borders', (2016), <https://drive.google.com/file/d/0B7uykMX1rDrWU3BRZTBMNzFwLVE/view>; *Olena Havrylchyk*, 'Regulatory Framework for the Loan-Based Crowdfunding Platforms', OECD Economics Department Working Papers No. 1513/2018, <https://www.oecd.org/officialdocuments/publicdisplaydocumentpdf/?cote=ECO/WKP(2018)61&docLanguage=En>; *Dirk A. Zetzsche/Christina Preiner*, 'Cross-Border Crowdfunding – Towards a Single Crowdfunding Market for Europe', European Business Organization Law Review 19 (2018) 217; *Deirdre Ahern*, 'Regulatory Arbitrage in a FinTech World: Devising an Optimal EU Regulatory Response to Crowdlending', (March 1, 2018), European Banking Institute Working

stance, have received varied legal classifications and consequent regulatory treatments, depending on the country:

a) as payment service providers (PSPs) or even as payment agents of EU PSPs when directly handling client money; nonetheless, platforms perform much more complex services than PSPs such as project owner selection, matching, pricing, information channelling, which better characterize crowdfunding activities and are not covered by rules governing PSPs; therefore, such relevant services remain unregulated (in e.g., Italy, Poland, the Czech Republic, Denmark, Sweden);

b) as intermediaries conducting a form of banking activity without the required authorization: in some countries, lending was formerly reserved to banks and therefore platforms could be considered as facilitators of an illegal activity performed by private lenders (Germany and France before the reform); other countries have regarded the platforms' activity as the collection of repayable funds from the public or simply as the facilitation of such collection. This characterization depends on the particular borders of the banking monopoly and the transposition of the Capital Requirement Directive/Regulation in each country (in, e.g., Italy and Belgium, where there is a prohibition on the collection of repayable funds from the public even if by non-professionals). However, this perspective appears to misread the reality of marketplace lending: in fact, platforms do not perform the typical economic functions of banks (maturity/liquidity transformation and money creation through the activity of receiving repayable deposits in order to provide loans), offer more limited kinds of services, and – at least under models other than the balance sheet model – do not lend at their own risk.[44] More complex business models deploying auto-bid systems or even individual portfolio management and guaranteed returns models, the use of contingent funds and investment advice, with crowd-lenders bearing credit and liquidity risks, indeed raise important regulatory issues but only from an in-

---

Paper Series 2018 No. 24, <https://ssrn.com/abstract=3163728>; *Sebastiaan N. Hooghiemstra/Karl de Buysere*, 'The Perfect Regulation of Crowdfunding: What Should the European Regulator Do?', in: Oliver Gajda/Dennis Brüntje (eds.), Crowdfunding in Europe – State of the Art in Theory and Practice, 2015; *Elif Härkönen*, 'Regulating Equity Crowdfunding Service Providers – An Innovation-Oriented Approach to Alternative Financing', NJCL 1 (2018), 201; *T. Jørgensen*, 'Peer-to-Peer Lending – A New Digital Intermediary, New Legal Challenges', NJCL 1 (2018) 231 (concerning the Nordic and Eastern European countries).

44 See *Claessens et al.* (fn. 30), p. 32; *Balyuk/Davidenko* (fn. 40), 38; *CGFS/FSB* (fn. 25), 31; *Olena Havrylchyk/Marianne Verdier*, 'The Financial Intermediation Role of the P2P Lending Platforms', Comparative Economic Studies 60 (2018) 115; *Boris Vallée/Yao Zeng* (fn. 39) (marketplace lending is characterized by joint information production by both platforms and investors); *Anjan V. Thakor*, 'Fintech and Banking: What Do We Know?', Journal of Financial Intermediation 41 (2020), 1.

vestment (not banking) law perspective (see below). Banking law issues can only arise in case of of lenders' instant redemption rights, absence of asset separation, or the absence of any decisional power over the destination of the funds to crowd-borrowers,;[45]

c) as credit brokers who professionally connect lenders and borrowers to allow the same to conclude loan contracts (e. g., Estonia and Finland for consumer loans, and Norway for all loans). Credit brokers are generally subject to light national regimes which are focused on borrower (not investor) protection. At the EU level, the discipline of credit intermediaries has only been partially harmonized by the Mortgage Credit Directive (2014/17/EU); furthermore, such EU law tends to apply only in the case of professional lenders (while crowd-lenders are considered nonprofessional; see Art. 1(1)b-c Consumer credit directive – CCD – No. 2008/48/CE and below);

d) as investment firms that perform, depending on the business model, reception and transmission of orders, placing without firm commitment, investment advice, individual portfolio management, or as managers of investment funds. The fact that they offer investment opportunities and channel relevant investment information makes the activity of platforms something closer to investment services than banking activity; nonetheless, MiFID II applies only in the case of investment services pertaining to financial instruments. However, not only does the identification of all of the typical features of such investment services depend on national interpretations that are not straightforward (see below) but, preliminarily, the legal characterization of loans as financial instruments is debated. In fact, while crowd-loans might recall debt securities (bonds) in terms of the obligation to repay capital and interest, they might not implicate the same standardization (in particular with respect to their size and applicable interest rate, which are sometimes set within a range based on an auction or matching, or even, in the case of auto-bid/portfolio management, on the composition of a personalized portfolio) or transferability rules. In particular, "financial instruments" are not defined except by example in MiFID II, and Member States traditionally employ different interpretations and criteria. Nonetheless, the Commission has identified their 'negotiability in the capital market' as their fundamental

---

45 Certain authors (*Havrylchyk/Verdier*, fn. 44; *Braggion et al.*, fn. 31, 2) recognize some similarities between marketplace lending and banking activity, specifically in the use of auto-investment mechanisms (portfolios of short-term loan liabilities invested in long-term loan liabilities) and credit scoring – because of the reliance on platforms' due diligence – and in the creation of liquidity for secondary markets. Nonetheless, they also recognize that significant differences remain, including the fact that investors bear the risks and also potentially provide instructions/orders.

feature, and described this as transferability in all contexts in which buyers and sellers of securities meet, clarifying that these 'contexts' might not correspond to regulated trading venues but instead refer to the absence of significant obstacles to transferability (e.g., with respect to contractual terms, legal restrictions, etc.).[46] Therefore, the transferability of crowd-loans on the same platform (through bulletin boards or kinds of secondary markets, especially when multilateral matching systems allow the conclusion of a contract) raises the issue of whether they can be characterized as transferable securities (as recognized in the Netherlands) and whether borrowers can be characterized as issuers (even when they are consumers);[47]

e) as alternative investment funds – when crowdfunding operations entail the use of a collective investment scheme, collecting funds from the public (e.g. in the form of shares and investing in companies' debt instruments), or acquiring loans or even directly providing the same, the Alternative Investment Fund Managers Directive (AIFMD) No. 2011/61/EU (and the related Regulations EuVECA No. 345/2013, EuSEF No. 346/2013 and ELTIF No. 2015/760, with specific reference to loan origination) should apply. This Directive subjects fund managers to general conduct and organizational requirements in addition to specific disclosures, but the rules about loan origination, leverage limits, retail investors' access, and marketing (at the product level) are not harmonized among Member States;[48]

f) finally, as a (generally) new financial intermediary subject to special regulation (e.g., in France, UK, and the Netherlands; applying the same regime to both marketplace investing and marketplace lending, Portugal, Spain, Belgium, Finland, and Lithuania). The regimes cover both consumer and business loans (UK and Spain; in France, only business and educational loans) or only business loans (Portugal, Netherlands, Lithuania, and Finland).

These regulations related to crowdfunding have in common the creation of a new kind of financial intermediary, authorized by the national or European fi-

---

46 *European Commission*, 'Questions and Answers on the MiFID Directive 2004/39/EC', p. 1, 22, <https://ec.europa.eu/info/sites/info/files/business_economy_euro/banking_and_finance/docu ments/mifid-2004-0039-commission-questions-answers_en_0.pdf>.

47 See in more detail *Eugenia Macchiavello*, 'Financial-return' (fn. 2), 689; *Id.*, 'FinTech Regulation from a Cross-sectoral Perspective, in Veerle Colaert/Danny Busch/Thomas Incalza (eds.), European Financial Regulation: Levelling the Cross-Sectoral Playing Field, 2019, p. 63, p. 69; *Id.*, 'European Crowdfunding Service Providers' (fn. 15)'; *Id.*, 'What to Expect' (fn. 2); *Id.*, 'Disintermediation' (fn. 15).

48 See *ESMA*, 'Key Principles for a European Framework on Loan Origination by Funds – Opinion', (11 April 2016), ESMA/2016/596.

nancial authority after verification of the "fit and proper" qualifications of the managers and directors, an adequate business plan, business continuity arrangements, professional insurance (in some places, such as in Spain, Portugal, and Finland, as an alternative to a certain amount of minimum capital) and, in some countries, proper corporate organization (Spain and Portugal). These actors are subject to a lighter and more flexible regulatory regime than banks or investment firms focused primarily on informational requirements, but in general the borrower remains the only party responsible for information about the project and the borrower him or herself.[49] Crowdfunding providers are also subject to other general conduct rules, such as requirements to act honestly, fairly, and professionally towards clients (both crowd-lender and crowd-borrowers), with policies in place to avoid and manage conflicts of interest, In some countries, crowd-borrowers are considered at least in part to have the same status as consumers under consumer credit legislation (UK, Netherlands, Finland, Lithuania). A general duty to avoid money laundering tends also to be recognized.[50]

Organizational requirements, when imposed (e. g., Spain and Portugal), are not detailed, relying and rely on the discretion of platforms over their business organization. The UK has, however, recently introduced more demanding requirements in terms of risk management with respect to more complex models such as loan pricing services and portfolio management that promise a certain level of return; even simple models must meet a minimum level of internal governance (e. g., an independent risk management function, an independent internal audit function, and a compliance function) on a proportionality principle basis, mirroring the requirements placed on dealers and investment managers.[51]

---

49 Relevant information, especially about the lender, the proposed investments and their risks and costs, and past performance, with warnings about the absence of traditional safeguards, must be presented on the website and in a document that takes the place of a prospectus (under an exemption from prospectus requirements, where applicable to investment products other than transferable securities) that is not approved by the relevant authority. In certain countries, the law or the authority mandates the use of a standard document (France and Portugal) but the document is required everywhere to be concise and easy to understand.

50 While Austria, Germany, and France have extended AML/CT rules to platforms, the regimes in the UK, Spain, and Portugal only require that platforms have an AML/CT policy.

51 Platforms that price loans are required to gather sufficient information about the borrower, to categorize borrowers according to their credit risk in a systematic and structured way (taking into account the probability of default and the loss in the event of default), and set a fair and appropriate price reflecting the risk profile of the borrower. Platforms that also offer portfolio management with a guaranteed return must have a risk management framework ensuring that they can achieve the stated target rate of return with a reasonable degree of confidence; they must be able to evaluate loans, at least when originated, in the event of default, and when the platform is facilitating an investor's exit. When advertising a certain return, platforms

Prudential requirements are generally absent, save in the UK, Lithuania and – when loans intermediated exceed €2 million – Spain, the last of which also mandates certain own funds requirements.

On the other hand, crowdfunding providers everywhere face significant limitations on their permissible activities; for example, activities reserved to other intermediaries, in particular investment services or payment services, are prohibited except when specifically authorized. In addition, save in the UK and the Netherlands, the size of loan requests from the same borrower in 12 months is generally limited to somewhere between €1 million and 5 million,[52] and there are limitations on the maximum investable amount contributed by each retail crowd-lender per project and per year.[53]

The majority of jurisdictions do not require platforms to assess the appropriateness of an investment for the crowd-lender, but there are exceptions such as in the Netherlands (for investments above €500), Belgium, Lithuania, and, starting in 2019, the UK. Platforms are generally only required to disclose the criteria deployed in pre-screening applicants, but in Spain and the Netherlands there is an explicit duty of due diligence in selecting crowd-borrowers. Only a few jurisdictions recognize a right of withdrawal for crowd-lenders (the UK and the Netherlands).

Most regimes also allow traditional financial institutions to conduct crowdfunding operations (except in Spain), without the limitations and constraints of crowdfunding platforms in terms of services and offer/investible amounts, but generally subject them, in addition to the regulations specific to their regime, to requirements specifically applicable to crowdfunding (e. g. disclosure duties and other investor protection measures).[54]

---

should be able to demonstrate the use of appropriate data and a robust modelling capability, and disclose actual historical returns against target rates: *FCA* (fn. 27); *Id*, 'Loan-based ('peer-to-peer') and Investment-based Crowdfunding Platforms: Feedback to CP18/20 and Final Rules', (June 2019), PS19/14, 10 – 13, <https://www.fca.org.uk/publication/policy/ps19-14.pdf>.
52 The maximum threshold is €1 million in France and Portugal, €2 million in Spain, and €5 million in Lithuania and Finland. In the Netherlands, the reference is the general exemption from the prospectus obligation for maximum consideration, which corresponds to € 2.5 million.
53 In France, the maximum size of the investment for retail investors is €2,000 per project and per issuer on a given platform; in Spain and Portugal, it is €3,000 per issuer and €10,000 per year in total on all platforms (these limits do not apply to institutional investors or to legal persons or individuals with an income above certain levels); and €80,000 in the Netherlands.
54 In Lithuania, regulated firms must respect the higher prudential requirements and the stricter "fit and proper" requirements between the ones set in the crowdfunding regulations and those applicable to their own regimes (Art. 7(6) and 8(7) Crowdfunding Law). In Portugal, Article

All of these differences in regulations applicable to marketplace lending trace back, on the one hand, to the above-mentioned variety of business models and, on the other, to the persistent differences in legal traditions and implementation of EU Directives, and to the presence of a number of unharmonized areas (e. g. company law and lending activity) despite recent efforts to create Capital Markets and Banking Unions. For instance, Member States offer different definitions or identification criteria applicable to certain investment services, financial instruments, and transferable securities; EU financial law (e. g. MiFID, the Prospectus Regulation, MAR, etc.) must be implemented in the face of these differences[55] and in the face of varied thresholds and coverages (e. g., transferable securities versus investment products) applicable to the prospectus exemption.[56]

Thus, marketplace lending platforms interested in offering cross-border crowdfunding services face significant regulatory obstacles because their activity is potentially subject to oversight by different authorities and to additional national rules. This situation applies even when certain portions of a platform's activity are covered by a European passport; for instance, in case of a crowdfunding platform authorized as a payment service provider services offered by the same other than payment services, such as credit scoring, debt collection, etc., might fall outside the scope of the passport. Furthermore, the diversity in the regimes applied to marketplace platforms in the territory of the EU clashes with the current objective of creating a real single market (in terms of regulatory arbitrage, European freedoms, equal investor protection, etc.). In light of these problems, it is no surprise that the level of cross-border activity in Europe, although increasing, remains limited.[57]

---

15 of *Regulamento* 1/2016 requires banks to comply with their own rules when offering crowdfunding.

55 For instance, in Poland, Italy, Denmark, and Sweden, the shares of private limited liability companies are not considered transferable securities, while this is not the case in Hungary. See *Macchiavello*, 'Financial-return' (fn. 2) 698. See, more recently, concerning the characterization of crypto-assets in various Member States and different interpretations of the concept of financial instrument/transferable security, *ESMA*, 'Initial Coin Offerings and Crypto-Assets. Advice', (9 January 2019), ESMA50 – 157– 1391.

56 Ranging, under the previous EU Prospectus Directive No. 2003/71/CE, from €100,000 (for a mandatory exemption) to €5 million (for an optional exemption) in total consideration per offer in 12 months and, under the recent EU Regulation No. 2017/1129/EU, from €1 million to €8 million in 12 months.

57 For recent data about investments and requests for funds across European borders, which have been increasing in recent years, see *Klaes et al.* (fn. 43); *Ziegler et al.*, 'Shifting' (fn. 1), p. 48 – 51; *Karsten Wenzlaff et al.*, 'Crowdfunding in Europe: Between Fragmentation and Harmonization', in: Roten Shneor/Liang Zhao/Bjørn-Tore Flåten (eds) Advances in Crowdfunding, 2020, 373, p. 376 – 78.

4 The European Crowdfunding Service Provider Regulation in Light of Marketplace Lending Challenges: How Effective Is It?

4.1 An Analysis of the ECSP Regulation: The Most Controversial Issues

The ECSP Regulation, which is aimed at creating a single crowdfunding market while protecting investors, represents a great advancement for the crowdfunding sector.

As mentioned above (§1), since the Commission's Proposal for a Regulation on European Crowdfunding Service Providers for Business of March 2018, the legislative process has progressed slowly, in part because of differing views about financial-return crowdfunding intermediation emerged during trilateral negotiations (see in particular the European Parliament's resolution of 27 March 2019[58] and the very different Council suggestions of 24 June 2019[59]).[60] The text adopted in October 2020, therefore, contains several fundamental revisions from the original proposal.[61]

In the following paragraphs, we will analyse the ECSP Regulation through the lenses of the main legal and policy issues presented above. In particular, we will assess whether, first, the ECSP Regulation is able to provide solutions for the entire single market and second, whether the regime is designed to respond to the main risks presented by crowdfunding. Furthermore, we will evaluate, in light of the regulatory choices made in the adopted Regulation (also as compared to the original proposal) and the overall design of the regime, which

---

58 *European Parliament*, 'Legislative Resolution of 27 March 2019 on the Proposal for a Regulation of the European Parliament and of the Council on European Crowdfunding Service Providers (ECSP) for Business (COM(2018)0113 – C8–0103/2018–2018/0048(COD)), <http://www.europarl.europa.eu/RegData/seance_pleniere/textes_adoptes/provisoire/2019/03-27/0301/P8_TA-PROV(2019)0301_EN.pdf>.
59 *Council of the European Union*, 'Proposal for a Regulation of the European Parliament and of the Council on European Crowdfunding Service Providers (ECSP) for Business and amending Regulation (EU) No 2017/1129 – Mandate for negotiations with the European Parliament – Compromise proposal', (24 June 2019), <https://data.consilium.europa.eu/doc/document/ST-10557-2019-INIT/en/pdf>.
60 In this respect, see *Macchiavello*, 'What to Expect' (fn. 2).
61 Again, for a detailed analysis of the ECSP Regulation, please see *Macchiavello*, 'The European Crowdfunding Service Providers Regulation' (fn. 15); *Id.*, 'Marketplace Lending' (fn. 15); *Id.*, 'Disintermediation in Fund-raising' (fn. 15).

function of marketplace lending platforms has been recognized and how the ECSP Regulation has addressed the platform dilemma. Finally, we will attempt to forecast the future impact of the ECSP Regulation on the European crowd-funding market.

4.2 Is the ECSP Regulation Creating the Conditions for a Single Crowdfunding Market?

4.2.1 Authorization Process and Supervisory Authority Powers

The Regulation introduces a mandatory European regime for crowdfunding plat-forms, requiring any legal person willing to offer crowdfunding services covered by such Regulation to apply for a new authorization (Artt. 3(1); 12), and benefit-ing, once authorized, from a specific European passport modelled after that of MiFID II. No exemption is envisaged for platforms operating only nationally or with low volumes, which, after a transitional period (ending 10 November 2022), which can be extended by the Commission by an additional 12 months: Art. 48(3)), will be required to comply with the ECSP regime. Already-regulated entities (banks, investment firms, e-money providers, etc.) that are interested in offering crowdfunding services need also to apply for ECSP authorization, but can take advantage of simplifications (in terms of procedure and documen-tation) and exemptions (e. g., to capital requirements for operational risk when already complying with their own capital requirement) in order to avoid duplica-tion (recital 35, Artt. 12(14)-(15) and 11(3)).

The licensing and supervising authority is the national competent authority (NCA) of the Member State where the applicant is established (instead of the ESMA, as originally proposed), which will request that ESMA enter the author-ized ECSP into a public register that it will set up and maintain.[62]

The requirements to obtain the authorization are harmonized and consist not only of certain ordinary requirements (minimum capital, insurance policy coverage, a programme of operations, proper internal organization, "fit and proper" managers) and plans for business continuity, but also of a description and evidence of compliance with certain prudential safeguards and a number

---

62 The ESMA registry will also indicate which crowdfunding services the authorized ECSP can offer, additional activities it can carry out, the Member States in which it can operate, the super-visory authority, and penalties that may be imposed (Art. 14).

of other conduct and organizational requirements[63] (see below §§4.3.1 ss.). Since the ECSP Regulation is a maximum harmonization instrument, Member States cannot impose stricter or additional requirements and, in particular, according to Art. 1(3), cannot impose on platforms the same requirements of banks or require crowd-borrowers/crowd-lenders to obtain a banking license or an express dispensation or exemption.

The powers of the NCA are harmonized in an extremely detailed way (Art. 30 ff)[64] and the ESMA's RTSs will further harmonize standard forms, templates, and procedures related to the authorization application, requirements, and reporting, taking into account the nature, scale, and complexity of the services offered (Artt. 12(16); 16(3)). The NCA will, however, determine the frequency and depth of the compliance assessment, which will take place in part via on-site inspections, again 'having regard to the nature, scale and complexity of the activities' of the ECSP.

Therefore, as regards the authorization process and supervision, the ECSP regime seems designed to adequately ensure harmonization, not only with respect to the authorization requirements but also with respect to supervisory practices, while ensuring that NCAs will be entrusted with a supervisory role.

4.2.2 Scope and Limitations with Respect to Activities and Products

It is possible that the goal of creating a single internal market in the crowdfunding sector may be frustrated by the limited scope of the ECSP Regulation. The Regulation, in fact, applies only to identified crowdfunding services. Crowdfunding services are defined as 'the matching of business funding interests of investors and project owners through the use of a crowdfunding platform' but identified, as regards marketplace lending, in the 'facilitation of granting of loans' (Art. 2(2)), with exclusive reference to business loans.

Consumer loans are expressly excluded under the justification that consumer loans are already covered by the CCD and also in line with the Capital Markets

---

63 E.g., in terms of systems and procedures for risk management; data processing; complaint handling; verification of the completeness, correctness, and clarity of the information provided; and investment limits.

64 NCAs will receive annual confidential reports from ECSPs about the projects funded, specifying for each project the project owner and the amount raised, the instrument issued, and aggregated information about the investors and invested amount (by fiscal residency and type of investor). This report will be transmitted to the ESMA in an anonymized form to facilitate the publication of aggregated statistics about the EU crowdfunding market (Art. 16).

Union's focus on business financing. Nonetheless, as anticipated (§3), the CCD only applies to loans provided to consumers by a professional lender and therefore tend not to apply to P2P loans where the lender is also a consumer,[65] despite the platforms' professional role in the lending process, including the provision of contractual documentation. However, certain countries have adopted a broader interpretation in their national consumer credit laws or have specifically extended the CCD to P2P platforms.[66] The Commission is considering revising the CCD in order to extend its coverage to P2P loans,[67] but it is unlikely that a comprehensive regime (e. g. including an authorization) for crowdfunding platforms can be accommodated under the CCD. The consumer lending segment represents the most relevant (and delicate, concerning a 'contractually weak' party) part of marketplace lending in Europe (see §1) and seems to be used by entrepreneurs even for their business activities.[68]

Furthermore, the definition of "loan" as 'an unconditional obligation to repay [the capital] with the accrued interest' might exclude from the Regulation's scope not only interest-free loans but also subordinated loans (conditioned on previous satisfaction by another creditor) and loans for which the lender's remuneration is conditioned on the investee's profits, that is, profit-participation loans (which are closer to equity investments).

The platform's "facilitation" activity mentioned above, as explained in recital 11, might, under the basic model, simply entail presentation of projects on the website and matching of the interests of crowd-lenders and crowd-borrowers. However, the recently adopted version has also allowed the activities of more complex models, subject to additional requirements, activities like scoring and pricing of investments and loans and the individual portfolio management of

---

65 E.g., in Belgium, Italy, and Poland.

66 Respectively, Denmark, Finland, Estonia; and the UK, the Netherlands, Finland, and Lithuania.

67 *European Commission*, 'Staff Working Document – Impact Assessment – Legislative Proposal for an EU Framework on Crowd and Peer To Peer Finance', (30 October 2017), 32–33, <https://ec.europa.eu/info/law/better-regulation/initiatives/ares-2017-5288649_en>; *Id.*, 'Evaluation of the Consumer Credit Directive (Directive 2008/48/EC). Summary Report – Public Consultation', (May 2019), 6, <https://ec.europa.eu/info/law/better-regulation/have-your-say/initiatives/1844-Evaluation-of-the-Consumer-Credit-Directive/public-consultation>; *Id.*, 'Consumer Financial Services Action Plan: Better Products, More Choice', (Communication) COM(2017) 139 final (23 March 2017), 8; *Id.*, 'Consumer Credit Agreements–Review of EU Rules. Inception Impact Assessment', (23 June 2020), p. 1, <https://ec.europa.eu/info/law/better-regulation/have-your-say/initiatives/12465-Consumer-credit-agreements-review-of-EU-rules>.

68 *Ziegler/Shneor* (fn. 25) 76 report that a large number of business crowd-borrowers are actually using consumer crowd-loans to support their business activities.

loans, as suggested by the European Parliament and reflecting recent market developments (see above §2). The latter consists of the 'allocation by the crowd-funding service provider of a pre-determined amount of funds of an investor, which is an original lender, to one or multiple crowdfunding projects on its crowdfunding platform in accordance with an individual mandate given by the investor on a discretionary investor-by-investor basis' (new Art. 2(1)c). The Regulation defines portfolio management as the use of 'automated processes whereby funds are automatically allocated by the crowdfunding service provider to crowdfunding projects in accordance with, as under the non-automatic port-folio management, parameters and risk indicators predetermined by the investor (such as interest rate, maturity, risk category, target return), so called auto-investing' (recital 20).[69] The use of filtering systems that display results based on criteria relating to purely objective product features (e. g., economic sector, interest rate, type of instrument) is expressly permitted and is not considered portfolio management as long as investors 'review and expressly take an investment decision in relation to each individual crowdfunding offer'; these filtering systems are not classified either as "investment advice" – a service explicitly excluded and subject to MIFID II – where the presentation is neutral, without a recommendation being formulated.

The Regulation also covers marketplace investing when it corresponds to a MiFID II placement without a firm commitment, in conjunction with reception and transmission of orders pertaining to transferable securities and – the new category of "admitted instruments", identified with the shares of limited liability companies that are not considered financial instruments under national law but are freely transferable. Therefore, debt instruments not considered to be transferable securities under national law seem to remain outside the ECSP regime. In any case, platforms must inquire about and comply with national rules and procedures pertaining to the transfer of such products (recital 14).

Various additional services and business models must find a governing legal framework outside the ECSP Regulation. For instance, because ECSPs cannot financially participate in projects (see below § 4.3.5), models providing that the platform will co-lend with the crowd-lenders (even when this is intended to align the interests of the platform and the investors) fall outside the Regulation and remain subject to national law (or EU law or a mix of the two; e. g., directly lent investment funds managed by AIFMs); they are therefore potentially excluded from any passport (in situations where the interpretation that such models are

---

69 In line with ESMA's position on automation in investment services. See *ESMA*, 'Guidelines on Certain Aspects of the MiFID II Suitability Requirements – Final Report', (28 May 2018).

not permitted at all does not prevail). Platforms willing to offer crowdfunding services equivalent to individual investment portfolio management, collective investment schemes, OTF/MTF, etc., should obtain the corresponding authorization which can coexist with the ECSP one: see § 4.2.1). In particular, investment funds directly providing loans (credit funds) shall obtain from the NCA an authorization as an AIFM and comply with national rules, since many relevant aspects of doing so, especially in terms of retail distribution and additional requirements for direct lending, have not yet been harmonized at the EU level, although this is currently under discussion.[70]

Additional ancillary services provided by ECSPs under national law (Art. 1(2) (b)) are also excluded from the ECSP framework.

Summing up, the ECSP Regulation seems not to cover a relevant part (at least in some geographic areas) of the market (e. g., subordinated and profit-participating loans) or certain business models (e. g. collective investment schemes, investment advice), potentially creating regulatory arbitrage and reducing market integration. Furthermore, it also leaves unregulated the market for consumer loans, the most delicate (for borrower protection concerns) and largest part of the market in terms of volumes and market size.

Maximum Offer Threshold and Space Left to National Regimes: To be covered by the ECSP Regulation, any offer from the same project owner (taking into account not only crowdfunding offers but also other offers exempted under the Prospectus Regulation) should not exceed €5 million in total consideration within 12 months. Member States that have set lower thresholds in the Prospectus Regulation framework will be able to maintain them with respect to crowdfunding only for a period of 24 months after entry into force (Artt. 1(2) and 49). Thus, harmonization in this regard will be reached, but only after a transitional period.

Furthermore, whether it is possible to regulate under national law the services and offers not covered by the ECSP Regulation is not clear nor, consequently, is it clear whether national crowdfunding regimes can still exist under certain conditions. Anyway, because the Regulation is a maximum harmonization instrument and because of its above-described scope, it should be inferred that national crowdfunding regimes, if still allowed, can only cover crowdfunding models outside the ECSP Regulation's perimeter; for instance, crowdfunding services characterized as investment advice (probably not, instead, as reception and transmission of orders only) and exempted from MiFID II through its Art. 3(1)

---

70 *European Commission*, 'Assessing the Application and the Scope of Directive 2011/61/EU [...] on Alternative Investment Fund Managers', (10 June 2020), SWD(2020) 110 final, p. 29; *Id.*, 'A Digital Finance Strategy for the EU', (Communication) COM(2020) 591 final, p. 7.

(see in France) and the facilitation of consumer loans (where not already covered by the new CCD). In such cases, offers might even pertain to transferable securities (even loans, if qualified as such) equal to or below the national prospectus exemption (which can be above €5 million and up to €8 million), and offers of admitted instruments well above €5 million. Instead, Member States seem to have lost the power to regulate business models characterized as placement without guarantee and/or as reception and transmission of orders, even as respects offers of transferable securities between €5 million and the maximum threshold under national prospectus laws or offers of admitted instruments, as well as the facilitation of business loans above €5 million (but a specification and clarification would appear appropriate). It is unclear, however, whether it is possible to set up and differently regulate hybrid business models entailing co-lending by the platforms. As a result, room for regulatory competition and obstacles to the formation of a true single market might still exist.

Finally, certain relevant aspects of the regulatory scheme, some of which are discussed below, are left to Member States, such as the transferability rules of admitted instruments, marketing rules, and the regime for civil liability arising from information provided. Member States' discretions, options or variations are allowed in certain areas, such as the language and *ex ante* notification of the main informational document (§4.3.2).

4.3 Does the ECSP Regulation Address All of the Relevant Crowdfunding Risks?

4.3.1 Overview

The ECSP regime mimics the MiFID regime in simplified form, and has the aim of balancing innovation and SMEs' access to finance with investor protection. The regime is in principle the same for marketplace lending and investing but special rules and additional requirements apply in the case of particular business models seen as more complex (and generally associated with marketplace lending). The required disclosures differ depending on the type of crowdfunding and product.

In any case, the approved version, following in part the Council's suggestions and the 2019 revisions to the lending-based crowdfunding regime in the UK,[71] but going beyond the usual rules of national crowdfunding regimes, has

---

71 See above footnote 51 and accompanying text.

significantly expanded the duties of ECSPs, not only in terms of conduct rules but also in terms of organizational, risk management, and prudential requirements, especially for certain marketplace lending models. However, proportionality considerations and ESMA/EBA RTSs will play an important role in the application and implementation of rules.

4.3.2 Risk of Fraud, Misleading Information, and Investor Protection: Conduct and Disclosure Duties

The main risks, as evidenced above (§2), relate to investor protection. The adopted version of the Regulation has correctly decided to reserve certain protective measures for non-sophisticated investors in order to limit the platforms' requirements of sophisticated ones (see below).

ECSPs are subject to the general conduct rule to act honestly, fairly, and professionally in accordance with the best interests of their clients (Art. 3(2)). From this general duty, it might be possible to infer a duty to select projects with some diligence (see recital 18), therefore reducing any information asymmetry which might benefit crowd-investors. The adopted version has also introduced an explicit duty that ECSPs undertake a minimum level of due diligence in respect of project owners (crowd-borrowers), but only with respect to a history of criminal behaviour (for infringements of laws relating to commercial activity, insolvency, financial services, AML/CT, fraud, and professional obligations) and their establishment in noncooperative jurisdictions (with respect to AML/CT) (Art. 5).

The Regulation contains numerous disclosure obligations: ECSPs are required to make available to clients and potential clients, before they enter into the contract and also at the marketing stage, in a non-discriminatory manner, fair, clear, and not misleading information about fundamental aspects of the business under consideration such as information about themselves, the costs of the services, the financial and other risks, charges related to crowdfunding services and investments, and project selection criteria. The adopted version also requires additional information about the lack of a deposit guarantee and securities compensation coverage, the four-day reflection period for non-sophisticated investors (see below)[72] and, when the platform performs a credit scoring

---

72 The ECSP must inform the investor immediately before his/her expression of interest or order of the existence of the reflection period and its duration, and the modalities available to revoke his/her order or expression of interest; immediately after receipt of the offer to invest or of the

or pricing, the calculation method used and whether or not it uses audited financial statements; the method used must also comply with ESMA's RTS concerning the format and elements to be included (Art. 19).

Moreover, the adopted version has dedicated an entire article to requiring ECSPs, only when engaging in marketplace lending, to disclose annually and in a prominent part of their website, the default rates of the crowdfunding projects offered over at least the last 36 months and publish an outcome statement at the end of each financial year detailing: a) the expected and actual default rate of all loans by risk category; b) a summary of the assumptions used to determine the expected default rates; and c) in the case of portfolio management of loans where a target rate has been indicated, the actual return achieved (Art. 20). Specifications about the methodology for calculating such default rates will be provided by ESMA, in close cooperation with the EBA, through draft RTSs.

With reference to individual offers, ECSPs must provide clients with a Key Investor Information Sheet (KIIS) based on the KID-PRIIPs model;[73] the information in the KIIS must be prepared by the project owner and be fair, clear, and not misleading (Art. 23(7)).

Besides containing certain information specified in the annex pertaining to the project owner and its project (including activities and products offered, a hyperlink to financial statements when available, and key financial figures/ratios), the crowdfunding process (e.g., the minimum target and deadline for reaching it), the main risks and costs, and redress procedures, the KIIS must contain a number of warnings distinguishing crowdfunding from traditional loan activities, such as the lack of supervisor control and approval, guarantee schemes, or an appropriateness test. It shall also underline particular risks (e.g., illiquidity), as well as the opportunity to not invest more than 10 percent of the client's net worth (NW). The additional information required depends on the type of product: in the case of loans, the KIIS must contain information also about the nature, duration, and terms of the loan; interest rates or other compensation; risk mitigation measures; the repayment schedule; any defaults on credit agreements by the project owner within the past five years; and the servicing of the loan. Additional technical aspects regarding the requirements and content of the model for the KIIS, the types of main risks that are associated with crowd-

---

expression of interest (or, in the case of portfolio management of loans, receipt of the mandate), the ECSP must inform the investor that the reflection period has begun (Art. 22(8)).

73 See Regulation (EU) No 1286/2014 of the European Parliament and of the Council of 26 November 2014 on key information documents for packaged retail and insurance-based investment products (PRIIPs) (OJ L 352, 9.12.2014, p. 1. The authorities are considering substituting the KID for the KIIS when ECSP and PRIIPS Regulations both apply (Art. 23(15)).

funding offers, the use of certain financial ratios, and the commissions, fees, and transaction costs will be provided by ESMA through draft RTSs (Art. 23(16)).

To increase investor protection, the adopted version has favoured the KIIS language rules, which are similar to but less onerous than those of the prospectus summary,[74] instead of the base prospectus language proposed by the Commission, which allowed, as a general rule, the use of a language accepted in international finance (Art. 23(2)-(3)).[75] However, Art. 23(5) requires NCAs to inform ESMA about the KIIS languages that they accept, which creates the opportunity for regulatory competition and further harmonization in the longer term. NCAs can now require the seven-day ex ante notification (not the approval) of the KIIS (Art. 24(14)). In any case, marketing rules remain national, with ESMA publishing the relevant ones on its website to assist the platforms (Artt. 27–28).

The KIIS is prepared by the project owner (except in the case of portfolio management of loans). The original proposal required ECSPs to verify only the completeness and clarity of the KIIS and request that the project owner correct it when they identified an omission, mistake, or inaccuracy. However, the approved version also refers to the ECSP's duty to verify the 'correctness' of the same (Art. 23(11)): this expression seems to refer to the requirement of non-misleading and fair language or at least to the absence of evident mistakes in filling out the form (in terms of a correspondence between the type of information and the box filled out). However, the Regulation should be clearer about the extent of ECSPs' duties in this respect so that they can avoid liability for the lack of truthfulness of any information provided by the project owner. Otherwise, this would transform platforms into gatekeepers with a role not only comparable to but even more onerous than is assumed by lead underwriters.

Liability rules have not been harmonized, and therefore, the solutions and practical effects of platforms' co-responsibility might diverge nationally. As under the PR, Member States are required to ensure an adequate national liability regime for misleading or inaccurate information and omissions of key infor-

---

74 Therefore, the KIIS must be written in one of the official languages of the NCA's Member State or in a language accepted by such NCA and translated into the official or accepted language of each country in which the crowdfunding offering is made available. The investor can always request a translation and, in case the ECSP does not comply, should be advised not to invest. The effects of such choices will be evaluated by the Commission in its report due 36 months after the Regulation's entry into force, followed, if necessary, by a revision proposal (Art. 45(2)l).

75 The final version has surprisingly maintained the investor's right to require a translation into his/her language, and, should the ECSP refuse, a prohibition on the ECSPs sale of the product to that investor. This made more sense in the context of the Commission's proposal (Art. 23(13)).

mation from the KIIS, at least with respect to the project owner and its related entities. The KIIS must also disclose the names of the people responsible for the information (Art. 23(9)-(10)).

Furthermore, special conduct rules have been introduced in the cases of individual portfolio management of loans and the provision of scoring/pricing services. ECSPs offering portfolio management must disclose to investors the relevant decision-making process, take all necessary steps to pursue the client's best interest, and respect at least two parameters of preference chosen by investors.[76] Furthermore, specific additional disclosure duties apply (Artt. 3(4)-(5); 6(1)-(2); 12); in particular, the ECSPs must provide investors with a description of the systems and procedures deployed to conduct a credit risk assessment (Art. 6(2); see also below § 4.5), and, on a continuous basis or upon request, information about the composition of the portfolio.[77] For each loan, key information such as interest rate, maturity date, risk category, payment schedule, and risk mitigation measures shall be provided. Moreover, information must be provided about defaults within the past five years by any project owner, any fee in respect of the loan, and, if the ECSP has carried out a valuation of a loan, certain information about the most recent one valued (Art. 6(4)).[78] Special information requirements apply when the ECSP has set up and operates a contingent fund, including a description and explanation of the contingent fund's functioning[79] and a warning about the risk of not obtaining a payout and about ECSP's discretion with respect to such payout and its amount. These ECSPs must also disclose on a quarterly basis the performance of the fund, in particular information about the size of the contingency fund as compared to the total amounts outstanding on loans and the ratio between the payout made to the total amounts outstanding on loans (Art. 6(6)). Further specifications about the information to be disclosed and its format will be provided through RTSs drafted by the EBA in cooperation with ESMA (Art. 6(7))

---

76 These parameters are 1) the minimum and maximum interest rate payable; 2) the minimum and maximum maturity date; 3) the range and distribution of risk categories; and 4) if an annual target rate of return on an investment is offered, the likelihood that the selected loans will enable the investor to achieve that rate with reasonable certainty.

77 Including its weighted average annual interest rate and loan distribution according to risk category (in percentages and absolute terms).

78 E. g., the valuation date, why it performed the valuation, and a fair description of the likely actual return, taking into account fees and default rates.

79 E. g., about the source of the money paid into the fund, how the fund is governed, to whom the money belongs, the considerations taken into account and the process followed when making a discretionary decision concerning whether or how to pay out from the fund and how the money paid into the fund will be treated in the event of insolvency (Art. 6(5)).

Finally, ECSPs offering portfolio management of loans (instead of project owners as with other services) have a responsibility to prepare, update, and correct the KIIS and to ensure that no information has been omitted or is materially misleading or inaccurate (Art. 24). The content of the KIIS reflects the type of service and replicates in part the information mentioned above: in addition to information about the ECSP and the people responsible for it, it must contain information about the prospective composition of the portfolio (see above concerning client parameters), the key elements of the internal methodology for credit risk assessment and risk categories, procedures and criteria for the selection of projects, characteristics of applicable guarantees, servicing of the loan, risk diversification strategies, and fees to be paid by the project owner or the investor (Art. 24; annex I, parts H-I).

ECSPs offering only scoring/pricing systems must publish the policies and procedures used for the credit risk assessment performed (see below §4.5) and its calculation method (Art. 4(4); 19(6)).

As anticipated, certain special protections are reserved to 'non-sophisticated' investors. This is a new category not contained in MiFID II and applies to investors not falling within the categories of professional investors or sophisticated investors (a new category as well). In particular, sophisticated investors are identified as investors who would otherwise fall into the retail investor category but request to be treated as sophisticated and who declare that they are aware of the relative consequences and present evidence of significant NW or investment experience.[80] The aim is to protect only the most fragile investors while lowering compliance costs for investors able to understand the risks and therefore not deserving of certain protective measures.

The first measure reserved to non-sophisticated investors is the "entry-knowledge test", according to which ECSPs, before investors can access the offers, must perform, every two years, a test aimed at verifying whether and

---

80 As specified in annex II, this applies to 1) legal entities meeting one of the following conditions: *a)* at least €100,000 in own funds; *b)* a turnover of at least €2 million; and *c)* a balance sheet of at least €1 million; 2) natural persons meeting at least two of the following conditions: *a)* personal gross income of at least €60,000 or a financial instrument portfolio (including cash deposits and financial assets) exceeding €100,000; *b)* professional experience in the financial sector in a position requiring knowledge of the transactions or services envisaged or an executive position in the legal entities listed under 1) for at least 12 months; *c)* operations on the capital markets of significant size at an average frequency of 10 per quarter over the previous four quarters. Providers must take reasonable steps to ensure that investors requesting to be categorized as sophisticated and warned about the consequences effectively qualify as such, but the providers can approve the request unless it has reasonable doubt that the information provided is correct.

which crowdfunding services are appropriate for non-sophisticated investors, considering their past investments in transferable securities, admitted instruments, and loans, and their understanding of risks and professional experience with crowdfunding. In case of a negative test result (because of an investor's insufficient knowledge, skills, or experience), the ECSP can proceed with the order only after issuing a risk warning and receiving the investor's acknowledgement (Art. 21(1)-(4)). This test is similar to an appropriateness test but is less product-specific and performed at an earlier stage.[81]

Second, ECSPs must require non-sophisticated investors, before accessing the offers and every year, to undertake a loss simulation test in order to verify their ability to bear losses, calculated as 10 percent of their NW, based on certain information.[82] Again, irrespective of the results, investors can invest after simply acknowledging the risks (Art. 21(5)-(6)). ESMA will draft an RTS about the required information and how to carry out both tests.

ECSPs must issue a warning and receive the explicit consent of the investor and evidence of his/her understanding of the investments and risks (this can consist of a positive result on the entry-knowledge test) in case of investments above €1,000 or 5 percent of the non-sophisticated investor's NW (Art. 21(7)). Finally, non-sophisticated investors have the right to a four-day reflection period, during which and before its expiration they are entitled to withdraw their investment at no cost and without providing a reason.

Thus, the ECSP Regulation has assigned a large role to disclosure and other conduct duties but with significant differences based on business model and type of investor. Investor tests seem correctly simplified. Some doubts remain about the possibility of keeping the KIIS short and effective despite the volume of information required, as well as about the ability of the KIIS to serve as an adequate informational document for both professional/sophisticated and non-sophisticated investors. Furthermore, the standardization of KIIS and its assimilation to a more traditional informational document might reduce the innovative and alternative character of crowdfunding (not taking into account nonfinancial aspects and motives as well as non-traditional types of information,

---

81 The approved Regulation now requires ECSPs to collect information also about clients' investment objectives and the financial situation (as under a suitability test and as suggested by the Parliament), although the evaluation pertains to the investor's knowledge, skills, and experience.

82 Regular income and total income and whether earned on a permanent or temporary basis; assets, including financial investments and cash deposits, but excluding personal and investment property and pension funds; and financial commitments.

signalling, etc.) and the positive 'rational herding' effect,[83] although the KIIS can in principle include additional information.

4.3.3 Client Money

We have analysed above the measures used to protect clients from financial loss by means of the diligent selection of projects and information disclosure, among other things, but a few aspects of this concern should be further underlined.

ECSPs are not allowed, per se, to hold client money or other assets. Nonetheless, they can provide payment services and take custody of financial instruments after they obtain relevant authorizations and comply with the specific regime (Art. 12(13)). In this case, client assets are protected under the usual financial regulation framework.

As mentioned above (§4.3.2), ECSPs must warn their clients that the money invested or lent and the instruments subscribed to through the platform are not covered by deposit protection or investor compensation schemes. Should ECSPs establish a contingent fund (apparently, only when providing portfolio management of loans), they assume additional organizational and disclosure duties (§§4.3.2 and 4.3.5).

The choice to rely on existing authorizations for holding client money appears rational, although the presence of admitted instruments (which are not financial instruments) and loans might have required some adaptations.

4.3.4 Investor Liquidity Risk

As anticipated, one of the downsides of crowdfunding investments, is the limited liquidity of loans (which generally cannot be transferred without following certain procedures, such as a notary act and/or formal notification to the borrower of the transfer, following an agreement between the original and the new creditor) or stakes in private limited companies. As mentioned, LBC platforms in particular have created forms of exchange between users to increase liquidity.

Under the ECSP Regulation, platforms can set up systems allowing clients to advertise their buying/selling interests pertaining to products previously subscribed to through the platform ('bulletin boards', Art. 25). Nonetheless, these cannot present the characteristics of a trading venue, i.e., bringing together buying

---

83 See above fn. 35.

and selling interests in a way that results in a multilateral contract. Therefore, users must negotiate and finalize the agreement outside the platform; it is uncertain whether the platform can even provide standard contracts. Moreover, ECSPs must specify that these systems are not regulated trading venues, that any exchanges take place under the exclusive responsibility of investors, and, where there is a suggested reference price, that it is not binding. The ECSP must also substantiate the suggested reference price.

The intention seems to be not only to require an authorization as the operator of a trading venue in case platforms want to set up a multilateral exchange for transferable securities, but also to prohibit multilateral exchanges in loans (unless permitted under national law and limited to the national territory) in order to limit regulatory arbitrage and ensure a level playing field with regulated intermediaries, as well as to limit the platform's role as an intermediary. Of course, this might reduce the effectiveness of bulletin boards and consequently the liquidity of the market.

In the adopted version, ECSPs must require prospective sellers to make the KIIS available and must ensure that non-sophisticated prospective buyers receive the required information and the risk warning. Moreover, in the case of loans, ECSPs must provide buyers with updated information about the default rates of the loans offered on such bulletin boards (Art. 25(3)c): this improves investor protection and the efficiency of such bulletin boards as exchanges but also assigns a greater gatekeeper role to marketplace lending platforms.

4.3.5 Market Integrity, Efficiency, and Stability: Organizational and Prudential Requirements

ECSPs must also establish adequate measures to ensure effective and prudent management, including the segregation of duties, provisions for business continuity, and conflicts of interest prevention and management (similar to provisions in MiFID II: Art. 8(3)-(5)); management of the operational risk that results from outsourcing; and the proper handling of complaints (complying with certain of the requirements set forth in Art. 7).

Special organizational requirements apply, once again, depending on the specific business model. Only in the case of marketplace lending (even under the basic models) does the adopted version require 'appropriate systems and controls to assess the risks related to the loans intermediated on the crowdfunding platform' (Art. 4(2), first period).

When platforms offer portfolio management of loans, they need to have in place robust internal processes and methodologies for risk management and financial modelling (Art. 4(2), second period) and to ensure compliance, using appropriate data, with the requirements set forth in Art. 6(1)-(2) concerning respect for the parameters chosen by investors (see above §4.4). They also need to assess the credit risk of individual crowdfunding projects selected for an investor's portfolio and of the portfolio itself, as well as the project owners' prospects of meeting their obligations. When offering and operating contingent funds, ECSPs must adopt policies, procedures, and organizational arrangements to be specified in an RTS drafted by the EBA in cooperation with ESMA (Art. 6(7)).

When providing scoring/pricing services (but, it seems, according to the wording, only in respect of loans or possibly debt securities), ECSPs must establish, implement, and maintain clear and effective policies and procedures to enable them to carry out a reasonable assessment of the credit risk of offers and project owners, an assessment that must be based on adequate information,[84] price fairness, and an adequate risk management framework; the ECSPs must keep a record of the evidence of compliance with these criteria. With particular reference to loans, ECSPs must conduct a valuation of each of them at least: a) at the time of origination; b) when the project owner is unlikely to fulfil its obligations to repay the loan in full and the ECSP does not enforce any relevant security interest or take steps with analogous effect; c) after a default; and d) when the ECSP is facilitating a lender's exit before the maturity date (Art. 4(4)). The information and factors that ECSPs are required to consider in such an assessment to ensure price fairness, as well as the related minimum governance and organizational requirements, will be further specified by the EBA in close cooperation with ESMA (Art. 19(7)).

In this respect, the regime appears quite rigid, especially as regards marketplace lending and scoring (see §§4.4, 4.5), and might consequently limit innovation when market-based or more generalized AI solutions (such as certification of the algorithm used, together with disclosure, forums/feedback, borrowers' rights to object, etc.) might have assisted such innovation.

Finally, the adopted version has also embraced the Council's suggestion to introduce prudential safeguards for operational risk (Art. 11), which represents the main business risk for marketplace lending platforms. These can consist of CET1 requirements as an alternative to or in combination with professional insurance equal to the higher of €25,000 and one-quarter of the overhead in the pre-

---

84 Including information about audited accounts where available, information of which the ECSP is aware, information obtained from the project owner, and other information needed to perform a reasonable credit risk assessment.

vious year.[85] Such funds are intended to cover, as revealed by the requirements set for the insurance policy, the risks created by misleading information (possibly only when directly provided by the ECSP: see §4.3.2); a breach of legal and regulatory obligations; a breach of a duty of skill and care towards clients; lacking or defective procedures to prevent conflicts of interest; losses from business disruption, system failures, or process management; and gross negligence in pricing (Art. 11(7)), among other things.

The introduction of prudential requirements for all ECSPs reflects the recent reform of prudential requirements for investment firms (in the IFD/IFR package), which has eliminated the original art. 4(1)2 CRR II exemption from capital requirements for investment firms offering the services of reception/transmission of orders or offering investment advice without holding client money (art. 62(3) b IFR) and introduced a prudential requirement for operational risk even for Class 3 firms (that conduct more broker-like activity). The same reform has reduced or eliminated the differentiation in capital requirements (both initial capital and Basel capital adequacy) based on the type of investment service offered to focus more on effective risks, and even revised the definition of credit institutions. The new Art. 4(1)1 CRR II (as revised by Art. 62(3) IFR), in fact, now assigns relevance to identifying banks not only according to their activities and associated functions but also based on the systemic relevance of certain investment activities.[86] In any case, we should take into account, in this regard,

---

85 This requirement recalls the capital requirements of Class 3 firms under the Investment Firms Regulation (IFR 2019/2033) and Directive (IFD 2019/2034) but is potentially lower since the IFD/IFR requirement depends on the minimum capital requirement of the particular service provided; the lowest of these is €75,000.

86 This new article provides that 'credit institution' means an undertaking the business of which consists of any of the following: (a) to take deposits or other repayable funds from the public and to grant credits for its own account; (b) to carry out any of the activities referred to in points (3) and (6) of Section A of Annex I to Directive 2014/65/EU of the European Parliament and of the Council, where one of the following applies, but the undertaking is not a commodity and emission allowance dealer, a collective investment undertaking or an insurance undertaking: (i) the total value of the consolidated assets of the undertaking is equal to or exceeds EUR 30 billion; (ii) the total value of the assets of the undertaking is less than EUR 30 billion, and the undertaking is part of a group in which the total value of the consolidated assets of all undertakings in that group that individually have total assets of less than EUR 30 billion and that carry out any of the activities referred to in points (3) and (6) of Section A of Annex I to Directive 2014/65/EU is equal to or exceeds EUR 30 billion; or (iii) the total value of the assets of the undertaking is less than EUR 30 billion, and the undertaking is part of a group in which the total value of the consolidated assets of all undertakings in the group that carry out any of the activities referred to in points (3) and (6) of Section A of Annex I to Directive 2014/65/EU is equal to or exceeds EUR 30 billion, where the consolidating supervisor, in consultation with the super-

that platforms do not operate in the traditional financial sector and that they must issue warnings to make investors aware of the lack of traditional safeguards. The rationale for preserving trust and stability through strict regulation – which applies to banks and investment firms – is here instead weak.[87]

Furthermore, the ECSP Regulation fails to explicitly address cyber-security risks, even though these comprise a relevant part of crowdfunding operational risk (and of FinTech in general). However, the Digital Operational Resilience Act (DORA) Proposal,[88] which was recently presented within the Digital Finance Package,[89] should be applicable also to ECSPs, filling the gap.

Finally, the Regulation does not directly impose duties on ECSPs under the V AML/CT Directive, although the possibility of extending these duties to ECSPs will be evaluated by the Commission in its review (Art. 45(2)p). Checks that take place pursuant to this Directive are in fact to be performed by the payment services provider involved, i. e., the ECSP itself under a separate authorization, or a partner holding a payment service provider authorization. This choice links AML checks with the holding and transferring of money, but ECSPs might be in the best position to perform them, irrespective of the fact that they also offer payment services.

4.3.6 Agency Costs and Conflicts of Interest

Agency costs, as has been mentioned, represent a typical risk in crowdfunding since the financial risk rests with investors but at least the initial selection of borrowers is performed by platforms. Agency costs are particularly high when the platform's fees are linked to the volume of the loans intermediated or equivalent figures, which creates negative incentives for platforms. As has been mentioned, certain platforms, in order to assure investors about the diligent selection of loans, co-lend with the investors.

---

visory college, so decides in order to address potential risks of circumvention and potential risks for the financial stability of the Union".

87 Actually, the ECSP Regulation, which allows banks and investment firms to hold at the same time their specific authorization and a ECSP one, might have the effect of rising systemic risk through increased interconnections and potential investor confusion.

88 *European Commission*, 'Proposal for a Regulation [...] on Digital Operational Resilience for the Financial Sector [...]', COM/2020/595 final. The regime would apply to all firms across the financial sector and aims at ensuring their ability to withstand all types of ICT-related disruptions and threats. Furthermore, it also provides a design for an oversight framework for ICT service providers deemed critical to the financial sector (e. g., cloud computing).

89 *European Commission*, 'A Digital Finance Strategy' (fn. 70), p. 10, 17.

The above-described general duties of conduct should contribute to reducing agency risk and, in the case of pricing/credit scoring, the ECSP Regulation provides very detailed rules in terms of disclosure and the organization and functioning of such pricing/scoring systems. Under the ECSP Regulation, platforms cannot have any financial participation in offers, not even when it would be aimed at aligning the interests of platforms and clients (as proposed by the Parliament). However, models in which platforms would partially invest in the intermediated loans under certain conditions (such as when it would help align the interests of platforms and investors) should not have been banned per se since they might create virtuous incentives that require only some additional rules related to credit risk management.

Furthermore, the Regulation remains silent about platform fees and related perverse incentives. The general requirement that there be effective conflicts of interest policies and procedures (with rules echoing the general rules of MiFID II) might mitigate risks related to these fees but, given the particularity of the risk to the crowdfunding model, explicit and tailored solutions would have been preferable; for instance, creating incentives for the platforms to charge fees based on loan performance.

Also with respect to conflicts of interest, the ECSP Regulation prohibits platform managers, employees, or controlling shareholders from acting as project owners. These persons can, however, operate on the platform as investors, conditioned on disclosure on the website and equal terms (Art. 8).

Finally, as we have seen, co-lending with institutional investors can contribute to reduce information asymmetries when transparency and equal terms are guaranteed but might otherwise lead to a cherry-picking phenomenon at the expense of retail investors. The ECSP regulation does not address this issue. Instead, platforms should be required to allow non-sophisticated investors to invest along with professional investors (e. g., after paying an additional fee) but also to disclose the details and terms of the investments made by professional investors.

4.4 A Special Focus: Loans versus Investments and Borrower Protection

The general design of the Regulation is to partially assimilate the loan regime and the investment regime, since they both share similar functions and characteristics in a digital context and the aim is to improve investor protection and trust. However, it is worth highlighting that the marketplace lending regime appears somehow stricter and more rigid than the regime for marketplace investing. As an example, even under the basic model, the ECSP Regulation requires appropriate systems and controls to assess the risks related to loan products only; in addition, the loan regime imposes additional disclosure requirements (disclosure of the default rate and outcome statement; disclosure regime in case of bulletin boards involving loans).

Moreover, in the case of pricing services, detailed rules are set only for the creditworthiness assessment, not for the pricing of investments or at least equity instruments. This is the case despite the fact that marketplace lending is, in principle, less risky than similar forms of credit intermediation that are generally subject, in the traditional sector, to simplified requirements (e. g., for credit brokers, manufacturers of PRIIPs, and AIFMs).[90]

As regards portfolio management of loans, the regime is strict not only compared to the recent British regime which likely inspired it,[91] but also compared to the corresponding traditional investment models, such as investment portfolio management (except for, e. g., product governance requirements)[92] or the management of alternative investment funds. For instance, the requirements as respects the procedures for pricing and portfolio management appear more detailed and prescriptive than those for investment portfolio management (set forth in MiFID II and Art. 47 et seqq. Commission delegated Regulation No. 2017/565 concerning disclosure, reporting to clients, and asset valuation) or alternative collective investment schemes (Art. 15 and 19 AIFMD, detailing general obligations related to due diligence in the selection and identification of investments and the management and monitoring of risks, and the Commission Delegated Regulation No. 231/2013). Even banks, which are not comparable to platforms in terms of the variety of services they offer, their structures for bearing risk, their deposit-taking and the related costs of capital, induced trust, and their systemic relevance (see above §2), have been left quite free to evaluate the creditworthiness of borrowers (within the parameters set by Basel/CRDV-CRR,

---

90 See in more detail, e. g., *Macchiavello* 'Financial-return' (fn. 2) 674.

91 The ECSP regime appears stricter and less flexible in certain respects as compared to the British regime, both in general (additional organizational requirements are imposed in the UK only in the case of guaranteed returns, not for every form of portfolio management) and in terms of credit-risk assessment (which in the UK is required only when the platform prices loans, not when it just intermediates them), outcome statements (required by the FCA only when pricing services are offered), factors to be included in the credit-risk assessment (the ECSP Regulation requires the use of audited financial statements), and different levels of credit-risk analysis (e. g.. at the project, project owner, and portfolio levels).

92 Art. 45(2)f requires the Commission to assess whether the requirements for portfolio management of loans remain 'appropriate to pursue the objectives of this Regulation, in the light of MiFID II investment portfolio management.

unless offering residential consumer loans), since, because they bear the risk of borrower defaults, they should have sufficient incentives to adequately perform this activity. Nonetheless, the financial crisis and the recent surge in nonperforming loans (NPLs) have created the conditions for the adoption of the EBA's guidelines on loan origination and monitoring[93] (based on a 'comply and explain approach'); this was after the European Central Bank Guidelines for Fintech Banks had imposed specific requirements for creditworthiness assessment performed by technology-based banks.[94] Consequently, banks will be required (for new loans, starting June 2021) to comply with a new set of detailed internal governance requirements (best practices) for the granting and monitoring of credit, loan origination procedures for each type of borrower, pricing, collateral valuation, and the proper framework for monitoring.

The services that entail a creditworthiness assessment are indeed of fundamental importance for investors' decisions, opaque[95] and a source of potential agency problems/conflict of interest (since the crowd-lender bears the credit risk of the loans and the platforms are at least partially remunerated based on loan volume),[96] while being so far unregulated. Nonetheless, instead of relying more on disclosure of the methods and the general adequacy of structures and procedures, the ECSPR regime has very detailed rules about platform organization and the factors that platforms must take into account in the credit assessment, without considering the need to preserve innovation in the sector[97] and the possibility that they could rely, at least partially, on reputational capital (many

---

93 *EBA*, 'Guidelines on loan origination and monitoring – Final Report', (20 May 2020), <https://eba.europa.eu/sites/default/documents/files/document_library/Publications/Guide
lines/2020/Guidelines%20on%20loan%20origination%20and%20monitoring/884283/EBA%
20GL%202020%2006%20Final%20Report%20on%20GL%20on%20loan%20origination%20and
%20monitoring.pdf>.
94 *European Central Bank*, 'Guide to Assessments of Fintech Credit Institution Licence Applications', (March 2018), <https://www.bankingsupervision.europa.eu/ecb/pub/pdf/ssm.201803_
guide_assessment_fintech_credit_inst_licensing.en.pdf?1c99fa2126f6ef80eb61a276bab94379>.
95 These innovative creditworthiness assessment methods, DON especially when proprietary, are not clearly disclosed by platforms: *CGFS-FSB* (fn. 25) 11–12: *Ziegler/Shneor* (fn. 25) 77–79.
96 See *Paolo Giudici/Branca Hadji Misheva*, 'P2p Lending Scoring Models: Do They Predict Default?', J. Digit. Bank. 2018, 2, 353; *Paolo Giudici/Branca Hadji-Misheva/Alessandro Spelta*, 'Network Based Scoring Models to Improve Credit Risk Management in Peer to Peer Lending Platforms', Front. Artif. Intell. 2019.
97 See, for instance, a study attesting to the fact that a lender selecting loans by applying a profit scoring system using multivariate regression outperforms the results obtained by using a traditional credit scoring system. See *Carlos Serrano-Cinca/Bego Gutiérrez-Nieto*, 'The Use of Profit Scoring as an Alternative to Credit Scoring Systems in Peer-to-peer (p2p) Lending', Decis. Support Syst. 2016, 89, 113.

crowd-lenders are returning investors[98]) and the incentives that would result from performance-based fees.

The assimilation of the loans and securities regimes has also had the effect of moving the protection of borrowers to the background. Borrowers benefit from the general conduct and disclosure duties of ECSPs (§4.3.2), including these duties as they apply to the selection process. Organizational rules set forth for scoring systems and portfolio management are aimed at ensuring fairness in the evaluation of borrowers (§4.3.5). However, as the recent Regulation on online intermediation services (No. 2019/1150, not even mentioned in the ECSP Regulation) has underlined, attention should also be paid to platforms' business counterparties, who are in a weaker contractual position. Therefore, in the case of SMEs, protections consisting of express warnings (e. g., about the consequences of default, the information provided in the KIIS, and specific risks), a right to dispute certain scoring results or criteria, and a right of withdrawal, should be introduced or made more explicit.

4.5 Addressing the Core Question: How Does the ECSP Regulation Deal with the Platform Dilemma? Effects on Market Structure

The approved version has filled in some relevant gaps in the original proposal and seems to respond to the most important risks of marketplace lending platforms, although it contains certain limitations.

As regards its approach to the platform dilemma, the ECSP Regulation correctly and clearly differentiates marketplace lending from banking. Nonetheless, the numerous revisions in the text of the Regulation made during negotiations also reflect a change in attitude toward the regulation of crowdfunding, moving from flexible, agile, and optional to detailed, rigid, mandatory, and stricter. The

---

98 The research of *Balyuk /Davydenko* (fn. 40) seems to evidence market discipline among platforms, which appear to have a tendency to improve screening in response to investor threats of withdrawal. Nonetheless, Thakor and Merton provide evidence that banks (and other deposit-taking institutions) have stronger reputational incentives than P2P lenders because of the presence of deposits and the trust these create; however, they also underline that reputation (e. g. avoiding a default crisis) is important for nonbank lenders since they would not be able to recover from an erosion of trust. This means that fee-based incentives are fundamental: *Richard T. Thakor/Robert C. Merton*, 'Trust in Lending', NBER Working Paper No. 24778/2018, https://www.nber.org/papers/w24778 (version updated September 2019 available at <https://www.researchgate.net/publication/326473894_Trust_in_Lending>); *Thakor* (fn. 44), p. 6.

original ECSP proposal attempted to characterize marketplace lending/investing platforms as "neutral" intermediaries (reflecting many national crowdfunding laws) and to balance, on the one hand, a light regime with relevant limitations on maximum offering size and permissible products/activities, with, on the other hand, investor protection and containing project owner costs, using new, technologically based, and simplified measures (e. g., the entry-knowledge test and loss simulation) and synthetic and comprehensible information. The approved version, even though it fills in some relevant gaps, seems to share the same vision only partially and aims instead at "re-intermediating" marketplace lending/investing. In fact, it has significantly increased the number and detail of requirements that ECSPs are subject to. They will also be subject to numerous future EBA/ESMA rules that will be issued in light of the nature, scale, and complexity of crowdfunding services.[99] The approach appears particularly rigid in the case of loans, an area that is not yet harmonized and, in many countries, is less regulated than banks or investment firms. The aim seems to consist of amending the duties and roles of crowdfunding providers so that it is closer to those of traditional investment firms (e. g., in terms of conduct and organizational requirements, liability, and language rules governing prospectuses); the final Regulation looks at ECSPs as gatekeepers, not just managers of marketplaces. Such further assimilation to the role of traditional investment firms, although aimed at reducing regulatory arbitrage and ensuring a level playing field in the sector, does not properly take into account that MiFID firms are able to offer a varied set of services across borders with fewer restrictions, while relying on government support with respect to, for instance, investor compensation, access to credit bureaus, and state assistance and facilitation during COVID-19, etc.[100] Unfortunately, this results in an undervaluing of the alternative (i. e., not involving investor trust and the consequent implications for stability) character of marketplace lending, as well as its need to offer innovative solutions and operate under flexible rules.

---

99 E. g., rules that will address pricing/scoring criteria and factors; default rate calculations and disclosures; portfolio management clients' standards and contingent funds; and governance and procedures for risk management and complaint handling.
100 See   <https://www.crowdfundinsider.com/2020/03/159570-what-crowdfunding-platforms-do-in-times-of-covid19-and-why-governments-should-use-crowdfunding-to-battle-the-economic-impact-of-socialdistancing/>; *Ziegler* et al. (fn. 10) 88 – 89. The SEC has temporarily eased crowdfunding regulation requirements for SMEs, which has expedited the offering process: <https://www.sec.gov/rules/interim/2020/33-10781.pdf>; <https://www.orrick.com/en/Insights/2020/05/SEC-Provides-Temporary-Relief-from-Certain-Regulation-Crowdfunding-Requirements-in-COVID-19-Response>.

The exact borders of the gatekeeper role of platforms remains uncertain in light of the many possible issues that this may implicate, including the extent of the diligent selection of projects, platforms' duties to check the correctness of KIISs, platforms' civil liability, and their role in bulletin boards. These have not been clearly defined and have largely been left to national and market responses.

Finally, as has already been underlined, a portion of the adopted rules for marketplace lending has been drawn from the UK framework. In the UK, the market is particularly mature, receives government support (e. g., referrals under the 2015 Small Business, Enterprise and Employment Act), and most platforms have moved to more complex models closer to traditional intermediaries'. ECSPR rules also apply to local-only platforms with low volumes unless the reference to the proportionality principle is to be interpreted broadly, even to the point of creating a tension with ECSP rules. Therefore, the ECSP Regulation seems to anticipate the market's evolution and might appear less appropriate for some less-developed and more "alternative" markets, for which a regime relying more on initial local exemptions, reputational capital, general risk management requirements, market-based mechanisms, and certification mechanisms (e. g. concerning the adequacy of the algorithms used) would have worked better (§§4.3.5, 4.3.6; 4.4).

Furthermore, the subtle line between the use of filtering systems under the basic model and the model of automatic portfolio management – a difference that entails relevant consequences in terms of the applicable rules since portfolio management is subject to a stricter regime – might affect ECSPs' choice of business model and therefore market development.

All this, together with the exclusion of certain business models from its scope of application, suggests that the ECSP Regulation might be able to significantly affect market structures, making platforms' choices about business models more dependent on the relative regulatory regime than on true business/market choices, an effect that might not be desirable in a sector that is, in many countries, so immature and innovation-dependent.

5 Conclusions

Marketplace lending is an innovative and puzzling kind of intermediation. According to the Court of Justice's decisions in *Uber* and *Airbnb* (§1), its services can be regarded as services for the information society offered through a pre-existing market (lending), but its decisive influence over the underlying lending services, at least under the most widespread models, is undeniable: platforms select borrowers, provide contractual documentation, and often set prices (at least within a range). Anyway, in a financial sector context, we cannot disregard the existence of several reserved activities at both the European and national level and the corresponding principles and regulatory objectives.

Under this perspective, marketplace lending is clearly distinguishable from banking (strong intermediation) because of the absence of maturity/liquidity transformation and money creation; it is even different from lending (under the basic model, in which the platform does not engage in co-lending) since the funds are made available and put at risk by crowd-lenders only. Platforms connect lenders with borrowers as credit brokers, but the area is not completely harmonized and, with respect to consumer credit, the relevant EU law (e. g., CCD) tends not to apply and, in any case, would not respond to the complex set of risks and issues raised, including those related to investor protection and the platforms' organizational requirements.

The services offered by platforms (e. g., information channelling and screening and sometimes creditworthiness assessments and matching) are of fundamental relevance for crowd-lenders, potentially affecting their investment decisions.[101] The investment aspect of the platforms is clearly evident, with their role most resembling that of investment firms (weak intermediation), but involving the creation of a new asset class. Their services are, depending on the particular business model, similar to –(and mixing some characteristics of) brokerage, markets, portfolio management, and placing but pertain to financial products (loans) instead of financial instruments, unless the free transferability of loans though bulletin boards and an innovative and harmonized interpretation of the financial instrument concept are able to change this perspective. Furthermore, the platforms seem to complement financing by incumbents, serving otherwise underserved clients with lower loan amounts, instead of competing with them,[102] ensuring a faster process and therefore limiting the need for a perfectly

---

101 See *Douglas J. Cumming/Lars Hornuf*, 'Marketplace lending for SMEs', CESifo Working Paper 8100/2020, <https://papers.ssrn.com/sol3/papers.cfm?abstract_id=3541448> (investors decide whether to participate based mostly on a platform's ratings, disregarding other – financial – indicators, such as income, assets, liabilities, etc.). See also *Serrano-Cinca et al.* (fn. 5) (recognizing as relevant to investor decisions and predictions about the likelihood of default other factors, such as the purpose of the loan and the borrower's annual income, current housing situation, credit history, and indebtedness).
102 See the references and relevant text in footnote 7 of *Giorgio Barba Navaretti et al.*, 'Fintech and Banking. Friends or Foes?' (January 10, 2018), <https://ssrn.com/abstract=3099337>. However, see also *Havrylchyk/Verdier* (fn. 44) (FinTech substitutes for banks in areas hardest hit by the crisis); *Huan Tang*, 'Peer-to-Peer Lenders Versus Banks: Substitutes or Complements?', The Review of Financial Studies 32(5) (2019) 1900 (as regards the US's unsecured consumer credit mar-

level regulatory playing field. The role played by the platforms is also extremely relevant from the borrower's side, since the opportunity to even receive a loan, its economic conditions, and the post-contractual management of the parties' rights and obligations strongly depend on the tasks undertaken by the platforms.

Consequently, platforms appear to satisfy traditional financial needs but, thanks to technology (i.e., platforms and data analytics), through new business models, creating a new asset class, and a new subsector (P2P lending), which is less systemically important than traditional intermediaries'. However, this subsector is characterized by the need to balance investor protection with access to finance, borrower protection, innovation, and competition goals. All of this bolsters arguments in favor of special regulations for marketplace lending. We therefore welcome the EU's choice to introduce a special EU-wide framework for financial-return crowdfunding, which certainly takes a step forward with respect to the platform dilemma, but is subject to some criticisms as set forth in our analysis.[103]

First of all, the idea of creating a single market for crowdfunding, while adequately pursued in terms of maximum harmonization in the authorization process and supervisory practices, is undermined by the limited scope of the ECSP Regulation; in fact, it applies only to certain services and products instead of covering the entire crowdfunding universe (e.g., it excludes consumer crowdloans, certain conditional loans, and some business models such as credit funds), potentially creating regulatory arbitrage and an unlevel playing field. Still uncertain is the interplay of the ECSP Regulation with national crowdfunding regimes and other EU frameworks; in addition, certain relevant aspects of crowdfunding remain unharmonized (platforms' civil liability, marketing rules, etc.) (§4.2).

With respect to the overall regime, we support the choice to design the legal framework for both marketplace lending and investing following the traditional regulatory model for investment services, with simplifications justified by the different types of markets, assets, and activities, and by their beneficial effects and alternative characters. The regime is grounded on the proportionality principle and contains differences applicable to activities that involve different levels of complexity and risk. The ECSP Regulation also correctly focuses on disclosure (with warnings about the alternative character of each sector) and conduct rules. The adopted version seems to provide an extremely detailed and strict

---

ket, FinTech lenders seem to substitute for banks, serving riskier borrowers when a crisis hits the banking sector, but also to complement banks by providing smaller loans).

103 See also *Macchiavello*, 'European Crowdfunding' (fn. 15); *Id.*, 'What to Expect' (fn. 2).

framework from an organizational point of view, especially for marketplace lending platforms (although much will depend on the future ESMA/EBA RTSs and the application of the proportionality principle), with limited space given to innovative solutions and technology (e. g. RegTech solutions) (§§4.1 ss).

Looking at the specific choices made by the Regulation, it correctly addresses certain peculiar risks of crowdfunding intermediation. Investor protection has been increased in the adopted version, balanced with considerations of the needs of ECSPs and correctly focusing on unsophisticated investors. Disclosure duties are especially detailed and strict and envisage the provision of information about selection mechanisms, scoring, and past and actual performance – important and previously overlooked aspects of marketplace lending – but the KIIS as designed might not be effective in conveying the right information to all types of investors (§4.3.2). Client assets are protected under the general financial regulation framework (§4.3.3). Nonetheless, the strict approach towards the function of bulletin boards aimed at defending the monopoly of trading venues might result in a failure to adequately address investors' liquidity risk, despite some efforts in this regard, especially with respect to loans (§4.3.4).

Organizational and prudential requirements reflect a recent turn towards more attention being given to operational risk and the systemic relevance of non-bank intermediaries. Nonetheless, such requirements would appear to be rigid and particularly burdensome for certain marketplace lending business models in a way that does not seem to take into account the need for innovative and flexible models and the "alternative" character of the sector (§4.3.5). Conflicts of interest rules are also rigid and appear not to fit with the chosen "reintermediation" approach. For instance, more flexible rules prohibiting platforms' remuneration based exclusively on the volume of loans intermediated and instead incentivizing methods partially based on loan performance could have been considered. Furthermore, rules should have limited the risk that professional investors would appropriate to themselves the benefits of investments meant for non-sophisticated investors and taken advantage of co-investing for its related reductions in information asymmetries (§4.3.6).

Finally, adopting an investment perspective on crowd-loans should not cause us forget about the need to also introduce protective measures for crowd-borrowers, even when they are entrepreneurs, in line with the recent online intermediation Directive.

In conclusion, the approved version has distanced itself from the original Commission view of ECSPs as neutral intermediaries, "re-intermediating" through marketplace lending/investing. However, the exact borders of such intermediation, and consequently, the approved version's response to the platform dilemma, appear blurred. In fact, the adopted version has significantly increased the detailed requirements placed on ECSPs, with the aim of changing the duties and roles of crowdfunding providers to be closer to those of traditional investment firms (e. g., in terms of conduct and organizational requirements, liability, and language rules about prospectuses), viewing them as important gatekeepers. This change seems to only partially take into account that MiFID firms traditionally perform a more systemically relevant role (which affects investor trust in official financial markets), are able to offer a varied set of services across borders, and rely on government support. In fact, the ECSP Regulation appears uncertain about the platforms' role as gatekeeper, swinging from one extreme to the other (see above about bulletin boards). Furthermore, certain aspects of the Regulation (the exact limits of the KIIS correctness check, civil liability rules, the need to diligently select borrowers, etc.) will significantly affect the resulting design of the intermediating role of platforms, but appear to be left to national solutions, which implies a fragmented approach.

In any case, the regime appears unbalanced in its favouring of marketplace investing over marketplace lending in a way that is not consistent with the existing general financial law framework. It seems to anticipate market evolution (already realized in the US and the UK) and might appear inappropriate for less-developed crowdfunding markets. This, coupled with the exclusion of certain business models and services, seems to suggest a potentially important (and undesirable) impact of the ECSP Regulation on existing market structures. Platform choices about the business model to use might not follow the existing market and client needs or features but only the relevant legal framework (§§4.2, 4.4 and 4.5).

Paolo Giudici and Guido Ferrarini

Digital Offerings and Mandatory Disclosure: A Market-Based Critique of MiCA

Abstract: In this paper we argue that, as market mechanisms have worked acceptably well and there has been no investor protection crisis, ICOs and IEOs have so far failed to offer arguments in favour of a mandatory prospectus-like regime. Investors in the blockchain space know where to get information and what they risk. Accordingly, we offer a preliminary market-based critique of MiCA's white paper regulation, arguing that blockchain offering securities or utility tokens should be left free to decide what information to offer to investors, as long as the information provided is free from false or misleading statements, and does not omit any material fact. We also argue, contrarily to the Commission's proposal, that to facilitate private enforcement the burden of proof in liability actions should be on the issuer and not on the investor. This approach would offer a chance to reduce red tape and return to a more manageable regime, where general provisions against fraud and misrepresentation are applied with well-defined private liability rules and burden of proof allocations. As a result, blockchain startups would not only be left free to signal their quality and develop their channels of communication with potential investors, but concurrently also be effectively responsible for the information provided.

Table of Contents

Paolo Giudici, Professor of Business Law, Free University of Bozen-Bolzano, Italy
Guido Ferrarini, Emeritus Professor of Business Law, University of Genova, Italy

∂ OpenAccess. © 2022 Paolo Giudici and Guido Ferrarini, published by De Gruyter. (cc) BY-NC-ND This work is licensed under the Creative Commons Attribution-NonCommercial-NoDerivatives 4.0 International License.
https://doi.org/10.1515/9783110749472-004

1 Introduction

Initial Coin Offerings (ICOs) and Initial Exchange Offerings (IEOs) have raised a lively international debate on whether digital tokens issued by blockchain start-ups should be characterized as securities (US) or financial instruments (EU) and therefore whether registration requirements (US) or prospectus regulation (EU) should apply to token offerings. In a paper co-written with a financial economist, we argued that under the European Prospectus Regulation[1] a large part of token offerings should be treated as financial instrument offerings.[2] However, the debate has not been accompanied by a wider discussion concerning policy issues. There has been discussion on the benefits of not suffocating the rising digital market with excessive regulatory burdens, also considering that ICOs have a worldwide dimension with teams and target investors potentially operating in any part of the world. Nevertheless, a deeper analysis of the overall policy issues concerning mandatory disclosure in securities regulation has not been conducted with respect to the ICO phenomenon. We would like to raise this issue here, also in the light of the new proposal for a regulation on Markets in Crypto-assets submitted by the Commission on 24.9.2020 ("MiCA").[3]

The paper proceeds as follows. We start from the theoretical underpinning of mandatory disclosure and the empirical evidence regarding its allegedly positive effects, in order to show that the consensus over the virtues of this regulatory technique is only apparent (sections 2 and 3). We then analyse some recent cases where the role of mandatory disclosure has been debated, namely equity

---

1 Regulation 2017/1129 [2017] OJ EU L168/12.

2 *Dmitri Boreiko/Guido Ferrarini/Paolo Giudici*, "Blockchain Startups and Prospectus Regulation", European Business Organization Law Review 2019, 20, 665. See also *Guido Ferrarini/Paolo Giudici*, Transferable Securities and Prospectus Regulation: The Case of ICOs, in: Danny Busch/Guido Ferrarini/Jan Paul Franx (ed.), Prospectus Regulation and Prospectus Liability, 2020, p. 129; *Philipp Hacker/Chris Thomale*, "Crypto-Securities Regulation: ICOs, Token Sales and Cryptocurrencies under Eu Financial Law", European Company and Financial Law Review 2018, 15, 645.

3 See the Proposal for a Regulation on Markets in Crypto-assets, and amending Directive (EU) 2019/1937, COM(2020) 593/3 2020/0265 (COD). The proposal is available at https://eur-lex.europa.eu/legal-content/EN/TXT/?uri=CELEX%3A52020PC0593 (last access 5 February 2021).

crowdfunding regulation and high leveraged loan securitizations (section 4). Then we move to ICOs and IEOs, to show how blockchain startups have sought to signal quality through their white papers and other communication mechanisms, and how the academic literature has assessed those attempts (paras. no. 5 and 6). We then offer a brief analysis of MiCA, focusing exclusively on the mandatory disclosure regime that the proposal would like to apply to crypto-assets and on the liability regime that it presents, which curiously is not favourable to investors (section 7). In the last section we present our tentative proposals and conclusions.

2 The Debate Concerning the Theoretical Underpinnings of Mandatory Disclosure

The proposed inclusion in MiCA of a white paper regime with mandatory disclosure requirements, similar to the prospectus regime, for utility tokens might appear so obvious that it requires no discussion. As the argument goes, more information is better than none; and almost anybody dealing with mandatory disclosure regimes has pointed out that they are aimed at solving the problem of asymmetric information, which gives rise to a market failure.[4] A believer in mandatory disclosure would also argue that the uncontested theoretical literature is in favour of mandatory disclosure and that this should be sufficient to justify the extension of mandatory disclosure to any type of digital offerings.

However, the views in the theoretical literature are more nuanced. With regard to securities regulation, several arguments have been offered to justify its extensive disclosure regime, whose essential goals relate to the protection of investors and market efficiency. However, many of these arguments contradict one another and the different views are far from settled. We cannot review here all the extensive literature that discusses the pros and cons of a mandatory disclosure regime in securities regulation, but can only quickly refer the reader to that literature. The relevant scientific discussion concerns the extent of mandatory financial disclosure and its real purpose;[5] the selection of the most appropriate

---

4 "Recall that the essential problem with the public offering of truly new securities is the adverse selection that arises from a situation of severe information asymmetry. (...) Without solutions to this information-asymmetry problem, the market will unravel" *Merritt B. Fox*, "Regulating Public Offerings of Truly New Securities: First Principles", Duke LJ 2016, 66, 673, 719.
5 Cf *Paul G. Mahoney*, "Mandatory Disclosure as a Solution to Agency Problems", University of Chicago Law Review 1995, 62, 1047; *John C. Coffee Jr.*, "Market Failure and the Economic Case for

regulator, with particular reference to the costs and benefits of regulatory competition compared to those of centralized or highly harmonized regulation;[6] and the possibility of any serious cost and benefit analysis in the field of securities regulation and mandatory disclosure.[7]

We would like to point out here, with regard to what we will discuss vis-à-vis MiCA, that there is an aspect of the debate that is not sufficiently stressed. The arguments in favour of mandatory disclosure and, in particular, mandatory disclosure in connection with public offerings by issuers who are new to the market, being based on the asymmetric information problem, are articulated with no distinction between retail and professional investors, since asymmetric information concerns any person and entity different from the issuer. However, both US and European law accord exemptions to private placements, thereby recognizing that market-based solutions can work when professional investors are concerned, mostly because the collective action problems that are at the basis of the asymmetry of information rationale can be sorted out. With regard, in particular, to European law, the Prospectus Regulation provides for an exemption when the offer of securities is addressed solely to qualified investors and there is no admittance of the securities to trading on a regulated market within the EU.[8] If the securities are offered to qualified investors and are traded on a multilateral trading facility, there is no prospectus obligation, even though the listing

---

a Mandatory Disclosure System", Virginia Law Review 1984, 70, 717; more recently, *Luca Enriques/Sergio Gilotta*, Disclosure and Financial Market Regulation, in: Niamh Moloney/Eilís Ferran/Jennifer Payne (ed.) The Oxford Handbook of Financial Regulation, 2015, p. 511; *Kevin Haeberle/Todd Henderson*, "A New Market-Based Approach to Securities Law", University of Chicago Law Review 2018, 85, 1313; *Henry T. C. Hu*, The Disclosure Paradigm: Conventional Understanding and Modern Divergences, in: Danny Busch/Guido Ferrarini/Jan Paul Franx (ed.), Prospectus Regulation and Prospectus Liability, 2020, p. 99.

6 *Paul G. Mahoney*, "The Exchange as Regulator", Virginia Law Review 1997, 83, 1453; *Roberta Romano*, "Empowering Investors: A Market Approach to Securities Regulation" Yale Law Journal, 1998, 107, 2359; *Stephen J. Choi*, "Regulating Investors Not Issuers: A Market-Based Proposal", California Law Review 2000, 88, 279. See also *Emilios Avgouleas/Guido Ferrarini*, A Single Listing Authority and Securities Regulator for the CMU and the Future of ESMA: Costs, Benefits, and Legal Impediment, in: Danny Busch/Emilios Avgouleas/Guido Ferrarini (ed.), Capital Markets Union in Europe, 2018, 4.01.

7 *Eric Posner/E. Glen Weyl*, "Benefit-Cost Analysis for Financial Regulation", 103 American Economic Review 2013, 103, 393; *John C Coates IV*, "Cost-benefit analysis of financial regulation: Case studies and implications", Yale Law Journal, 2014, 124, 882; *Omri Ben-Shahar/Carl E Schneider*, "The futility of cost-benefit analysis in financial disclosure regulation" The Journal of Legal Studies 2014, 43, S253.

8 *Frank Graaf*, Private Placements in the Capital Market Union, in: Danny Busch/Emilios Avgouleas/Guido Ferrarini (ed.), Capital Markets Union in Europe (fn. 6), ch. 14.

rules of the trading facility could require some voluntary light prospectus requirement. Accordingly, the mandatory disclosure regime should actually be referred to retail investors exclusively, since both EU and US law do not mandate disclosure in offerings addressed to professional, accredited or institutional investors. Thus, the prospectus regime is mainly a retail investor's regime of protection, and should be treated and discussed as such.

Unsurprisingly, therefore, securities regulation and its mandatory disclosure regime have been imitated in many different areas of regulation concerning consumer protection. A significant number of influential papers have pointed out, however, that this particular form of protection has been a spectacular failure, since consumers and retail investors do not read standard form contracts, prospectuses and disclosure documents, as any reader who is also a consumer can easily confirm through her own experience.[9] Accordingly, prospectus regulation is a large and expensive mandatory disclosure regime aimed at protecting people that do not read prospectuses.[10]

3 The Empirical Research on Mandatory Disclosure is Moot

Researchers have tried to understand the value, if any, of mandatory disclosure through empirical studies. These studies are not restricted to prospectus regula-

---

9 *Omri Ben-Shahar/Carl E Schneider*, More than you wanted to know: The Failure of Mandated Disclosure, 2014; *Omri Ben-Shahar/Carl E. Schneider*, "The Failure of Mandated Disclosure", University of Pennsylvania Law Review 2011, 159, 647; *Ian Ayres/Alan Schwartz*, "The no-reading problem in consumer contract law", Stanford Law Review, 2014, 66, 545.
10 See *Emilios Avgouleas*, "The Global Financial Crisis and the Disclosure Paradigm in European Financial Regulation: The Case for Reform", European Company and Financial Law Review, 2009, 440, 466, advocating the use of economics experiments to test the impact of disclosure rules on investors and, in particular, lay investors; John Armour/Daniel Awrey/Paul Lyndon Davies/Luca Enriques/Jeffrey Neil Gordon/Colin P Mayer/Jennifer Payne, Principles of Financial Regulation, 2016, p. 160 et seqq.. *Luca Enriques*, EU Prospectus Regulation: Some Out-of-the-Box Thinking, www.law.ox.ac.uk/business-law-blog/blog/2016/05/eu-prospectus-regulation-some-out-box-thinking (accessed 7 February 2021): "when an offer is made with a view to having securities admitted to trading on a regulated market (ie, in IPOs), mandating disclosure may only serve the purpose of laying down once and for all the information items that sophisticated buyers and investment analysts would anyway deem necessary in order to price the securities. Retail investors are not users of issuer disclosures in this context. Rather, they free ride on the mechanisms (usually in the form of the bookbuilding process) that lead to setting an IPO price reflecting available information".

tion, but cover mandatory disclosure in general. Empirical research does not support the mandatory disclosure paradigm. Indeed, it is a moot point whether mandatory disclosure increases global welfare. In a widely cited paper, Leuz and Wysocki review the literature on disclosure and financial reporting in search for an empirical ground for regulatory measures. However, they point out that researchers are far from being able to perform appropriate quantitative cost-benefit analysis, as there is no real evidence of the welfare effects of disclosure and reporting regulation.[11] In fact, studies increasingly consider as totally unrealistic the idea that disclosure provides a public good that can be easily used by investors. Reading and understanding lengthy information takes time and therefore requires a private investment, which transforms the apparent public good in a private one.[12] For example, there has been much discussion on whether financial statements have become less informative over time, since in the past investors used to respond immediately to financial statement releases that contained significant changes, while this announcement effect is currently less pronounced. In a recent and important paper, Cohen, Malloy and Guyen find that the lack of announcement returns is not caused by financial statements having become less informative, but by investors' lack of attention, which the authors suspect can be attributed to the increase in complexity and length of financial reports over the last 25 years.[13] This research outcome is important because it confirms that information acquisition is an expensive task and that information overload has economic effects.[14]

4 Crowdfunding and High Leveraged Loan Securitizations

Empirical studies try to insulate situations where markets evolved without mandatory disclosure, in order to see what happened and infer policy indications for

---

11 *Christian Leuz/ Peter Wysocki*, "The economics of disclosure and financial reporting regulation: Evidence and suggestions for future research", Journal of Accounting Research 2016, 54, 525.
12 *Elizabeth Blankespoor/Ed deHaan/ Ivan Marinovic*, "Disclosure processing costs, investors' information choice, and equity market outcomes: A review" Journal of Accounting and Economics 2020, 70, 1.
13 *Lauren Cohen/Christopher Malloy/Quoc Nguyen*, "Lazy Prices", The Journal of Finance, 2020, 75, 1371.
14 *Troy Paredes*, "Blinded by the Light: Information Overload and its Consequences for Securities Regulation", Washington University Law Quarterly 2003, 81, 417.

other markets. Two interesting natural experiments have been recently reported by the law literature. The first concerns investment-based crowdfunding. In the EU, investment-based crowdfunding is regulated also with respect to disclosure, but with a light-touch approach and less stringent requirements than for IPOs.[15] In fact, the securities distributed through crowdfunding platforms are offered in amounts which are usually set below the thresholds fixed either by the European Prospectus Regulation for its applicability (EUR 1,000,000) or by the individual Member States (under the option granted to them under the European Prospectus Regulation to increase this threshold up to EUR 8,000,000).[16] Consistently, the European Crowdfunding Services Providers Regulation will only apply to securities offered for a consideration below EUR 5,000,000.[17] In addition, the disclosure regime included in this Regulation is milder than that found both in the European Prospectus Regulation and in MiFID II.[18] Before the Crowdfunding Services Providers Regulation and the Prospectus Regulation were adopted, the regime applicable to investment-based crowdfunding under *ad hoc* legislation in the Member States was similarly milder as to disclosure than that provided for public offers under the rules on prospectuses and on investment services.[19]

The lighter treatment of crowdfunding under national laws has contributed to the remarkable rise of crowdfunding in several Member States.[20] As one of us

---

15 *John Armour/Luca Enriques*, "The Promise and Perils of Crowdfunding: Between Corporate Finance and Consumer Contracts" Modern Law Review 2018, 81, 51; *Guido Ferrarini/Eugenia Macchiavello*, "Fintech and Alternative Finance in the CMU", in: Danny Busch/Emilios Avgouleas/ Guido Ferrarini (ed.), Capital Markets Union in Europe, 2018, 208, 10.45.

16 See Articles 1 (3) and 3 (2) Prospectus Regulation. On the treatment of small offerings under this Regulation, see *Kitty Lieverse*, The Obligation to Publish a Prospectus and Exemptions, in: Danny Busch et al., Prospectus Regulation (fn. 2), 145, 7.25.

17 See Art. 1 (2) (c) of Regulation (EU) 2020/1503 of 7 October 2020 on European crowdfunding service providers for business and amending Regulation (EU) 2017/1129 and Directive (EU) 2019/ 1937, OJEU L347/1.

18 See *Eugenia Macchiavello*, "The European Crowdfunding Service Providers Regulation and the Future of Marketplace Lending and Investing in Europe: the 'Crowdfunding Nature' Dilemma", forthcoming in European Business Law Review 2021, 3, available at https://ssrn.com/abstract=3668590 or http://dx.doi.org/10.2139/ssrn.3668590.

19 See *Guido Ferrarini/Eugenia Macchiavello*, Investment-based Crowdfunding: Is MiFID II Enough?, in: Danny Busch/Guido Ferrarini (ed.), Regulation of the EU Financial Markets: MiFID II and MiFIR, 2016, p. 659.

20 See the Explanatory Memorandum to the Commission's Proposal for a Regulation of the European Parliament and of the Council on European Crowdfunding Service Providers (ECSP) for Business, Brussels, 8.3.2018 COM(2018) 113 final, 2018/0048 (COD), and the accompanying Com-

has argued in a previous paper from a comparative perspective, crowdfunding laws tend to favour capital formation by reducing transaction costs, while trying to protect investors from fraud.[21] However, the costs that crowdfunding investors face when assessing a new company are great in comparison to the amount invested by a single user. Such information costs are even higher with innovative start-ups, which typically do not provide a reasonable basis for forecasting future earnings and face the inherent uncertainty of innovation.[22]

Strengthening mandatory disclosure obligations to solve this problem may not be a viable solution since start-ups have no historical data nor relevant track records. The possibility for evaluating them may derive from the chance to analyse the quality of their innovations. However, in the absence of exclusive rights on such innovations, the indirect costs of disclosure would be particularly high. Crowdfunding investors should then benefit from market-based mechanisms of indirect disclosure, as when the funders have previously used the products or known the people that they decide to support and benefitted from the information received by their online or offline network. In the case of innovative start-ups, whose products or services cannot yet be tested, such voluntary mechanisms are more sophisticated and include patents, ties with venture capitalists and the services provided by crowdfunding portals.[23]

Accordingly, in the crowdfunding space market-based mechanisms are very important and probably are more effective than regulatory measures aimed at imposing mandatory disclosure. Indeed, it is reported that at least one jurisdiction decided to get rid of any form of mandatory information with regard to equity crowdfunding without negative consequences. A recent paper highlights the success of crowdfunding in New Zealand, where disclosure is purely voluntary and where no market unravelling has occured so far.[24]

The second natural experiment is probably even more interesting, given the volumes of the relevant markets. Elisabeth De Fontenay has shown that high leveraged loans are functionally similar to high yield bonds also with regard to the production of information by issuers (corporate debtors, in the loan

---

mission Staff Working Document including the Impact Assessment, where data on the EU crowd-funding market.

21 See *Guido Ferrarini/Andrea Ottolia*, "Corporate Disclosure as a Transaction Cost: The Case of SMEs", European Review of Contract Law 2013, 9, 363, 375 seq.

22 *Gerrit K.C. Ahlers/Douglas Cumming/Christina Guenther/Denis Schweizer*, "Signaling in Equity Crowd-funding", Entrepreneurship Theory and Practice 2015, 39, 4, 955.

23 See *Ferrarini/Ottolia* (fn. 20), 380, where the reader can find further references.

24 *Andrew A. Schwartz*, "Mandatory Disclosure in Primary Markets", Utah Law Review 2019, 5, 1069.

world) who find appropriate incentives to inform even in the absence of mandatory disclosure.[25] ICOs similarly concern investor protection in truly primary offers and suggest another natural experiment.

5 ICOs and Mandatory Disclosure

When ICOs started and literally exploded in 2017 as a financial phenomenon, teams generally disregarded the possibility or even the risk that the offering could be characterized as a securities offering and therefore subject to registration with the SEC in the US or with national securities authorities elsewhere. There were many reasons for this general disregard of securities regulation, amongst which the idea that tokens could work and be considered like money, therefore escaping the rigours of securities regulation, or that utility tokens were very different from financial investments.

We do not want to repeat here the arguments that can draw token offerings either inside or outside securities regulation. We stress, however, that a large part of the ICOs which occurred in 2017–2018 had features that would certainly fit the arguments of believers in mandatory disclosure, apart from any legal assessment on whether the tokens offered in those ICOs could be characterized as securities or not. Consider, for instance, the so called "utility tokens", which present some type of functional utility to their owners, who use them to get access to a blockchain platform that offers some product or service. Utility tokens distributed through ICOs are almost invariably admitted to trading on crypto-exchanges through the efforts of their promoters. Investors can be interested to buy a token either in order to get cheaper access to the utilities that the pertinent platform will offer or to hold and then trade a crypto-asset that might increase in value in the future and be easily exchanged within the eco-system at issue or in crypto-exchanges.

No doubt, one of the reasons for their success is that ICOs help to solve the coordination problems that any new platform raises. Platforms benefit from network effects, since a user's utility increases with the number of those utilising the platform. The promoters try to solve this coordination problem by offering a stake in the future success of the platform to early potential users, who are therefore incentivized to embrace and support the platform, counting on the sec-

---

25 *Elisabeth De Fontenay,* "Putting the Securities Laws to the Test", Regulation 2014, 37, 22; *Elisabeth de Fontenay,* "Do the Securities Laws Matter? The Rise of the Leveraged Loan Market", Journal of Corporation Law 2014, 39, 725.

ondary market of tokens as a mechanism to trade future cash flows for present ones. Indeed, thanks to token tradability, early adopters can sell their tokens at a higher price when the platform is successful, thereby becoming vested in its success. As a result, lower incentives are needed to get early users to access the platform, thus reducing overall transaction costs.

In essence, and this is what concerns us here, tradable utility tokens are equivalent to equity, not as an investment in the company, but as an investment in the platform that the blockchain startup wishes to develop.[26] Consequently, token offerings are very similar to offerings of new securities and present many of the same problems that pushed securities regulators to the adoption of mandatory disclosure. The initial main target of those regulators were the problems created by newly formed companies with ambitious purposes, selling shares to the public for the first time. In particular, as argued by Paul Mahoney in a well-known paper, the mandatory disclosure system was introduced in order to combat a specific agency problem – the promoters' propension to use the cash raised by the sale of stock to enter into pre-arranged transactions between the newly formed company and entities owned by the promoters or their family and friends, with the purpose of getting part of the money contributed to the company by investors.[27]

From this perspective, ICOs truly represent a return to the past, also considering that they are structured as one round of financing. Since raising funds is not staged in ICOs and therefore is not a repeated game such as, for instance, in venture capital financing, there is a significant danger of fraud.[28] When promoting teams ask for money needed to finance grandiose change-the-world projects through the blockchain, there are huge opportunities for self-enrichment through pre-arranged related party transactions at the expenses of gullible investors attracted by the lure of easy gains. Thus, ICOs offer a step back in history, in addition to being a natural experiment of what can happen today where mandatory disclosure does not exist.

---

26 *Dmitri Boreiko/Guido Ferrarini/ Paolo Giudici* (fn. 2), 470 et seqq.
27 *Mahoney* (fn. 5).
28 *Lars Klöhn/Nicolas Parhofer/Daniel Resas*, 'Initial Coin Offerings (ICOs): Economics and Regulation' (2018) available at https://papers.ssrn.com/sol3/papers.cfm?abstract_id=3290882 (last access 8 February 2021); *Dmitri Boreiko/Gioia Vidusso*, "New blockchain intermediaries: do ICO rating websites do their job well?" The Journal of Alternative Investments 2019, 21, 67.

6 Signalling Quality in the ICO World

It is not a surprise that a large number of studies have sought to analyse what actually has happened in ICOs. The relevant papers show that investors have used several information sources to assess the quality of the token sale, such as GitHub, Twitter, Telegram/Slack/Discord, Bitcoinwiki, Facebook, Bitcointalk. As to issuers, many papers agree that good blockchain startups have been quite effective in signalling their quality. Yermack et al. find that liquidity and trading volume are higher when issuers offer voluntary disclosure, credibly commit to the project, and signal quality.[29] Rosemboom et al. find projects that disclose more extensive information to investors (i.e. have a higher profile rating) are more successful in fundraising, and experience more post-ICO project success; in addition, they find that a higher rating by cryptocurrency experts on both the quality of the project and project team is associated with more success in fundraising and better ex-post performance.[30] Zhang and others find that an ICO whitepaper narrative with more readable disclosures is likely to result in a higher initial return for ICO investors.[31] Fisch argues that a technical whitepaper and a high-quality code are associated with increased ICO funding.[32] According to these results, blockchain startups can effectively and efficiently signal their quality to investors.[33] However, ratings do not seem to be indicative of ICOs' success and are so far not very informative.[34]

These results are not undisputed. Momtaz finds that firms exaggerate information in white papers; a moral hazard in signalling that investors only learn in the aftermarket, when the token price plummets.[35] Accordingly, Momtaz argues

---

29 *Sabrina T Howell/Marina Niessner/David Yermack*, "Initial coin offerings: Financing growth with cryptocurrency token sales", The Review of Financial Studies 2020, 33, no. 9, 3925.
30 *Peter Roosenboom/Tom van der Kolk/Abe de Jong*, "What determines success in initial coin offerings?", Venture Capital 2020, 22, 161.
31 *Shuyu Zhang and others*, "Readability of token whitepaper and ICO first-day return", Economics Letters 2019, 180, 58.
32 *Christian Fisch*, "Initial coin offerings (ICOs) to finance new ventures", Journal of Business Venturing 2019, 34. 1.
33 Albrecht et al find evidence of significant relationships between startups' raised volume and a) the general blockchain discourse as measured by search trends; b) their average Twitter sentiment; c) increasing emotionality in their tweets towards the ICO end date: *Simon Albrecht/Bernhard Lutz/Dirk Neumann*, How Sentiment Impacts the Success of Blockchain Startups-An Analysis of Social Media Data and Initial Coin Offerings (2019)
34 *Boreiko/Vidusso* (fn. 27), 11.
35 *Paul P Momtaz*, "Entrepreneurial Finance and Moral Hazard: Evidence from Token Offerings", forthcoming, Journal of Business Venturing (available online 14 March 2020, 106001).

that, in the logic of the classic Akerlof model, the moral hazard in signalling may even entail a 'market for lemons,' and that good firms cannot credibly distinguish themselves from bad ones.[36] However, the same author recognizes that, even though the ICO market has been criticized for providing fertile soil for scams, using a conservative definition of what constitutes a scam, their number appears not so high (less than 40, measured presumably at the end of 2018).[37] Cohney et al. show that many ICOs failed even to promise that they would protect investors against insider self-dealing, and fewer still manifested smart contracts in code. Indeed, the authors point out that a significant fraction of issuers retained centralized control through a previously undisclosed code permitting modification of the entities' governing structures.[38] However, their important paper does not analyse whether these problems affect capital raising and therefore does not offer evidence that decisively contradicts the signalling argument. Also Hornuf at al. seek to understand the incidence of fraud in ICOs.[39] Their working paper reports a high incidence of fraud. However, the authors classify as fraud a large number of situations, among which frauds that are induced by persons not related to the issuer, such as pump-and-dump schemes and, more importantly, phishing and hacking attacks, which the authors report as the most frequent example of fraud in their sample. As to issuer's and team's frauds, they classify as such, for instance, violations of registration requirements and ensuing SEC's actions, which they call "securities frauds" but which of course are not cases of fraud but cases of violation of mandatory disclosure rules. The most significant cases reported by the authors are "exit frauds", where the promoters get the money or the cryptomoney and then disappear. They report 21 suspected and 25 confirmed cases of exit fraud out of 1,393 ICOs considered in their sample, a number which looks extraordinarily low and which in any event should be assessed in the light of the money syphoned off more than the mere number of occurrences.[40] Thus, research does not seem

---

36 *George A. Akerlof*, "The Market for "Lemons": Quality Uncertainty and the Market Mechanism" Quarterly Journal of Economics 1970, 84, 488.

37 *Paul P. Momtaz*, "Initial Coin Offerings", Plos One 2020 (available online, last access 25 February 2021). The author makes reference to a presentation by Lars Hornuf and Armin Schwienbacher, concerning a paper that is commented infra in the text.

38 *Shaanan Cohney and others*, "Coin-operated capitalism" Columbia Law Review 2019, 119, 591.

39 *Lars Hornuf/Theresa Kück/Armin Schwienbacher*, "Initial coin offerings, information disclosure, and fraud" CESifo Working Paper No. 7962, 2019, available at SSRN (last access 25 February 2021).

40 The concern should be on the ability of fraudsters to convince gullible investors to give money for nothing, and therefore an overall measure of this ability should consider how much money was taken in exit frauds compared to the overall money raised in ICOs.

to support the view that market mechanisms are not able to function when issuers have to signal their quality.

When moving from research papers to real life cases, there are no strong arguments that offer clear evidence that in the ICO market a mandatory disclosure regime is really needed in order to protect gullible investors. No doubt, there have been scams, but there is no clear evidence of significant cases showing the true capacity of fraudulent offerings to lure disingenuous investors. In the US there are class actions against many token issuers, but these class actions mainly claim that issuers did not comply with securities regulation and therefore cannot be used as evidence that prospectus regulation would have avoided the investors' problems and that prospectus regulation costs would be inferior to prospectus regulation benefits.[41]

Without any clear sign that voluntary disclosure is not working well or, from a different perspective, that the absence of a mandatory disclosure system has drawn millions of naïve investors around the world to put their wealth at risk in irrational token bets, ICOs might be a signal that it is time to rethink the mandatory disclosure paradigm. Possibly, today retail investors are different from those that populated the markets a century ago. In a world of social networks and open access to information, it is perhaps better to incentivize retail investors to find information through the channels that they prefer rather than insisting on their reading hundreds of prospectus pages, requiring issuers to draft them and regulators to take charge of the issue. It has been pointed out that rather than relying on traditional sources of information such as financial statements and SEC filings, professional investors have started looking at alternative data such as satellite imagery, social media posts, insurance policy,[42] and patents.[43] The ICO market seems to show a similar trend, but also referred to nonprofessional investors.

In the light of these conclusions, the regulation of ICOs and IEOs could be a starting point for a new approach to information regulation in primary markets, which gradually abandons the great regulatory costs of prospectus regulation and embraces a new era, for instance one with lesser micro-regulation of information channels and templates and more widespread enforcement of rules concerning true and correct information and against material omissions. The proposed MiCA instead follows the prospectus regulation paradigm, albeit with an apparent light touch.

---

41 On the complexities of cost and benefit analysis in this area see *supra*, fn. 7.
42 *Hu* (fn. 5), 110
43 *Ferrarini/Ottolia* (fn. 20), 18 et seq.

7 The European Commission's Proposal for a Regulation on Markets in Crypto-Assets

7.1 MiCA in brief

On 24 September 2020, the European Commission published a much anticipated proposal on the establishment of an EU-level regime for crypto-assets, the Markets in Crypto-Assets Regulation (MiCA).[44] On the same day, the Commission also published a proposal for a regulation on a pilot regime for market infrastructures based on DLT.[45] The draft text of MiCA sets out a regime to regulate issuers of crypto-assets and providers of crypto-asset services, including exchanges, custodians, and firms providing investment type services in respect of crypto-assets. The effect of the MiCA proposal, if ultimately adopted, would be to bring substantially all crypto-assets within the perimeter of EU financial services regulation. The proposal would represent a significant expansion of the EU's regulatory perimeter and likely result in a significant upheaval for firms wanting to operate or promote a crypto-asset project in the EU or to provide services in respect of crypto-assets.

The Proposal of MiCA stresses that crypto-assets which qualify as financial instruments are already subject to the Markets in Financial Instruments Directive (MiFID). However, the Proposal does provide some crossover insofar as firms authorized under other EU directives and regulations could issue crypto-assets, provided that they comply with the additional disclosure obligations under MiCA. The Proposal then distinguishes the following types of crypto-assets: (i) e-money tokens, which are defined as crypto-assets the main purpose of which is to be used as a means of exchange, and that purport to maintain a stable value by referring to the value of a fiat currency that is legal tender; (ii) asset-referenced tokens, which are defined as those crypto-assets that purport to maintain a stable value by referring to the value of several fiat currencies that are legal tender, one or several commodities or one or several crypto-assets, or a combination of such assets; (iii) crypto-assets other than asset-referenced tokens and e-money tokens. The third class includes "utility tokens," which are defined as a type of crypto-asset intended to provide digital access to a good or a service

---

44 *Supra*, fn. 1. For a preliminary comment of MiCA see *Dirk Zetzsche et al.*, "The Markets in Crypto-Assets Regulation (MICA) and the EU Digital Finance Strategy", 2020, available at https://papers.ssrn.com/sol3/papers.cfm?abstract_id=3725395 (last access 8 February 2020).
45 See the Proposal for a regulation on a pilot regime for market infrastructures based on distributed ledger technology (COM(2020) 594 final), 2020/0267 (COD).

available on DLT and accepted only by the issuer of that token. However, it is not clear from the Proposal if there are "crypto-assets other than asset-referenced tokens and e-money tokens" that are not utility tokens. Recital no. 9 seems to imply that utility tokens make up the whole class, but not so Article 4(3), where it is assumed that utility tokens are a part of that class. Whatever the correct answer, the utility token category is used principally in relation to disclosure requirements for projects that are not yet in operation and that carry a risk that the proposed good or service may never be provided.

MiCA imposes investor disclosure requirements on issuers of all crypto-assets covered by the regulation, although more onerous obligations apply to issuers of asset-referenced tokens and e-money tokens. We consider exclusively crypto-assets other than asset-referenced tokens and e-money tokens, since these are the tokens that mainly concern blockchain startups that are not involved in the attempt to create new, private forms of money.

7.2 MiCA's Provisions on Crypto-Assets other than Asset-Referenced Tokens and E-money Tokens

For a general crypto-asset to be offered to the public in the EU or to be admitted to a crypto-asset trading platform in the EU, the issuer must be a legal entity and must first draft a "white paper." This provision seems to confirm that the market comes first and then regulation ensues. Indeed, we are not aware of any significant successful ICO that raised capital without a white paper; the term is new in EU financial and consumer regulation and comes from market practices.

The contents of the white paper, which must be dated, are provided for in Article 5. The white paper must contain a detailed description of the issuer and a presentation of the main participants involved in the project. ICO white papers are usually very detailed in the description of the team participants, even though less so with regard to the issuer entity. Annex 1 sketches in further detail the information that must be presented on the issuer.

The white paper must contain a detailed description of the issuer's project and the planned use of the fiat currency or other crypto assets collected via the offer to the public. According to Annex I, where the offer to the public of crypto-assets concerns utility tokens, the key features of the products or services developed or to be developed must also be contained in the white paper. This type of information is richly offered by ICO white papers. As mentioned, no ICO has any prospect of success if this type of information is not voluntarily provided for.

The white paper must describe the type of crypto asset that will be offered to the public or for which admission to trading is sought; once again, this is a type of information that is always voluntarily provided by white papers. The white paper must also explain the reasons why the crypto assets are offered to the public or for which admission to trading is sought, another type of information that is almost invariably provided by white papers in practice.

The white paper must contain a detailed description of the characteristics of the offer to the public, in particular the number of crypto-assets that will be issued or for which admission to trading is sought, the issue price of the crypto-assets and the subscription terms and conditions; a detailed description of the rights and obligations attached to the crypto-assets and the procedures and conditions for exercising those rights; information on the underlying technology and standards applied by the issuer of the crypto-assets allowing for the holding, storing and transfer of those crypto-assets; a detailed description of the risks relating to the issuer of the crypto-assets, the crypto-assets, the offer to the public of the crypto-asset and the implementation of the project. Generally speaking, this type of information is less detailed in ICO white papers, especially with regards to risk factors; but the most successful ICOs have generally offered similar information to purchasers.

All information must be fair, clear and not misleading. The crypto-asset white paper must not contain material omissions and must be presented in a concise and comprehensible form. It must state that the issuer is solely responsible for its content and that the white paper has not been reviewed or approved by any competent authority in any Member State of the European Union. The crypto-asset white paper must not contain any assertions on the future value of the crypto-assets, and must warn investors that the crypto-assets may lose their value in part or in full, may not always be transferable, may not be liquid, and where the offer to the public concerns utility tokens, that such utility tokens may not be exchangeable against the good or service promised in the crypto-asset white paper, especially in case of failure or discontinuation of the project.

Every crypto-asset white paper must contain a statement from the management body of the issuer of the crypto-assets, confirming that the crypto-asset white paper complies with MiCA requirements and that the information it presents is correct and that there is no significant omission. As usual for modern prospectus regulation, MiCA also requires that the white paper must contain a summary.

The white paper must be registered with (but not approved by) a designated EU authority in one of the Member States where the crypto-asset will be marketed or admitted to trading on a crypto-asset trading platform, and published on the issuer's website. However, issuers of general crypto-assets need not be established in the EU; nor do they have to be authorized under any EU directive. From this perspective, MiCA should remove fragmented national regimes, and provide the ability for a general crypto-asset to be marketed on a pan-EU basis from a single point of entry, including by non-EU issuers. The scope of MiCA as an anti-fragmentation measure seems to be more important than does its scope as a mandatory disclosure instrument that sorts out unresolved market failures.

The notification to the regulator must explain why the crypto-asset is not to be characterized as a financial instrument – a topic on which MiCA offers no clarification to issuers who can be in doubt on how to characterize their offer.

MiCA contains a provision on marketing communications (Article 6) and another on offers that are limited in time (Article 9). Article 11 provides that issuers must modify their published crypto-asset white paper and published marketing communications to describe any change or new fact that is likely to have a significant influence on the purchase decision of any potential purchaser or on the decision of holders of such crypto-assets to sell or exchange the same. This is the link between information to primary market investors and information to secondary market investors. Accordingly, MiCA covers also *ad hoc* information. The issuer must immediately inform the public through its website of the notification of a modified crypto-asset white paper and has to provide a summary of the reasons for the changes. The amendments must be time-stamped.

Issuers of crypto-assets, other than asset-referenced tokens and e-money tokens, must offer 14-day right of withdrawal to consumers who buy directly from the issuer or from a crypto-asset service provider that places the crypto-assets on behalf of that issuer. However, the right of withdrawal does not apply where the crypto-assets are admitted to trading on a trading platform for crypto-assets.

Issuers of crypto-assets, other than asset-referenced tokens or e-money tokens, must act honestly, fairly and professionally; they must communicate with the holders of crypto-assets in a fair, clear and not misleading manner; they must prevent, identify, manage and disclose any conflicts of interest that may arise; they must maintain all of their systems and security access protocols to appropriate Union standards. Moreover, they must act in the best interests of the holders of such crypto-assets and treat them equally, unless any preferential treatment is disclosed in the crypto-asset white paper and in the marketing communications. If the offer is cancelled, the issuer must return the funds to the purchasers.

7.3 MiCA's Implications

MiCA assumes that a large part of utility tokens cannot be characterized as negotiable securities and, without any guidance on how to distinguish crypto-assets that are to be considered financial instruments from crypto-assets that are not, creates an *ad hoc* prospectus regime for the latter. This position, however, would have significant implications for the interpretation of EU financial law. Since all MiCA's regulation mirrors existing financial regulation, and since MiCA explicitly recognizes that utility tokens can be traded and custodied through crypto-asset service providers and exchanges that reflect and readapt the traditional financial market infrastructures to blockchain, *de facto* MiCA would elicit the importance of the reference to capital markets contained in the definition of transferable securities provided for by Article 4(1)(44) MiFID II.[46] If and when MiCA becomes effective, the crypto-asset world will be transformed into an almost perfect reflection of the traditional (even though simplified) capital market regulation; and the presence of crypto-asset brokers, custodians and exchanges will no longer be sufficient to argue, as we have done in our previous paper, that those professional figures are typical features of the capital markets and contribute to making the crypto assets that are traded through them 'transferable securities' under EU law (especially when there is an investment component on the purchasers' side).[47] Unfortunately, however, the boundary between transferable instruments and crypto-assets as defined in the Proposal is blurred, creating uncertainty as to the applicable regulation and opening numerous arbitrage opportunities to the interested parties to the extent that MiCA includes a lighter regime, for instance with regard to non-approval of the white paper by the registration authority.

As to mandatory disclosure in particular, MiCA mirrors prospectus regulation and introduces a prospectus-like regime with regard to crypto-assets that are not to be considered as financial instruments. An easy forecast is that these crypto asset prospectuses will become lengthy and not particularly useful for retail investors who will no longer read them, since they will be packed with legalese and will be written simply to appease the authority that will receive the notification and will register the white paper – rather than the geek audience to whom white papers were originally addressed in the blockchain space – and to defensively escape liability and litigation, even though in this area, as we point

---

46 Please refer for a more thorough analysis of this specific point to *Boreiko/Ferrarini/Giudici* (fn. 2), 678–682.
47 *Boreiko/Ferrarini/Giudici* (fn. 2), 678–682.

out in next paragraph, MiCA is not aimed at facilitating investors' claims, rather counterintuitively given its investor protection fanfare.

7.4 MiCA's Liability Regime

MiCA would also introduce an *ad hoc*, detailed liability regime, which is unusual in European financial regulation. A special European liability regime is foreseen with regard to rating agencies,[48] but the rest of EU financial regulation does not include common liability rules and contains broad provisions on liability. Article 11 of Prospectus Regulation, for instance, provides that Member States ensure that responsibility for the information given in a prospectus, and any supplement thereto, attaches to at least the issuer or its administrative, management or supervisory bodies, the offeror, the person asking for the admission to trading on a regulated market or the guarantor, as the case may be. Pursuant to Article 11, the persons responsible for the prospectus, and any supplement thereto, have to be clearly identified in the prospectus by their names and functions or, in the case of legal persons, their names and registered offices, as well as declarations by them that, to the best of their knowledge, the information contained in the prospectus is in accordance with the facts and that the prospectus makes no omission likely to affect its import. Nothing is stated, accordingly, on the nature of the liability regime or the allocation of the burden of proof.[49]

According to the proposal, where an issuer of crypto-assets, other than asset-referenced tokens or e-money tokens, and/or its management body have infringed Article 5 – by providing information which is not complete, fair or clear, or by providing information which is misleading in the crypto-asset white paper (or in a modified one) – a holder of such crypto-assets may claim damages from that issuer or its management body for damages caused to her as a result of the infringement. Any exclusion of civil liability shall have no effect. However, the effectiveness of the liability provision is fully diluted by the adoption of a standard burden of proof regime, where it is on the holder of crypto-assets to offer evidence indicating that the issuer has infringed Article 5 and that such an infringement has had an impact on her decision to buy, sell or ex-

---

48 *Giorgio Risso*, "Investor Protection in Credit Rating Agencies' Non-Contractual Liability: the Need for a Fully Harmonised Regime", *European law review* 2015, 5, 706.

49 On European liability rules concerning financial information and transparency see *Paolo Giudici*, Private Enforcement of Transparency, in: Vassilios Tountopoulos/Rüdiger Veil (ed.), Transparency of Stock Corporations in Europe: Rationales, Limitations and Perspectives, 2019, p. 297.

change the crypto-assets. In jurisdictions with no fee-shifting mechanisms, no collective litigation instruments and, above all, no recourse to discovery, this burden of proof might become unsurmountable.[50] If this is the intention, it clashes with a regulatory framework that is expressly addressed at protecting investors and that seeks to reduce the intervention of public authorities, for example by eliminating the prospectus approval procedure. More important, this approach conflicts with the widespread view that private enforcement matters – apart from any assessment on whether it is more or less important than public enforcement in the construction of efficient capital markets – and that regulation in Continental Europe is excessively oriented towards public enforcement and puts too much reliance on administrative bodies.[51] From this critical perspective, MiCA would be in line with a criticisable European tradition of great regulatory frameworks and poor enforcement, where regulation gives with one hand and takes away with the other.

8 Our Tentative Proposals and Conclusions

Our conclusions are tentative. The ICO explosion has offered a chance to rethink mandatory disclosure of public offerings. Rather than creating a parallel framework that mirrors Prospectus Regulation, it could be worth investigating the possibility of exempting from prospectus-like regulation any offering regarding tokens (whether securities or utility tokens), where the issuer is a blockchain startup, the entity issuing the tokens and the persons involved in the offering are clearly identified, and no intermediary is involved in the placing of the offer-

---

50 *Guido Ferrarini/Paolo Giudici*, Financial scandals and the role of private enforcement: the Parmalat case, in: John Armour/Joseph A. McCahery, After Enron: Improving Corporate Law and Modernizing Securities Regulation in Europe and the US, 2006, p. 159, 193 et seqq.

51 The literature on the issue is huge and mainly concerns antitrust law and securities law. With regard to the latter, cf. *Rafael La Porta et al.*, "What Works in Securities Laws?" Journal of Finance 2006, 61, 1 (who find little evidence that public enforcement benefits stock markets, but strong evidence that laws facilitating private enforcement benefit stock markets); *Howell E. Jackson/Mark J. Roe*, "Public and Private Enforcement of Securities Laws: Resource-Based Evidence" Journal of Financial Economics 2009, 93, 207 (reversing the results on both liability standards and public enforcement). Both works find evidence about the importance of mandatory disclosure, but we do not think that they contrast the arguments we have presented in the first part of the work, since their reference to mandatory disclosure mainly concerns disclosure in secondary markets. See also the literature mentioned in *Ferrarini/Giudici* (fn. 49), 193 et seqq.; *Giudici* (fn. 48), 300 et seqq.

ing.[52] For example, blockchain startups could be left free to decide what information to offer to investors, so long as the information provided to investors is free from false or misleading statements, and does not omit anything that can make the statements false or misleading. A regime of this type is provided for by Rule 506 of Regulation D in the US, and we think that it might be sufficient at this stage, especially if coupled with a standard of strict liability on the issuer or a reversal of the burden of proof. From this perspective, ICOs could be a great chance to return to a more manageable regime, where general anti-fraud provisions are applied with well-defined private liability rules and burden of proof allocations, and startups are left free to signal their quality and develop their channels of communication with potential investors.

The MiCA proposal goes in the opposite direction by mirroring, even though in small scale, the EU framework of financial regulation. However, we know from past experience that there is no way to escape from political pressure to expand regulation when a statute is aimed at protecting investors and some scams happen. At that point in time the debate will not centre on whether the statute was really necessary, but on the measures to be taken to enlarge its scope and provide more detailed rules in to prevent future scandals. In this way, regulation gets out of control and is potentially able to hold back EU competitiveness in the blockchain space for a long period.

MiCa looks also well-rooted in the EU tradition of designing grandiose regulatory frameworks aimed to protect investors without offering the protected parties effective instruments of private enforcement of their rights.

---

52 The last requirement reflects the idea that, of course, intermediaries placing products on behalf of issuers have a strong incentive to push sales and sell free advice to clients on the advantages of the product. Nevertheless, we believe that if intermediaries are involved in the placing of products, they have to be held liable for their recommendations as financial advisors and a mandatory prospectus regime is not necessary.

Carsten Gerner-Beuerle

Algorithmic Trading and the Limits of Securities Regulation

Abstract: Since the infamous flash crash of 2010, instances of unexplained high volatility in financial markets, often driven by algorithmic and high-frequency trading, have received increased attention by policy makers and commentators. A number of regulatory initiatives in the EU and US deal specifically with the perceived risks that algorithmic and high-frequency trading pose to market quality. However, their efficacy is disputed, with some claiming that they are unlikely to prevent the future misuse of HFT practices, while others caution that the additional regulatory burden may have unintended and counterproductive consequences for market efficiency. This paper examines whether existing regulatory techniques, notably disclosure, internal testing and monitoring systems, and the regulation of structural features of the trade process, such as order execution times and circuit breakers, are adequate to address the risk of extreme market turbulence. It draws on market microstructure theory in arguing that regulation in the EU and the US takes in sufficient account of the mechanics of automated trading in modern financial markets.

Table of Contents

Carsten Gerner-Beuerle, Faculty of Laws, University College London, Email: c.gerner@ucl.ac.uk.
I am grateful to the participants of workshops at the University of Helsinki and the UCL Department of Computer Science for helpful comments and suggestions. Special thanks are due to Emilios Avgouleas, Guido Germano and Heikki Marjosola. All remaining errors are mine.

∂ OpenAccess. © 2022 Carsten Gerner-Beuerle, published by De Gruyter. [CC] BY-NC-ND This work is licensed under the Creative Commons Attribution-NonCommercial-NoDerivatives 4.0 International License.
https://doi.org/10.1515/9783110749472-005

1 Introduction

According to some calculations, high frequency trading now accounts for more than 50% of trading volume in US equity markets, 40% in European equity markets, and between 60% and 80% in futures markets.[1] Algorithmic trading, of which high-frequency trading is a special case,[2] is responsible for the clear majority of trades in many markets.[3] As algorithmic and high frequency trading have proliferated, so have the regulatory initiatives to address their perceived harmful consequences. Algorithms have been held responsible for sudden violent market movements that have become frequent since the mid-1990s,[4] such as the infamous "flash crash" of May 2010.[5] They, or at least certain types of

---

[1] Thierry Foucault/Sophie Moinas, "Is Trading Fast Dangerous?" in Walter Mattli (ed.), Global Algorithmic Capital Markets: High Frequency Trading, Dark Pools, and Regulatory Challenges (OUP 2019); Rena S. Miller/Gary Shorter, High Frequency Trading: Overview of Recent Developments, Congressional Research Service Report (2016), 1. For more detailed data that reports significant variation across EU trading venues, see also Steffen Kern/Giuseppe Loiacono, High Frequency Trading and Circuit Breakers in the EU: Recent Findings and Regulatory Activities, in Mattli, Ibid. at 308, 312.

[2] Algorithmic trading is defined by the Markets in Financial Instruments Directive (Directive 2014/65/EU of the European Parliament and of the Council of 15 May 2014, [2014] OJ L173/349 (MiFID II)) as "trading in financial instruments where a computer algorithm automatically determines individual parameters of orders such as whether to initiate the order, the timing, price or quantity of the order or how to manage the order after its submission, with limited or no human intervention", MiFID II, Art 4(1), subsection (39). High-frequency trading is an algorithmic trading strategy that makes use of infrastructure intended to minimise network and other types of latencies, for example co-location, proximity hosting or high- speed direct electronic access; generates, routes and/or executes orders without human intervention; and the algorithmic trader has a high message intraday rate as regards orders, quotes or cancellations, MiFID II, Art 4(1), subsection (40). An intraday message rate is regarded as high if two or more messages per second are submitted with respect to a single financial instrument or four or more messages per second with respect to all financial instruments traded on a trading venue, Commission Delegated Regulation (EU) 2017/565 of 25 April 2016 supplementing Directive 2014/65/EU of the European Parliament and of the Council as regards organisational requirements and operating conditions for investment firms and defined terms for the purposes of that Directive, [2017] OJ L 87/1, Art 19(1).

[3] Yesha Yadav, "How Algorithmic Trading Undermines Efficiency in Capital Markets" (2015) 68 Vand. L. Rev. 1607, 1619.

[4] Irene Aldridge/Steven Krawciw, Real-time risk: what investors should know about fintech, high-frequency trading, and flash crashes (Wiley 2017), 111.

[5] For a comprehensive analysis of the flash crash of May 2010, see Commodity Futures Trading Commission (CFTC) and Securities / Exchange Commission (SEC), Findings regarding the market events of May 6, 2010 (September 2010). Discussions of the causes of the flash crash from the

high frequency traders, have been criticised for reducing liquidity,[6] expending valuable resources on a socially wasteful "arms race" with the goal of reducing latency by a matter of milliseconds,[7] and placing other investors at a persistent informational disadvantage similar to traditional insiders who exploit inside information.[8]

However, there are probably few regulatory initiatives that stand on weaker theoretical and empirical ground than the requirements imposed on algorithmic and high frequency traders in the EU's Markets in Financial Instruments Directive (MiFID II)[9] or Regulation NMS – Regulation of the National Market System in the United States.[10] Empirical evidence shows predominantly that algorithmic and high frequency trading have, under most circumstances, positive effects on market quality and price formation.[11] Regulatory interference with the trading

---

literature include *Eric M. Aldrich/Joseph A. Grundfest/Gregory Laughlin*, "The Flash Crash: A New Deconstruction" (2017), available at SSRN: https://ssrn.com/abstract=2721922; *David Easley/Marcos M. López de Prado/Maureen O'Hara*, "The Microstructure of the "Flash Crash": Flow Toxicity, Liquidity Crashes and the Probability of Informed Trading" (2011) 37 J. Portf. Manag. 118; *Andrei Kirilenko/Albert S. Kyle/Mehrdad Samadi/Tugkan Tuzun*, "The Flash Crash: High-Frequency Trading in an Electronic Market" (2017) 72 J. Fin. 967.

6 *Andrei A. Kirilenko/Andrew W. Lo*, "Moore's Law versus Murphy's Law: Algorithmic Trading and Its Discontents" (2013) 27 J. Econ. Perspect. 51, 60.

7 *Eric Budish/Peter Cramton/John Shim*, "The High-Frequency Trading Arms Race: Frequent Batch Auctions as a Market Design Response" (2015) 130 Q. J. Econ. 1547. This issue has been popularised by *Michael Lewis*, Flash Boys: A Wall Street Revolt (W.W. Norton 2014).

8 *Yesha Yadav*, "Insider Trading and Market Structure" (2016) 63 *UCLA L. Rev.* 968.

9 Directive 2014/65/EU (fn. 2).

10 17 CFR §§ 242.600 – 242.613, promulgated by the SEC pursuant to Section 11 A of the Securities Exchange Act of 1934. For a critical assessment of Regulation NMS, see *Jennifer V. Dean*, "Paradigm Shifts / Unintended Consequences: The Death of the Specialist, the Rise of High Frequency Trading, / the Problem of Duty-Free Liquidity in Equity Markets" (2012) 8 *FIU L. Rev.* 217; *Paul G. Mahoney*, "Equity Market Structure Regulation: Time to Start Over" (2020), Virginia Law and Economics Research Paper No. 2020 – 11, available at SSRN: https://ssrn.com/abstract=3622291; *Steven McNamara*, "The Stock Exchange as Multi-Sided Platform and the Future of the National Market System" (2018) *BYU L. Rev.* 969.

11 *Jonathan Brogaard/Terrence Hendershott/Ryan Riordan*, "High-frequency trading and price discovery" (2014) 27 Rev. Financ. Stud. 2267; *Allen Carrion*, "Very fast money: High-frequency trading on the NASDAQ" (2013) 16 J. Financial Mark. 680; Peter Gomber et al., High-Frequency Trading, report commissioned by Deutsche Börse Group (March 2011), p. 59; *Joel Hasbrouck/Gideon Saar*, "Low-latency trading" (2013) 16 J. Financial Mark. 646; *Terrence Hendershott/Charles Jones/Albert Menkveld*, "Does Algorithmic Trading Improve Liquidity?" (2011) 66 J. Fin. 1. Overviews of the literature are given by *Gaia Balp/Giovanni Strampelli*, "Preserving Capital Markets Efficiency in the High-Frequency Trading Era" (2018) 2018 U. Ill. J.L. Tech. & Pol'y 349, 356 – 364; *Gianluca Piero Maria Virgilio*, "High-frequency trading: a literature review" (2019) 33 Financial Mark. Portf. Manag. 183.

process, for example through so-called circuit breakers that seek to curb volatility if price changes exceed pre-defined levels, has been found to be often counterproductive and to entail unintended consequences, such as volatility spillovers into other markets.[12]

This paper argues that much of the current regulatory framework continues to be centred around the classical disclosure paradigm of securities regulation, and hence around the role of information in financial markets, without taking sufficient account of the changes in the process of price discovery brought about by the rise of automated trading.[13] Regulation based on the disclosure paradigm, which can be traced back to the US Securities Act of 1933 and Securities Exchange Act of 1934, has been credited with enhancing liquidity and reducing volatility.[14] However, new challenges have arisen in modern digital capital markets. Information no longer simply contributes to the formation of fundamentally efficient prices[15] through the "wisdom of crowds", but it does so increasingly often in circumstances where an algorithm is interposed between the "crowds" (informed investors) and the process of price formation. This can lead to distortions, especially where algorithms are executed so quickly that it is difficult to identify unintended consequences in real time and intervene accordingly. For example, as in the flash crash of 2010, algorithms may trigger dynamics that move prices within seconds increasingly further away from an equilibrium representing fundamental value.

The paper makes two contributions. First, methodologically, it suggests that the disclosure paradigm of securities regulation of the pre-automation age should be enriched with an account of the mechanics of price formation at the microstructure level of securities markets. This means that regulation needs to appreciate how, for example, the configuration of the limit order book, the matching algorithm used by a marketplace, or the operation of an execution, market making, or arbitrage algorithm deployed by an investment firm affect market dynamics and by extension the efficient market paradigm. The

---

12 The effects of circuit breakers will be discussed in detail in section 3.2.2 below.

13 A similar observation has been made in the economic literature, for example *Kirilenko/Lo* (fn. 6), 52, but less so in legal scholarship.

14 An important early study identifying a reduction in the dispersion of abnormal returns (i. e., a reduction in issue-specific risk), rather than in increase in mean returns, as the main effect of the Securities Act of 1933 is *Carol J. Simon*, "The Effect of the 1933 Securities Act on Investor Information and the Performance of New Issues"(1989) 79 *Am. Econ. Rev.* 295. For an overview of the debate, see *John Armour* et al., Principles of Financial Regulation (OUP 2016), 164.

15 Prices are fundamentally efficient if they rationally reflect fundamentals, *Lawrence H. Summers*, "Does the Stock Market Rationally Reflect Fundamental Values?" (1986) 41 J. Fin. 591, 592.

paper draws on market microstructure theory[16] to illustrate how certain economic concepts that describe the operation of modern, mostly automated capital markets, for example the relationship between order volume, execution speed and price impact, can be used to assess the effectiveness of regulation. Such a discussion is largely absent from the legal literature.[17] Second, against the backdrop of market microstructure theory, the paper critically reflects on current regulatory tools concerning algorithmic and high frequency trading. It argues that the empirical support for regulatory intervention (other than in the case of manipulative behaviour[18]) is weak and policy makers should, therefore, proceed with caution. In particular, circuit breakers, as currently calibrated, are likely to overreach and impede efficient price discovery by restricting price movements that represent fundamental volatility.

The remainder of this paper is structured as follows. Section 2 discusses the operation of typical algorithmic trading strategies and reviews the findings of market microstructure research in order to assess whether, and when, algorithms disrupt orderly market operations. Section 3 draws normative lessons from the technical discussion in section 2. It focuses on three central regulatory strategies: disclosure obligations and organisational requirements imposed on investment firms engaged in HFT, trading halts when price movements exceed specified thresholds, and the design of the matching mechanism used by a market. It explores whether market quality is negatively affected because trading is automated and/or executed at high frequency and discusses whether the risks to which automated trading gives rise are adequately addressed by current regulation, considering the available empirical evidence.[19] Section 4 concludes.

---

16 Foundational works in market microstructure theory include *Maureen O'Hara*, Market Microstructure Theory (Blackwell 1995) and *Joel Hasbrouck*, Empirical Market Structure (OUP 2007).
17 Notable exceptions include *Balp/Strampelli* (fn. 11); *Merritt B. Fox/Lawrence R. /Gabriel V. Rauterberg*, Naked Open-Market Manipulation and Its Effects in *Mattli* (fn. 1), 199; *Yadav* (fn. 3 and 8); *Yesha Yadav*, Algorithmic Trading and Market Regulation in *Mattli* (fn. 1) 232; *Yesha Yadav*, "The Failure of Liability in Modern Markets" (2016) 102 Va. L. Rev. 1031.
18 Algorithmic trading techniques that satisfy the definition of market manipulation, such as quote stuffing, layering and spoofing, or "pump and dump", and possible regulatory responses to these techniques, are outside the scope of this paper.
19 For example, a flash crash may be caused by the manual submission of a large order or by the execution of an algorithm that submits a number of child orders in short succession that deplete liquidity, see the simulation by *Paul Brewer/Jaksa Cvitanic/Charles R. Plott*, "Market Microstructure Design and Flash Crashes: A Simulation Approach" (2013) 16 J. Appl. Econ. 223. Regulatory strategies that target only algorithmic or high-frequency trading, such as the increased regulatory requirements imposed by MiFID II (see sections 3.1 and 3.2), are justified if certain features of automated trading make the occurrence of a flash crash more likely and regulation develops an effective response to these features.

2 Algorithmic Trading and Unintended Consequences

2.1 Types of Trading Algorithm

Algorithms are pervasive in modern financial markets. According to their function, they can be broadly grouped into market making algorithms, arbitrage or directional trading algorithms, and execution algorithms. Market making algorithms serve to provide liquidity, arbitrage algorithms seek to exploit market inefficiencies or price fluctuations around news announcements, and execution algorithms are used to minimise the market impact of a large trade by splitting the trade into several so-called "child orders" that are executed according to certain criteria.

Market makers provide liquidity by posting limit buy and limit sell orders. In doing so, they incur inventory risk, that is, the risk of posting a limit buy order in a downward trending market and a limit sell order in an upward trending market, and the risk that the market maker's limit orders are matched with orders of better informed traders.[20] Market making algorithms make use of different parameters to manage these risks, including the number of ticks away from the market price at which limit orders are placed, possibly as a function of volatility (given that limit orders that are further away from the market price are more likely to be executed in high-volatility conditions than in low-volatility conditions), the fact that a market is trending or mean-reverting, the level of liquidity in a market, and order flow (the difference in trade volume between buyer-initiated and seller-initiated trading activity, which has been shown to become directional while news is impounded into market prices[21]).[22]

Arbitrageurs and information traders seek to exploit market inefficiencies or an informational advantage. Algorithms used by them may thus be based on models to calculate the fundamental value of a security and identify deviations from that value or deviations in price levels of correlated financial instruments or baskets of financial instruments.[23] Other algorithms exploit the fact that news announcements are often not, or only partially, incorporated into prices in-

---

20 *Irene Aldridge*, High-frequency trading: A practical guide to algorithmic strategies and trading systems (Wiley, 2nd ed. 2013), 167.
21 *Ryan Love/Richard Payne*, "Macroeconomic News, Order Flows, and Exchange Rates" (2008) 43 J. Financ. Quant. Anal. 467.
22 *Aldridge* (fn. 20), 168–192.
23 *Ibid.* at 131–144.

stantaneously, and will only be fully incorporated via the order flow.[24] Such algorithms may, for example, estimate likely price responses to particular types of news based on historical data and trade directionally before the market can reach a new equilibrium price level.[25]

Finally, execution algorithms are used to offload large positions. Typical execution algorithms are Time-Weighted Average Price (TWAP), Volume-Weighted-Average-Price (VWAP) and participation or Percentage-of-Volume (POV) algorithms. The three types of execution algorithm have in common that they split a large order into several smaller child orders to minimise the market impact of the sale. The simplest execution algorithm is TWAP, which breaks up a large order into child orders of equal size that are placed at equal time intervals in the market.[26] In contrast to TWAP, in a VWAP algorithm, the size of child orders is a function of the average volume traded in the instrument during the same time of the trading day (using historical trading data, for example, from the preceding month), on the assumption that intraday volume patterns are persistent and predictable. The size of child orders is larger when historical trading volume is higher, and smaller when it is lower, which allows for a more cost-effective execution of the orders.[27] Participation (POV) algorithms differ from VWAP algorithms in that they calculate the size of child orders as a percentage of the total volume traded over a specified time interval preceding the execution of each child order, rather than based on historical averages.

The large market movements during the flash crash of 2010 have been ascribed to a feedback loop caused by a POV algorithm that was used by a "fundamental trader",[28] Waddell & Reed, to unwind a large position in S&P 500 futures ("E-Mini") contracts, and contemporaneously trading HFTs.[29] The POV algorithm sent orders into the market representing 9% of the trading volume calculated

---

24 *Love/Payne* (fn. 21).

25 *Aldridge* (fn. 20), 148.

26 *Ibid.* at 253–254.

27 *Ibid.* at 254–257.

28 CFTC/SEC (fn. 5), 2 define "fundamental traders" as "market participants who are trading to accumulate or reduce a net long or short position".

29 *Kirilenko/Lo* (fn. 6), 58; *Didier Sornette/Susanne von der Becke*, "Crashes and High Frequency Trading: An evaluation of risks posed by high-speed algorithmic trading", UK Government Foresight Project, The Future of Computer Trading in Financial Markets, Foresight Driver Review DR 7 (2012), 11; *Jean-Pierre Zigrand*, "Feedback effects and changes in the diversity of trading strategies", UK Government Foresight Project, The Future of Computer Trading in Financial Markets, Foresight Driver Review DR 2 (2012), 4, 8. For a detailed discussion of algorithmic trading and feedback loops, see *Government Office for Science*, Foresight: The Future of Computer Trading in Financial Markets, Final Project Report (2012), 61–85.

over the previous minute, without containing any further conditions with regard to price or time, selling Waddell & Reed's position in E-mini contracts rapidly within 20 minutes.[30] This alone would not have been enough to trigger the flash crash, but other traders reacted to the POV algorithm by quickly reselling the contracts initially sold by Waddell & Reed. The volume effects of the POV algorithm thus did not dissipate, but became self-reinforcing, exerting ever greater pressure on the sale side of the order book.[31]

A participation algorithm is a dynamic trading strategy, since each child order depends on the evolution of market conditions during a specified time interval before the next child order is executed, for example the previous minute. In contrast, static trading strategies are completely determined based on past market information before the strategy is executed.[32] Examples of static execution algorithms are TWAP and VWAP. Dynamic strategies such as POV have been criticised for giving rise to selling pressure and depleting liquidity, and thus meriting regulatory attention.[33] However, whether they have detrimental consequences that are different from the consequences that arise whenever a large order is submitted depends on the precise structure of the algorithm and its interaction with other trading strategies. In principle, dynamic strategies, just as static strategies, do not destabilise the market if they are properly coded. The next section illustrates this point by evaluating the price effects of a typical execution algorithm that splits a large order into several child orders.

2.2 Price Effects

It is empirically well established that the execution of a metaorder (a large order divided into several child orders, as in a POV or VWAP algorithm) has a market impact that follows certain regularities, referred to as the "square root impact

---

30 CFTC/SEC (fn. 5), 2.

31 See CFTC/SEC (fn. 5), 3: "[L]acking sufficient demand [for the sell orders of Waddell and Reed] from fundamental buyers or cross-market arbitrageurs, HFTs began to quickly buy and then resell contracts to each other – generating a 'hot-potato' volume effect as the same positions were rapidly passed back and forth." See also *Albert J. Menkveld/Bart Zhou Yueshen*, "The Flash Crash: A Cautionary Tale About Highly Fragmented Markets" (2019) 65 Manag. Sci. 4470; *Zigrand* (fn. 29), 8.

32 *Aldridge* (fn. 20), 252.

33 *Riccardo Cesari/Massimiliano Marzo/Paolo Zagaglia*, "Effective Trade Execution" in *H. Kent Baker/Greg Filbeck* (eds.), Portfolio Theory and Management (OUP 2013), 411, 422.

law".[34] The square root law models the price impact I of a metaorder of quantity Q that is executed over a time horizon T as follows:[35]

$$I = Y\sigma_T \left(\frac{Q}{V_T}\right)^\delta \tag{1}$$

where Y is a numerical coefficient that varies depending on the security in question, σ_T is volatility (standard deviation) over the same time horizon T, V_T is the total volume of the instrument traded over T, and δ is a parameter that can be shown to be close to 0.5 (hence, the name "square root law") for values of $Q \ll V_T$.[36] If the last condition holds and the size of the metaorder is significantly smaller than the total traded volume, the impact of the child orders is therefore not additive, but decreases in Q.[37] It should also be noted that I is not dependent on T, and it is consequently, in principle, irrelevant whether the algorithm is executed over a short or a long period of time. However, importantly, I is dependent on contemporaneous volatility and volume. Where $Q \ll V_T$ does not hold, the market impact of the metaorder depends, crucially, on the execution schedule. If execution is sufficiently slow, impact remains a concave function of Q, but where child orders are submitted too quickly for the order book to refill, the function becomes convex.[38] This may have occurred during the flash crash of 2010. As mentioned, Waddell & Reed used an algorithm that was designed to sell 9% of the currently traded volume, which is below the threshold where empirical studies indicate that $Q \ll V_T$ no longer holds.[39] However, the sell orders were executed in an unusually short period of time. Initial liquidity provided by the buyers of the E-mini contracts, mostly HFTs and intermediaries, quickly dissipated as the buyers sought to reduce their long positions and accordingly also entered sell orders.[40] The CFTC and SEC investigation into the flash crash concluded that the combined selling efforts of the algorithm and the HFTs and

---

34 For references, see *Jean-Philippe Bouchaud/Julius Bonart/Jonathan Donier/Martin Gould*, Trades, Quotes and Prices: Financial Markets under the Microscope (CUP 2018), 243–244; *Bence Tóth/Yves Lemperiere/Cyril Deremble/Joachim de Lataillade/Julien Kockelkoren/Jean-Philippe Bouchaud*, "Anomalous Price Impact and the Critical Nature of Liquidity in Financial Markets" (2011) 1 Physical Review X 021006.
35 This formulation of the square root law is from *Bouchaud et al., Ibid.* at 234.
36 The precise value seems to vary with tick size, *Ibid.* at 235.
37 For an economic explanation see *Ibid.* at 236.
38 A more detailed discussion of these dynamics can be found *Ibid.* at 237–238.
39 It has been suggested that I is a concave function of Q if $Q/V_T \lesssim 0.1$, *Ibid.* at 238.
40 CFTC/SEC (fn. 5), 14–16.

intermediaries almost completely depleted buy-side market depth in the E-Mini, which had fallen to less than 1% by the time the algorithm had sold E-Minis for about 15 minutes, compared to the same morning. As a result of the vanishing buy-side liquidity, prices dropped rapidly until the circuit breaker of the Chicago Mercantile Exchange was triggered.[41]

How does the price impact of a metaorder—that is, a sequence of orders typically entered by an algorithm—compare with the impact of a single order of the same size that is entered manually? As before, a substantial amount of empirical work indicates that the relationship between market impact and the size of an order is not linear, but concave. Impact as a function of the volume traded, accordingly, takes a similar form to equation (1) above. Parts of the literature have argued that the empirical evidence supports the following relationship:[42]

$$I = Y \bar{s}_t \left(\frac{v}{\bar{V}_{best}} \right)^{\delta} \qquad (2)$$

As in (1), Y is a numerical coefficient that depends on the asset class and δ is a parameter that varies with tick size. The volume of the submitted order v is normalised by the average volume at the opposite side best quote $\bar{V}_{best}$ and $\bar{s}_t$ is the average spread over a small time interval just before the arrival of the order. The parameter δ has been found to be smaller than 0.5.[43] (2) is therefore more strongly concave than (1), and market impact approximates a constant with $I = Y \bar{s}_t$ for small-tick stocks where $\delta \cong 0$ (in other words, the market impact of orders concerning small-tick stocks tends not to be dependent on volume). Figure 1 depicts the association between market impact and volume for different parameter values of δ.

It has been argued that the strong concavity of the impact response function of a single market order is partly the result of a conditioning effect. The probability density of the ratio of order volume and volume at the opposite side best quote at the time of order arrival is highest where $v/V_{best} = 1$ (and, surprisingly, it generally spikes where the ratio equals a simple fraction or round number, for example 0.5 or 2).[44] This means that traders often submit orders that equal the available volume at the best quote (so-called selective liquidity taking). It is rare to find orders that exceed the available volume, and somewhat less rare

---

41 *Ibid.* at 15.
42 *Bouchaud* et al. (fn. 34), 217.
43 *Ibid.*
44 *Ibid.* at 218–219.

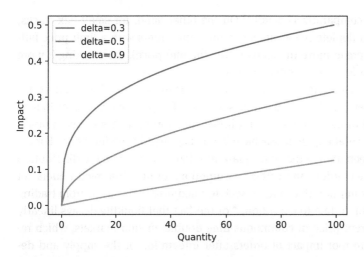

Figure 1: Market Impact as a Function of Order Volume.
Figure 1 shows the price impact of a metaorder according to the square root impact law for different values of δ. Q is defined so that the condition Q≪V_T holds after full execution of the metaorder, with the total volume of the metaorder equalling 0.1*V_T. Y and $σ_T$ are both assumed to equal 1. It can be seen that price impact increases linearly with δ close to 1, and the impact function becomes more strongly concave with smaller δ.

to find orders that are smaller than the available volume (thus, the probability density for $v/V_{best} < 1$ is greater than for $v/V_{best} > 1$, but smaller than for $v/V_{best} = 1$). If all traders submitted orders that matched exactly the volume at the best quote, the price would go up or down accordingly and market impact would be independent of order volume (disregarding any second order market effects, such as trades induced by the information content of the initial order). The relationship is not strictly constant because some orders are larger than the volume at the best quote and move the price by more than one tick and some orders that do not match the volume at the best quote may still have an impact on the market owing to their information content. Furthermore, as mentioned, there is empirical evidence that the relationship is less strongly concave for large-tick stocks than small-tick stocks (that is, δ is larger for large-tick stocks). This has been attributed to the fact that the bid-ask spread (the difference between the highest price among buy limit orders and the lowest price among sell limit orders) is typically equal to the minimum possible size of one tick in the case of a large-tick stock, but wider in the case of a small-tick stock. Hence, for large-tick stocks, price moves require that the volume on one side of the order book is completely depleted, which is more likely if the available volume is comparatively small.[45] On the other hand, for small-tick stocks, both orders that deplete the available volume and orders with a limit price falling inside the spread move the market (i.e., the mid-price), thus making it more likely that an order has an impact irrespective of its size.[46]

It is not well understood why the impact response function changes for metaorders, where, as discussed, δ takes a value of approximately 0.5, or indeed why the impact of metaorders is not a linear function of their size, as intuition may suggest. Several explanations have been suggested in the literature. For example, it has been argued that the square root law follows from the distribution of the size of metaorders and certain assumptions of how informed traders set prices,[47] the assumption that traders seek to maximise their payoff from trading subject to a desired time to execution,[48] or the fact that liquidity decays linearly around the current price in continuous-time double-auction markets, which results in a square root impact of orders after integration of the supply and demand curves.[49] None of these explanations is undisputed, but the important point is that the empirical fact that they seek to explain—the square root impact law—has, within the law's domain of application,[50] been corroborated by a large number of studies in different contexts.[51]

From a normative perspective, the empirical findings direct attention to two considerations. First, to reiterate, if the square root law applies, the marginal impact of a metaorder does not increase, but decreases in size. As discussed above, it is a precondition for the application of the law that the size of a metaorder is significantly smaller than the total volume traded over the time horizon of the execution of the order. That this must be so is intuitive. If the size of a child order is so large that it consumes much of the available volume on the opposite side of

---

45 *Ibid.* at 118, 217. See also figure 11.4, *Ibid.* at 219, showing that an average-size order equals about 30% of the available volume if that volume is of average size, but almost all if it is unusually small, say 10% of the average volume at the best quote, and only 20–25% if it is unusually large, say twice the size of the average volume at the best quote. In other words, average order size does not grow linearly, but sub-linearly, in available volume. Smaller orders consume, on average, a higher proportion of the available volume than larger orders consume of the correspondingly larger available volume.

46 *Ibid.* at 118.

47 *J. Doyne Farmer/Austin Gerig/Fabrizio Lillo/Henri Waelbroeck*, "How efficiency shapes market impact" (2013) 13 Quant. Finance 1743.

48 *Xavier Gabaix/Parameswaran Gopikrishnan/Vasiliki Plerou/H. Eugene Stanley*, "A Theory of Power-Law Distributions in Financial Market Fluctuations" (2003) 423 Nature 267.

49 *Tóth et al.* (fn. 34), 021006 – 1.

50 See text to notes 36-41.

51 See fn. 34 above.

the order book, the impact of subsequent child orders is increasing, not decreasing.[52] Destabilising effects of an algorithm executing a sequence of orders are therefore not a function of the size of the orders individually or in aggregate as such, but of the available volume in the order book. The latter, in turn, is affected by the speed of execution of the metaorder. If the order book is given sufficient time to refill, an algorithm such as POV or VWAP, on its own, does not entail price dynamics that could result in a flash crash.[53] Therefore, the focus of regulation should be on slowing down trading, rather than halting it altogether.[54]

The second important point is that the main risk of the emergence of price dynamics without stable fixed points results generally from the interaction effects of two or more algorithms, rather than the operation of an algorithm in isolation.[55] Regulation should therefore be designed so that interaction effects can be assessed, and harmful effects identified. This can be achieved through the provision of appropriate testing environments and transparency. This regulatory strategy is discussed in section 3.1 below.

3 Regulatory Solutions

In the following sections, three central regulatory strategies will be presented and their effectiveness critically evaluated in light of the technical discussion in section 2: transparency and internal control requirements imposed on invest-

---

52 Impact becomes a convex function of size, see text to fn. 38 above.

53 The orders executed by the algorithm may, of course, result in a significant price drop, but if this is a result of genuine buy and sale interests and not merely a mismatch in execution speed between orders on the two sides of the order book, there is no reason for regulatory intervention. In this case (and under the assumption of rational behaviour on the part of market participants), the price drop would reflect the market's assessment of the issuer's fundamentals, and regulatory intervention would distort the process of efficient price formation.

54 A suspension of automatic order execution, followed by a call auction after several minutes, is technically similar to mechanisms suggested in the literature to slow down trading. These mechanisms rely on a call market where orders that arrive during specified time intervals are collected, priority ordered according to price and executed at the price that maximises the volume that can be traded, see e. g., *Brewer et al.* (fn. 19), 239–240. Thus, the process of order execution is the same under both approaches. The difference is the time interval over which orders are collected. Conventional circuit breakers halt trading for several minutes (see section 3.2.1: typically, 5 or 10 minutes), whereas a call market may use intervals as short as a few seconds or fractions of a second, see the simulation in Brewer et al. (fn. 19), 241 and Budish et al. (fn. 7) (suggesting that the continuous limit order book should be replaced with uniform price double auctions conducted every tenth of a second).

55 See the discussion of the flash crash in the text to nn 39-41 above.

ment firms engaged in algorithmic and high-frequency trading; order resting times or delays in the processing of orders when price movements exceed specified thresholds (circuit breakers); and the design of the matching mechanism used by a market. It will be seen that many of these strategies are not well calibrated and are either too far-reaching and ineffective, or not sufficiently far-reaching.

3.1 Disclosure and Internal Risk Control Systems

Current European regulation, laid down in MiFID II, requires investment firms that engage in algorithmic trading to "have in place effective systems and risk controls ... to ensure that its trading systems are resilient and have sufficient capacity, are subject to appropriate trading thresholds and limits and prevent the sending of erroneous orders or the systems otherwise functioning in a way that may create or contribute to a disorderly market."[56] The systems must be fully tested and properly monitored.[57] The competent authorities of the firm's home Member State and the trading venue(s) at which the firm engages in algorithmic trading must be notified of the fact that the investment firm employs algorithmic trading strategies.[58] The home state authority "may require the investment firm to provide, on a regular or ad-hoc basis, a description of the nature of its algorithmic trading strategies, details of the trading parameters or limits to which the system is subject, the key compliance and risk controls that it has in place ... and details of the testing of its systems", and it may request further information about the firm's algorithmic trading and systems.[59] The competent authorities of the trading venues where the algorithmic trader operates can request that the disclosed information be communicated to them by the home Member State regulator.[60] Additional record-keeping requirements apply to high-frequen-

---

56 MiFID II, Art 17(1). The requirements have been implemented by Commission Delegated Regulation (EU) 2017/589 of 19 July 2016 supplementing Directive 2014/65/EU of the European Parliament and of the Council with regard to regulatory technical standards specifying the organisational requirements of investment firms engaged in algorithmic trading, [2017] OJ L87/417, Arts 1–18.
57 MiFID II, Art 17(1).
58 Art 17(2), first subparagraph.
59 Art 17(2), second subparagraph.
60 Art 17(2), third subparagraph.

cy traders,[61] and additional organisational and operational requirements to algorithmic traders that pursue market making activities.[62]

It is evident that algorithmic traders should have systems in place that test and monitor their algorithms to ensure that they are correctly coded, do not send erroneous orders, or otherwise function in an unintended manner. However, if it is correct that the *interaction effects* of two or more algorithms are typically detrimental to market stability and efficient price discovery, rather than the price effects of an algorithm in isolation, there are limits to how well an individual firm can assess the impact of their algorithms on the market as a whole. Conventional backtesting is unsuitable to identify harmful interaction effects. Simulations that model the interaction of a firm's algorithms with other typical trading strategies are more promising,[63] but there is a risk that algorithms will produce unintended consequences once they are deployed in the market and interact with idiosyncratically coded trading strategies. Testing and monitoring at the level of the investment firm, while important,[64] is therefore unlikely to be sufficient.

MiFID II also requires trading venues to provide environments to facilitate the testing of algorithms, including simulation facilities that replicate the production environment and allow for the modelling of specific scenarios, for example service disruptions.[65] Members must certify that they have tested their algorithms before deploying them.[66] Again, it is important to recognise that the

---

61 MiFID II, Art 17(3), last subparagraph. The record-keeping obligations are implemented in Commission Delegated Regulation (EU) 2017/589, Art 28 and Annex II.

62 MiFID II, Art 17(3). Market making strategies are defined in Art 17(4).

63 For examples of how such a simulation could be designed, see *Brewer et al.* (fn. 19); *Iryna Veryzhenko/Lise Arena/Etienne Harb/Nathalie Oriol* "Time to Slow Down for High-Frequency Trading? Lessons from Artificial Markets" (2017) 24 Intell. Sys. Acc. Fin. & Mgmt. 73; *Nathalie Oriol/Iryna Veryzhenko*, 'Market structure or traders' behavior? A multi agent model to assess flash crash phenomena and their regulation" (2019) 19 Quant. Finance 1075.

64 See, in particular, Commission Delegated Regulation (EU) 2017/589, Arts 5 – 7.

65 MiFID II, Art 48(6), implemented by Commission Delegated Regulation (EU) 2017/584 of 14 July 2016 supplementing Directive 2014/65/EU of the European Parliament and of the Council with regard to regulatory technical standards specifying organisational requirements of trading venues, [2017] OJ L87/350, Arts 9, 10. The provision of access to production environment simulations is required pursuant to Art 10(2). For a detailed description of one such simulation facility, the London Stock Exchange's Customer Development Service (CDS), see London Stock Exchange (LSE), MIT501 – Guide to Testing Services, Issue 20 (2020), 8 – 11. The CDS replicates the full market structure of the live service, simulates market activity through the interaction between customers on the service, and uses scripted scenarios to facilitate the development and testing of different routines to deal with the scenarios.

66 Commission Delegated Regulation (EU) 2017/584, Art 10(1).

effectiveness of a trading venue's testing regime in identifying harmful consequences of an algorithmic trading strategy depends not only on an accurate replication of the venue's trading systems, but also a replication of interactions between customers comparable to what would occur on the live service. Since market maker and participant details will inevitably vary to some degree,[67] disruptive effects that are a function of the interaction of two or more trading algorithms may not be captured.

Likewise, existing disclosure obligations fall short of establishing effective safeguards. First, there is no universal obligation to disclose information on trading strategies and compliance and risk control systems, but competent authorities are merely *authorised* to request such information, either on a regular or an ad-hoc basis. Second, the disclosed information includes details of the trading parameters, but MiFID II does not require the actual code to be disclosed. Full disclosure of algorithms to the market would certainly be resisted by algorithmic traders, for whom innovative algorithms constitute valuable trade secrets. It may also be harmful, since it would stifle financial innovation and potentially encourage herding behaviour. However, full transparency is unnecessary. If the greatest risk to stability derives from the interaction of algorithms, disclosure to the competent authority is sufficient and would allow the regulator to assess—within the limits of what is technically possible and feasible, given the available resources—the algorithms that are used in the market and their interaction effects.[68] Third, MiFID II does not provide for an automatic exchange of information between competent authorities. Since algorithms, particularly arbitrage strategies, may operate on more than one market, which conforms to the aim of MiFID II to promote integrated financial markets within the EU, it is essential that the competent authorities of all affected marketplaces have full information. Indeed, in order to facilitate effective and cost-efficient supervision, and given that algorithms may target any market in the course of a trading session depending on where opportunities arise, it is counterproductive that supervision

---

67 See, e.g., LSE (fn. 65), 9.

68 For a similar suggestion, see *Yadav* (fn. 3), 1670. However, it has also been pointed out that the practical difficulties of designing an effective testing environment may be significant, because the number of possible combinations of algorithms is likely to be high and algorithms may be programmed to learn and evolve over time. For this reason, the UK Government Office for Science (fn. 29), 101–102 recommended not to adopt any notification requirements. Further research is required to explore the technical feasibility and cost-efficiency of a regulator-level notification and testing system. Nevertheless, it is important to stress that the disclosure obligations currently laid down in MiFID II are likely to impose costs on investment firms without generating commensurate benefits (this was also noted by the UK Government Office for Science (fn. 29), 101).

(and the possible simulation of market effects) is located at the level of the Member State, rather than the EU.

3.2 Circuit Breakers

3.2.1 Circuit Breakers around the World

Most exchanges have systems in place that halt trading in individual securities or the market as a whole temporarily when certain volatility thresholds are exceeded. The US equity, options and futures exchanges have adopted two so-called national market system plans that set out their policies and procedures to mitigate high market volatility.[69] Since all US exchanges participated in the formulation of the plans, uniform procedures are in place to respond to episodes of volatility concerning securities traded in the national market system.[70] The first plan establishes a market wide circuit breaker (MWCB) that results in the coordinated temporary halt of all trading in equities and options on all exchanges.[71] The MWCB is triggered if the S&P 500 Index experiences a decline of 7%, 13% or 20% as compared to the closing price of the S&P 500 for the immediately preceding trading day. A decline of 7% and 13% entails a halt in trading for 15 minutes when the respective threshold is reached for the first time during a trading day, and trading is suspended for the remainder of the day if a 20% decline occurs.[72]

The second plan, known as the Limit Up/Limit Down (LULD) Plan, is intended to prevent trades in securities from occurring outside of specified price bands.[73] If the national best offer equals the lower price band or the national

---

69 National market system plans are formulated by two or more national stock exchanges and filed with the SEC for approval under Rule 608 of Regulation NMS.

70 The securities that are covered are defined in Rule 600(b)(47) of Regulation NMS.

71 The plan was first approved by SEC Release No. 34–67091, Order Approving, on a Pilot Basis, the National Market System Plan to Address Extraordinary Market Volatility, May 31, 2012. For the most recent amendments, see SEC Release No. 34–88406, Notice of Filing of the Twentieth Amendment to the National Market System Plan to Address Extraordinary Market Volatility, March 17, 2020; and SEC Release No. 34–88704, Order Approving the Twentieth Amendment to the National Market System Plan to Address Extraordinary Market Volatility, April 21, 2020.

72 See, for example, New York Stock Exchange, Rule 7.12.

73 Approved by the same release as the MWCB, SEC Release No. 34–67091 (fn. 71). For information on the operation of the plan, see Limit Up/Limit Down, Annual Report for 2019 of the Op-

best bid[74] equals the upper price band (the security enters a so-called limit state) and the limit size quotations are not executed or cancelled in their entirety within 15 seconds (because bids remain below the lower band or offers above the upper band), the primary listing exchange[75] declares a five-minute trading pause, which halts trading in the security on all venues.[76] If the national best bid is below the lower band but the national best offer is above the lower band, or the national best offer is above the upper band and the national best bid is below the upper band (a so-called straddle state), the primary listing exchange has discretion to declare a trading pause if it deems trading in the security to deviate from normal trading characteristics.[77] After the trading pause, trading is reopened in the usual manner,[78] that is, with a call auction.[79] In addition to pausing continuous trading in a security that is in a limit (and potentially a straddle) state, exchanges will reprice sell orders that are below the lower band and buy orders above the upper band to the respective limit price band (but not buy orders below the lower band or sell orders above the upper band, which are non-executable since they are outside the price bands and may result in a limit or straddle state).[80] Figure 2 visualises the limit and straddle states and the repricing of orders below or above the price bands.

In the EU, MiFID II requires regulated markets to be able to halt trading "if there is a significant price movement in a financial instrument on that market or a related market during a short period".[81] MiFID II and the relevant implementing legislation do not specify the operational details of trading halts, but impose

---

erating Committee of the Plan to Address Extraordinary Market Volatility, available at http://www.luldplan.com.

74 National best bid and national best offer are defined in Rule 600(b)(43) of Regulation NMS.

75 The primary listing exchange is the exchange on which the security has been listed the longest, Plan to Address Extraordinary Market Volatility Submitted to the Securities and Exchange Commission pursuant to Rule 608 of Regulation NMS under the Securities Exchange Act of 1934, 20th Amendment Version (2020), Section I(O).

76 Plan to Address Extraordinary Market Volatility, Section VII(A). The price bands are calculated by adding and subtracting between 5% and 20% depending on type of security and previous closing price to a reference price, which equals the arithmetic mean price of transactions over the last five minutes. The reference price is updated every 30 seconds, provided a new reference price is at least 1% away from the current reference price, Plan to Address Extraordinary Market Volatility, Section V and Appendix A.

77 Plan to Address Extraordinary Market Volatility, Section VII(A)(2).

78 *Ibid.* at Section VII(B)(1).

79 See, for example, New York Stock Exchange, Rules 7.11(b), 7.35, 7.35(A).

80 See, for example, *Ibid.* Rule 7.11(a)(5).

81 MiFID II, Art 48(5), first subparagraph; Commission Delegated Regulation (EU) 2017/584, Art 18(1)(b).

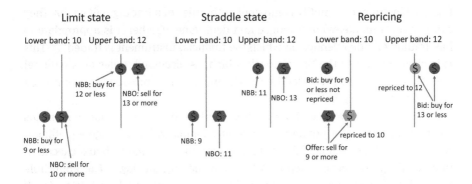

Figure 2: Limit and Straddle States; Repricing of Orders (US law)
Figure 2 shows examples of a limit state and a straddle state on US exchanges. Note that an offer to sell below the lower price band or a bid to buy above the upper price band will be repriced to the respective band, thus resulting in a limit state if the national best bid is also below, or the national best offer above, that price band.

an obligation on trading venues to test their circuit breakers before implementation and periodically thereafter, continuously monitor them, and allocate IT and human resources to the design, maintenance and monitoring of the circuit breakers.[82] ESMA has developed common standards that are "to be taken into consideration by trading venues for the calibration of their circuit breakers and ... to ensure consistent application of the provisions" of MiFID II.[83] Criteria set out by the guidelines include the nature and liquidity profile of the financial instrument (with tighter parameters applying to more liquid instruments), trading mode (with tighter parameters applying in the case of continuous auctions and quote driven systems), and type of reference price (stipulating that both a static and a dynamic reference price should be used).[84] Otherwise the design of circuit breakers is within the discretion of the trading venue.

MiFID II seeks to achieve the necessary coordination across trading venues by requiring a venue that is "material in terms of liquidity"[85] in the respective

---

82 Commission Delegated Regulation (EU) 2017/584, Art 19(2).
83 ESMA, Guidelines on calibration of circuit breakers and publication of trading halts under MiFID II, 6 April 2017, ESMA70 – 872942901– 63, para 6.
84 *Ibid.* at paras 11– 13.
85 Material market in terms of liquidity is, for shares, depositary receipts, exchange-traded funds, certificates and similar financial instruments, the trading venue with the highest turnover within the Union for that financial instrument, and for other financial instruments the regulated market where the financial instrument was first admitted to trading, Commission Delegated Reg-

financial instrument to notify competent authorities of a trading halt so that they can devise "a market-wide response and determine whether it is appropriate to halt trading on other venues on which the financial instrument is traded".[86] This is in clear contrast to the US approach, which, as discussed, relies on a national market system plan formulated by the US exchanges to provide for coordinated cross-market trading halts.

To give a few examples from Europe, the London Stock Exchange monitors whether the price of a potential execution remains within a range equalling a predetermined percentage above and below the last order book execution price or the most recent auction price from the current day.[87] The applicable thresholds depend on the type of security and segment on which it is traded.[88] If a security breaches a price monitoring threshold, automatic execution is suspended for five minutes and a call auction is held to allow for the formation of a reliable price. Should the auction fail to generate a price that is within applicable tolerance levels around the dynamic reference price, the call period is extended by another five minutes. After this additional extension period, orders will be matched to the extent possible and executed irrespective of price monitoring tolerance levels.[89] The Frankfurt Stock Exchange and the Euronext markets rely on similar mechanisms involving price bands around a dynamic and a static reference price and the suspension of continuous trading, followed by a call auction, if the price bands are breached.

While the basic design of circuit breakers is thus comparable on the three exchanges, the circuit breakers operate according to different parameters, which can result in conflicting responses to market volatility. On Euronext, the price monitoring bands applicable to equities range from 3% to 10%, while

---

ulation (EU) 2017/570 of 26 May 2016 supplementing Directive 2014/65/EU of the European Parliament and of the Council on markets in financial instruments with regard to regulatory technical standards for the determination of a material market in terms of liquidity in relation to notifications of a temporary halt in trading, [2017] OJ L87/124, Art 1.

86 MiFID II, Art 48(5), second subparagraph.

87 London Stock Exchange (LSE), MIT201 – Guide to the Trading System, Issue 15 (2020), Sections 7.3, 7.4.

88 The thresholds are set out in London Stock Exchange, Millennium Exchange and TRADEcho Business Parameters (2020), available at https://www.londonstockexchange.com/trade/equity-trading (see tab "Sector Breakdown"). For example, for the most liquid shares included in the FTSE 100, the thresholds are +/- 8% of the static reference price (the most recent auction price) and +/- 3% of the dynamic reference price (the last order book execution price). Price bands become increasingly wider as securities are less liquIbid.

89 *Ibid.* (see tab "Trading Service Breakdown").

they are wider on the London Stock Exchange (3% to 25%).[90] An interruption of continuous order execution lasts at least two minutes on the Frankfurt Stock Exchange, three minutes on Euronext, and five minutes on the London Stock Exchange.[91] In addition, the consequences of a breach of the price bands differ. On the Frankfurt Stock Exchange, a so-called volatility interruption is initiated if the execution price of an order would be outside either the dynamic or the static price range.[92] In contrast, the Euronext markets distinguish between a breach of the dynamic and static price bands (called "collars"). Securities included in the benchmark indices of the most significant stocks on the Euronext markets, such as the CAC40, are subject to so-called collar confirmation logic.[93] This means that an order that would be executed at a price outside the dynamic collars is rejected, but trading remains in continuous mode. The member can confirm the order within 30 seconds with the same price. If the confirmed order still entails a collar breach, the reference price is updated to the collar crossing price, new collars are calculated and the trade is executed, provided it is now within the updated collars. An order can be confirmed two times and, if it remains outside the collars, will then be rejected (but continuous trading is not interrupted). Other securities are not subject to collar confirmation logic, and trading will be halted (the security "reserves"[94]) if a matching price is outside the dynamic collars. Likewise, collar confirmation logic does not apply to breaches of the static collars, which are higher than the dynamic collars.[95]

Figure 3 gives an example of a dual-listed company with shares traded on both the London Stock Exchange and Euronext. As can be seen, it is possible that trading in dual-listed shares is suspended on one exchange, while it continues on the other.

---

90 Euronext Rule Book I (2019), Rules 4403/1, 4403/2; Euronext, Trading Manual 4–01 for the Optiq Trading Platform (2019), Section 4.2 and Appendix. The Frankfurt Stock Exchange discloses only the method for calculating the dynamic and static reference prices, but not the actual price bands, Deutsche Börse, Exchange Rules for the Frankfurter Wertpapierbörse (FWB) (2020), §§95, 96; Deutsche Börse, T7 Release 8.1: Market Model for the Trading Venue Xetra (2020), Section 9.1.

91 See above and Deutsche Börse, Trading Parameters Xetra Frankfurt (2020), available at https://www.xetra.com/xetra-en/trading/trading-models (follow hyperlink "Trading parameters & tick sizes"); Euronext, Trading Manual 4–01 (fn. 90), Section 4.2.4.

92 Deutsche Börse, T7 Release 8.1 (fn. 90), Section 9.2.1.

93 Euronext, Trading Manual 4–01 (fn. 90), Section 4.2.1.1.

94 *Ibid.* at Section 3.4.2.

95 *Ibid.* at Section 4.2.2. Dynamic collars start at 3% and static collars at 8% for the securities with the highest liquidity, *Ibid.*, Appendix (see tab "Appendix to 4–01 Manual OPTQ", columns "Col C" and "Static Col").

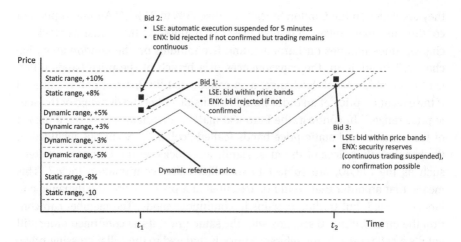

Figure 3: Volatility Bands in the UK and the EU

Figure 3 depicts three scenarios where circuit breakers are initiated idiosyncratically after the submission of identical orders to buy a dual-listed stock. For example, Just Eat Takeaway.com N.V. is listed on both Euronext Amsterdam (ENX) and the London Stock Exchange (LSE). It is a constituent company of the AEX and the FTSE 100, but does not belong to the most liquid FTSE 100 index constituents. As such, it is subject to dynamic collars of 3% and static collars of 8% on Euronext Amsterdam and a dynamic price monitoring threshold of 5% and a static threshold of 10% on the LSE. Bid 1 represents an order falling outside the dynamic ENX thresholds, but inside the dynamic LSE thresholds. Bid 2 represents an order falling outside the dynamic thresholds on both exchanges, and bid 3 an order that is inside the dynamic thresholds on both exchanges, but outside the static thresholds on ENX. Collar confirmation logic according to the Euronext rules applies to Just Eat Takeaway.com, hence neither bid 1 nor bid 2 result in a suspension of continuous trading on Euronext Amsterdam, but the bids must be confirmed and will otherwise be rejected. In contrast, collar confirmation logic does not apply to bid 3, which breaches the static collars. Consequently, a reservation period of three minutes ensues and a call auction will be held to facilitate price formation. On the London Stock Exchange, only bid 2 falls outside the price monitoring thresholds and will result in a suspension of automatic execution.

3.2.2 Efficiency of Circuit Breakers

The description of the operation of circuit breakers in section 3.2.1 gives rise to three related questions, which are ultimately empirical in nature. First, the case for regulatory intervention in the form of trading halts or the suspension of automatic order execution requires that it can be shown that circuit breakers have a positive effect on price discovery. Second, circuit breakers need to be calibrated carefully, both with regard to the conditions under which they are activated and the type and length of market intervention they entail. Finally, if a case in favour of the adoption of circuit breakers can be made, the question arises whether, and how, circuit breakers operating on different exchanges should be coordinated, in particular where financial markets are closely integrated, such as in the United States or the EU, but also between the EU and the UK or Switzerland.

(1) Effects on Volatility, Liquidity and the Efficiency of Price Discovery

The effects of circuit breakers on volatility, liquidity and price discovery are hotly debated.[96] Both theoretical models and empirical studies offer mixed findings. The traditional argument in favour of circuit breakers, the so-called cooling-off hypothesis, posits that circuit breakers contribute to price stability and the efficiency of price formation by curbing overreaction and dissuade market manipulation.[97] This argument builds on the empirically well supported claim that markets exhibit "excess volatility", that is, securities prices are more volatile than

---

96 Recent studies include *Benjamin Clapham/Peter Gomber/Martin Haferkorn/Sven Panz*, "Managing Excess Volatility: Design and Effectiveness of Circuit Breakers" (2017) SAFE Working Paper No. 195, available at SSRN: https://ssrn.com/abstract=2910977 (finding that circuit breakers decrease excess volatility, but also liquidity); *Peter Gomber/Martin Haferkorn/Marco Lutat/Kai Zimmermann*, "The Effect of Single-Stock Circuit Breakers on the Quality of Fragmented Markets" in *Fethi A. Rabhi/Peter Gomber* (eds.), Enterprise Applications and Services in the Finance Industry (Springer 2012), 71 (finding that a decline in market volatility after the activation of a circuit breaker comes at the cost of higher spreads and weakened price discovery in satellite markets); *Cyrille Guillaumie/Giuseppe Loiacono/Christian Winkler/Steffen Kern*, Market impacts of circuit breakers – Evidence from EU trading venues (2020) ESMA Working Paper No. 1, 2020 (finding that price volatility is significantly lower after the use of a circuit breaker); *Zeguang Li/Keqiang Hou/Chao Zhang*, "The impacts of circuit breakers on China's stock market" (2020) Pacific-Basin Finance Journal (available online) (finding that circuit breakers hinder efficient price discovery); *Steven Shuye Wang/Kuan Xu/Hao Zhang*, "A microstructure study of circuit breakers in the Chinese stock markets" (2019) 57 Pacific-Basin Finance Journal 101174 (finding no evidence of a reduction in market volatility or order book imbalances after market-wide circuit breakers are triggered). For an overview of the theoretical and empirical literature, see *David Abad/Roberto Pascual*, "Holding Back Volatility: Circuit Breakers, Price Limits, and Trading Halts" in *H. Kent Baker/Halil Kiymaz* (eds.), Market Microstructure in Emerging and Developed Markets: Price Discovery, Information Flows, and Transaction Costs (Wiley 2013), 303; *Imtiaz Mohammad Sifat/Azhar Mohamad*, "Circuit breakers as market stability levers: A survey of research, praxis, and challenges" (2019) 24 Int. J. Finance Econ. 1130.
97 *Christopher K. Ma/Ramesh P. Rao/R. Stephen Sears*, "Volatility, price resolution, and the effectiveness of price limits" in *Franklin R. Edwards* (ed.), Regulatory Reform of Stock and Futures Markets (Springer 1989), 67.

predicted by the efficient markets hypothesis.[98] In addition, it has been argued that trading halts encourage the provision of liquidity.[99] After a halt, trading resumes with a call auction. In contrast to continuous order execution, a call auction involves the execution of all orders collected during the call period that can be matched (that is, all market orders and limit orders that can be executed at the limit price or better). The auction (or "uncrossing") price is typically the price at which the executable volume is maximised.[100] Thus, call auctions reduce the risk that limit orders remain unexecuted. Suspending continuous order execution during times of high volatility, the argument goes, therefore gives an incentive to place limit orders during normal times.[101]

Most of the theoretical arguments, however, go both ways. The main argument against circuit breakers and other forms of trade interruptions is that trades carry informational content, and trading halts therefore delay price discovery.[102] Several studies have found evidence of inefficiencies in price discovery on markets with circuit breakers, measured, for example, as deviations of stock returns from a random walk path.[103] Furthermore, it is clear that circuit breakers interfere with trading strategies and interrupt execution schedules, which may result in losses for traders that could have been avoided without the interruption.[104] It has also been argued that circuit breakers may have the perverse effect of increasing volatility, rather than reducing it. This can be expected both on the primary market of a security, because traders anticipate a halt in trading as the price of a security approaches the threshold at which a circuit breaker is triggered and advance their trades to ensure that they are executed before trading is paused,[105] and on secondary markets without coordinated circuit breakers, be-

---

98 *Robert J. Shiller*, "Do Stock Prices Move Too Much to be Justified by Subsequent Changes in Dividends?" (1981) 71 Am. Econ. Rev. 421.

99 *Sifat/Mohamad* (fn. 96), 1145.

100 For an example of a call action execution algorithm, see LSE, MIT201 – Guide to the Trading System (fn. 87), Section 7.2.5.

101 See section 3.3 below for a more detailed comparison of call auctions and continuous order execution.

102 *Eugene F. Fama*, "Perspectives on October 1987 or What Did We Learn from the Crash" in *Robert J. Barro et al.* (eds.), Black Monday and the Future of Financial Markets (Irwin, 1989).

103 For an overview of the research, see *Sifat/Mohamad* (fn. 96), 1152–1154.

104 *David M Serritella*, "High Speed Trading Begets High Speed Regulation: SEC Response to Flash Crash, Rash" (2010) 2010 U. Ill. J.L. Tech. & Pol'y 433, 441–442; *Sifat/Mohamad* (fn. 96), 1154–1155.

105 *Avanidhar Subrahmanyam*, "Circuit breakers and market volatility: A theoretical perspective" (1994) 49 J. Fin. 237 (hereinafter "Circuit breakers and market volatility"). This phenomenon has been called the "magnet effect". Empirical evidence of the magnet effect has been found in several markets, see, e.g., *Edward Curran/Vito Mollica*, Magnet Effects of Price Limits: Evidence

cause traders migrate to these markets and thus transfer price variability from the primary to the secondary markets.[106] Finally, the migration of price variability to secondary markets has been shown to be accompanied by a transfer of market liquidity and trading volume in the same direction.[107] Thus, if these studies are correct, there is a tension between the policy goals of reducing volatility and preserving market liquidity that is difficult to resolve with circuit breakers. In conclusion, given the absence of clear empirical support, the normative case for circuit breakers is weak.

(2) Calibration of Circuit Breakers

The previous section suggested that caution should be exercised when devising regulatory tools that interfere in the trading process. This section will discuss whether it is possible to attenuate the detrimental effects identified by empirical studies by calibrating circuit breakers appropriately. A first possibility concerns the criteria that trigger a circuit breaker. In theory, an efficient trigger would distinguish between what has been called fundamental (or permanent) and transitory volatility.[108] Fundamental volatility is a function of new information concerning the fundamentals of an investment. Efficient price formation requires that such information is quickly and fully absorbed by the market. Mechanisms that reduce volatility beyond certain thresholds, therefore, impede the efficiency

---

from a Market Liberalization Experiment (2018), available at SSRN: https://ssrn.com/abstract=3115844. The fact that traders anticipate the initiation of a circuit breaker and accelerate their trades implies that discretion-based circuit breakers are preferable to circuit breakers operating with bright-line trigger points, *Avanidhar Subrahmanyam*, "On rules versus discretion in procedures to halt trade" (1995) 47 J. Bus. Econ. 1 (showing that discretion-based halts attenuate the magnet effect).

106 *Bei Cui/Arie E. Gozluklu*, "Intraday rallies and crashes: Spillovers of trading halts" (2016) 21 Int. J. Finance Econ. 472; *Charles S. Morris*, "Coordinating circuit breakers in stock and futures markets" (1990) 75 Federal Reserve Bank of Kansas City Economic Review 35. However, again, the empirical evidence is mixed. *Benjamin Clapham/Peter Gomber/Sven Panz*, "Coordination of Circuit Breakers? Volume Migration and Volatility Spillover in Fragmented Markets" (2017) SAFE Working Paper No. 196, available at SSRN: https://ssrn.com/abstract=2906719, find no evidence of volatility spillovers into satellite markets, but rather that the market share of the main market increases during a circuit breaker. For similar findings, see *James Brugler/Oliver Linton/Joseph Noss/Lucas Pedace*, "The Cross-Sectional Spillovers of Single Stock Circuit Breakers" (2018) 4 Market Microstructure and Liquidity 1950008; Guillaumie et al. (fn. 96), 31–38.

107 *Subrahmanyam*, "Circuit breakers and market volatility" (fn. 105), 250.

108 *Abad/Pascual* (fn. 96), 317; *Joel Hasbrouck*, "Modeling market microstructure time series" in *G.S. Maddala and C. Radhakrishna Rao* (eds.), Handbook of Statistics 14: Statistical Methods in Finance (Elsevier 1996), 647, 648–649.

of price discovery to the extent that market movements represent fundamental volatility and breach applicable price bands. Transitory volatility, in contrast, refers to deviations of prices from their fundamental value because of market friction, for example a lack of liquidity, manipulative trading activity, or irrational investor behaviour, such as herding or a trading strategy based on the law of small numbers.[109] Reducing this form of volatility evidently enhances the efficiency of prices. The main challenge in devising an efficient circuit breaker, therefore, is to develop criteria that allow the identification of transitory volatility.

It is questionable whether volatility can be decomposed precisely into a fundamental and a transitory part. Often (albeit not always, the Black Monday stock market crash of 19 October 1987 is a famous example), transitory volatility is triggered by a change in fundamentals. Statistically, the distinction can be captured by decomposing securities prices into a random part, which represents fundamental volatility (the error term in a simple random walk model), and a stationary part, which represents transitory volatility.[110] In some contexts, the random variable that represents transitory volatility is observable or can be modelled indirectly, thus allowing decomposition, in others this is not possible.[111] The parameters used in current regulation are, in any case, not suitable to differentiate between fundamental and transitory volatility.[112] As we have seen, circuit breakers in operation in the US and Europe employ a simple rule based on price moves over a trading day, expressed in percentage deviations from a static or dynamic reference price.[113]

However, even if it is not possible to decompose volatility precisely into a fundamental and a transitory part, it may be possible to identify certain patterns that are indicative of volatility occurring without a change in fundamentals. The activation of a circuit breaker could then be made conditional on the observation of such patterns. Where they are absent, a policy maker may either refrain from activating a circuit breaker altogether, given the weak empirical support for a positive effect of circuit breakers on volatility and liquidity, or impose higher thresholds in terms of percentage deviations from a reference price. The discussion in section 2 above suggests that a clear case for regulatory intervention exists when price impact changes from being a concave function of size to a convex

---

109 *Abad/Pascual* (fn. 96), 317.
110 *Hasbrouck* (fn. 108), 653–654.
111 An example of observable transitory volatility is the deviation from an efficient price that results from the bid-ask spread charged by market makers, see *Ibid.* at 654–656.
112 See, for example, ESMA, Guidelines on calibration of circuit breakers (fn. 81), 6–8.
113 Section 3.2.1 above.

function. In this case, it is likely that two or more algorithms interact in unintended ways and price movements do not (solely) reflect fundamental volatility. For the calibration of circuit breakers, this means that dynamic or static reference price bands should be combined with other measures that capture the marginal price impact of orders over a defined period of time. Further research is required to determine the most appropriate such measures in light of price dynamics typically exhibited by flash crashes.[114] As currently calibrated, circuit breakers, in any case, do not distinguish between fundamental and transitory volatility and are, therefore, likely to overreach.

A second approach to attenuating potential inefficiencies of circuit breakers could focus on the form of market intervention that ensues when a circuit breaker is triggered. As mentioned in section 3.2.1, circuit breakers in the US and Europe typically halt trading for 5 or 10 minutes. However, an analysis of the price impact of algorithms executing metaorders suggests that regulatory intervention that slows down trading is preferable to intervention that halts it altogether.[115] Trading can be slowed down by switching from continuous order execution to a call auction mechanism for a limited period of time. Empirical evidence concerning the effects of switching from continuous to periodic order execution will be reviewed in section 3.3 below.

(3) Coordination Issues

Fragmented markets and interrelated assets call the effectiveness of trading halts into question if circuit breakers are not coordinated across securities exchanges and across markets within the same exchange, in particular between cash and derivative markets. This was illustrated by the flash crash of 2010, when circuit breakers were triggered on the Chicago Mercantile Exchange, where the E-Mini contracts were traded, but initially not on NYSE, where the underlying cash products were listed, leading to a mismatch in the processing of equity orders and

---

114 The literature has made some suggestions for identifying patterns indicative of harmful volatility, see, e. g., *David Easley/Marcos M. López de Prado/Maureen O'Hara*, "Flow Toxicity and Liquidity in a High-frequency World" (2012) 25 Rev. Financ. Stud. 1457 (introducing a "VPIN toxicity metric" based on volume imbalance and trade intensity); *Easley/de Prado/O'Hara* (fn. 5) (arguing that order flow as captured by the VPIN metric indicated high toxicity in the hours before the flash crash of 2010, which contributed to the withdrawal of liquidity during the flash crash).
115 See section 2.2.

derivative hedges.[116] Algorithms also typically reroute orders if they cannot be executed on one exchange, which may propagate volatility if circuit breakers are calibrated differently.[117]

Regulation NMS in the United States seeks to address these problems by institutionalising the formulation of national market system plans that provide for uniform policies and procedures to mitigate high market volatility.[118] As mentioned, in response to the flash crash of 2010, all US securities exchanges adopted two such plans, one concerning a market wide circuit breaker[119] and the other (Limit Up/Limit Down (LULD) Plan) individual securities that cross certain price bands.[120] The LULD Plan applies to so-called NMS stocks, which comprise all NMS securities except rights and warrants.[121] The relevant price bands differentiate between the most liquid ("Tier 1") securities, in particular stocks included in the S&P 500 and Russell 1000 indices and certain exchange-traded funds, and less liquid ("Tier 2") securities,[122] but they are otherwise aligned and provide for a synchronised, market-wide treatment of both derivative instruments and underlying equity and debt securities.

In the EU, in contrast, coordination across markets is, so far, limited. Following a common strategy in EU capital markets law, MiFID II imposes reporting and notification requirements on trading venues and seeks to achieve coordination at the level of market regulators. More precisely, MiFID II requires regulated markets to report the parameters for a halt in trading to their national competent authorities, which in turn report them to ESMA.[123] When a circuit breaker is triggered on a market that is "material in terms of liquidity",[124] the trading venue has to notify the competent authorities of the trading halt. The competent authorities will then consider whether trading should be halted on other markets.

Empirical evidence concerning the effectiveness of this system of notification and regulator-level coordination is limited. The most detailed study, an ESMA-led assessment of circuit breakers in the EU, does not address the question of coordination directly. However, for a sample of cross-listed shares, it analyses

---

116 *Avanidhar Subrahmanyam*, "Algorithmic trading, the Flash Crash, and coordinated circuit breakers" (2013) 13 Borsa Istanbul Review 4, 7. Likewise, the initial regulatory response to the Flash Crash was criticised for its limited coverage, see *Serritella* (fn. 104), 441.
117 See n 106 above and accompanying text.
118 See section 3.2.1 above
119 See the references in fn. 71 above.
120 See the references in fn. 73 above.
121 Regulation NMS, § 600(b)(48).
122 LULD Plan, Appendix A.
123 MiFID II, Art. 48(5), second subparagraph.
124 See fn. 85 above for a definition.

the effect that the activation of a circuit breaker on one market has on trading activity on satellite markets.[125] In a substantial number of cases, circuit breakers on satellite markets are not triggered and trading continues, but the study identifies a "hidden circuit breaker effect". As trading is halted on the primary market, trading activity and volatility also decrease on satellite markets and, as a consequence, bid-ask spreads widen. When trading resumes on the primary market, the order book refills quickly on the satellite markets and volatility increases.[126] If these findings are corroborated, they imply that the response of market participants to the activation of a circuit breaker on one market achieves a de facto coordination across markets. Regulatory action, either in the form of an alignment of circuit breaker parameters similar to Regulation NMS or the ad-hoc extension of a trading halt to other markets, may accordingly be less important. The ESMA study also observes that an alignment of circuit breakers is difficult to implement in practice, since volatility parameters, such as price collars, will have different effects in markets that differ in terms of liquidity and other market conditions.[127] Thus, it is unlikely that a simple replication of parameters would be effective. On the other hand, it should be noted that the evidence on volatility spillovers is mixed and several studies find that circuit breakers have negative effects in the absence of coordination.[128] More research is required to investigate these questions and understand the comparative effectiveness of the EU and US approaches to coordination of circuit breakers.

3.3 Auction Design

Typically, a continuous double auction mechanism is used to trade securities on exchanges. In a double auction, buyers and sellers submit bids and offers at a particular size and price level (or at multiple price levels). The orders are time stamped and executed, usually according to priority by price and then time.[129] In contrast, in a call auction, bids and offers are collected over specified intervals. At the closing of the auction, the auction platform determines a single price that maximises the volume of trades. Periodic call auctions are used at

---

125 *Guillaumie et al.* (fn. 96), 31–38.
126 *Ibid.* at 32–33.
127 *Ibid.* at 39.
128 See n 106 above for references.
129 Thus, limit orders are ordered from highest to lowest on the buy side and lowest to highest on the sell side, irrespective of the time when they were submitted, and then matched according to time priority.

the open and close of a market, and also when trading resumes after it was halted because a circuit breaker was triggered.[130]

Several studies have examined the effects of continuous double auction and call auction mechanisms on volatility and liquidity. Some have used a simulated market environment to test how extreme price movements are absorbed by markets with continuous and periodic order execution. They have found that switching from a continuous double auction to a periodic call auction, with auction call periods ranging between one second and one minute, was more effective in restoring liquidity and reducing price variability after a flash crash than halting trades.[131]

Other studies have gone further and suggested that frequent call auctions, conducted, for example, every tenth of a second, are generally superior to continuous order execution in the presence of high frequency trading, even if new information that affects the value of a financial instrument is symmetrically observed by all traders.[132] When new information becomes publicly available, trading firms that provide liquidity to the market will seek to cancel their existing quotes and submit new quotes that reflect the updated valuation of the instrument. Simultaneously, arbitrageurs will seek to buy at the old ask before liquidity providers can adjust their quotes. In a market with a continuous limit order book, requests to cancel and orders are processed in order of receipt. Whether the liquidity providers are able to cancel before arbitrageurs buy at the now stale price therefore depends on the speed of order submission, and there is a high likelihood that liquidity providers will sell at the incorrect price at least some of the time.[133] This situation gives rise to two inefficiencies. First, even in a perfectly competitive market without asymmetric information about fundamentals, the bid-ask spread will be positive in order to incorporate the cost of liquidity provision associated with the arbitrage opportunity. Second, liquidity

---

130 *Andrew Ellul/Hyun Song Shin/Ian Tonks*, "Opening and Closing the Market: Evidence from the London Stock Exchange" (2005) 40 J. Financ. Quant. Anal. 779.

131 *Brewer et al.* (fn. 19); *Ravi Jagannathan*, "On Frequent Batch Auctions for Stocks" (2020) J. Financ. Econom., nbz038.

132 *Eric M. Aldrich/Kristian López Vargas*, "Experiments in high-frequency trading: comparing two market institutions" (2020) 23 Exp. Econ. 322; *Budish et al.* (fn. 7); *J. Doyne Farmer/Spyros Skouras*, "Review of the benefits of a continuous market vs. randomised stop auctions and of alternative Priority Rules (policy options 7 and 12)", UK Government Foresight Project, The Future of Computer Trading in Financial Markets, Economic Impact Assessment EIA11 (2012); *Elaine Wah/Michael Wellman*, "Latency Arbitrage, Market Fragmentation, and Efficiency: A Two-Market Model" in Proceedings of the Fourteenth ACM Conference on Electronic Commerce (ACM 2013) 855.

133 *Budish et al.* (fn. 7), 1553–1554.

providers and arbitrageurs have an incentive to engage in a wasteful high-frequency "arms race" with the goal of reducing latency.[134] It has been shown that both inefficiencies can be eliminated by processing orders in discrete rather than continuous time using uniform-price auctions.[135] This strand of research has important implications for market microstructure design and regulation. Notably, it directs attention to the fact that many widely discussed pathologies of high-frequency trading are not a function of trading at high frequency as such,[136] but of flawed market design.[137]

These two strands of research reinforce the arguments from section 3.2.2(2) above. While more work is required to better understand the relationship between the time interval between auctions, the severity of a flash crash, and the efficiency of price discovery,[138] the available research suggests that current circuit breakers halt trading for inefficiently long periods of time.[139]

4 Conclusion

The traditional disclosure paradigm of securities regulation cannot give clear guidance to policy makers in the world of algorithmic and high-frequency trading, where market inefficiencies are often a result of market design, rather than informational asymmetries. This article highlights the importance of market microstructure theory as a foundation for the regulation of algorithmic and high-frequency trading. While many questions have not yet been answered conclusively, research in market microstructure theory holds important lessons that can inform the scope and type of regulatory intervention. Where the empirical evidence in support of regulatory intervention is weak, regulators should act with caution. In the absence of clear evidence, it is particularly important to calibrate regulatory mechanisms carefully and explore alternatives to traditional approaches. For example, in the case of circuit breakers, switching from continuous trading

---

134 *Ibid.* at 1554–1555.

135 *Ibid.* at 1597–1601.

136 As mentioned, the empirical evidence suggests that high-frequency trading generally has positive effects on market quality and price formation, see the references in n 11 above.

137 *Budish et al.* (fn. 7), 1557.

138 See, e.g., *Jagannathan* (fn. 131), 2 (also pointing out that the consequences of switching from continuous to periodic order execution can only fully be assessed if it is well understood how different types of trader would change their trading strategies in response to periodic auctions).

139 See section 3.2.1.

to a call auction, with a short auction call period, may be preferable to halting trading altogether. In addition, market microstructure theory draws attention to issues at the intersection of the mechanics of trading and securities regulation that warrant further research. For example, it is not well understood when algorithms interact in ways that give rise to harmful feedback loops, or how price movements that result from feedback loops can be distinguished from fundamental volatility that reflects the availability of new information. This article reviews findings in market microstructure theory and makes suggestions for refining regulatory mechanisms in order to take account of these insights, or for limiting the scope of regulation where further research is required to produce clearer evidence.

Katja Langenbucher and Patrick Corcoran
Responsible AI Credit Scoring – A Lesson from Upstart.com

Abstract: Modern FinTech companies are disrupting the traditional credit scoring model for loan decision-making by turning to artificial intelligence and machine learning systems. They use those systems to assess creditworthiness based on "alternative data" like banking activity or education history. Such AI scoring has the potential to extend credit to those whose creditworthiness is not captured by standard scores. At the same time, it presents new concerns that current regulatory schemes are ill-equipped to address. This paper raises these concerns and compares the current U.S. and EU regulatory regimes insofar as they may apply to the emerging AI scoring industry. The first issue is data privacy in AI credit scoring. The EU regulates this under the omnibus approach of the General Data Protection Regulation, in the United States it implicates the Fair Credit Reporting Act. The second issue is discrimination in AI-based lending, which falls under the U.S. Equal Credit Opportunity Act and a number of European Anti-Discrimination Directives. The paper discusses the discrimination issue in the context of the U.S. Consumer Financial Protection Bureau's decision to grant the no-action letter requested by FinTech lender Upstart. In a postscript, we discuss the EU's recent proposal for an Artificial Intelligence Act and provide some preliminary thoughts on the Proposal's provisions in the context of the challenges of AI scoring regulation raised in this paper.

Table of Contents

Katja Langenbucher and Patrick Corcoran, Katja is tenured at Goethe University, House of Finance, Frankfurt, affiliated professor at Leibniz Institute for Financial Research SAFE and SciencesPo, Paris, and visiting at Fordham Law School, NYC. Patrick holds a JD of New York University School of Law, and is admitted to the bar in NYC. The authors are most grateful to feedback received during the conference to which this ECFR issue is devoted, excellently organized by Emilios Avgouelas and Heikki Marjosola. We would also like to thank Iris Chiu, UCL London, and Udo Milkau, Frankfurt, for their feedback on prior versions of this paper. Needless to say, remaining errors are ours.

᧠ OpenAccess. © 2022 Katja Langenbucher and Patrick Corcoran, published by De Gruyter.
[CC BY-NC-ND] This work is licensed under the Creative Commons Attribution-NonCommercial-NoDerivatives 4.0 International License. https://doi.org/10.1515/9783110749472-006

1 Introduction

"Traditional credit scores leave people behind. We use artificial intelligence to expand access to reasonably priced credit." This is how Upstart.com advertises its services to consumers. The company's website invites visitors to choose from a drop-down menu their personal credit goal (such as refinancing or making a purchase), and to "check your rate." Further questions concern the applicant's approximate credit score, details on his level of education and primary source of income, and a number of personal details. After providing this information and some supporting documentation, the applicant may choose his loan and the terms offered by Upstart.[1]

What distinguishes lenders like Upstart from a traditional bank? Traditional lenders—including, most prominently, the major banks and credit card compa-

---

1 For a more detailed description see Upstart's request for a no action letter, p. 1 et seq., available at: https://files.consumerfinance.gov/f/documents/201709_cfpb_upstart-no-action-letter-request.pdf (last accessed 22 January 2021) (hereinafter "Request for a no action letter").

nies—rely mainly on a predetermined set of factors when evaluating a loan applicant's creditworthiness based on his credit history. The factors determining a traditional FICO score include the applicant's history of on-time or late payments, the percentage of their available credit that they use, the length of their credit history, the variety of their credit (e. g. credit cards, mortgages, and installment loans), and the recent acquisition of new credit.[2] Upstart, on the other hand, does not rely exclusively on these factors, at least not for all applicants. Instead, it employs an artificial intelligence-based model that distills an alternative credit score from non-FICO data points looking at probability of repayment based on future salary. Upstart also operates online without brick-and-mortar locations, but partners its AI platform with a traditional bank which actually originates loans approved under Upstart's model.

At the heart of what distinguished Upstart from traditional lenders is its AI scoring model, which focuses on borrowers' level of education and high-income potential in order to predict future salary, hence, probability of repayment.[3] If an applicant's credit score is below Upstart's minimum credit underwriting requirements, Upstart will accept him only if he has graduated from or is currently enrolled in an associate, four-year bachelor, or more advanced degree at an accredited school.[4] The underlying business idea seems compelling: Instead of narrowing the assessment of a future borrower to FICO-score criteria and past credit history, further variables are taken into account. These alternative data give a richer picture of financial capacity and likelihood to repay a loan, especially for applicants with short credit histories.[5] Young borrowers or recent immigrants enrolled in school or with a job offer present an attractive market, undertargeted by traditional lenders because they lack the history of interaction with credit markets that is required to achieve an adequate FICO score. At the same time, specific groups of potential borrowers are deliberately left out.[6] Worried that this might raise concerns of direct discrimination or disparate impact, Up-

---

2 Fair Isaac Corporation (FICO), What's in my FICO Scores?, (22 November 2020), https://www. myfico.com/credit-education/whats-in-your-credit-score (last accessed 22 January 2021).
3 On the potential of digital data to more accurately predict future events see: Communication from the Commission to the European Parliament, the Council, the ECON and the Committee of the Regions, 24.9.2020, COM (2020) 591 final, p. 3.
4 See Request for a no action letter (fn. 1), p. 2.
5 See ibid., p. 3.
6 For a critique of bias in consumer lending, see Student Borrower Protection Center, Educational Redlining (February 2020), https://protectborrowers.org/wp-content/uploads/2020/02/Education-Redlining-Report.pdf (last accessed 22 January 2021).

start applied for a no-action letter in 2017 which we will discuss in more detail below.

The CFPB's decision to issue a no-action letter to Upstart is both an indication that major changes to the consumer lending industry are inevitable, and a reminder that such change will create new regulatory challenges as existing rules are applied to technologies that their drafters did not anticipate. The Bureau's acknowledgement of alternative credit scoring opens the door for companies like Upstart to fulfill their promises of more efficient and inclusive lending. At the same time, the CFPB's acceptance of alternative data and AI modelling could prove a difficult fit with current regulations including the Fair Credit Reporting Act (FCRA) and Equal Credit Opportunity Act (ECOA).

This paper will examine the regulatory scheme formed by these and other statutes in the U.S. and EU to better understand how the fintech companies embracing alternative credit scoring fit into those schemes, and where these regulations may need to be adjusted to account for AI scoring methods. Part 2.1 summarizes and compares the relevant consumer lending and data privacy regulations of the U.S. and EU as they apply to lenders and scorers. Part 2.2 analyzes these jurisdictions' anti-discrimination regulations. 3 identifies questions arising from the Upstart no-action letter specifically and discusses how alternative scoring models may implicate discrimination. Part 4 analyzes how the Upstart case may apply generally and suggests how data and model quality may be improved as a result. Part 5 concludes, and Part 6 revisits these questions in the context of the EU Proposal for an Artificial Intelligence Act of April 21, 2021.

2 Which Regulatory Framework for Non-Traditional Data?

Algorithmic scoring models have started to attract regulatory scrutiny for two main reasons. The first has to do with the data collected, processed and transferred to third parties. The second concerns the hidden potential for discriminatory outcomes when using alternative data.

2.1 Data Privacy Regulation

2.1.1 The Lender

One immediate application of algorithmic scoring models is for the lender itself to apply his model to proprietary data it has already collected about the borrower. Such data may stem from a prior contractual relationship with the borrower, like a previous loan or existing bank account. In the course of this relationship, the borrower will have provided the lender with data about himself. This may include, for instance, data submitted in past applications to take out loans or open accounts. Such data encompasses names, addresses, phone numbers, and sometimes credit card account and social security numbers, income and credit histories. It may also extend to information about what kinds of stores the borrower shops at, how much he borrows, his account balance or the dollar value of his assets, what the borrower has purchased with a debit or credit card,[7] whether credit card applications have been denied, or his traditional credit score.

Lenders have naturally decided to use this type of data in the past when making a creditworthiness assessment, and several data privacy regulations apply to such use. In the U.S., the Gramm-Leach-Bliley Act (GLBA) provides the main regulatory framework, and the Financial Credit Reporting Act (FCRA) includes data-sharing rules for those who receive credit reports. State laws such as the California Consumer Privacy Act and the proposed New York Privacy Act impose additional obligations on companies handling consumer data. However, the California law makes exception for data shared among consumer reporting agencies and their furnishers, as that information is already subject to FCRA regulation.[8] In the EU, the General Data Protection Regulation (GDPR) has so far constituted the only relevant regime. The credit reporting infrastructure as such differs from country to country in the EU and there is no EU legislation in place. The proposed AI Act offers a regulatory framework for the use of AI scoring applications. Most of the Act's requirements concern the developer of the application, not necessarily the lender that utilizes the AI system (see *infra* Part 6).

---

7 Credit and debit purchases are considered nonpublic personal information under the Gramm-Leach-Bliley Act, and therefore can only be shared with nonaffiliated third parties if the consumer is given clear and conspicuous notice and an opportunity to opt out of the disclosure, 15 U.S.C. § 6802 (a)–(b).

8 See, e.g., California Consumer Privacy Act (CCPA), Transunion, https://www.transunion.com/consumer-privacy (noting that "personal information related to your credit report is not subject to the CCPA") (last accessed 22 January 2021).

The GLBA requires financial institutions to safeguard certain sensitive data.[9] To comply, financial institutions have to "develop, implement, and maintain a comprehensive information security program that [...] contains administrative, technical, and physical safeguards."[10] Additionally, financial institutions have to explain their data-sharing practices to their customers.[11] If they share information with certain third-party non-affiliates, i.e. companies which are not part of the same corporate group, customers must be notified.[12] There are some disclosures for which financial institutions are not required to provide the consumer with notice and an opportunity to opt out, such as when no customer relationship has been established or the information is being shared with an affiliate entity.[13]

Going beyond the GLBA, under the FCRA a financial institution which has received information from a consumer reporting agency and intends to share that information with an affiliate becomes a credit reporting agency (CRA) for FCRA purposes and is subject to the same notice and information-sharing requirements as CRAs.[14] That said, under the FCRA a financial institution can still share information relating to transactions between the consumer and that institution,[15] and may share consumer report information with entities with which it is affiliated or shares common ownership provided that consumers are provided with notice and opportunity to opt out.[16]

A core feature of both the FCRA and GLBA is the somewhat permissive (as compared to EU regulation) approach towards lenders who wish to utilize consumer data they have collected. While it has to safeguard certain data, the lender is at liberty to use consumer data as it sees fit to evaluate applicants' creditworthiness (subject, of course, to the antidiscrimination regulations discussed below). This approach goes hand in hand with placing the burden to take initiative on the borrower. Lenders who plan to share data with affiliates or non-affiliates must notify the borrower, but it is the borrower who has to speak up and opt out – if a right to opt out exists, that is. As of now, the regulatory regime is the

---

9 Safeguards Rule, 16 Code of Federal Regulations (CFR) § 314, implementing sections 501 and 505(b)(2) of the Gramm-Leach-Bliley Act.
10 16 C.F.R. §314.3.
11 16 C.F.R. § 313.3(b).
12 16 C.F.R. § 313.4 – 313.6.
13 16 C.F.R. § 313.4(b).
14 *Chris Brummer*, Fintech Law in a Nutshell, 2020, p. 320 et seq.
15 15 U.S.C. § 1681a(d)(2)(A) ("the term 'consumer report' does not include [...] information solely as to transactions or experiences between the consumer and the person making the report").
16 12 C.F.R. § 1022.20 et seq.

same regardless of whether a lender is using traditional or alternative, AI-driven scoring models.

EU law follows a considerably less liberal regime as to data protection. Art. 6 GDPR requires there to be a legitimate reason for any form of data collection or processing. A lender who makes use of data, even if it is proprietary data he has collected about the borrower, qualifies as a "data processor" under Art. 4 para. 2 GDPR: "any operation [...] which is performed on personal data [...] such as collection, recording, organization, structuring, storage." Instead of requiring the borrower to take the initiative to opt out, it is the lender who must show that its handling of data is legal under Art. 6 para. 1 (a) GDPR ("Processing shall be lawful only [...]"). Additionally, if employing an algorithm entails profiling, special safeguards apply under Art. 22 para. 1 GDPR. The GDPR provides for a general prohibition on decisions based solely on automated processing ("The data subject shall have the right not to be subject to a decision based solely on automated processing, including profiling, which produces legal effects concerning him or her [...]"), allowing for exceptions in its para. 2 (necessity to enter into a contract, authorization under Union or Member State law, explicit consent by the data subject). For specially protected categories of data, even fewer exceptions apply.[17]

2.1.2 The Scoring Agency

Algorithmic credit scoring, especially when based on non-traditional data, will often be done not by traditional lenders, but by third party FinTech companies. Traditionally, credit bureaus have delivered credit scores (e. g. by the German SchuFa) or credit reports (e. g. by Experian, TransUnion and Equifax in the U.S.), the latter of which form the basis for the applicant's FICO[18] score. FinTech companies such as ZestFinance[19] and Underwrite.ai[20] offer novel scoring models which go beyond the traditional variables underlying the FICO score. AI, machine learning, and related technologies enable these companies to model and predict creditworthiness based on a more complex analysis of relevant consumer data. AI-based scorers of this type may rely exclusively on the proprietary data of

---

17 Art. 22 para. 2, Art. 9 para. 2 (a), (g) GDPR.
18 FICO is a leading analytics software company that delivers the software to compute credit scores to many of the largest U.S. lenders, but is not itself a credit reporting agency, FICO, About Us, https://www.fico.com/en/about-us#our-company (last accessed 22 January 2021).
19 https://www.zest.ai (last accessed 29 January 2021).
20 https://www.underwrite.ai (last accessed 29 January 2021).

the lender itself. Such seems to be the case for Underwrite.ai, which adds value by applying more sophisticated analysis to the data contained in a lender's pre-existing data on cured loans. Underwrite.ai's approach has no need for the collection of additional data, while other companies, like Upstart, rely on new sources of data to supplement traditional FICO elements.

Beyond delivering novel scoring models to be applied to lenders' data, FinTech companies like Upstart collect their own data in addition to running it through their AI-based models to compute a score. Often, these companies source borrowers, but a bank originates the loan. In the case of Upstart, Cross River Bank, operating under a New Jersey charter, is the originator. FinTech business models vary in detail. Some have the issuing bank take care of the entire process of debt collection while others are involved in servicing, funding and debt collection and may even buy back the loan.

Algorithmic scoring models rely heavily on data. Of course, all statistical credit scoring uses data to some degree, but AI scoring is unique in the sheer volume of data processed and the number of variables that may be analyzed in creating and applying models. While companies like Underwrite.ai and Gini-Machine[21] use only the lender's own historical lending data, others acquire explicit permission from customers to access more data.[22] Petal, for example, requires that applicants with little to no credit history link their bank accounts in order to apply for certain products.[23] Models may include variables which the user does provide, but where he does not necessarily understand the way in which they are important in a credit context. An often-cited example concerns a specific font found on a user's electronic device which correlated with the use of an online gambling site.[24] Others ask potential borrowers to grant broad access to some form of digital footprint, like a PayPal or Amazon account, a mobile phone or a fitness tracking app. They then correlate such data points with their proprietary data on probability of repayment. This is where machine learning comes in to analyze the relationships and interactions between hundreds of potentially relevant variables, and thereby discover the predictive power of data

---

21 https://ginimachine.com (last accessed 29 January 2021).
22 See GiniMachine, "How it works: An End-to-End Scoring Platform", https://ginimachine.com/product/ (explaining that models are based on records of previously issued loans) (last accessed 22 January 2021).
23 Petal, "What do you do with my bank information?", https://support.petalcard.com/hc/en-us/articles/360012518794-What-do-you-do-with-my-bank-information- (last accessed 22 January 2021).
24 On Kreditech see the report on p. 23 at https://www.european-microfinance.org/sites/default/files/document/file/Inclusive-credit-scoring-Final.pdf (last accessed 22 January 2021).

points that might otherwise never be realized as predictive of a likelihood to repay.[25]

EU regulation will usually understand scoring agencies as "data process-ors."[26] Under the GDPR's omnibus regime, this includes "data collection" as well as "disclosure by transmission, dissemination or otherwise making availa-ble." In order for data processing to be legitimate, it must qualify under one of the GDPR's exceptions. The most natural exception is under Art. 6 para. 1 (a): if the data subject gave his consent. Consent has to be in the form of a "freely given, specific, informed and unambiguous indication of the data subject's wish-es."[27] If the non-traditional data involves protected categories, Art. 9 GDPR lays down a stricter regulatory framework, asking for explicit (rather than "freely given") consent.

The European Court of Justice (ECJ) has just started to specify what it consid-ers necessary features for consent. A pre-checked box on a website does not meet the court's standard of "active" consent. In an *obiter dictum*, the ECJ raised doubts whether behavioral nudges, such as making continuation in an online gambling game dependent on giving consent to the processing of one's data, are legal.[28] If there is no consent, processing may be legitimate if it "is necessary for the purposes of the legitimate interests pursued by the controller or by a third party," as long as these legitimate interests outweigh the interests and funda-mental rights and freedoms of the data subject.[29] However, it is certainly doubt-ful that the legitimate interests of a scoring agency will ever outweigh the inter-est of the data subject in preventing access to their private data without their consent, likely rendering this exception ineffectual in this context.

In a 2020 Whitepaper on artificial intelligence, the EU Commission began to outline a "European approach to excellence and trust" that addresses privacy protection when employing AI, among other concerns.[30] The report highlights

---

25 On the basis of (limited, non-representative) empirical research the authors of this paper have done, scoring agencies always ask for consent. Put differently: we have not seen agencies which scrap the internet for publicly available information on potential borrowers. Of course this is not to say that such business models do not exist.
26 Art. 4 para. 2 GDPR.
27 Art. 4 para. 11 GDPR.
28 ECJ, 1 October 2019, Planet49, C-673/17, ECLI:EU:C:2019:801, mn. 64.
29 Art. 6 para. 1 (f) GDPR.
30 White Paper on Artificial Intelligence – A European approach to excellence and trust, p. 10 et seq., available at: https://ec.europa.eu/info/sites/info/files/commission-white-paper-artificial-intelligence-feb2020_en.pdf (last accessed: 14 February 2021); the Public Consultation on the AI White Paper, Final Report on the public consultation is available at: https://ec.europa.eu/digital-

that, while a regulatory framework is already in place, regulators must continue to consider proper enforcement and, possibly, the need for adjustments to existing regulations. As mentioned above, the Whitepaper did not specifically address AI scoring.

FinTech companies equipped with a banking license and originating the loan themselves will have to comply with the GDPR's regulation on "profiling" and on "decisions based solely on automated processing." Recital 71 of the GDPR explicitly refers to a prohibition of (fully) automated refusals of an online credit application on the basis of profiling, unless Union or Member State law allows for them. Companies which are involved in scoring only, i.e. whose models propose to issue the loan which is then granted by an originating bank, will usually still be involved in automated processing under the GDPR.

Under U.S. law, the FCRA applies to entities which qualify as a "consumer reporting agency" (CRA) and to data which can be considered a "consumer report." CRAs are agencies that compile and maintain public information and credit account information "for the purpose of furnishing reports to third parties bearing on a consumer's credit worthiness."[31] A consumer report is any communication "bearing on a consumer's credit worthiness [...] which is used or expected to be used [...] as a factor in establishing the consumer's eligibility for" credit, insurance, or employment.[32]

Under the FCRA, a CRA may not report information adverse to the consumer if that data is over seven years old.[33] The CRA may only furnish a credit report for certain enumerated purposes, including the evaluation of applicants for credit, insurance, and employment.[34] To ensure they comply with this requirement, CRAs must require their clients (i.e. the lender, insurer, or employer) to identify themselves and their purposes for requesting the consumer report.[35] The fees a CRA charges for reports must be reasonable.[36]

The statute also imposes responsibilities on the entities that furnish the CRA with consumer information. These 'furnishers' constitute a wide variety of good

---

single-market/en/news/white-paper-artificial-intelligence-public-consultation-towards-euro pean-approach-excellence (last accessed: 14 February 2021), see pp. 12, 14 on privacy.

31 15 U.S.C. § 1681a(p).

32 Id. at § 1681a(d)(1).

33 15 U.S.C. § 1681c(a).

34 15 U.S.C. § 1681b(a)(3).

35 15 U.S.C. § 1681e(a).

36 15 U.S.C. § 1681 g(f)(8).

and service providers with whom consumers directly interact.[37] Furnishers must notify consumers when negative information is sent to a CRA,[38] and must not furnish information that a consumer has told them or they otherwise have reason to know is inaccurate.[39] Consumers are entitled to know the sources of the information in their credit report,[40] and to dispute the accuracy of information directly with the entity that furnished it.[41]

Summing up, artificial intelligence models' reliance on big data and FinTech lenders' interest in a wider array of data points to inform alternative credit scoring models will inevitably bring those lenders within the scope of various data privacy regulations. Though such regulations will generally require the consent of and disclosures to the borrower when lenders access and use data to make credit decisions, data privacy regulations alone cannot guarantee that borrowers understand the scope of any alternative data accessed, and how nontraditional data points might affect their credit decision.

2.2 Anti-Discrimination Regulation

A perhaps less evident concern when dealing with P2P lending and AI-based credit scoring is the regulation of discriminatory lending practices. Withholding credit solely on the basis of certain characteristics of the borrower, such as gender, race or religious affiliation, is prohibited in both the U.S. and the EU. These regulations obviously rule out AI-based models which explicitly make their credit decision dependent on these characteristics. However, the problem with AI-based models is a more complicated one. The larger the data pool from which machine learning algorithms pull the correlations they use, the higher the risk that a correlation indirectly discriminates or – in U.S. terminology – has a dispa-

---

37 Furnishers mostly consist of "automobile dealers; banks, clothing, department, and variety stores; finance agencies; grocery and home furnishing dealers; insurers; jewelry and camera stores; contractors; lumber, building materials, and hardware suppliers; medical-care providers; national credit card companies and airlines; oil companies (credit card divisions); personal services other than medical; mail-order houses; real estate agents; hotel keepers; sporting goods and farm and garden supply dealers; utilities; fuel distributors; government agencies (e.g. the Federal Housing Administration and the Veterans Administration); wholesalers; advertisers; and collection agencies." Frederick H. Miller/Alvin C. Harrell/Daniel J. Morgan, Consumer Law: Cases, Problems, and Materials, 1998, 296.
38 15 U.S.C. § 1681s-2(a)(7).
39 15 U.S.C. § 1681s-2(a)(1).
40 15 U.S.C. § 1681 g(a).
41 15 U.S.C. § 1681s-2(a)(8)(E).

rate impact on protected groups. This is because an AI system can find correlations between a high likelihood of debt repayment and complex combinations of input variables, some of which may have no obvious relationship to a person's financial tendencies or responsibility. For example, an algorithm might recognize that applicants who shop online at Website X and communicate with Messenger App Y are less likely to stay on top of credit card payments. However, the intersection of those two variables may well serve as a proxy for a particular race even if race itself is not being considered as a standalone variable, and the scorer may not even realize that race or other protected classes are indirectly influencing their model's calculations in this way.

Upstart provides a compelling illustration of this concern. In the U.S., education is significantly correlated with race. A 2015 report by the U.S. Census Bureau indicated that among people aged 25 and older, 36% of white people had attained at least a bachelor's degree, compared to 23% of Black people and 16% of Hispanic people. For the same population, 14% of white people held advanced degrees, compared to 8% of Black people and 5% of Hispanic people.[42] A study by the Student Borrower Protection Center shows that Upstart's education-dependent model leads to higher costs (e. g. interest rates and origination fees) for students of Historically Black Colleges and Universities and Hispanic-Serving Institutions than for students of non-minority serving institutions.[43] When refinancing student loans with Upstart, this study found, a hypothetical Howard University graduate[44] is charged almost $3,500 more over the life of a five-year loan than a NYU graduate, all other inputs held constant.[45] A hypothetical graduate with a B.A. from New Mexico State University, a Hispanic-Serving Institution, is charged almost $1,800 more over the life of a five-year loan than a NYU graduate.

The approaches to anti-discrimination regulation in the U.S. and EU mirror the two jurisdictions' approaches to data protection: U.S. law relies on a sectoral legal regime prohibiting discriminatory lending practices, while the EU provides for more general anti-discrimination rules.

---

42 *Camille L. Ryan/Kurt Bauman*, Educational Attainment in the United States: 2015, U.S. Census Bureau (March 2016), https://www.census.gov/content/dam/Census/library/publications/2016/demo/p20-578.pdf (last accessed 22 January 2021).
43 Student Borrower Protection Center (fn. 6) p. 15 et seq.
44 Howard University is a historically Black University.
45 Student Borrower Protection Center (fn. 6) pp. 4, 7.

Setting aside fundamental human rights protections and how they impact contract law,[46] EU law provides for a number of Directives which prohibit discrimination in specific situations such as employment or social security. EU Directive 2000/43/EC is intended to implement the principle of equal treatment between persons irrespective of racial or ethnic origin. Under Art. 2 para. 2 (a), (b) and Art. 3 para. 1 (h), the Directive prohibits direct and indirect discrimination in relation to "access to and supply of goods and services which are available to the public, including housing." To consider credit scoring and loan contracts as qualifying for that rule, those agreements would have to be standardized services, rather than individualized agreements. Art. 3 EU Directive 2004/113/EC prohibits direct and indirect gender discrimination as to the offer of goods and services which are available to the public, except for some goods related to private and family life. With its broader wording, scoring and loan provision will in many cases qualify.

In its Whitepaper on AI, the EU Commission expressed its awareness of the potential for discrimination that AI presents.[47] The report highlights both "flaws in the overall design of AI systems" and issues arising "from the use of data without correcting possible bias."[48] Drawing conclusions from such preliminary work, the Proposal for an AI Act sets up a regulatory framework with the explicit goal of prohibiting harmful practices which "contradict Union values of respect for human dignity, freedom, equality, democracy and the rule of law and Union fundamental rights, including the right to non-discrimination, data protection and privacy."[49]

In the U.S., the ECOA makes it unlawful for any creditor to discriminate against any applicant on the basis of race, color, religion, national origin, sex, marital status, or age.[50] Creditors also cannot discriminate because an applicant derives all or part of their income from public assistance, or because an applicant has in good faith exercised their rights under the Consumer Protection Act.[51] The ECOA also creates a private right of action for applicants against creditors who have discriminated against them.[52] The Act includes both direct or in-

---

46 In more detail at *Katja Langenbucher*, "Responsible AI-based Credit Scoring – A Legal Framework", 31 European Business Law Review 2020, 527, 544 et seqq.

47 See White Paper (fn. 30), 1, 10 ("opaque decision-making"); Final Report (fn. 30), pp. 14, 16, 17.

48 Final Report (fn. 30), p. 11.

49 Proposal, Recital (15).

50 15 U.S.C. § 1691(a)(1).

51 Id. at § 1691(a)(2)–(3).

52 15 U.S.C. § 1691e(a).

tentional discrimination based on the aforementioned factors, and indirect or "disparate impact" discrimination in which the lender's practices have "a disproportionately negative impact on members of a protected class—and the lender is unable to demonstrate that the practice is justified by a legitimate business need and cannot reasonably be achieved by other less discriminatory needs."[53]

The ECOA also requires lenders to notify applicants of adverse actions (e. g. denying credit or offering credit on less favorable terms) within 30 days.[54] That notice must contain the specific reasons for which the decision was made or a promise to deliver that explanation upon the applicant's request. Broad statements that the adverse action was based "on the creditor's internal standards or policies, or that the applicant [...] failed to achieve a qualifying score on the creditor's crediting system are insufficient."[55] In other words, regardless of how complex a scoring algorithm might be, incorporating myriad variables and interactions, the decisions it recommends must be explainable in a way that is comprehensible. However, depending on the complexity of a model and the number and variety of variables bearing on its decision, an explanation comprehensible to the average consumer may necessarily fall short of identifying all the factors contributing to the decision, and a fully accurate explanation may prove too verbose and intricate to be readily understood. Even if the lender can clearly explain the workings of its particular model, such disclosures could also implicate the scorer's proprietary decision algorithm.

ECOA applies to all creditors, which the statute defines as any person who "regularly extends, renews, or continues credit; any person who regularly arranges for the extension, renewal, or continuation of credit; or any assignee of an original creditor who participates in the decision to extend, renew, or continue credit."[56] Under this definition, a company like Underwrite.ai or GiniMachine that sells its AI technology to lenders but does not extend credit itself would not face liability if its model's decisions were not sufficiently explainable. However, there would seem to be some responsibility on the scorer to provide a scoring model that can at the very least be transposed into traditional credit factors for the sake of explaining decisions to consumers. As it stands, lenders would likely have to impose this responsibility on AI scorers via contract. If such contracts shifted liability for ECOA explainability violations to the scorer, scorers

---

53 *Brummer* (fn. 14), p. 337.
54 15 U.S.C. § 1691(d)(1).
55 12 C.F.R. § 1002.9(b)(2).
56 15 U.S.C. § 1691a(e).

may be incentivized to develop models the decisions of which are not a "black box" to the average consumer.

The Truth in Lending Act, which regulates and standardizes the terms used to explain credit offerings in order to ensure consumers' understanding of the lending agreements they enter, also applies.[57] The Act's disclosure requirements are detailed and vary based on the specific type of credit or transaction at issue, but in general a credit card lender must disclose any mandatory minimum payments and the annual percentage rate,[58] and must also regularly update the consumer about their balance and charges. In order to prevent terms from being hidden in fine print, CFPB regulations require that these disclosures be "clear and conspicuous."[59] While the use of AI scoring over traditional scores does not change the terms used in the ultimate credit agreement, lenders employing alternative scoring should be aware of how that technology might affect the clarity of any routine disclosures.

3 The Upstart No-Action Letter

Worried that the use of its statistical model could violate ECOA and Regulation B or more general disparate impact principles, Upstart requested a no-action letter from the U.S. Consumer Financial Protection Bureau (CFPB) in 2017. The CFPB has primary regulatory authority over a range of consumer lending activities, including credit cards.[60] A no-action letter is a statement by the bureau that it has "no present intention to recommend initiation of an enforcement or supervisory action against the requester," and intended to prevent current regulations from "hinder[ing] the development of innovative financial products that promise substantial consumer benefit because, for example, existing laws and rules did not contemplate specific products."[61]

Insisting that its model does not lead to discriminatory lending practices, Upstart has compared applicant outcomes under its own model against outcomes that would result from a model using only traditional variables.[62] If an applicant scored well under the traditional model, Upstart's non-traditional vari-

57 15 U.S.C. § 1601.
58 15 U.S.C. § 1663.
59 12 C.F.R. § 226.5(a)(1).
60 Brummer (fn. 14), p. 30.
61 Policy on No-Action Letters; Information Collection, 81 Fed. Reg. 8,686 (22 February 2016).
62 See Request for a no action letter (fn. 1), p. 14.

ables would not affect the loan decision.[63] By contrast, if an applicant did not meet the minimum requirements for traditional creditworthiness but fulfilled Upstart's additional tests, he would be eligible for a loan that otherwise would have been denied or offered at higher costs. In this sense, Upstart claimed to offer an arguably fair regime: some people will be better off, and no one will be worse off than under a purely FICO score-based system. The CFPB granted Upstart the no-action letter.[64]

3.1 The Argument in Upstart

To understand Upstart's reasoning, it might be useful to recall its focus on education variables. Enrollment at an elite institution, so Upstart claims on the basis of its model, makes a higher-paying job more likely, and is therefore a natural variable to be considered by a lender.[65] Furthermore, Upstart argues, traditional scoring based on FICO variables also results in Black Americans qualifying for loans at higher interest rates than white Americans in comparable financial circumstances.[66] As with traditional lenders, using alternative data and AI models to inform credit decisions will see some level of disparate outcomes across protected classes, a phenomenon which is not unique to FinTech lenders. Upstart might point out that the fact that probability of repayment is statistically lower for Black and Hispanic Americans than for white Americans, while deplorable, reflects existing inequality. Furthermore, Upstart showed, all the "promising individuals with limited credit history"[67] are better off. No applicant is worse off than under a traditional scoring model, because the additional variables are used only if the traditional score is too low.[68]

---

63 Ibid., p. 3 et seq.
64 For more details see the Bureau's request for information, available at: https://files.con sumerfinance.gov/f/documents/20170214_cfpb_Alt-Data-RFI.pdf (last accessed 22 January 2021) (hereinafter "Request for information").
65 A counterargument has been put forward by the Student Borrower Protection Center which claims that there is only a slight correlation between institutional selectivity and increased earnings Student Borrower Protection Center (fn. 6) p. 10.
66 See Student Borrower Protection Center (fn. 6), p. 6.
67 See Request for a no action letter (fn. 1), p. 1.
68 See ibid., p. 1: "complementing (not replacing) traditional underwriting signals." This would presuppose that if nobody is worse off, the possibility that some are being denied the opportunity to be better off based on a protected characteristic is not actionable at all. This issue will not be discussed in detail here, but see 4.1 further below.

3.2 Intentional Discrimination

Considering whether there was intentional discrimination, the CFPB noted that "[m]achine learning algorithms that sift through vast amounts of data could unearth variables, or clusters of variables, that predict the consumer's likelihood of default [...] but are also highly correlated with race, ethnicity, sex, or some other basis protected by law."[69] For example, "a variable indicating subscription to a magazine exclusively devoted to coverage of women's health issues"[70] might serve as a proxy to gender.

There is overt discrimination if the scoring agency should *explicitly* use non-traditional data involving protected categories: "If the scorer/lender is aware of this correlation," using proxies like these allows "ill-meaning lenders to intentionally discriminate and hide it behind a curtain of programming code."[71] Hence, if Upstart had intentionally used educational data in order to screen out members of protected classes (i.e. race, color, religion, sex, marital status, age, or national origin),[72] this would have constituted a violation of the ECOA.

However, due to the intricacies of machine learning models, not every scorer or lender will be aware of correlations in their model that may serve as proxies for membership in protected classes. Thus, even well-intentioned lenders relying on complex or black-box algorithms may end up working with scores which disparately impact protected groups.

Even if a scoring agency is aware of the relevant correlation, as was the case for Upstart, it does not usually focus intentionally on race. Instead, Upstart insists on only looking at correlations produced by its machine-learning algorithm on the basis of "a mix of all the variables used in Upstart's underwriting model."[73] Against this background, the fact that graduates from historically black colleges and universities (HBCUs) or Hispanic-serving institutions (HSIs) pay considerably more for a similar loan if compared to an NYU graduate is "a result of the model" – a reflection of the world as it is, out of Upstart's

---

69 See Request for information (fn. 64), p. 19.
70 Ibid.
71 Ibid.
72 15 U.S.C. § 1691(a)(1).
73 Upstart letter p. 4: "the model only processes variables in concert; it does not process variables in isolation"; on the discussion on HUD's interpretation of the Fair Housing Act in 2019 see *Talia B. Gillis*, False Dreams of Algorithmic Fairness: The Case of Credit Pricing, p. 10 (available at: https://papers.ssrn.com/sol3/papers.cfm?abstract_id=3571266 [last accessed 30 January 2021]).

reach, as it were.[74] "Such correlations are not per se discriminatory,"[75] the Bureau found.[76]

This is where one of the obstacles to applying traditional anti-discrimination laws to new technologies becomes evident. While traditional antidiscrimination doctrine asks for intentional discrimination on a basis such as race or gender, a lender relying on algorithmic scoring can point to the math behind the model, arguing that it is "the machine" making the decision. The EU Proposal addresses this "tendency of automatically relying or over-relying on the output produced by a high-risk AI system" as "automation bias."[77] Establishing intent would then require showing that the scorer (or lender) deliberately picked the offensive variable to "mask"[78] its bias, which will rarely be the case. Duties to review and backtest the models employed, on which the EU Proposal largely rests, will not suffice to establish *intentional* discrimination but could perhaps provide the basis for a claim of indirect discrimination.

3.3 Indirect Discrimination/Disparate Impact

When intent to discriminate cannot be established, the usual next step is to move on to a claim of disparate impact. This doctrine does not require the claimant to show intent but focuses on discrimination by statistical differences in aggregate outcomes across groups. Disparate impact would capture a facially neutral model that affects members of a protected group differently than members of another group.[79] The ECJ has long accepted what it calls "indirect discrimination" claims and the relevant anti-discrimination Directives incorporate this doctrine. The U.S. Supreme Court, on the other hand, is much more hesitant to do so outside of housing and employment law.[80] In 1971, the Court adopted the theory

---

74 Ibid. p. 18.

75 Request for information (fn. 64), p. 19.

76 The CFPB went on to state that there "may be fair lending risks" but did not elaborate in detail.

77 Art. 15 para. 4 lit. b.

78 *Solon Barocas/Andrew D. Selbst*, "Big Data's Disparate Impact", California Law Review 2016, 671, 692 et seqq.

79 In the context of credit scoring see *Gillis* (fn. 73), p. 27 et seq.

80 See U.S. Supreme Court, 30 March 2005, *Smith v. City of Jackson*, 544 U.S. 228 (2005) (affirming disparate impact claim brought under Age Discrimination in Employment Act); U.S. Supreme Court, 25 June 2015, *Texas Department of Housing and Community Affairs v. The Inclusive Communities Project*, 576 U.S. 519 (2015) (holding that disparate housing claims were cognizable under the Fair Housing Act); ECJ, 23 March 2004, *Collins*, C-138/02, ECLI:EU:C:2004:172.

of disparate impact when interpreting the Civil Rights Act of 1964[81] and the doctrine was codified in the Civil Rights Act of 1991. However, the court has since limited the doctrine by requiring plaintiffs to show discriminatory intent for some claims[82] and allowing discrimination based on bona fide occupational qualifications.[83] Today, the extent to which U.S. courts and agencies are open to applying disparate impact principles has remained an open question. While the CFPB and some U.S. courts have been open to applying disparate impact theory in the context of the ECOA, no Supreme Court guidance is available yet. Those arguing for a more narrow approach insist on the proximity between intentional discrimination and disparate impact, understanding the latter only as "an evidentiary tool used to identify genuine, intentional discrimination – to 'smoke out,' as it were, disparate treatment."[84] Others frame the principle more broadly as concerning "the consequences of [...] practices, not simply the motivation."[85] However, even such a broader interpretation of the principle does not necessarily justify a disparate impact claim which requires (i) a difference in treatment and (ii) the absence of a reasonable business rationale.[86]

In Upstart's case, establishing a disparate impact claim would, *first,* require proof that students of HBCUs and HSIs have been treated differently by Upstart's model than students of non-minority serving institutions. The reason for this is some version of a "don't compare apples with oranges" argument. Discrimination presupposes that one group has been treated differently than another group that is otherwise equal in all relevant respects. But "the devil is in the detail" in this case, particularly with regard to the assessment of what we are prepared to treat as *equal in all relevant respects.* The disparate treatment may simply reflect existing inequality. Such inequality in financial capacity, Upstart may have claimed, will have to be taken into account by a lender because he is required to run a realistic risk assessment.[87] Hence, the entire exercise is far from a mathematical one. Normative issues arise in deciding on the characteristics of the baseline population against which to compare the allegedly discriminated-against group.[88] For instance, should the "control group" consist of any-

---

81 U.S Supreme Court, 8 March 1971, *Griggs v, Duke Power Co.,* 401 U.S. 424 (1971).
82 U.S Supreme Court, 7 June 1976, *Washington v, Davis,* 426 U.S. 229 (1976).
83 U.S Supreme Court, 27 June 1977, *Dothard v. Rawlinson,* 433 U.S. 321 (1977).
84 U.S. Supreme Court, 29 June 2009, *Ricci v. DeStefano* 557 U.S. 595 (2009) (Scalia J., concurring).
85 U.S Supreme Court, 8 March 1971, *Griggs v, Duke Power Co.,* 401 U.S. 424 (1971).
86 *Gillis* (fn. 73), p. 24 et seqq.
87 In more detail at *Langenbucher* (fn. 46), 552 et seq.
88 On this point: *Gillis* (fn. 73), p. 89.

one who could objectively be interested in a loan, anyone who actually applied for a loan, or anyone who is in the exact same position save for enrollment in a HBCU or HSI? Once a plaintiff has established the relevant groups, they must show disparate treatment. The more off-the-rack and standardized a credit contract appears, the more straightforward this exercise is. By contrast, the more individualized the pricing scheme, the more complex and normatively challenging it will be to establish disparate treatment. Lastly, one will have to settle on the level of outcome disparity one is willing to accept: is a small difference in borrowing conditions acceptable? If so, how small?

Second, even if disparate impact has successfully been established, it might still be justified. The U.S. Supreme Court looks for a "business necessity" and the need for "practical business choices" underlying the disparately impactful practice.[89] Similarly, the ECJ accepts practices that are "objectively justified by a legitimate aim [if] the means of achieving that aim are appropriate and necessary."[90] Both courts ask defendants to show that there is no alternative practice available that would produce less discriminatory results.[91] Establishing a business necessity defense will usually be a very straightforward exercise, as long as the scorer/lender can show that his model, diligently developed,[92] suggests a higher statistical probability of default for the relevant group.

4 Generalizing Upstart?

4.1 The Argument that "everyone is better off"

Upstart received the first no-action letter issued by the CFPB concerning a Fin-Tech lender in the context of disparate impact prohibitions. While some of its reasoning has to do with the specifics of Upstart's business model, the focus of this last part is to understand the extent to which the decision has more far-reaching implications. One of the charms of Upstart's model is that it offers a second chance to borrowers who are ineligible under traditional scoring models without treating other borrowers differently. Compared to a world without Up-

---

89 U.S. Supreme Court, 25 June 2015, *Texas Department of Housing and Community Affairs v. The Inclusive Communities Project*, 576 U.S. 519, 531–532 (2015); *Gillis* (fn. 73), 27 fn. 76, 80, 213.
90 ECJ, 14 March 2017, *G4S Secure Solutions*, C-157/15, ECLI:EU:C:2017:203 (citing EU Directive 2000/78/EC of 27 November 2000 establishing a general framework for equal treatment in employment and occupation).
91 In more detail at *Langenbucher* (fn. 46), p. 554 et seq.
92 See below at 4.2.

start, no one seems to be worse off than before. Against this background, it is tempting to understand the no-action letter as relying on this (specific) business model of Upstart.

However, the CFPB made very clear that an alternative scoring model would not necessarily run afoul of its rules even if it left some borrowers worse off. "It is important to note," states the Bureau's request for information, "that to the extent alternative data or modeling techniques could help a creditor identify consumers who are *more and less* likely to default than their current credit score suggests, alternative data could in fact *decrease or increase* a given consumer's likelihood of receiving credit, or could *raise or lower* the price that any individual is offered for that credit."[93] The CFPB seems unfazed: "Though this could be seen as a detriment to consumers who are less likely to receive credit (or whose prices increase), it could also be seen as an improvement in risk assessment, which may provide greater certainty and allow a lender to increase credit availability for those who qualify. Indeed, in the longer term consumers whose credit scores understate their true risk may be better served if they do not obtain additional credit that they cannot repay."[94]

Hence, while Upstart presents a specific case in that "everyone is better off," even if the extent to which this is true still varies across white, Black and Hispanic Americans, the CFPB did not stress this argument. Instead, it explicitly embraced denying credit on the basis of an AI model, arguing that AI models deliver better predictions on the probability of repayment.

4.2 Ensuring Quality

We have said further above[95] that a business necessity defense requires a carefully and diligently developed AI scoring model. This points towards the enormously complex question of how to assess the quality of the data and of the model. Not only courts dealing with discrimination lawsuits, but also banking supervisory authorities will have to address the choice of scoring methodology and input data.[96] Following Upstart's argument, we have so far assumed that the non-traditional scoring model succeeds in producing better quality results

---

93 Request for information (fn. 64), p. 14.
94 Ibid.
95 See section 3.3. above.
96 *Gillis* (fn. 73), p. 49 et seq.; on the latter *Langenbucher* (fn. 46), p. 561 et seq.

than the traditional one. Indeed, in a joint statement, the CFPB and other financial regulators accepted that alternative data may "improve the speed and accuracy of credit decisions" and may allow extension of credit to those underserved in the "mainstream credit system."[97] However, there are number of potential issues to keep in mind.

4.2.1 Quality of the Data and "biased AI"

The CFPB has found that alternative data may raise "accuracy concerns because the data are inconsistent, incomplete, or otherwise inaccurate."[98] The Bureau is aware that traditional scoring models raise such concerns, too. However, because non-traditional data are not often sourced for the purpose of a credit rating, the CFPB worries that quality standards may be lower.[99]

Additionally, the regulatory framework applicable to traditional credit bureaus provides safeguards for borrowers who want to know which data has been used and/or correct mistakes.[100] The FCRA entitles credit applicants to the information in their report, and they may dispute the completeness or accuracy of that information with the CRA, which must notify furnishers of the dispute and update or delete the disputed information within 30 days.[101] In this way, inaccurate data which might have entered a scoring model can be rectified, allowing for the eventual score to more accurately reflect reality. Not all of these legal safeguards apply to non-traditional data. Even if the aforementioned rights to access the data and correct errors exist, consumers might not understand how and which data impacts their credit standing, and therefore not proceed with such claims.

The use of alternative data has the potential to complicate the FCRA regulatory scheme in a number of ways. Traditional FICO scores only require furnishers to send data relevant to the basic FICO factors, like a consumer's credit usage and repayment history, which are generally well-documented by furnishers and borrowers alike. Some alternative data points, on the other hand, are neither well documented nor well understood by consumers, making it difficult to know

---

97 Board of Governors of the Federal Reserve System et al., "Interagency Statement on the Use of Alternative Data in Credit Underwriting", 3 December 2019, https://files.consumerfinance.gov/ f/documents/cfpb_interagency-statement_alternative-data.pdf (last accessed 22 January 2021).
98 Request for information (fn. 64), p. 16.
99 Request for information (fn. 64), p. 17.
100 Request for information (fn. 64), p. 17.
101 15 U.S.C. § 1681i(a)(1)(A).

when and how to exercise their FCRA/GDPR rights to access, challenge, and correct inaccurate information. Depending on the number of variables that factor into a model, the sheer number of data points could make the exercise of those rights impracticable. Furthermore, it may be difficult under the FCRA for furnishers to determine whether information they have provided is 'negative' and therefore requires notice to be sent to the consumer. This determination is straightforward for the traditional FICO factors, all of which have a binary set of outcomes: on-time payments are good and late payments are bad, lower credit usage is good and higher usage is bad, etc. Furnishers can easily understand these dichotomies, but may have no way of knowing whether, for example, a consumer's choice to frequent certain websites or live in a particular zip code would have a positive or negative effect on that person's creditworthiness. This also impacts the "explainability" of their credit decisions. The CFPB points out that traditional scoring agencies have been transparent about most of the input they use and about how consumers may work on behavioral changes in order to better their score.[102] This is why the ECOA expects lenders to explain why they reached an adverse credit decision in specific terms which will be comprehensible to the applicant.[103] Safeguards such as these do not work as well when dealing with alternative data. Explainability presupposes precise understanding of the model, which is not necessarily a given when black-box algorithms are used. Some FinTech lenders, such as, for instance, Underwrite.ai,[104] have started to address this issue by trying to ensure that their models' decisions come with explanations that correspond to the categories of explanation that have traditionally been given to denied applicants.[105]

If the accuracy concerns identified by the CFPB have discriminatory potential, they are often addressed as "biased AI."[106] A correlation the algorithm de-

---

102 Request for information (fn. 64), p. 17.

103 15 U.S.C. § 1691(d)(1).

104 Underwrite.ai also uses machine learning to generate scores, but relies only on data of past cured loans, Underwrite.ai, About Us, https://www.underwrite.ai/about (last accessed 22 January 2021).

105 Underwrite.ai, Frequently Asked Questions, https://www.underwrite.ai/faq (claiming that their model can explain exactly why it reached a lending decision in a way that its fully FCRA-compliant) (last accessed 22 January 2021).

106 *Karen Hao*, "This is how AI bias really happens—and why it's so hard to fix", MIT Technology Review (4 February 2019), https://www.technologyreview.com/2019/02/04/137602/this-is-how-ai-bias-really-happensand-why-its-so-hard-to-fix/ (Explaining that AI is biased because models are programmed "for various business reasons other than fairness or discrimination," datasets are "unrepresentative of reality[...] or reflect[...] existing prejudices," and bias may be

tects may be rooted in historical (discriminatory) data which no longer represents today's reality.[107] When this happens, the score the algorithm computes is based on an outdated legal restriction or threshold. If this restriction or threshold no longer reflects today's world, it rules out borrowers who may in fact have an attractive risk profile.

An example for quality concerns due to biased AI are gender discrimination claims. In many countries, the law required a husband's signature for his wife to take out a loan. If a woman was unmarried, even if her income was secured, this would have lowered her score. An AI trained on historical data would have "learned" that being married is "better" than being unmarried. Once the law changes, the AI not only discriminates against unmarried women, but also turns away potentially good customers, thus raising a further-reaching quality issue.

Against this background it is worth noting that in its Whitepaper on AI, the EU Commission envisages "obligations to use data sets that are sufficiently representative."[108] The Proposal on an AI Act includes more detailed provisions on data quality management.[109] However, while some such data quality issues may be easily recognized and fixed by re-training the AI, historically biased data of this type is often hidden and detected only by chance – or not at all.

4.2.2 Quality of the Model

A related but distinct problem arises when the underlying data is bias-free but the software itself suffers inadequacies that disproportionately affect certain groups. A much-cited example concerns researchers at MIT finding that Amazon's facial recognition software had more difficulty identifying the gender of female and darker-skinned faces.[110] Another example is provided by an algorithm used by a health insurance company. The model assigned risk scores on the

---

introduced "during the data preparation stage" when variables are selected.") (last accessed 22 January 2021).

107 *See, e.g., Alexander D'Amour et al.,* "Underspecification Presents Challenges for Credibility in Modern Machine Learning" (2020), at https://arxiv.org/abs/2011.03395 (last accessed 22 January 2021) (expressing concern that machine learning systems like national language processors rely on "shortcuts that reinforce societal biases around protected attributes such as gender.").

108 White Paper (fn. 30), p. 19, also on record-keeping.

109 See Art. 10.

110 *James Vincent,* "Gender and racial bias found in Amazon's facial recognition technology (again)", The Verge (25 January 2019), https://www.theverge.com/2019/1/25/18197137/amazon-re kognition-facial-recognition-bias-race-gender (last accessed 22 January 2021).

basis of total health-care costs per year, not taking into account that – statistically – black people went to see a doctor later than white people. This resulted in them having to be sicker before being referred to additional help. The "faulty" variable was found by mere chance, when the health insurance let a university use its data for research purposes.[111] Hence, to fully address bias, lenders utilizing AI should be aware that discriminatory decision-making may arise from biased data,[112] biased software, and the interaction between the two.

Models which rely on variables which have to do with the behavior of a borrower raise further concerns. Traditional scores address behavior which is subject to change, such as the number of credit cards used or the paying back of a loan in time. By contrast, some of the scoring agencies working with alternative data focus on behavioral clues to the borrower's personality. These agencies may often lack any interest in consumers changing the relevant behavior. If these companies rely heavily on non-traditional data such as friends on social networks,[113] fonts used in text messages[114] or performance in fitness tracking apps,[115] they may prefer that the correlations discovered between those alternative data points and credit risk retain their predictive power.

The German FinTech Kreditech provides an illustration. The company had found a strong correlation between a specific font found on electronic devices of applicants for a loan and probability of repayment. Borrowers with the specific font on their device presented a high-risk group. Kreditech has speculated that the reason for this statistical correlation is that online gambling sites use the same font.[116] Finding the font in text messages is a statistical clue that this person may engage in online gambling, which lowers their statistical probability of repaying a loan on time. An obvious data quality issue emerges: not everybody using the font will be an online gambler, and not every online gambler presents

---

111 See *Ziad Obermeyer/Brian Powers/Christine Vogeli/Sendhil Mullainathan*, "Dissecting racial bias in an algorithm used to manage the health of populations", Science 2019, 447.

112 See, e. g., *Philipp Hacker*, "A Legal Framework for AI Training Data", 13 Law, Innovation & Technology (forthcoming 2021) (discussing various ways bias can distort the data used to train AI models, and therefore the models themselves).

113 Report Sachverständigenrat für Verbraucherfragen (SVRV), Consumer-friendly scoring, p. 52, available at: https://www.svr-verbraucherfragen.de/wp-content/uploads/Report.pdf (last accessed 22 January 2021).

114 Ibid., p. 62.

115 Ibid., p. 101 et seq.

116 Id., p. 62; referencing *Karsten Seibel*, "Gegen Kreditech ist die Schufa ein Schuljunge", WELT, https://www.welt.de/finanzen/verbraucher/article139671014/Gegen-Kreditech-ist-die-Schufa-ein-Schuljunge.html (last accessed 22 January 2021).

a bad credit risk.[117] Let us further assume the consumer learns that his credit assessment is based (among other things) on the font he uses. He now ceases use of this font on his devices, while his online gambling habits remain the same. Because the algorithm has lost the statistical indicator, it will become less precise. Companies using non-traditional data may therefore have an incentive to not be transparent about such indicators and their relation to consumer behavioral traits. Revealing this information would open up their models to the challenge of "gaming the system."[118] The consumer changes the font but goes ahead with his gambling habit. The statistical clue is then open to manipulation, raising yet another quality issue. The same story could not be told for traditional scoring bureaus, which rely on financial indicators that can only be 'manipulated' by actually improving one's capacity for repayment. These traditional scoring models are not interested in withholding information on how consumers may better their FICO score because traditional data are not used as statistical clues, pointing towards more hidden behavioral traits, in the way the text message font pointed towards an online gambling habit.

Looking beyond the world of heavily regulated and supervised financial institutions, AI scoring also raises issues in the context of other, more predatory lending models. We have so far assumed that the AI models used are trained to "assess creditworthiness." However, this is an oversimplification. Models are used by a scorer/lender with a specific business model in mind. The lender might train his model to detect a borrower with a high likelihood of paying back a long-term loan with market interest rates. However, he might also train his model to detect borrowers who seem likely to default in the long run but show a high probability of performance over the first couple of months—perhaps at very high interest rates. In the words of the CFPB, these consumers are "more likely" to default, but this does not rule out a business model under which they may be attractive customers. Payday loan companies, for example, issue small

---

117 Perhaps unsurprisingly, Kreditech is insolvent, as well as its successor "monedo": *Caspar Tobias Schlenk*, Kreditech-Nachfolger: Die Hintergründe der Monedo-Insolvenz, Finance Forward, 8 September 2020, https://financefwd.com/de/monedo-insolvenz/ (last accessed 22 January 2021).

118 Strandburg and Cofone assert that disclosing the methodology of a decision-making algorithm such that its subjects can game the system is socially desirable "when the potential for socially undesirable gaming is low," and that algorithm creators may act strategically in deciding whether and what to disclose to consumers, *Ignacio Cofone/Catherine Strandburg*, "Strategic Games and Algorithmic Transparency" (Working Paper) p. 3, available at https://www.law.nyu.edu/sites/default/files/Strategic%20Games%20and%20Algorithmic%20Transparency.pdf (last accessed 30 January 2021).

loans (usually $500 or less) to be repaid in a single payment on the borrower's next payday. Payday lenders often do not consider an applicant's ability to repay, but charge fees of $10 to $30 per $100 borrowed (for reference, a $15 fee per $100 borrowed is the equivalent of a 400% annual interest rate).[119] Though traditional FICO scores don't serve the payday lending model well, such lenders could employ AI scoring models to identify those likely to make the single lump-sum repayment on payday.

5 Conclusion

Upstart's business model and the CFPB's no-action letter have served as a useful illustration of problems in applying the traditional regulatory frameworks for credit scoring and data privacy to AI-based scoring. Despite the promise to offer more attractive credit options to traditionally underserved borrowers, alternative scoring models give rise to important risks. Some of these seem somewhat technical, but are no less salient. Such issues concern the quality of data and models used in algorithm-based credit scoring as well as the applicability of procedural safeguards such as access to data, the right to rectification of errors and to contradict the use of data, and the efficient enforcement of rights. The complex question of how to apply anti-discrimination laws shows the pitfalls of alternative scoring that aspires to create more fair lending.

Other risks are less technical. They have to do with the fairness of scoring as such.[120] What makes a scoring model "fair" is the subject of ongoing debate, and traditional scoring models also implicate fairness concerns. That said, the "unfair" label would certainly apply to models that violate the ECOA's antidiscrimination provisions, and because AI models may create more overlap between variables that predict likelihood to repay and variables correlated with membership in protected classes, those models may well raise questions of fairness. The CFPB's Request for Information on alternative credit scoring touches upon the matter very briefly when it claims that "using some alternative data, especially data about a trait or attribute that is beyond a consumer's control to change, even if not illegal to use, could harden barriers to economic and social mobility, particularly for those currently out of the financial mainstream."[121] Let us be re-

---

119 Consumer Financial Protection Bureau, What is a payday loan?, (2 June 2017), https://www.consumerfinance.gov/ask-cfpb/what-is-a-payday-loan-en-1567/ (last accessed 22 January 2021).
120 On the concept of "fair" scoring and on remedies and sanctions see in more detail *Langenbucher* (fn. 46), p. 527 et seq, p. 565 et seq.
121 Request for information (fn. 64), p. 18.

minded, again, that traditional credit scoring exercises have held the same potential. The underserved borrowers, those with a "thin file" who may be ineligible for traditional scores, have faced barriers to economic and social mobility for a long time. Despite its promise to serve the unbanked, AI-based scoring may well deepen this problem.

One reason for this is the opaqueness of behaviorally oriented models such as the gambling site font example set forth above. While traditional scoring models rely on variables which are open to behavioral change, such as, for instance, reducing late payment on bills, AI models that use the correlation between probability of repayment and a certain behavior may provide fewer opportunities for such change because borrowers may remain unaware of which variables influenced their credit decision, and to what degree. Lenders/scorers are not interested in disclosing the use of these variables because they wish to disallow "gaming the system." In many instances, depending on the complexity of the AI or the efforts of the lender/scorer, the scorer might not even be aware of the impact of such variables in their model.

Another reason AI scoring might deepen disparities in access to credit is the seductive allure of AI modeling which the EU has referred to as "automation bias." Many have praised machine learning for its potential to detect previously unanticipated correlations and to replace human bias when making a loan decision, relying on the "objectivity" of machines.[122] Even if just as many others have pointed to flaws in that reasoning,[123] psychological research teaches us that it can be very appealing to outsource responsibility for decision-making. In other words, when responsibility for a decision can be shared with or transferred to another person (or to a decision-making computer program), the individual sharing responsibility is less likely to work to remedy the issue than if they bore full responsibility.[124] Linking this to the quality problems of data and models, we risk overstating what an algorithm can deliver.

---

122 *Cass R. Sunstein*, "Algorithms, Correcting Biases", 86 Social Research 2019, 499, 504 (Finding that, "for purposes of law and policy, some of the most important empirical research finds" that algorithms are unbiased, and that "well-designed algorithms should be able to avoid cognitive biases of many kinds.").

123 *Barocas/Selbst* (fn. 78), 678; *Talia B. Gillis/Jann L. Spiess*, "Big Data and Discrimination", 86 University of Chicago Law Review 2019, pp. 459, 475.

124 *Frederike Beyer/Nura Sidarus/Sofia Bonicalzi/Patrick Haggard*, "Beyond self-serving bias: diffusion of responsibility reduces sense of agency and outcome monitoring", 12 Social Cognitive Affective Neuroscience 2017, PP. 138, 144 (concluding that the presence of other actors reduces one's sense of responsibility in remedying a problem).

This is also where the Bureau's assessment, that "in the longer term consumers whose credit scores understate their true risk may be better served if they do not obtain additional credit that they cannot repay," risks missing the point. "Understating risk" requires the modeler to define risk and to determine what the model will understand as "success."[125] It depends, as we have seen, on the quality of the data and the model, both in a narrow sense of the care with which the data/model have been sourced/developed, but also in a broader sense of biases inherent to the data or model. On the one hand, these circumstances hold a real risk of creating a new group of underserved borrowers, again ossifying existing inequalities. On the other hand, overly liberal expansion of credit to different groups could result in a crisis of indebtedness at a social scale. Effective regulation may play an important role in steering FinTech lenders clear of these extremes.

The most intricate problem linked to the fairness of scoring arises even if we assume an ideal world in which all data could be de-biased and lenders could efficiently screen all models for discriminatory effects. Linking credit outcomes to behavioral traits increases the risk that a model will reproduce and even worsen deeply embedded social biases and inequalities. Not only one's ZIP code or payment history, which are – at least in theory – subject to change, but also one's hobbies or friends, taste in restaurants or shopping habits, efficiency in filling out a web form, model of smartphone or amount of spelling mistakes, age or health might be considered predictive of success. Graduating from a HBCU could hurt an applicant's chances if compared to graduating from a non-minority-serving institution, as could a preference for budget supermarkets as opposed to more expensive organic grocers, using an Apple instead of an Android smartphone,[126] going online during the day or at night, using price comparison websites or not,[127] and the list goes on. A lack of disclosure and explainability undermine the applicant's opportunities to learn from a credit decision and adapt their

---

125 *Cathy O'Neill*, Weapons of Math Destruction, 2016, p. 21 et seqq.

126 See *Marianne Bertrand/Emir Kamenica*, "Coming Apart? Cultural Distances in the United States Over Time", National Bureau of Economic Research, Working Paper No. 24771, 2018 (showing research relating brand of phone owned with income).

127 See *Tobias Berg/Valentin Burg/Ana Gombović/Manju Puri*, "On the Rise of FinTechs—Credit Scoring Using Digital Footprints", Michael J. Brennan Irish Finance Working Paper Series, Paper No. 18–12, 2019 ("For example, customers coming from a price comparison website are almost half as likely to default as customers being directed to the website by search engine ads", p. 3).

behavior accordingly. ECOA's central tenet, to offer equal credit opportunities, seems severely compromised in such circumstances.[128]

6 Post Scriptum: AI Credit Scoring under the EU Proposal for an AI Act

The European Commission has on 21st April 2021 published a Proposal for a Regulation to lay down harmonized rules on artificial intelligence. Once passed, a Regulation is binding law in every Member State. In contrast to a Directive, it is directly applicable without the need to be transposed, Art. 288 para. 2 TFEU. However, this pan-European scope is not the only reason for a closer look at the Proposal. Its rules will apply to providers of AI systems within the EU as well as in third countries such as the United States. It will cover users of AI systems in third countries if the output they produce is used in the EU. Most importantly, the Proposal aims to shape global norms and standards. Given a trend called the "Brussels effect,"[129] an observation on how multinational companies have progressively adopted European standards on, for instance, data privacy, consumer safety, and antitrust, the claim to contribute once again in this fashion might not be entirely without merit and companies may well follow suit on AI regulation as well.

The Proposal should be understood against the context of a number of previous studies and official documents, such as the report of the High-Level Expert Group on AI on "Ethics Guidelines for Trustworthy AI" which we mentioned above. Additionally, in February 2020 the EU Commission published the White Paper on AI, accompanied by a Report on safety and liability implications. The European Parliament adopted resolutions on civil liability for AI, on an ethical framework for AI, and on related issues of intellectual property. Next steps for the Proposal to become law include first and second readings by the co-legislating bodies, the European Parliament and the Council, internal debates in Member States' national parliaments, and European and global lobbying efforts.

The Proposal starts from the assumption that several fundamental principles and standards apply horizontally across all AI use cases. Among these use cases, the Proposal singles out unacceptable and high-risk applications. Unacceptable

---

128 Once again, thoughts on potential solutions and preferable approaches to regulatory governance in this area are reserved for future papers. See also *Langenbucher* (fn. 46), 527 et seq, 565 et seq.

129 *Anu Bradford*, The Brussels Effect: How the European Union Rules the World, 2020.

use cases will be prohibited. For high-risk applications, the Proposal prescribes a variety of requirements of *ex ante* testing, certification, technical documentation, and monitoring, as well as *ex post* controls. By contrast, the Proposal explicitly encourages AI applications which qualify as neither unacceptable nor high-risk, posing only low or minimal risk. For these uses, the Proposal seeks to ensure an attractive environment for investment by combining legal certainty with effective enforcement and allowing for regulatory sandboxes while preventing market fragmentation.

6.1 A Risk-Based Approach

The drafters of the Proposal chose what they call a "risk-based approach." They frame this approach as the best answer to the tension between "promoting the uptake of AI and of addressing the risks associated with certain uses of such technology." According to the Proposal, risks are unacceptable, if they are "manipulative, exploitative and social control practices." Such risks "contradict Union values" and will be prohibited. Against this background, Art. 5 para. 1 of the Proposal lists AI practices which qualify as unacceptable. Among these we find the use of biometric identification systems in publicly accessible spaces for the purpose of law enforcement. The same goes for some cases of social scoring by public authorities, as set forth in Art. 5 para. 1 lit. c of the Proposal.

While few AI use cases are considered unacceptable and prohibited, the list of high-risk applications is longer. One Annex to the Proposal enumerates products for which Union legislation as to safety precautions is already in place, covering products as diverse as toys, explosives, medical devices, and civil aviation. AI systems which are used as safety components in such products will be considered high-risk. A second Annex to the Proposal lists areas of use, rather than products. These include biometric identification, operation of critical infrastructure, employment, access to essential private services, law enforcement, migration and administration of justice.

AI systems that "evaluate the creditworthiness of natural persons or establish their credit score" are listed as one instance of access to "essential private services." Interestingly, neither the High Level Expert Report nor the White Paper had taken up decisions about creditworthiness. The policy reasons for including AI scoring in the Proposal surface in Recital (37). Starting from the fundamental role of access to financial resources, the Proposal stresses the much-debated risks of AI scoring. These include "discrimination of persons or groups," dangers that these applications may "perpetuate historical patterns of discrimination, for example based on racial or ethnic origins, disabilities, age, sexual orientation," and the creation of "new forms of discriminatory impacts." Of course, the EU, like the United States, possesses a large body of law which prohibits discrimination – and in both jurisdictions, courts and scholars have been grappling with the challenges raised by the "new forms of discriminatory impacts" which the Proposal cites. Still, the document does not explicitly take up questions of algorithmic fairness, historic bias or discrimination as such. Instead, its approach brings product design to mind: certification procedures, data and model quality checks, technical documentation and *ex post* monitoring duties abound. Public authorities supervise, but private enforcement instruments are not included. This fundamental tension between the anti-discriminatory policy goal and the product-oriented, formalistic regulatory design shapes the Proposal.

6.2 Applying the EU Proposal to Algorithmic Credit Scoring

6.2.1 How to Distinguish High-Risk Credit Scoring from Prohibited Social Scoring

Algorithmic scoring has raised enormous concerns globally insofar as it is used for surveillance of private citizens, a practice usually addressed as "social scoring." The Proposal defines specific forms of social scoring which would be prohibited in the EU. These are:

"AI systems (placed on the market put into service or used) by public authorities or on their behalf for the evaluation or classification of the trustworthiness of natural persons over a certain period of time based on their social behaviour or known or predicted personal or personality characteristics, with the social score leading to either or both of the following:

(i) detrimental or unfavourable treatment of certain natural persons or whole groups thereof in social contexts which are unrelated to the contexts in which the data was originally generated or collected;

(ii) Detrimental or unfavourable treatment of certain natural persons or whole groups thereof that is unjustified or disproportionate to their social behaviour or its gravity;[130]

---

130 Art. 5.

Under this definition, AI credit scoring done by private entities does not qualify, unless performed on the behalf of a public authority. To the extent that public authorities engage in any form of credit scoring, application of the provision hinges on what "trustworthiness" entails. The Proposal does not offer a definition nor explains how "trustworthiness" differs from "creditworthiness." Recital (17), which sets out the policy goal for the prohibition, talks about "social scoring of natural persons for general purpose" and of "detrimental or unfavourable treatment of natural persons or whole groups thereof in social contexts." While it seems intuitive to understand creditworthiness as a sub-category of the more general term "trustworthiness," the Proposal seems to have a different, namely a "social" context in mind. Arguably, future work on the Proposal would profit from a brighter line between trustworthiness and creditworthiness, and between extending credit and "treatment (...) in social contexts" as listed above under (ii). Should these provisions apply to AI credit scoring, the use of alternative data like that posited above to generate credit scores could be found to constitute the use of data in contexts "unrelated to the contexts in which the data was originally generated or collected."

6.2.2 How to Ensure Compliance with the Proposal

Leaving public authorities (or work done on their behalf) aside, AI models intended for creditworthiness assessments and credit scoring qualify as high-risk, Art. 6 para. 2, Nr. 5 b Annex III. AI use cases which qualify as high-risk have to comply with the Proposal's risk and quality management framework. The Proposal follows an omnibus approach across all areas of AI applications, including medical, law enforcement, machinery and credit scoring.

This horizontal, omnibus approach differs markedly from the U.S. regulatory framework we have outlined above, which works with application area-focused legal rules such as, for instance, the ECOA, the FCRA, and the HUD. While the Proposal's approach offers legal security across different use cases, its requirements must be tailored to a variety of AI applications. The Proposal somewhat vaguely suggests doing so with the "intended purpose of the high-risk AI system and the risk management system" in mind.[131]

---

131 Art. 8 para. 2.

6.2.2.1 Risk Management and Quality Management Systems

An adequate risk management system is one of the core pillars of the Proposal. Such a system "shall consist of a continuous iterative process run throughout the entire lifecycle of a high-risk AI system, requiring regular systematic updating." Risks have to be identified and analyzed, estimated and evaluated.[132] Risk management concerns "known and foreseeable risks" as well as "risks that may emerge when the high-risk AI system is used in accordance with its intended purpose and under conditions of reasonably foreseeable misuse."[133] A post-marketing system is added,[134] and residual risks have to be "judged acceptable" and "shall be communicated to the user."

The need to adapt these general, omnibus requirements to the specifics of AI scoring systems surfaces clearly. "Risk" will come in very different shapes and forms across different AI use cases. As to AI scoring and creditworthiness assessments, the Proposal seems to understand "risk" as related to fundamental rights, and, more specifically, to discriminatory outcomes. However, "risk" is as vague a term as "fundamental rights" or "non-discrimination." How to apply non-discrimination doctrine to AI scoring is as hotly debated in the EU as in the U.S. Some of the relevant concerns that this ambiguity creates have surfaced in our discussion of the Upstart case. The decision to go ahead with this approach illustrates the built-in tension and the ambitiousness of the decision to use a formal, product-oriented regulatory design in order to realize substantive goals such as non-discrimination.

In addition to a risk management system, the Proposal requires "providers," the developers of AI systems, to ensure that compliance and quality management systems are in place,[135] Art. 16, 17, and that conformity assessments are undergone. Written documentation of the quality management system is expected, including, for instance, a strategy for regulatory compliance, test and validation procedures, procedures for data management, for post-market monitoring and for communication with national competent supervisory authorities, as well as an accountability framework setting out the responsibilities of management and staff. If the provider is a credit institution regulated by Directive 2013/36/EU ("CRD IV"), the obligation to put a quality management system in place is deemed to be fulfilled by complying with Art. 74 of CRD IV. Post-market monitoring is required of any provider under Art. 61, and is thus not limited to high-risk

---

132 Art. 9 para. 2 (a), (b).
133 Ibid. para. 2 (b).
134 Art. 9 para. 2 (d), Art. 61.
135 Art. 16, 17.

systems. However, Art. 62 provides that only high-risk providers have an obligation to report malfunctions to market surveillance authorities.

6.2.2.2 Data and Data Governance

Data and data governance are a core ingredient of AI scoring applications. Art. 10 of the Proposal lays down quality criteria for training, validating and testing with data sets. These concern design choices, data collection and preparation, the formulation of assumptions, examination of biases, the identification of gaps and more.

Data sets must be "relevant, representative, free of errors and complete" and have "appropriate statistical properties."[136] Again, the terms used are vague and need further interpretation. A data set will probably never be "free of errors" nor "complete." The relevance of data is often in the eye of the beholder, and it would be useful to further specify what may count as "representative."

A conscious choice has been made as to bias monitoring. While the extent to which one may use protected categories of data such a "race" in order to uncover bias is subject to debate under the U.S. framework. By contrast, the Proposal allows processing of such data if it "is strictly necessary for the purpose of ensuring bias monitoring, detection and correction."

6.2.2.3 Technical Documentation and Record-keeping, Accuracy, Robustness, and Cybersecurity

A number of requirements concern technical documentation, record keeping and conformity assessments. Technical documentation must be drawn up *ex ante*, and kept up to date. Logs for the automated recording of events have to be installed,[137] and kept by the providers.[138] Additionally, high-risk systems have to achieve an appropriate level of accuracy, robustness, and cybersecurity.[139] Machine learning applications, a standard feature of many AI scoring systems, have to address feedback loops which the Proposal defines as "possibly biased outputs due to outputs used as input for future operations."[140]

---

136 Art. 10 para. 3.
137 Art. 11, 12.
138 Art. 20.
139 Art. 15.
140 Art. 15 para. 3.

Art. 16, under the heading of "obligations of providers," lists these as well as other requirements specified in the Proposal. The Proposal does not address whether this is to be understood as an obligation giving rise to a private right of action, leaving the matter to the national law of the Member States. If the provider is established outside the Union and an importer cannot be established, the third country provider must establish an authorized representative.[141]

6.2.2.4 Transparency and Information

Seen from a U.S. perspective, informing retail borrowers about the data used for scoring, explaining basic workings of the scoring model and allowing for rectification constitute core elements of credit scoring regulation. By contrast, in the EU not only credit scoring regulation as such but also the institutional set-up of relevant scoring institutions differs between Member States. Taking this together with the EU GDPR providing for a reasonable degree of data protection (including rectification and some explainability), it is maybe unsurprising that there are no provisions in the Proposal on how to inform a borrower.

Importantly, transparency and the provision of information to "users," which Art. 13 requires, is not about informing borrowers. "Users," as defined in Art. 3 para. 4, means "any natural or legal person, public authority, agency or other body using an AI system under its authority." The end consumer (or "end borrower") is not herself "using" the AI system. She is rather, as it were, its object. Obligations towards this group of end consumers are limited to a number of specific instances such as, for example, emotion recognition, biometric categorization, or systems creating deep fakes.[142]

The "users" toward whom the AI system must be transparent are those who employ the system in their own business. This could be a lender, who uses an AI system for its own rating of borrowers. It could also be a scoring agency using AI systems as part of its scoring process. These users of AI systems are the beneficiaries of the duties of disclosure which the Proposal imposes on providers. Providers must furnish information on, among other things, the intended purpose of the AI system, the level of accuracy, potential risks for fundamental rights, the expected lifetime of the system and human oversight measures.

---

141 Art. 25.
142 Art. 52.

Users of high-risk systems have to comply with the instructions of use which includes certain monitoring instructions. Logs must be kept, if these are under the control of the user (not the provider).[143]

6.2.2.5 Human Oversight

The Proposal requires that high-risk AI systems feature an element of human oversight. Art. 14 explicitly mentions risks to fundamental rights, which have caused growing concern in AI scoring systems, and assumes that human oversight can prevent or minimize these risks.[144] Human oversight is to serve a monitoring function, allowing for detection of "dysfunctions and unexpected performance."[145] This section also addresses "automation bias,"[146] and requires that AI-based decision making systems leave open the possibility of foregoing use of the AI application in a particular case.[147]

6.2.3 Enforcement

The Proposal relies heavily on public enforcement of its regulations. Member States have to designate a notifying authority to carry out the conformity assessments required by Art. 30 of the Proposal, and to issue certificates of compliance under Art. 44. The Proposal stresses that these bodies must be competent, independent, objective and impartial.[148] Art. 48 requires that providers draw up declarations of conformity for AI systems they put on the market. The product-design framework of the Proposal is especially obvious in Art. 48 and 49, which address an EU declaration and a CE marking of conformity.[149] Art. 71 sets forth a framework for administrative sanctions including fines and penalties for non-compliance.

---

143 Art. 29 para. 5.
144 Art. 14 para. 2.
145 Art. 14 para. 4 (a).
146 Art. 14 para. 4 (b).
147 Art. 14 para. 4 (d).
148 Art. 33 para. 5.
149 The "CE" mark indicates that products traded in the European Economic Area meet the EU's safety, health, and environmental protection standards. European Commission, "CE marking" https://ec.europa.eu/growth/single-market/ce-marking_en (last accessed 5 August 2021).

National supervisory authorities are in charge of market surveillance.[150] An exception from the omnibus approach is made for financial institutions. If the AI system is used or placed on the market by a financial institution, the relevant financial supervisory authority is competent to regulate the system's use, mirroring the jurisdiction of specialized bodies such as the CFTC and the FTC in the United States.

The intent to allow for and support innovation is behind the regulatory sandbox regime established in Art. 53. Competent authorities are encouraged to establish controlled environments which facilitate the development and testing of new AI systems. Art. 54 grants exemptions from the GDPR's prohibition of data processing in these cases. Small-scale providers and start-ups get priority access to sandboxes under Art. 55.

6.3 Conclusion

By issuing Upstart its no-action letter, the CFPB acknowledged that the commercial lending industry, like many other fields, may be imminently and fundamentally changed by the introduction of artificial intelligence and machine learning technologies. These technologies hold legitimate promise for extending credit opportunities to those excluded by traditional credit scoring methodologies, but their complex, data-driven nature necessarily creates difficulties in the application of regulations attuned to more traditional methods of credit scoring. The data and algorithms used by FinTech lenders may replicate discriminatory outcomes. The complexity of AI models may limit the modeler's ability to anticipate and account for unintended disparate outcomes as well as the applicant's capacity to understand adverse decisions. A combination of updated regulations and careful use of AI by these lenders may go far in addressing these issues. However, CFPB's ready acceptance of Upstart's model—which relies heavily on education level, a variable with particularly great potential to introduce bias—raises questions of whether the regulatory environment is prepared for AI credit scoring to eventually permeate consumer lending practices. Time will tell whether more ambitious AI scoring methods, such as those relying on novel cell phone and search history data, gain sufficient prominence to warrant targeted changes to the regulatory frameworks in the United States.

The EU Proposal for an AI Act has ventured a first step in providing a regulatory framework specific to AI applications. The Proposal highlights the perils of

---

150 Art. 63.

bias and discrimination, and its risk-based approach takes up core quality and risk management issues. Needless to say, these will have to be adapted to the specifics of each AI application. Due to the omnibus approach underlying the Proposal, there is almost no guidance as to how different use cases (ranging from civil aviation to medical devices and credit scoring) would be treated. More importantly, there is a fundamental tension between the Proposal's policy goal to protect fundamental human rights and its risk-based philosophy. For financial institutions, the possibility to measure and evaluate risk with an eye on capital adequacy requirements is crucial. Translating the relative weights of conflicting human rights principles into computable variables of risk management is a daunting task. It remains to be seen whether, in its final form, the Proposal will include more concrete rules on risk and quality management.

Iris H-Y Chiu

Building a Single Market for Sustainable Finance in the EU-Mixed Implications and the Missing Link of Digitalisation

Abstract: This article critically analyses the EU's sustainable finance reforms and argues that the interaction between its regulative and enabling aspects creates mixed messages for governance and market-building. The Regulations adopt an incentive-based approach towards market-building for quality sustainable finance, but lower-level products are not shut out. However, if the market responds to quality signals facilitated by regulatory reforms, the article predicts that market-building may be concentrated in passively-managed indexed products which appeal to retail investors. This market may be dominated by large investment intermediaries who may gain an advantage precisely because of more stringent governance imposed on them. The article further argues that retail investors can be helped by policy bridging between sustainable and digital finance, such as adjustments to the legal duty of suitability to cater for investment advice incorporating sustainability preferences, including robo-advisory channels. The connection between digital and sustainable finance can be highly synergistic in attracting both institutional and retail demand.

Table of Contents

Iris H-Y Chiu, Professor of Corporate Law and Financial Regulation, University College London. Email: hse-yu.chiu@ucl.ac.uk. I am grateful to Emilios Avgouleas, Iain MacNeil and Eva Micheler for comments and questions on the presentation of this paper at the EU Digital Capital Markets webinar, 2 September 2020, and comments from Parker Hood at the Edinburgh Centre for Commercial Law seminar, 11 November 2020. All errors and omissions are mine.

∂ OpenAccess. © 2022 Iris H-Y Chiu, published by De Gruyter. [CC] BY-NC-ND This work is licensed under the Creative Commons Attribution-NonCommercial-NoDerivatives 4.0 International License.
https://doi.org/10.1515/9783110749472-007

1 Introduction

Since the European Commission adopted an action plan for promoting sustainable finance in 2018,[1] legislative reform has been introduced for market building in sustainable finance products as well as to harmonise the regulative standards for them.[2] Regulation is intended to mobilise the mainstream investment fund sector to develop and provide choice in their offers of sustainable financial products, hence it can be regarded as enabling in nature. Harmonised European regulation also provides for sufficiently high-quality regulative and protective standards so that market development is carried out in a manner that inspires market confidence. This is consistent with the ordoliberal underpinnings[3] of single market regulatory measures in the financial sector. This article examines the Regulation on sustainability disclosures required of the financial services sector[4] and the Taxonomy Regulation[5] in their roles to make sustainable finance products widely marketised by the mainstream investment funds sector. It also queries how digitalisation in the EU, which is keenly promoted under the Digital Single Market strategy,[6] can further the marketization agenda that is promoted by the Regulations. Indeed the article argues that policy thinking on promoting and marketising sustainable finance has not plugged into the potential offered by digitalising finance.

Section 2 discusses the EU reforms to mobilise and regulate mainstream sustainable finance particularly in collective investments and portfolio management. This Section examines the finely balanced nature of the EU's governance of sustainable finance as its enabling and regulative elements interact. It is argued that the net result may send mixed messages to the market, which may

---

1 *EU High Level Expert Group in Sustainable Finance*, Financing a Sustainable European Economy, 2018, https://ec.europa.eu/info/sites/info/files/180131-sustainable-finance-final-report_en.pdf.
2 sect 2.
3 See *Josef Hien/Christian Joerges*, Ordoliberalism, Law and the Rule of Economics, 2017.
4 Regulation (EU) 2019/2088 of the European Parliament and of the Council of 27 November 2019 on sustainability-related disclosures in the financial services sector (Sustainability Disclosures Regulation 2019).
5 Regulation (EU) 2020/852 of the European Parliament and of the Council of 18 June 2020 on the establishment of a framework to facilitate sustainable investment, and amending Regulation (EU) 2019/2088 (Taxonomy Regulation 2020).
6 *European Commission*, Communication from the Commission to the European Parliament, the Council, the European Economic and Social Committee and the Committee of the Regions on the Mid-Term Review on the implementation of the Digital Single Market Strategy: A Connected Digital Single Market for All, 2017, SWD(2017) 155 final.

not lead to significant development in product choice. The Section further contends that the marketization of sustainable finance should connect with digitalisation of finance in order to appeal more broadly to retail investors. Section 3 discusses reforms to the duty of suitability in investment advice that may be key to how digitalisation can be woven into the sustainable finance governance framework. Section 4 concludes.

2 Mainstreaming Sustainable Finance in the EU

The Sustainability Disclosures Regulation 2019,[7] supported by the Taxonomy Regulation 2020,[8] introduces a governance regime that elevates the standards of responsibility in the investment sector across many types of fund management, while at the same time facilitating the marketization of sustainable finance products. This type of governance is highly characteristic of EU regulation where enabling harmonised legislation intended for market building[9] is framed in relatively high regulative standards to support the building of credible and responsible markets. One perspective on this is the 'law and finance' thesis that laws with sufficiently high standards that provide for investor protection and confidence are needed to build out strong and developed capital markets.[10] The other perspective is that economic development is not pursued as a singular and disembodied goal independent from wider notions of solidarity and responsibility, especially after the global financial crisis 2007–09.[11] Policy makers in the EU are developing market-building measures in more holistic ways, such as taking into account financial stability and consumer protection risks.[12] The impetus for sustainable finance has only grown in the wake of the Covid-19 pan-

---

7 Sustainability Disclosures Regulation 2019.

8 Fn. 5.

9 For eg *Eilis Ferran*, Building an EU Securities Market, 2003 on critically discussing the role of regulatory harmonisation in market-building. The EU has always viewed the role of law as key to capital markets building, see *Nicolas Véron/Guntram B. Wolff*, "Capital Markets Union: A Vision for the Long Term" Journal of Financial Regulation, 2016, 2, 130.

10 *Rafael La Porta/Florencio Lopez-De-Silanes/Andrei Shleifer*, "What Works in Securities Law?" Journal of Finance, 2006, 61, 1.

11 *Niamh Moloney*, "EU Financial Market Regulation after the Global Financial Crisis: "More Europe" or more Risks?" Common Market Law Review, 2010, 47, 1317.

12 *Jacques de Larosière*, Report of the High Level Group on Financial Supervision in the EU, 2009, https://ec.europa.eu/economy_finance/publications/pages/publication14527_en.pdf.

demic.[13] The governance of sustainable finance in this round of regulatory reforms reflects a careful balancing of market-building goals with regulative goals to improve financial intermediaries' conduct at the marketing front, their gatekeeping roles in supporting the credibility of sustainable finance, and ultimately, the social and public interest outcomes that sustainable finance is supposed to fund.[14]

2.1 Policy Context for Mobilising Investment Intermediaries in Relation to Sustainable Risks

Although financial intermediaries are not often directly responsible for harms to sustainability or bringing about sustainable outcomes, such as those embodied in the 30 UN Sustainable Development Goals,[15] their channelling of funds makes projects and activities possible, turning financial intermediaries into facilitating or 'complicit' actors who incentivise or disincentivise projects and activities. At this level of gatekeeping, debt intermediaries such as banks in project finance have become keenly aware of their proximity[16] to the creation of environmental and social harms, and many of them have implemented the voluntary Equator principles to minimise their legal risk and ameliorate social irresponsibility.[17] However, even the proximity of creditor-borrower relationships may not bring about optimal management of sustainability risks at the level of the borrower.[18]

---

13 'ESG passes the Covid Challenge' (Financial Times, 1 June 2020), https://www.ft.com/content/50eb893d-98ae-4a8f-8fec-75aa1bb98a48.
14 This 'co-habitation' regulatory model involving the public and private sectors is discussed in *Nicholas Dorn*, "Capital Cohabitation: EU Capital Markets Union as Public and Private Co-regulation" Capital Markets Law Journal, 2016, 11, 84.
15 https://sustainabledevelopment.un.org/?menu=1300; *Jesse Griffiths*, "Financing the Sustainable Development Goals (SDGs)" Development, 2018, 61, 62; Alma Pekmezovic, The New Framework for Financing the 2030 Agenda for Sustainable Development and the SDGs in: *Julia Walker/Alma Pekmezovic/Gordon Walker* (eds), Sustainable Development Goals: Harnessing Business to Achieve the SDGs through Finance, Technology, and Law Reform, 2019, 87.
16 *Kirk Herbertson/ David Hunter*, "Emerging Standards for Sustainable Finance of the Energy Sector" Sustainable Dev. L. & Pol'y, 2007, 7, 4.
17 Many leading multinational and national banks are signatories of the Equator principles, see https://equator-principles.com/members-reporting/.
18 *Douglas Sarro*, "Do Lenders Make Effective Regulators? An Assessment of the Equator Principles on Project Finance" German Law Journal, 2012, 13, 1500 relating to lack of monitoring and governance, therefore making lender governance a procedural and superficial phenomenon that lenders can brand themselves by, also *Patrick Haack/Dennis Schoenborn/Christopher Wickert*, "Exploring the Constitutive Conditions for a Self-Energizing Effect of CSR Standards: The Case

Investment intermediaries who channel funds to enterprises, projects and activities are arguably 'in less control' of their gatekeeping capacities, as they are often diversified and minority shareholders. Further, there is not always congruence between (a) investment intermediaries' legal duties to manage portfolios in a financially optimal manner and (b) their goals relating to sustainable behaviour or outcomes on the parts of their investee companies.[19]

As the investment sector wields significant influence, with global assets under management growing year over year and estimated to amount to USD $145 trillion by 2025,[20] policy makers have started looking to the gatekeeping capacities of the investment sector, so that these intermediaries in capital markets can play a useful part in the governance landscape that aligns economic behaviour with sustainable goals.[21] There is also increased appetite on the part of both institutional[22] and retail beneficiaries[23] in the EU for investing in pension and other collective investment funds that would meet sustainable objectives as well as provide a financial return, although different investors may prefer different mixes of the two objectives if there is a trade-off.[24]

---

of the "Equator Principles"", 2010, University of Zurich Institute of Organization and Administrative Science IOU Working Paper No 115 http://papers.ssrn.com/sol3/papers.cfm?abstract_id=1706267.

19 In the UK see *Cowan v Scargill* [1985] Ch 270. But *UNEPFI, Fiduciary Duty in the 21st Century,* 2019, revised from 2009, has since clarified that ESG issues can be material to investment performance and it is not beyond the scope of fiduciary duties to take them into account, also *Sarah Barker/Mark Baker-Jones/Emilie Barton/Emma Fagan,* "Climate Change and the Fiduciary Duties of Pension Fund Trustees – Lessons from the Australian Law" Journal of Sustainable Finance & Investment, 2016, 6, 211 where fiduciary interpretation in common law traditions are less of a hindrance to integrating ESG considerations.

20 *PwC,* Asset & Wealth Management Revolution: Embracing Exponential Change, 2017, https://www.pwc.com/ng/en/press-room/global-assets-under-management-set-to-rise.html.

21 Fn. 14.

22 *Lei Delsen/Alex Lehr,* "Value Matters or Values Matter? An Analysis of Heterogeneity in Preferences for Sustainable Investments" Journal of Sustainable Finance & Investment, 2019, 9, 240; *George Apostolakis/Frido Kraanen/Gert van Dijk,* "Pension Beneficiaries' and Fund Managers' Perceptions of Responsible Investment: A Focus Group Study" Corporate Governance, 2016, 16, 1.

23 *Charlotte Christiansen/Thomas Jansson/Malene Kallestrup-Lamb/Vicke Noren,* "Who are the Socially Responsible Mutual Fund Investors?", 2019, http://ssrn.com/abstract=3128432 points out that prosocial investors are still the minority. *Bernhard Zwergel/Anett Wins/Christian Klein,* "On the Heterogeneity of Sustainable and Responsible Investors" Journal of Sustainable Finance & Investment, 2019, 9, 282.

24 *Apostolakis et al,* 2016; *Riikka Sievänen/Hannu Rita/Bert Scholtens,* "European Pension Funds and Sustainable Development: Trade-Offs between Finance and Responsibility" Business Strategy and the Environment, 2017, 26, 912.

The EU's sustainable finance strategy has therefore turned to capital markets regulation. One aspect of this policy movement is the nudging of institutional investors to become engaged shareholders in their investee companies. In the UK, this expected level of investor conduct is known as 'stewardship' and covers a range of shareholder engagement behaviour in relation to companies' corporate governance as well as their footprint in environmental, social and governance (ESG) matters.[25] In the EU, the Shareholders' Rights Directive 2017 introduced a comply-or-explain regime for institutional investors[26] in order to nudge[27] them towards more engaged behaviour and the overall promotion of the long-term interests of beneficiaries.[28] To support investors' engagement role, the EU has introduced concomitant regulations requiring[?] listed companies to make relevant 'non-financial disclosures' in relation to environmental impacts, impact on employees, human rights, and anti-corruptions matters.[29] Further, shareholders' powers have also been increased by harmonised legislation, such as shareholders' mandatory say on executive pay every four years,[30] and powers to approve related-party transactions in order to mitigate strong managerial powers.[31] Tridimas[32] argues that the 'shareholder' in the EU context is framed as a gatekeeper and facilitator of EU policy strategies in capital markets regulation for the Single capital market.

The group of shareholders to be galvanised are institutional investors, whether in pension, wealth or retail investment management. There are different incentives and structures at work that affect these intermediaries' behaviour when engaging with companies generally,[33] and targeted engagement on sustainability issues is only emerging in some European countries,[34] with the trend ob-

---

25 Principles 9 – 11, UK Stewardship Code, https://www.frc.org.uk/getattachment/5aae591d-d9d3-4cf4-814a-d14e156a1d87/Stewardship-Code_Dec-19-Final-Corrected.pdf.

26 Art 3 g.

27 *Marina Madsen* Behavioural Economics in European Corporate Governance: Much Ado about Nudging, European Business Law Review, 2021, 32, 295.

28 Arts 3 h and 3i.

29 Art 19a, enhanced by amendments in the Taxonomy Regulation 2020 to align environmental disclosures.

30 Article 9a and 9b.

31 Article 9c.

32 Keynote speech at Enforcing Shareholder Duties Conference, Glasgow, September 2017.

33 See *Roger M Barker/Iris H-Y Chiu*, Investment Management and Corporate Governance, 2019, which discusses significant investment fund vehicles and the structures, incentives and obstacles to shareholder engagement by them.

34 *Ian Hamilton/Jessica Eriksson*, "Influence Strategies in Shareholder Engagement: A Case Study of All Swedish National Pension Funds" Journal of Sustainable Finance and Investment,

served to be weaker in Anglo-American jurisdictions.[35] However, a common barrier to engaging with sustainability issues, except for funds expressly reserved for 'socially responsible investing' (SRI),[36] is the legal interpretation of investment intermediaries' fiduciary duties to their clients. A narrow interpretation focuses upon the need to invest prudently and in a diversified manner in order to achieve financial return to meet beneficiaries' needs.[37] This could mean that non-financial considerations that may interfere with that primary discharge of fiduciary duty are not permitted.[38] Although legal interpretation with regard to investment intermediaries' fiduciary duties has changed with times in order to allow more modern and salient considerations to factor into the discharge of fiduciary duties,[39] risk aversion can still affect investment intermediaries.[40] Alternatively, such risk aversion may be an excuse for those that do not wish to change from the conventional manners of financially-driven investment management methodologies.[41]

In an opposite, bottom-up development, some investment intermediaries have identified market opportunities for SRI. The universe of SRI is however populated with financial products of varying standards in terms of selection and performance,[42] and mis-selling risks to well-meaning investors exist.[43]

2011, 1, 44; *Frank A J Wagemans/ CSA (Kris) van Koppen/Arthur PJ Mol*, "Engagement on ESG issues by Dutch Pension Funds: Is It Reaching Its Full Potential?" Journal of Sustainable Finance & Investment, 2018, 8, 301.

35 *Beate Sjåfjell*, Achieving Corporate Sustainability: What is the Role of the Shareholder? In: *Hanne S Birkmose* (ed), Shareholders' Duties, 2017, ch. 18.

36 There are a number of strategies in this universe, from exclusion to stock-picking, and to shareholder activism.

37 In the UK see *Cowan v Scargill* [1985] Ch 270.

38 *Friederike Johanna Preu/Benjamin J. Richardson*, "German Socially Responsible Investment: Barriers and Opportunities" German Law Journal, 2011, 12, 865; *Benjamin Richardson/Wes Cragg*, "Being Virtuous and Prosperous: SRI's Conflicting Goals" Journal of Business Ethics, 2010, 92, 21.

39 UNEPFI report, 2019.

40 *Joakim Sandberg*, "Socially Responsible Investment and Fiduciary Duty: Putting the Freshfields Report into Perspective" Journal of Business Ethics, 2011, 101, 143.

41 *Kenneth Amaeshi*, "Different Markets for Different Folks: Exploring the Challenges of Mainstreaming Responsible Investment Practices" Journal of Business Ethics, 2010, 92. 41, arguing that sustainable finance requires different methodologies and mindsets altogether in its management.

42 *Julia Puashunder*, "On the Emergence, Current State, and Future Perspectives of Socially Responsible Investment (SRI)" Consilience, 2016, 16, 38; *Henry Schäfer*, "Sustainable Finance", 2012, http://ssrn.com/abstract=2147590; *Christin Nitsche/ Michael Schröder*, Are SRI Funds Conventional Funds in Disguise Or Do They Live Up to Their Name? in: Sabri Boubaker, Douglas

The harmonised legislative instrument in the Sustainability Disclosures Regulation 2019 intends to achieve two policy goals: legal clarification and market regulation. It introduces a mandatory duty with regard to sustainability risks for investment intermediaries. This duty supports and accompanies the governance regime for the marketing of sustainably-labelled financial products, which need to meet minimum standards.

2.2 Mandatory Responsibility for Investment Intermediaries

Financial markets participants who engage in portfolio management or fund management (whether as mainstream pension or collective investment schemes, or as alternative investments funds)[44] must make mandatory disclosures as to how they integrate sustainability risks in their investment decision-making.[45] This also includes financial services providers who offer investment-based products as part of an insurance product. In this manner, through mandatory disclosure, the Regulation has arguably brought about a new expectation for investment intermediaries in terms of their investment management conduct. This expectation cannot be avoided by narrow pursuits of financial performance in the name of compliance with fiduciary duties. This is a 'baseline' standard applicable to all investment intermediaries within the scope above. Large investment intermediaries are subject to additional regulatory obligations as follows.

Investment intermediaries of a certain scale, defined as having at least 500 employees or being a parent company of such an undertaking,[46] are mandated to account for adverse sustainability impacts, from 30 June 2021. This applies whether or not such financial services providers engage with sustainably-labelled products. They must account for any adverse impact of their investment decision-making processes on sustainability risks, how adverse impacts are discovered and what due diligence policies are deployed.[47] Smaller providers may declare that they do not consider adverse impacts on sustainability risks in their investment decision-making process, but must clearly explain why and

---

Cumming, and Duc Khuong Nguyen (eds), Research Handbook of Investing in the Triple Bottom Line, 2018, ch19.

43 'Report finds some ethical funds are 'misleading' investors' (5 Nov 2019) at https://www.moneyobserver.com/news/report-finds-some-ethical-funds-are-misleading-investors.

44 Sustainability Disclosures Regulation 2019, Art 2.

45 Ibid, Art 3.

46 Arts 4(3), (4), ibid.

47 Art 4(1)(a), ibid.

whether this practice cuts across all their products.[48] This means that smaller providers still need to disclose how they integrate sustainability risks as discussed above, but are not specifically tied to the prescribed mandatory disclosures of due diligence policies and measurement of adverse sustainability impact.

Further, by 30 December 2022, financial services providers mandated to integrate and disclose sustainability risks in relation to adverse impacts must also make that information available at the level of each financial product.[49] These disclosures are also regarded as pre-contractual in nature.[50]

As the integration of sustainability risks refers to material sustainability risks, it is arguable that the transparency obligation for large investment intermediaries to disclose adverse sustainability impact imposes on them the duty to account for double materiality. This means that large firms are accountable for not only material sustainability risks relevant to investment performance but other adverse sustainability impact as such. Mandatory disclosure in relation to adverse sustainability impact would be made according to the highly prescribed template proposed by the European Securities and Markets Authority (ESMA). ESMA's technical standards[51] provide for templates of types of adverse impact that investment intermediaries should engage with and measure. The prescriptive measure can on the one hand result in a compliance-based mindset, as investment intermediaries seek to meet the requirements of each 'box to tick.'[52] However, compelling those intermediaries to engage with a standardised set of sustainability risks in this manner allows them to learn and develop knowledge in areas that they cannot be selective about, so that the connection to public interest goals can be made. Such disclosures theoretically attract regulatory enforcement and also allow for the exercise of market discipline. Investors are able to enjoy comparability in disclosures made by investment intermediaries in order to facilitate choice and competition. Further, the list of adverse impacts that need to be measured is not inflexible, as it would be introduced in delegated Commission legislation that can be amended relatively easily. Designating the information to be disclosed as pre-contractual disclosures would allow investors

---

48 Art 4(1)(b), ibid.
49 Art 7, ibid.
50 Art 6, ibid.
51 draft technical standards as of 23 April 2020, at https://www.esma.europa.eu/press-news/esma-news/esas-consult-environmental-social-and-governance-disclosure-rules.
52 *Kimberly D Krawiec*, "Cosmetic Compliance and the Failure of Negotiated Governance" Washington University Law Quarterly, 2003, 81, 487.

to exercise *ex post* discipline in litigation for misrepresentation or mis-selling.[53] Retail investors in the UK can be a force of discipline to be reckoned with as they can seek redress from the Financial Ombudsman in out-of-court remedy for up to £150,000 in case of misrepresentation or mis-selling.[54] Nielsen and Parker argue that such compliance can produce a changed culture in time, as the need to change processes and methodologies could permeate organisational strategies and activities.[55]

However, the mandatory duty discussed above applies only to larger investment intermediaries. As mentioned above, smaller providers are able to declare and explain why they do not consider adverse impacts on sustainability risks in their investment decision-making process.[56] This exception is arguably based on proportionality, i.e. the cost of compliance for smaller firms may be significant. This exception thus leaves it to market discipline to determine if smaller investment intermediaries who are agnostic about ESG risks are sufficiently competitive or may be 'penalised' by investor choice. Regulators might also take enforcement action in view of poor or inadequate explanations. However, the inadequacy of a disclosure is often difficult to pin down if there is no falsehood or misrepresentation. Nevertheless, smaller firms are still subject to the general duty to integrate sustainability risks as a baseline. However, the lack of prescription in relation to what 'integration' means and how this should be implemented may result in a meta-regulatory phenomenon of fragmented and uneven implementation amongst firms. Firms may opt to implement the regulation in a manner suitable for their business models. In a positive way, firms could take advantage of the flexibility to develop standards and processes suitable for their business models. [57] However, it is also possible that meta-regulatory implemen-

---

53 This would overcome investment management arrangements seeking to exclude advisory duties, for eg *Cassa di Risparmio della Repubblica di San Marino SpA v Barclays Bank Ltd* [2011] EWHC 484 (Comm).
54 Part XVI, Financial Services and Markets Act 2000. Retail redress is often the precursor for hard law reforms for conduct of business, *Eilis Ferran*, "Regulatory Lessons from the Payment Protection Insurance Mis-selling Scandal in the UK" European Business Organisations Law Review, 2012, 13, 247.
55 *Christine Parker/Vibeke Lehmann Nielsen*, "Corporate Compliance Systems: Could They Make Any Difference?" Administration and Society, 2009, 41, 3.
56 Art 4(1)(b), Sustainability Disclosure Regulation 2019.
57 *Christine Parker*, The Open Corporation, 2000 offers a positive view of meta-regulatory implementation.

tation can result in minimalist self-regulation,[58] such as being a mere signatory to the UN Principles of Responsible Investment.[59]

As the threshold for a 'large' investment intermediary is set at 500 employees minimum, many investment fund and portfolio managers would not be caught within the more stringent tier of compliance. It is queried if this can normalize the market practice of declaring agnosticism with regard to adverse sustainability impact. For example, well-known names in the asset management industry such as Jupiter or Acadian have fewer than 500 employees. The efficacy of the mandatory duty may be perceived to be more marginalised as one realises that a large quarter of the investment sector consists of mid-size firms that are therefore not covered within the Regulation's scope. However, it may be argued that the more stringent tier of compliance only applies to large investment fund managers because their ownership of corporate equity is likely extensive. In this way, their sustainability stewardship would have a systemic impact upon corporate sector behaviour. Examples of such investment fund managers would be Fidelity, Blackrock, State Street and Vanguard. These firms also have the capacity and resources to significantly enhance their research and due diligence capabilities to adhere to the Regulation's demands.[60]

On the other hand, excluding smaller firms from the stringent tier of compliance would arguably prejudice them, as larger firms subject to these duties have the opportunity to distinguish themselves. As discussed below, the compliance burden of the mandatory duty can be seen as a building block for market opportunities in sustainably-labelled financial products. In this manner, the market-building agenda in the EU Regulations can be rather skewed in favour of large investment intermediaries, equipping them to dominate the market for sustainably-labelled products. The competitive effects of this Regulation ought to be further studied.

Nevertheless, can it be argued that that imposing a mandatory duty upon larger investment intermediaries to integrate sustainability risks does not advance sustainable finance as such? Such a duty does not necessarily lead to a

---

58 *Julia Black*, "Paradoxes and Failures: "New Governance" Techniques and the Financial Crisis" Modern Law Review, 2012, 75, 1037.

59 *Soohun Kim/Aaron Yoon*, Analyzing Active Managers' Commitment to ESG: Evidence from United Nations Principles for Responsible Investment, 2020, https://papers.ssrn.com/sol3/papers.cfm?abstract_id=3555984.

60 For example large investment firms such as State Street is already equipping itself for ESG analytics, see 'State Street enhances ESG data and analytics offering' (30 May 2019), https://www.institutionalassetmanager.co.uk/2019/05/30/276154/state-street-enhances-esg-data-and-analytics-offering.

positive channelling of finance to sustainable projects, activities or outcomes, a similar critique levelled against SRI. Many SRI strategies can be exclusion-based,[61] i.e. designed not to channel funds to industries or companies with questionable ESG impact. Exclusion does not necessarily change behaviour, especially at the macro level, for discernible outcomes in sustainability.[62] However, the mandatory disclosure duty should be regarded as a baseline, so that firms wishing to offer sustainably-labelled products would need to do more to prove their credentials. In this manner, the Regulation provides opportunities (as well as compliance burdens) for the building of product markets with distinguished standards.

2.3 Market-building for Sustainable Finance

Market-building in sustainably-labelled investment products is underpinned by minimum standards to cater to market confidence and credibility. In this manner, the mainstreaming agenda of the Regulations' reforms is 'enabled' by regulative standards. Regulative standards contain two aspects: one relates to the substantive quality of sustainably-labelled financial products, and the second relates to marketing and disclosure standards at point of sale and post-sale.

Moving away from the market's minimalism in accepting SRI as based only on exclusion, it may be argued that the Regulations provide higher minimum standards for sustainably-labelled finance in that such investment products should positively achieve specified sustainable outcomes and at least do 'no significant harm' to environmental and social objectives as a whole.[63] The definition of 'sustainably-labelled' includes:

'an economic activity that contributes to an environmental objective, ... [such as], by key resource efficiency indicators on the use of energy, renewable energy, raw materials, water and land, on the production of waste, and greenhouse gas emissions, or on its impact on biodiversity and the circular economy, or an investment in an economic activity that contributes to a social objective, ...

---

61 *Alan Lewis/Carmen Juravale*, "Morals, Markets and Sustainable Investments: A Qualitative Study of 'Champions'" Journal of Business Ethics, 2010, 93, 483.
62 *Sander Quak/Johan Heilbron/Jessica Meijer*, "The Rise and Spread of Sustainable Investing in the Netherlands" Journal of Sustainable Finance & Investment, 2014, 4, 249. On divestment see *Liz Cooper*, Determining How to Invest More Responsibly As an Institution in: *Tessa Hebb/James P. Hawley/Andreas G. F. Hoepner/Agnes L. Neher/David Wood* (eds), The Routledge Handbook of Responsible Investment, 2015, ch 34.
63 Art 2 (17), Sustainability Disclosure Regulation 2019.

[such as] tackling inequality or that fosters social cohesion, social integration and labour relations, or an investment in human capital or economically or socially disadvantaged communities, provided that such investments do not significantly harm any of those objectives and that the investee companies follow good governance practices, in particular with respect to sound management structures, employee relations, remuneration of staff and tax compliance.'[64]

This higher departure point, i. e. the achievement of positive characteristics and the avoidance of significantly negative ones,[65] arguably accords more with investors' expectations in meeting hybrid objectives.[66] ESMA's disclosure template[67] would require investment intermediaries to measure their investments' positive contributions to sustainable objectives[68] and the methodologies for attaining them. Further, investees' companies' corporate governance, remuneration policies, tax compliance and employee relations need to be evaluated. At the very least, the template would also compel investment intermediaries to measure and ensure that no significant harm is done to sustainable objectives in general. The Taxonomy Regulation's provisions, however, represent a 'ceiling' benchmark of substantive quality for environmental sustainability. It prescribes six objectives that 'environmentally sustainable' financial products should meet, and relevant indicators for each. Investors would have the confidence that investments are being channelled to defined environmental outcomes.[69] However, the Taxonomy Regulation, being relatively more developed for output legitimacy in environmentally sustainable objectives, is only catching up to social objectives.[70]

---

64 *Ibid.*

65 Discussed critically below.

66 *Peer Osthoff*, What Matters to SRI Investors?' in: Tessa Hebb/James P. Hawley/Andreas G. F. Hoepner/Agnes L. Neher/David Wood (eds), The Routledge Handbook of Responsible Investment, 2015, ch54; *Lei Delsen/Alex Lehr*, "Value Matters or Values Matter? An Analysis of Heterogeneity in Preferences for Sustainable Investments" Journal of Sustainable Finance & Investment, 2019, 9, 240; Some investors are prosocial and willing to tradeoff financial returns, see *Andrea Hafenstein/Alexander Bassen*, "Influences for Using Sustainability Information In the Investment Decision-Making of Nonprofessional Investors" Journal of Sustainable Finance & Investment, 2016, 6, 186; *Gunnar Gutsche/Andreas Ziegler*, "Which Private Investors Are Willing to Pay for Sustainable Investments? Empirical Evidence from Stated Choice Experiments" Journal of Banking and Finance, 2019, 102, 193.

67 *EBA, ESMA, EIOPA, Consultation on Environment, Social and Governance Disclosure Rules* (2020), https://www.esma.europa.eu/press-news/esma-news/esas-consult-environmental-social-and-governance-disclosure-rules.

68 Art 2(17), Sustainability Disclosure Regulation 2019.

69 Taxonomy Regulation 2020, arts 5–11.

70 This is being addressed by the Social Taxonomy project in development, see *European Commission*, "Platform on Sustainable Finance" (2021), https://ec.europa.eu/info/sites/default/files/

Social objectives may be of a wider, vaguer scope and can be more susceptible to disagreement. Nevertheless, the EU's commitment to the United Nations' Sustainable Development Goals in its Agenda 2030,[71] and the Commission[72] as well as ESAs[73] are developing greater standardisation of environmental and socially sustainable indicators for mandatory transparency and evaluation. Empirical research also finds that there is a genuine need for developing socially-focused products, which have fallen by the wayside due to policy-makers' focus on the environment.[74] This is however not the approach taken in the UK, which has preferred to sidestep the vast and vaguer universe of social objectives, focusing on developing regulation for environmentally sustainable investment products, notably in relation to climate change.[75]

The question remains whether there is still a market for other socially-responsible investment products that are not sustainably-labelled. It is arguable that 'ESG-like' products that do not meet the requirements of the sustainable label, such as products in the current universe of SRI funds,[76] can still be offered. This is because the Taxonomy Regulation seems to allow providers to clearly distinguish their marketing disclosures in such a way that aspects of products that do not meet the Taxonomy's standards can be articulated.[77] Hence the Regulation's approach is geared towards incentivising markets for high standards and reserving the sustainability label for products that meet those standards, rather than outlawing 'lower-level' offerings. It provides incentive-based regulation for products, rather than product regulation as such. Products labelled as 'SRI', 'ESG' or 'hybrid value' may still be available within the gap that the Reg-

---

business_economy_euro/banking_and_finance/documents/finance-events-210226-presentation-social-taxonomy_en.pdf.

71 *European Commission*, "The 2030 Agenda for Sustainable Development and the SDGs" (2012), https://ec.europa.eu/environment/sustainable-development/SDGs/index_en.htm.

72 *European Commission*, "Proposal for a Corporate Social Reporting Directive" (2021), https://ec.europa.eu/info/publications/210421-sustainable-finance-communication_en#csrd.

73 *ESAs Consult on Environmental, Social and Governance Disclosure Rules* (2020), https://www.esma.europa.eu/press-news/esma-news/esas-consult-environmental-social-and-governance-disclosure-rules.

74 *Rajna Gibson Brandon/Philipp Krüger*, "The Sustainability Footprint of Institutional Investors" (ECGI Working Paper 2018), https://ssrn.com/abstract=2918926.

75 *Financial Conduct Authority*, "Enhancing Climate-Related Disclosures by Asset Managers, Life Insurers and FCA-Regulated Pension Providers" (2021), https://www.fca.org.uk/publications/consultation-papers/cp-21-17-climate-related-disclosures-asset-managers-life-insurers-regulated-pensions.

76 *Geoffrey Jones*, Profits and Sustainability: A History of Green Entrepreneurship, 2017, (ch. 8. Can Finance Change the World?)

77 Art 7, Taxonomy Regulation 2020.

ulations leave. The enabling nature of the Regulations therefore facilitates competition in quality but also arguably in cost, as lower-level products are less demanding in terms of compliance.[78]

In marketing sustainably-labelled financial products, mandatory disclosure is introduced to ensure that investors obtain clear pre-sale and post-sale information to make their choices, discussed below.

Investment intermediaries who provide sustainably-labelled products must explain how the environmental or social characteristics promoted by each product meets its characterisation, whether in active or passive management. In an actively managed product, disclosure is to be made of the strategies designed to meet the relevant characteristics, including how the financial services provider defines the sustainability objective,[79] and how it measures its attainment or otherwise.[80] ESMA will prescribe a template[81] for such disclosure so that such disclosure attains certain standards and comparability. In relation to a passively managed product, the financial services providers must disclose if the environmental or social characterisation is derived by benchmarking against indices for sustainable finance.[82] It is not sufficient that financial services providers merely refer to a designated index satisfied by a product's environmental or social characteristics. They must disclose how the index is aligned or consistent with those characteristics and how alignment with it differs from a broad market index.[83] Although financial services providers are in substance relying on an index provider's diligence and evaluation, there needs to be some level of intelligent engagement with indexers' various methodologies[84] and perhaps with their track record.

---

78 *Christin Nitsche/Michael Schröder*, Are SRI Funds Conventional Funds in Disguise Or Do They Live Up to Their Name? in: Sabri Boubaker/Douglas Cumming/Duc Khuong Nguyen (eds), Research Handbook of Investing in the Triple Bottom Line, 2018, ch19; *Arnim Wiek/Olaf Weber*, "Sustainability Challenges and the Ambivalent Role of the Financial Sector" Journal of Sustainable Finance & Investment, 2014, 4, 9.
79 As defined in Art 2(17), Sustainability Disclosure Regulation 2019.
80 Art 8, 10, above.
81 draft technical standards as of 23 April 2020, at https://www.esma.europa.eu/press-news/ esma-news/esas-consult-environmental-social-and-governance-disclosure-rules.
82 Art 8, 9, Sustainability Disclosure Regulation 2019.
83 Art 9(1)(b), ibid.
84 *Robert J. Bianchi/Michael E. Drew*, "Sustainable Stock Indices and Long-Term Portfolio Decisions" Journal of Sustainable Finance & Investment, 2012, 2, 303 on the differences between indices.

On the one hand, the above reform underpins confidence in the marketing of pan-European products such as UCITs[85] and other alternative investment funds that are sustainably-labelled and benefit from a European passport.[86] The perspective from the law and finance thesis discussed above would support higher expected levels of investor and market confidence as a result of such regulatory standardisation. Further, because the disclosures are designated as pre-contractual disclosures, investors can exercise discipline in relation to *ex post* litigation for misrepresentation and mis-selling. Further, in the UK for example, large scale mis-selling can result in the regulator's imposition of consumer redress schemes[87] that compel firms to compensate customers in an out-of-court but collective manner. However, investment intermediaries would pass the increased cost of transparency and compliance to investors, and it is uncertain whether institutional allocation will be attracted[88] by virtue of the substantive standards or put off by the increased cost. Institutions could continue to invest in 'lower-level' products labelled as SRI or ESG without meeting the sustainably-labelled standards. However, the existence of higher standards may cause beneficiaries to put pressure on institutions, in turn generating demand for sustainably-labelled investments above the market minimalism of SRI or ESG.

Some posit that in response to the market-building agenda in the EU's Regulations, investment intermediaries and institutions may converge upon passively-managed, sustainably-labelled products as a middle ground to signal change in their investment behaviour. This is because the compliance burden for passively-managed products, although needing to meet the enhanced requirements of being sustainably-labelled, are relatively less onerous than for actively-managed products. The market is already skewed[89] in this manner and it is uncertain if legislation should reinforce this.

The demands for mandatory disclosure could prove burdensome for actively-managed products. Would investment intermediaries have to undertake sustain-

---

85 Regulated by the UCITs Directive 2009, Consolidated text: Directive 2009/65/EC of the European Parliament and of the Council of 13 July 2009 on the coordination of laws, regulations and administrative provisions relating to undertakings for collective investment in transferable securities (UCITS) (recast).

86 Art 2, Sustainability Disclosures 2019 which refers to the European-regulated investment fund providers.

87 S404, Financial Services and Markets Act 2000.

88 See citations in fn. 23 on the increased popularity of sustainable finance products with pension funds.

89 'Europeans make record investments in sustainable funds' (Financial Times, 30 Jan 2020) at https://www.ft.com/content/c2952357-c28b-4662-a393-c6586640404f.

able outcomes evaluations themselves,[90] or can they rely on third-party gate-keepers like social responsibility ratings providers? The building up of in-house expertise is not likely a short-term achievement that can be attained, and different methodologies exist within the diverse social responsibility ratings industry.[91] If investment intermediaries rely on particular ratings providers, would that be sufficient for showing that investment products meet sustainability characteristics? Without due governance and accountability of ratings providers, can regulators and the market be convinced of the sustainable performance claimed in an investment product? Further, active management relies heavily on research, the practices for which have been impacted after the UK and EU's reforms to unbundle research charges from brokerage.[92]

This reform was meant to address the problem that brokerage customers paying for trading charges and fees generally pay an extra percentage that firms would then use to subsidise payment for research. Over the years, the benefit to customers has not justified the bloated amounts passed off as research charges.[93] Besides, in an environment of low yield since the global financial crisis 2007–2009, charges and fees could erode returns for investors. Commission legislation was ultimately introduced under the parent Markets in Financial Instruments Directive 2014[94] to compel investment firms to unbundle research charges from brokerage charges and fees. Firms are to set aside an annual research budget and obtain clients' consent to contribute to this on an *ex ante* basis, or otherwise absorb such costs themselves.[95] This reform adversely affect-

90 Elizabeth Corley, Sustainable Investment: The Golden Moment in *London Institute of Banking and Finance*, Banking on Change: The Development and Future of Financial Services, 2019, ch6 on innovation being modest in sustainable finance.

91 *Robert G. Eccles/Judith C. Stroehle*, "Exploring Social Origins in the Construction of ESG Measures", 2019, http://ssrn.com/abstract=3212685; *Robert G. Eccles/Jock Herron/George Serafeim*, Reliable Sustainability Ratings in: Tessa Hebb/James P. Hawley/Andreas G. F. Hoepner/Agnes L. Neher/David Wood (eds), The Routledge Handbook of Responsible Investment, 2015, ch 48; *Boonlert Jitmaneeroj*, "Reform Priorities for Corporate Sustainability: Environmental, Social, Governance, or Economic Performance?" Management Decision, 2016, 54, 1497.

92 Art 13, Commission Delegated Directive (EU) 2017/593 of 7 April 2016 supplementing Directive 2014/65/EU of the European Parliament and of the Council with regard to safeguarding of financial instruments and funds belonging to clients, product governance obligations and the rules applicable to the provision or reception of fees, commissions or any monetary or non-monetary benefits.

93 'Invest £10,000, pay £14,227 in fees: how fund charges erode your money by stealth' (The Telegraph, 22 June 2017) at https://www.telegraph.co.uk/investing/funds/invest10000-pay14227-fees-fund-charges-erode-money-stealth/.

94 Fn. 92.

95 Implemented in the UK FCA Handbook COBS 2.3B.

ed the lucrativeness of research, and the business models for research have been reorganised. For example, some investment firms moved research in-house and limited its scope, for example by focusing only upon listed companies. Specialist research firms have also emerged, but there is concern that a wide range of research such as covering niche or smaller companies has become less available.[96]

The research reform may affect the marketising of sustainably-labelled, actively-managed products in two ways. First, investment intermediaries who have little capacity to build up such specialist research would forego this market, as outsourcing to specialist firms can also be expensive. Second, the lack of research coverage of smaller or niche companies[97] may affect new and innovative enterprises with sustainable goals,[98] and the lack of coverage for them would adversely affect their access to funding. Investment intermediaries who wish to market sustainably-labelled products may not include these smaller companies if research on them is too thin, a problem that heightens intermediaries' legal risk in relation to their compliance with the disclosure requirements above. This issue is gaining attention, and policy-makers are proposing exemptions from research payment rules in order to promote bond and small company research.[99] However, as the Sustainability Disclosure Regulation compels large investment firms to become accustomed to taking stock of and measuring adverse sustainability impact in a rather prescribed manner, complying with the duty would arguably force large investment firms to build up relevant evaluative expertise in sustainability matters. Large investment intermediaries may not find it too forbidding to build upon their compliance needs and develop competitive research and evaluative capacities for sustainable outcomes, in order to support actively-managed products. Further, niche investment firms can also develop specialized products in the actively-managed space, such as impact investing.[100] In this manner, the Regulation can provide a mobilisation opportunity for marketing such products, therefore taking these products from fringe to mainstream, opening up opportunities for investors in a broad active management universe.

---

96 'MiFID II research rules 'hitting sector coverage and quality' (18 Feb 2019), https://www.ipe.com/mifid-ii-research-rules-hitting-sector-coverage-and-quality/10029553.article; 'UK and EU fund managers at odds over MiFID II revamp' (Financial Times, 25 May 2020), https://www.ft.com/content/dc7b9a26-83d4-484d-bb26-0c651c41f240.
97 See fn. 96.
98 *Francisco Szekely/Zahir Dossa*, Beyond the Triple Bottom Line: Eight Steps toward a Sustainable Business Model, 2017, ch9.
99 'EU fund managers back fee changes to Mifid II trading rules' (28 July 2020), https://www.ft.com/content/a0e8195e-aae1-4370-b8bb-82363e01cc93.
100 *Olaf Weber*, Impact Investing; Maximilian Martin, Building The Impact Investing Market in: Othmar M Lehner (ed), Routledge Handbook of Sustainable and Social Finance, 2016.

Many investment intermediaries may more likely be incentivised to provide passively-managed sustainably-labelled products. Although investment intermediaries still need to show that indices chosen would meet sustainable objectives in terms of the 'positive contribution' and 'do no significant harm' thresholds, the measurement obligations are arguably a shared burden, as index providers keen to compete in this market would go some way towards providing such evidence[101] that investment intermediaries can leverage upon in their disclosures. Established index providers such as the FTSE4Good or Dow Jones Sustainability Index[102] have significant evaluative expertise to draw upon, even if meeting ESMA's template requirements or the Taxonomy Regulation requirements would demand more. In this manner, Steven Maijoor has already opined that service providers in ratings and indices could play fundamental roles in securing market confidence in sustainable finance, and regulatory governance ought to be extended over them.[103] Of course such a pronouncement can be a double-edged sword, as it legitimises this industry but at the same time imposes compliance requirements and cost, which would have to be reflected in the cost of investing in these products.

In its market-building agenda, EU reforms could skew towards incentivising the development of the market for passively-managed sustainably-labelled products.[104] This may result in an adverse impact to innovation and choice. However, the reforms also achieve an elevation in the quality in passively-managed products as passive managers cannot totally rely on index providers' innovations. They are subject to an obligation to provide a comparative discussion between (a) the overall sustainability-related impact of the financial product with the impacts of the designated index and (b) the impacts of a broad market index through sustainability indicators. This disclosure is to be made in periodic reports to investors.[105] This may mean that the passively-managed product provider must nevertheless undertake measurement of the sustainability impact of the

---

101 There are different levels of sophistication and maturity in indices, see *Bianchi/Drew*, 2012.

102 *Steve Lydenberg/Alexi White*, Responsible Investment Indexes in: Tessa Hebb/James P. Hawley/Andreas G. F. Hoepner/Agnes L. Neher/David Wood (eds), The Routledge Handbook of Responsible Investment, 2015, ch40.

103 *Steven Maijoor*, 'Sustainable financial markets: translating changing risks and investor preferences into regulatory action' (Speech at European Financial Forum, 12 Feb 2020).

104 This trend is already on the rise, with large investment firms dominating the landscape, such as Blackrock's 6 new Exchange-traded Fund products that are both passively-managed and exchange-traded for liquidity, see 'BlackRock Expands and Enhances iShares Sustainable ETF Product Line' (12 Feb 2020), https://www.businesswire.com/news/home/20200212005388/en/%C2%A0BlackRock-Expands-Enhances-iShares-Sustainable-ETF-Product.

105 Art 11, Sustainability Disclosure Regulation 2019.

index-aligned financial product and not merely rely on the performance of the index.

Policy-makers require such disclosure as the Regulation's Preamble refers to investors' lack of information in relation to various sustainability outcomes apart from financial metrics.[106] Such comparison allows investors to see the sustainability difference that their investment has made. Indeed, this obligation is possibly the key obligation that forces providers of passively-managed products to account for sustainable performance. It is queried how investment funds are to discharge such a burden. What level of granularity and measurement should be undertaken for comparison, and can funds be prevented from adopting imprecise or broad-brush approaches, such as by referring merely to differences in portfolio composition? Where product providers select a particular sustainability index to align with, such as the FTSE4Good Index, would the FTSE All-share index serve as a comparable broad market index that they should adopt? It is queried to what extent providers may select a comparator, in order to enhance the comparative results they would like to present. As this requirement is placed in periodic reports, the quality expected of financial reporting in periodic reports may provide some guidance for the reporting of such comparison. The quality of financial reporting in periodic reports is condensed from annual reporting, but adheres to the same standards of financial rigour and prescription, although unaudited.[107] On this basis, it is arguable that the periodic reporting of sustainable performance for passively-managed funds is not expected to be vague and broad-brush, and should contain indicators and metrics against which the sustainable characterisation is measured—the same metrics applied as a comparison with a broad market index. ESMA's development of a template for periodic disclosure may signal towards this approach, which would prevent passively-managed product providers from merely relying on index providers to vouch for sustainable performance. In this manner, it is arguable that marketing sustainably-labelled products entails obligations of quality monitoring and adherence that make it impossible to be 'merely passive' in the conventional sense of investment management. It is arguable that such obligations come close to a form of product regulation and transform the nature of 'passive investment,' achieving a mid-way between active stock-picking and portfolio curation and slavish adherence to indices. Further, Gordon[108] argues that

---

106 Preamble 24, ibid.
107 eg see the quality of periodic reports for UCITs funds, Art 69(4), Directive 2009/65/EC (UCITS).
108 *Jeffrey Gordon*, "Rethinking Stewardship" (ECGI seminar, 23 Oct 2020), https://ecgi.global/content/rethinking-stewardship.

passive managers have the incentive to manage 'systematic' portfolio risks such as ESG risks that apply generally to the corporate sector, in demonstrating their engagement with investee companies consistent with the Shareholders' Rights Directive expectations.

A market distinguished by higher standards goes hand in hand with cost implications, differentiated from the market minimalism of SRI or ESG.[109] Would institutional investors respond and increase their demand, or would there be a race to the lower levels of the market which are not outlawed?

Institutions should engage in the best practices of structuring mandates for asset managers to incorporate sustainability objectives, including their interface with institutions' financial objectives,[110] and any trade-offs.[111] In this respect, the

---

109 *Benjamin Richardson*, Keeping Ethical Investment Ethical: Regulatory Issues for Investing for Sustainability, Journal of Business Ethics, 2009, 87, 555.

110 *Nitsche/Schröder* (2018), ibid; *Xing Chen/Bert Scholtens*, "The Urge to Act: A Comparison of Active and Passive Socially Responsible Investment Funds in the United States" Corporate Social Responsibility and Environmental Management, 2018, 25, 1154.

111 There is significant concern in empirical research trying to establish if socially responsible funds perform better or worse, *Federica Ielasi/Monica Rossolini/Sarah Limberti*, "Sustainability-themed Mutual Funds: An Empirical Examination of Risk And Performance" The Journal of Risk Finance, 2018, 19, 247 (positive); *Michael Schröder*, "Financial Effects of Corporate Social Responsibility: A Literature Review" Journal of Sustainable Finance & Investment, 2014, 4, 337 (positive); *Matthew W. Sherwood/Julia L. Pollard*, "The Risk-Adjusted Return Potential of Integrating ESG Strategies into Emerging Market Equities" Journal of Sustainable Finance & Investment, 2018, 8, 26 (positive); *Pablo Durán-Santomil/Luis Otero-González/Renato Heitor Correia-Domingues/Juan Carlos Reboredo*, "Does Sustainability Score Impact Mutual Fund Performance?" Sustainability Journal, 2019, 11, 2972 (positive); *Benjamin Tobias Peylo/Stefan Schaltegger*, "An Equation With Many Variables: Unhiding the Relationship Between Sustainability and Investment Performance" Journal of Sustainable Finance & Investment, 2014, 4 110 (finding an inverted u-shaped performance trajectory of sustainable finance funds initially performing better than conventional ones and then dips).

But more granular research at company level shows mixed results in relation to connecting ESG and financial performance, see *Marien de Haan/Lammertjan Dam/Bert Scholtens*, "The Drivers of the Relationship Between Corporate Environmental Performance and Stock Market Returns" Journal of Sustainable Finance & Investment, 2012, 2, 338; *Roger C. Y. Chen/Shih-Wei Hung/Chen-Hsun Lee*, "Does Corporate Value Affect the Relationship Between Corporate Social Responsibility and Stock Returns?" Journal of Sustainable Finance & Investment, 2017, 7, 188 (negative); for positive accounts, see *Gregor Dorfleitner/Sebastian Utz/Maximilian Wimmer*, "Patience Pays Off – Corporate Social Responsibility and Long-Term Stock Returns" Journal of Sustainable Finance & Investment, 2018, 8, 132; *N. C. Ashwin Kumar/Camille Smith/Leïla Badis/Nan Wang/Paz Ambrosy/Rodrigo Tavares*, "ESG Factors and Risk-Adjusted Performance: A New Quantitative Model" Journal of Sustainable Finance & Investment, 2016, 6 292; *Gunnar Friede/Timo Busch/Alexander Bassen*, "ESG and Financial Performance: Aggregated Evidence from More Than 2000 Empirical Studies" Journal of Sustainable Finance & Investment, 2015, 5, 210.

UK's open-ended Stewardship Code provides a template for institutions and their asset managers to integrate sustainability into their strategic and governance frameworks for investment management, a.k.a. 'stewardship'.[112] There also needs to be better integration of investors' sustainability preferences into the investment advisory duty so that retail investors' needs can be met. This is especially pertinent to the digital finance market for sustainable finance, particularly in the passively-managed range.

3 Connecting with the Digital Single Market for Finance

We argue that further policy thinking can be developed in the market-building for sustainably-labelled products, particularly where these are passively-managed products likely to appeal to retail investors in mutual funds. Leveraging connections between digital finance and sustainable finance could promote market development in the retail sector and galvanise EU citizens towards participating in sustainable objectives via finance. This approach potentially contributes to meeting Single market as well as public good objectives, integrating economic/financial lives with a wider purpose of social mobilisation.

Digitalisation can serve as a key means to attract retail investors. Retail investors have developed a keen appetite for digital access to financial services, as fintech revolutions, first in payment services, have provided user-friendly and low-cost options to consumers in a jaded market for payment services that features significant rent extraction.[113] On the investment front, robo-advisers have captured significant market share by offering user-friendly interfaces for invest-

---

112 UK Stewardship Code 2020, https://www.frc.org.uk/getattachment/5aae591d-d9d3-4cf4-814a-d14e156a1d87/Stewardship-Code_Dec-19-Final-Corrected.pdf, Principle 7. Existing literature has criticised the mixed quality of 'stewardship' in relation to investment intermediaries actively monitoring investee companies and influencing their conduct, see eg *Arad Reisberg*, "The UK Stewardship Code: On the Road to Nowhere", Journal of Corporate Law Studies, 2015, 15, 217. However, the 2020 Code explicitly empowers asset owners to shape their contractual mandates, such as including sustainability concerns. This can provide new impetus for asset managers to address sustainability in their offerings.

113 *Christopher Dula/David Kuo-Chuen Lee*, Reshaping the Financial Order in: Christopher Dula/David Kuo-Chuen Lee (eds), Handbook of Blockchain, Digital Finance and Inclusion, 2018, ch1.

ors.[114] Although robo-advisers do not provide comprehensive and tailor-made financial advice, and only offer highly standardised products in view of regulatory risk,[115] they have become very popular amongst retail investors.

Robo-advisers managed assets valued at about USD145 m in Europe in early 2020,[116] a figure growing at 38% year over year and expected to grow at least 24% in the following year. The most popular robo-adviser in the UK, Nutmeg, saw its assets under management grow by 41% in the year 2019,[117] despite the industry averaging at a growth rate of 13%. Moneyfarm, another popular robo-adviser in the EU and UK, also saw assets under management grow by 80% from 2018 to 2019.[118]

Retail investors' interest in digitalised modes of investing is not confined to conventional financial returns-based investing. This is reflected in retail investors' keen participation in online equity crowdfunding—where monies are directly channelled to projects or causes they identify with and support—as a matter of social and personal mobilisation, and not merely financial instrumentality.[119] Indeed, there is significant interest in reward-based crowdfunding where projects usually pertain to social or environmental causes.[120] The introduction of the EU Regulation on Crowdfunding, which standardises investor protection such as mandatory disclosure by issuers and duties for platforms, is widely expected to improve market confidence and galvanise growth in this area.[121]

---

114 Public Attitudes to Financial Advice Survey, 2016, https://bandce.co.uk/wp-content/uploads/2016/02/201602-Public-attitudes-to-advice.pdf; *Benjamin P. Edwards*, "The Rise of Automated Investment Advice: Can Robo-Advisers Rescue the Retail Market" Chi.-Kent L. Rev, 2018, 93, 97.

115 *Iris H-Y Chiu*, Transforming the Financial Advice Market – The Roles of Robo-advice, Financial Regulation and Public Governance in the UK, Banking and Finance Law Review, 2019, 35, 9.

116 https://www.statista.com/outlook/337/102/robo-advisors/europe.

117 'Nutmeg tops £2 m AUM' (31 Jan 2020) at https://www.moneymarketing.co.uk/news/nutmeg-tops-2bn-aum/.

118 'Moneyfarm goes from strength to strength' (26 Sep 2019), https://blog.moneyfarm.com/en/moneyfarm-news/moneyfarm-raises-36-million-as-it-launches-one-of-the-largest-digital-wealth-management-partnerships-in-europe/.

119 *Matthew Hollow*, "Crowdfunding and Civic Society in Europe: A Profitable Partnership?" Open Citizenship, 2013, 4, 68.

120 *Saman Adhami/Giancarlo Giudici/Huy Pham Nguyen Anh*, "Crowdfunding for Green Projects in Europe: Success Factors and Effects on the Local Environmental Performance and Wellbeing", 2017, http://www.crowdfundres.eu/wp-content/uploads/2017/11/Crowdfunding-for-green-projects-in-Europe-2017.pdf.

121 EU Crowdfunding Regulation 2020 text based on July 2020 version, see https://www.consilium.europa.eu/en/press/press-releases/2020/07/20/capital-markets-union-council-adopts-

Digital and sustainable finance can be connected by mobilising the availability of indexed sustainably-labelled financial products through digital platforms and robo-advice channels. However, this policy needs to be supported by clarifying how investment advisory duties can be discharged in a manner integrating investors' financial and sustainability needs. This may involve an amendment to the duty of suitability imposed on investment advisors, which will help to clarify and support the concerns of this industry in relation to their legal risk.

3.1 Integrating Sustainability Objectives into Investment Advice

A regulatory duty to advise of 'suitable' investments applies where a personalised recommendation has been made to a customer,[122] excluding forms of more informal,[123] generic or marketing information. Further, an investment services provider must categorise clients into one of three groups: the retail client, the professional client and the eligible counterparty.[124] The professional client is defined as certain financial and corporate institutions as well as natural persons meeting certain quantitative criteria such as investible assets and frequency of financial transactions carried out previously, as well as qualitative criteria in relation to his or her expertise, knowledge and experience with financial services and transactions.[125] The eligible counterparty would be regarded as belonging in a peer level to financial institutions.[126] These two categories of customers are owed a lesser extent of (a) the duty of suitability in relation to investment advice or portfolio management, and (b) the duty of appropriateness for other financial transactions or services.[127]

For advisory and portfolio management services, financial services providers have to ensure that their service or advice is 'suitable' for the customer,[128] but

---

new-rules-for-crowdfunding-platforms/. The relevance of investor confidence to market growth may be attributed to the 'law and finance effect', discussed in La Porta et al (2006).

122 Art 25, Markets in Financial Instruments Directive 2014/65/EU (MiFID); Art 9, MiFID (Markets in Financial Instruments Directive) Commission Delegated Regulation 2017/565.

123 *Redmayne Bentley Stockbrokers v Isaacs & Ors* [2010] EWHC 1504 (Comm).

124 FCA Handbook COBS 3.4, 3.5, 3.6.

125 FCA Handbook COBS 3.5.

126 FCA Handbook COBS 3.6.

127 Art 25(3), MiFID 2014, Arts 54, 55, MiFID Commission Delegated Regulation 2017/565.

128 'Suitability' is interpreted as meeting the client's investment objectives and risk tolerance, and that the client understands the nature of the product or service engaged with and is finan-

retail customers benefit from a more comprehensive information collection exercise than other customers, and the obligation of 'suitability' is more extensively owed to retail customers.[129] The duties of suitability and appropriateness have been developed in a highly procedural manner.

Where investment advice or portfolio management is concerned, firms need to collect three areas of prescribed information from customers—investment objectives, risk appetite and financial profile—in order to recommend products that meet the customer's investment objectives, suit his or her risk appetite, and whose risks are reasonably understood by the customer.[130] For other financial transactions, firms need to collect information on the customer's knowledge and understanding of the risks of the transaction concerned in order to proceed with the transaction. In sum, the duties of suitability and appropriateness, even when they apply in full, are highly procedural, and can mitigate a firm's legal risk as compliance is evidenced by adhering to sound procedures and systems[131] that give rise to the ultimate recommendation, providing *ex ante* safety against *ex post* allegations of negligence. Further, firms need to provide a suitability report[132] to their customers ahead of customers' decision-making in order to fully inform them of the basis for recommending certain products as suitable. This provides *ex ante* information to the customer but also plays a significant role in mitigating *ex post* litigation risk for the firm.

The duty of suitability is framed in financial terms as customers' investment objectives and risk tolerance, which are determined by eliciting relevant proxy indicators such as duration of investment horizon and purpose of saving (e. g. for a housing deposit or for education). Further, customers' risk tolerance is also defined in consideration of customers' financial ability to bear loss.[133] Sustainability objectives need to be integrated into investors' preferences and suitability assessments.[134] The potential complexification of legal risk for investment

---

cially able to bear those risks. For a retail customer, the financial services provider must be satisfied that all three elements are achieved and explained in a suitability report to the customer. See Art 54, Commission Delegated Regulation (EU) 2017/565.

129 See legislation citations, ibid. Sophisticated customers are assumed to be able to bear their own financial risk and to have requisite levels of knowledge regarding investment products.
130 Art 54, 55 MiFID Commission Delegated Regulation 2017/565.
131 *Maple Leaf Macro Volatility Master Fund v Jacques Rouvroy* [2009] EWHC 257 (Comm); [2009] 1 Lloyd's Rep 475.
132 Art 54, MiFID Commission Delegated Regulation 2017/565.
133 Art 54, MiFID Commission Regulation 2017/565.
134 See https://ec.europa.eu/info/law/better-regulation/have-your-say/initiatives/12068-Strength ening-the-consideration-of-sustainability-risks-and-factors-for-financial-products-Regulation-EU-

advisors needs to be addressed if the demand for investment advice on sustainably-labelled financial products increases. In a robo-advice context, the financial nature of the duty of suitability is singularly adhered to by adopting a procedural approach. Adjustments should be made to the duty of suitability in order to facilitate investment advice that supports the sustainably-labelled product market, and the robo-advice industry in particular can benefit from such adjustments.

3.2 Integrating Investors' Sustainability Objectives into Robo-advice?

Robo-advice is the shorthand for automated forms of investment management interfaces. A robo-adviser can provide an algorithm-generated list of investment options to customers based on customer data, leaving customers to take further action. Robo-advisers also include automated wealth management services where portfolios are constructed by algorithmic intelligence, monitored according to programmed parameters and automatically rebalanced according to those parameters.[135]

It has been observed that robo-advisors are accessible on-demand, 24/7 in the comfort of one's environment.[136] This seems to meet the access preferences of many investors.[137] Crucially, robo-advice is often accessible to those who have small amounts to save, exemplified by Nutmeg's promise to on-board customers saving from as little as £100 initially.[138] This has the potential to help with 'democratising finance' and increasing financial inclusion, an outcome already observed in the United States where robo-advisors have garnered over USD $400 billion assets under management and are looking to exceed USD$1.5 trillion by 2023.[139] The cost of use of robo-advisors is also generally lower than other forms of investment fund management, as annual charges can be three

---

2017-565; also "AI can drive ethical investment only if we grasp the messy reality" (Financial Times, 9 Nov 2020), https://www.ft.com/content/b238b8f2-8645-4654-a806-681c9a461d0b.

135 *Pablo Sanz Bayón/Luis Garvía Vega*, "Automated Investment Advice: Legal Challenges and Regulatory Questions" Banking and Financial Services Policy Report, 2018, 37, 1.

136 *Andrea L. Seidt/Noula Zaharis/Charles Jarrett*, "Paying Attention to That Man behind the Curtain: State Securities Regulators' Early Conversations with Robo-Advisers" U. Tol. L. Rev, 2019, 50, 501.

137 Public Attitudes to Financial Advice Survey (2016).

138 https://www.nutmeg.com/new-to-investing, but see Edwards, 2018, who finds that some robo-advisers allow savers to start investing from as low as $8.

139 *Facundo Abraham/Sergio L Schmukler/José Tessada*, "Robo-Advisors: Investing through Machines", World Bank Research and Policy Brief, 2019.

times lower.[140] From an affordability point of view, robo-advisers have the potential to incentivise access, and in the UK[141] and Germany,[142] the two largest robo-adviser markets in Europe, there is an upward trend in terms of growth in robo-advisers' market share.

However, robo-advice suffers from several limitations. Most robo-advisers are programmed to adopt diversification strategies adhering to Modern Portfolio Theory,[143] and recommend investing only in exchange-traded funds,[144] or in passive index-linked funds that are often seen as cost-effective and reliable in performance.[145] Further, they are often 'restricted advisers' that are tied to a limited range of products.[146]

Robo-advisers have benefited from the procedural implementation of the duty of suitability. Compliance with suitability entails the eliciting of customer information as prescribed, and then matching the profile of the customer with financial products that are categorised accordingly. The procedural approach in complying with suitability and appropriateness makes the advisory process programmable in terms of sequencing and matching. Indeed, financial products are sorted into only a few categories for matching purposes, principally by risk appetite,[147] and this allows the programming of a clear labelling strategy for robo-advisors in seeking matches with customers' profiles. Such strategies are highly standardised and designed to be cost-effective and fuss-free, meeting requirements of suitability and appropriateness. This business model presents a relatively low level of legal risk for robo-advisory firms. The incorporation of sustainability preferences presents new challenges in the design of questionnaires

---

140 *Wolf-Georg Ringe/Christopher Ruof*, "A Regulatory Sandbox for Robo Advice", ILE Working Paper, 2018, http://hdl.handle.net/10419/179514.

141 *Gregor Dorfleitner/Lars Hornuf/Matthias Schmitt/Martina Weber*, "The Fintech Market in Germany", 2016, https://papers.ssrn.com/sol3/papers.cfm?abstract_id=2885931.

142 ibid.

143 *Michael Faloon/Bernt Scherer*, "Individualization of Robo-Advice" Journal of Wealth Management, 2017, 31.

144 Meaning that are liquid and traded on an exchange within the day, see *Philipp Maume*, "Regulating Robo-Advisory" Texas International Law Review, 2018/9, forthcoming.

145 The outperformance of passive index-linked funds has often been touted as superior to actively managed 'stock-picker' funds, *Kevin R James*, "The Price of Retail Investing in the UK", FSA Occasional Paper, 2000; *Burton G Malkiel*, Efficient Markets and Mutual Fund Investing: The Advantages of Index Funds in: John D Haslem (ed), Mutual Funds: Portfolio Structures, Analysis, Management, and Stewardship, 2010, ch 7.

146 For example the largest robo-adviser Nutmeg in the UK has over £800 m in assets under management but is a restricted adviser recommending its own products only.

147 *Faloon/Scherer* (fn. 143); *Bernd Scherer*, "Algorithmic Portfolio Choice: Lessons from Panel Survey Data" Financial Markets Portfolio Management, 2017, 31, 49.

that would translate into clear decision pathways for robo-advisors, and may therefore raise legal risks for robo-advisers in discharging the duty of suitability, discussed below. We observe that many robo-advisors do not provide for clearly signposted 'sustainable' options. There is room for development in policy thinking to leverage retail investors' interest in digitalised investing and to provide a framework to mitigate providers' legal risk in offering such options.

First, the duty of suitability would have to accommodate investors' sustainable objectives. The duty as framed in the Markets in Financial Instruments Directive 2014 (MiFID) does not exclude sustainable objectives, although the conventional interpretation of investors' objectives relates to financial ones. Robo-advisors' conventional due diligence cannot accommodate such objectives at the moment. If 'sustainable' objectives are added to the mix, it may be complex for robo-advisers to map investors' objectives onto products. 'Sustainable' objectives can contain subjective elements, i.e. investors' personal preferences, and objective elements such as the time it takes for sustainable goals to be achieved. Further, investors' sustainable objectives can be vaguer than financial ones.

The Regulations arguably ameliorate the imprecision or complexity of sustainability objectives. The Regulations provide a minimum definitional framework for sustainable objectives under the Sustainability Disclosures Regulation 2019 and a 'ceiling' of precise objectives for environmentally-sustainable objectives under the Taxonomy Regulation 2020.[148] Investors' choice of sustainable objectives can be mapped according to the Regulations. In order to facilitate the robo-advisory market to incorporate sustainable objectives, legislative clarification is required to articulate that the duty of suitability *includes* investors' sustainable objectives. An amendment to the Commission Regulation as delegated legislation to the MiFID has been proposed, [149] and we make further suggestions in this article for more clarification.

In ascertaining investors' objectives, Article 25 of the MiFID also requires investment intermediaries to find out investors' ability to bear financial risks.[150] Robo-advisory models implement this aspect of the duty of suitability by ascertaining whether investors' financial profiles are consistent with their preferences along the risk/return trade-off spectrum. In light of the marketising agenda for

---

148 Discussed in Sect. 2.
149 Art 54, Commission Delegated Regulation (EU) 2017/565; and consultation on amendment is at https://ec.europa.eu/info/law/better-regulation/have-your-say/initiatives/12068-Strengthening-the-consideration-of-sustainability-risks-and-factors-for-financial-products-Regulation-EU-2017–565.
150 Ibid.

sustainable finance, it can be argued that this focus on customers' financial motivations and profiles is too narrowly-framed.

Empirical research shows mixed evidence regarding whether investing in sustainable objectives is aligned with financial performance,[151] and many investors may be willing to accommodate a trade-off in favour of sustainable objectives even if financial performance is somewhat sacrificed.[152] This preference should be fielded in robo-advisory questionnaires as this has an impact on categorisation of investors and selection of matching products. Sustainably-labelled products have been touted for entailing superior financial performance, but investors should not take this for granted.[153] Indeed, sustainably-labelled products may be managed with a restricted portfolio or constitute relatively less liquid investments. In this manner, certain fund compositions could entail a trade-off[154] between financial and sustainable performance of the product.

It is proposed that where investment intermediaries are aware of proxy characteristics in a product that may involve a trade-off between financial returns and attainment of sustainable objectives, they should provide investors with a clear warning that this may be expected and the reasons why, for example because of a more restricted portfolio. Such a warning can be attached to particular products offered on the robo-advisory platform. Robo-advisers developing their protocols with more integrated data on investors' sustainability preferences and product sustainability can ultimately provide more sophisticated categorisations to investors to match with a more comprehensive suite of conventional and sustainably-labelled products.

Thirdly, investment intermediaries need to ensure that investors understand the nature of the product they are investing in, so as to discharge the duty of suitability. It can be argued that sustainable finance may be more complex, given that it has mixed objectives and aims at creating hybrid value with perhaps trade-offs. This may intensify the need for investment intermediaries to be satisfied that investors understand these dilemmas. If investment intermediaries need to invest in educational tools, for example, in order to mitigate their legal risks, offering sustainable finance products can become burdensome and costly. It can however be argued that the Sustainable Disclosure Regulation 2019 ameliorates this risk. The Regulation's prescriptions for mandatory disclosure, to be made

---

151 See fn. 111.

152 *Hafenstein/Bassen* (fn. 66); *Gutsche/Ziegler* (fn. 66).

153 *Sekhar Amba*, "Corporate Sustainability: Do Executives and Investors Care?- An Empirical Study" International Journal of Management and Marketing Research, 2018, 11, 19; *de Haan et al*, 2012.

154 *Ielasi* et al (fn. 111).

more granular in Commission legislation, would provide pre-contractual information for investors in relation to both actively-managed and passively-managed products. Large firms subject to the mandatory duty to disclose adverse sustainability impact at product level from 2022 would in addition be able to inform investors that way. Further, the Commission is introducing amendments to product governance rules to ensure that manufacturers and distributors of investment products clearly envisage sustainably-labelled products for the appropriate target market.[155] In this manner, the reforms we propose to the duty of suitability build upon the advancements already made, but achieve more pinpoint protection for investors.

Further, it may be optimal for Commission legislation to specify that the mandatory disclosures be made in a manner that a lay person can access, in both non-technical and technical language. In an online context, cross-referencing to mandatory disclosures may be tiresome for an investor and robo-advisors have to give some thought as to how information can be signposted. Investors should be made to read salient information in a user-friendly interface.

Adjustments to the duty of suitability would be necessary to accommodate investors' needs in sustainable finance generally, as ESMA already foresees.[156] Providers of robo-advisory protocols can also be encouraged to develop more competitive and sophisticated data management and profiling programmes for appealing to a wide market of investors, as demand is increasing in this area.[157] The implementation of an adjusted duty of suitability in robo-advisory protocols is necessary to connect digital and sustainable finance. We think further policy frameworks may be necessary in due course, such as the development of a market for comparison websites for mutual funds and robo-advisors,[158]

---

155 *European Commission*, "COMMISSION DELEGATED DIRECTIVE (EU) .../... amending Delegated Directive (EU) 2017/593 as regards the integration of sustainability factors into the product governance obligations" (2021). https://eur-lex.europa.eu/legal-content/EN/TXT/?uri=PI COM:C (2021)2612.

156 *ESMA, Guidelines on Certain Aspects of the MiFID II Suitability Requirements* (2018), https://www.esma.europa.eu/sites/default/files/library/esma35-43-869-_fr_on_guidelines_on_suit ability.pdf, p6.

157 'Sustainable investing is set to surge in the wake of the coronavirus pandemic', CNBC News, 7 June 2020, https://www.cnbc.com/2020/06/07/sustainable-investing-is-set-to-surge-in-the-wake-of-the-coronavirus-pandemic.html.

158 These are now subject to regulation by the FCA in the UK, see FCA, PS16/15: Feedback on CP15/33 – Consumer credit: proposals in response to the CMA recommendations on high-cost short-term credit, 2016, https://www.fca.org.uk/publications/policy-statements/ps16-15-feed back-cp15-33-consumer-credit-proposals-response-cma in relation to comparison websites for high-cost short-term credit; FCA, Guidance on the: Selling of General Insurance Policies Through

and improvements to robo-advisors in relation to post-sale services like investor engagement.[159] These are however beyond the scope of this paper for now.

4 Conclusion

The EU has developed a pioneering framework for marketising and regulating sustainably-labelled financial products. This article critically analyses the resulting regime and argues that the interaction between its regulative and enabling aspects creates mixed messages for governance and market-building. The Regulations adopt an incentive-based approach towards market-building for quality sustainable finance, but lower-level products are not shut out. The article predicts that market-building may be concentrated in passively-managed indexed products, but such products cannot be developed along the same passive trajectories as in conventional fund management, given the positive obligations attached to monitoring and reporting on quality. Moreover, the introduction of more stringent governance for large investment intermediaries may lead to fragmentation in compliance and market fragmentation in favour of the domination of large investment fund houses. These regulatory reforms need to be complimented by mobilising institutions to demand quality sustainably-labelled investment products, and by making them available to retail investors too. Where retail investors are concerned, we argue that the policy gap lies in bridging sustainable and digital finance. Investment advice provided to retail investors must incorporate the needs of sustainable finance, and the legal duty of suitability should be adjusted. Although this is in progress at the level of the Commission, the proposed amendments seem minimal and can be further clarified to take into account of the complexities of sustainable investments. We further discuss how our proposals are necessary to and can be implemented in digital finance, via robo-advisory channels that are growing in popularity with retail investors. The connection between digital and sustainable finance can be highly synergistic in attracting both institutional and retail demand.

Price Comparison Websites, 2011, https://www.fca.org.uk/publication/finalised-guidance/fg11_17.pdf.

159 the question of whether investors in pooled funds can feed in preferences for institutional shareholder engagement for example, as argued in E. *McGaughey*, "Does Corporate Governance Exclude the Ultimate Investor?" Journal of Corporate Law Studies, 2015, 16, 221.

Rainer Kulms

Digital Financial Markets and (Europe's) Private Law – A Case for Regulatory Competition?

Abstract: The EU's Digital Finance Strategy assumes that regulations and private laws interact. National private law systems are to demonstrate sufficient evolutionary strength to cope with digital disruption. Regulatory competition is intended to produce adequate private law solutions if EU regulators bring up the right questions. This paper takes a private law perspective to assess the EU's strategy and highlight potential shortcomings. Payment services, outsourcing business models, crowd lending, robo-advice and blockchain applications are identified as test cases where the interface between FinTech regulation and private law is most acutely felt. This translates into a re-interpretation of (digital) contractual duties. Traditional liability rules need to evolve, and incoherent concepts under the EU's digital finance and data protection laws have to be reconciled. Blockchain law is a model case for the far-reaching impact of the interface between FinTech and private law. Member States have to improve the private law status of crypto-assets in order to attract business and address insolvency scenarios. Regulatory sandboxes are addressed as early warning mechanisms, alerting regulators and legislators to risks arising from innovative business models. As innovation intensifies, so will the evolutionary pressure on Member States' private law systems, likely to provoke demands for EU legislative action if Member States underperform.

Table of Contents

Rainer Kulms, Priv.-Doz., Dr. iur., LL.M., Senior Research Fellow, Max Planck Institute for Comparative and International Private Law, Hamburg, Germany.

∂ OpenAccess. © 2022 Rainer Kulms, published by De Gruyter. [CC BY-NC-ND] This work is licensed under the Creative Commons Attribution-NonCommercial-NoDerivatives 4.0 International License.
https://doi.org/10.1515/9783110749472-008

1 Digital Disruption and its Fallout

1.1 Introduction

FinTech and artificial intelligence have changed the infrastructure of financial markets[1]. Distributed ledger technology stimulates cross-border transactions generated through algorithms, accelerating the privatisation of rule-making[2]. As a corollary, applications of artificial intelligence and machine learning enhance interconnectedness between financial markets and institutions[3]. Networks are emerging which test the viability of private regulation, regulatory intervention and the concept of enforcement of norms in a cross-border scenario[4].

---

[1] *Xavier Vives*, Digital disruption in financial markets – Note, OECD – Directorate for Financial and Enterprise Affairs (Competition Committee), p. 5 et seq. (16 May 2019, DAF/COMP(2019)1) (available at https://one.oecd.org/document/DAF/COMP(2019)1/en/pdf), *José Manuel González-Páramo*, Financial Innovation in the Digital Age: Challenges for Regulation and Supervision, Banco de España, Revista de Estabilidad Financiera, Núm. 32 (May 2017), 11, 15 et seq., Financial Times online 19 November 2020, *Gillian Tett*, Artificial Intelligence is reshaping finance (available at https://www.ft.com/content/c7d9a81c-e6a3 – 4f37-bbfd-71dcefda3739). Cf. on FinTech business models in Germany: *Gregor Dorfleitner/Lars Hornuf*, FinTech and Data Privacy in Germany – An Empirical Analysis with Policy Recommendations, 2009, p. 85 et seq.

[2] See *Florian Möslein/Sebastian Omlor*, in: *id.* (eds), FinTech-Handbuch – Digitalisierung- Recht – Finanzen, 2nd ed. 2021), p. 4 et seq., on the interface between distributed ledger technology and privatisation of rule-making.

[3] Financial Stability Board (FSB), Artificial intelligence and machine learning in financial services Market developments and financial stability implications (1 November 2017), p. 31 (available at https://www.fsb.org/wp-content/uploads/P011117.pdf).

[4] *Yane Svetiev*, in: *Hans-W. Micklitz/Yane Svetiev* (eds,), A Self-Sufficient European Private Law – A Viable Concept?, European University Institute, Department of Law Working Paper 2012/31) (available at https://works.bepress.com/jan_smits/66/), *Fabrizio Cafaggi*, in: *Kai Purnhagen/Peter Rott* (eds.), Varieties of European Law and Regulation, Liber Amicorum für Hans Micklitz,

FinTech invites regulatory competition on a global scale[5] and among the legal orders of the Member States of the European Union (EU). In some areas, there is evidence that a race to the bottom is conceivable[6]. However, the interface between functioning digital markets and the commodification of financial data leaves regulators and practitioners with a complicated message. Particularly private blockchains operate on a set of rules mutually agreed upon or imposed by the gatekeeper of a permissioned system[7]. Here, legislators might be called upon to supplying private law remedies (with erga-omnes effects) to assure enforceability of the results generated by distributed ledger technology. In 2019, the United Kingdom (UK) Law Tech delivery panel launched a public consultation on the legal status of crypto-assets, distributed ledger technology and smart contracts under English law[8]. It was felt that in spite of the flexibility of English common law the financial community suffered from a lack of certainty about the legal status of these devices[9]. Switzerland has relied on a similar argument: When the Swiss government published the draft for a law on distributed ledger technology, it explained that openness towards innovation needs to be supported by rules on

---

2014, 259, 262 et seq. See also European Commission, Communication on a Retail Payments Strategy for the EU, sub # III. (Brussels 24 September 2020 (COM(2020) 592 final, available at https://eur-lex.europa.eu/legal-content/EN/TXT/PDF/?uri=CELEX:52020DC0592&from=EN), on the need to establish full interoperability for cross-border infrastructures for instant payments.
5 See on the competitiveness of the EU financial as a global standard: Expert Group on Regulatory Obstacles to Financial Innovation (ROFIEG), 30 Recommendations on Regulation, Innovation and Finance, Final Report to the European Commission (December 2019), p. 11 (available at https://ec.europa.eu/info/files/191113-report-expert-group-regulatory-obstacles-financial-in novation_en). From a practical perspective, Switzerland's blockchain law (see infra sub 3.4.) attracts EU banks to offer trading and custody services for digital assets from Switzerland: See Bitcoin.com – News 19 December 2020, Spain's Second Largest Bank BBVA Launches Bitcoin Trading and Custody in Switzerland (available at https://news.bitcoin.com/spains-second-largest-bank-bbva-bitcoin-trading-custody-switzerland/), Frankfurter Allgemeine online 14 December 2020, Kryptowährungen – Bitcoin bei der Bank (available at https://www.faz.net/aktuell/finan zen/digital-bezahlen/bbva-will-2021-in-der-schweiz-bitcoin-handel-anbieten-17102098.html).
6 See *Luca Enriques*, Welcome to Vilnius: Regulatory Competition in the EU Market for E-Money, Columbia Law School Blog 4 November 2019 (available at https://clsbluesky.law.columbia.edu/2019/11/04/welcome-to-vilnius-regulatory-competition-in-the-eu-market-for-e-money/).
7 See *Chris Reed/Andrew Murray*, Rethinking the Jurisprudence of Cyberspace, 2018/2020, 112 et seq., 117 et seq., on normative competition in cyberspace through norms emerging from user interaction and technological specificities.
8 UK Jurisdiction Task Force of the LawTech Delivery Panel, Public Consultation – The status of crypto-assets, distributed ledger technology and smart contracts under English private law (May 2019, available at https://www.lawsociety.org.uk/campaigns/lawtech/news/crypto-assets-dlt-and-smart-contracts-ukjt-consultation).
9 Ibid., p. 4.

commodification and tradability of financial instruments (i.e. blockchain-based tokens)[10]. Liechtenstein's new blockchain law is also inspired by this legislative approach[11].

Competition authorities emphasise the positive welfare effects of financial disruption through FinTech, arguing for a principle-based approach where technology is faster than law[12]. The Spanish Competition Commission favours market entry under transparency, and disclosure rules with respect to conflicts of interest[13]. From a legislative policy perspective, insistence on transparency reflects a policy choice for informed markets[14]. Less charitably, transparency might also point to legislative unwillingness to interfere with the negative side-effects of (cross-border) digital finance, placing the risk on investors to find out by litigation whether they have to bear the consequences of a fall-out from innovation. The allocative effects this policy approach to innovation[15] have to be absorbed by private actors and their (prescient) ability to design contracts unlikely to fail a reality test[16].

The current regulatory approach towards FinTech has been criticized for an inherent micro-transactional bias which relegates regulators to neglecting macro-level risks for the benefit of private business models[17]. It is posited that a technocratic micro-level focus on FinTech exacerbates self-referential growth

---

10 See Schweizerische Eidgenossenschaft, Bundesrat, Press Release 27 November 2019, Bundesrat will Rahmenbedingungen für DLT/Blockchain weiter verbessern (available at https://www.admin.ch/gov/de/start/dokumentation/medienmitteilungen.msg-id-77252.html).

11 Token- und VT-Dienstleister-Gesetz (TVTG), Liechtensteinisches Landesgesetzblatt [Liechtenstein Gazette] 2019, no. 301 of 2 December 2019, *Josef Bergt*, Token als Wertrechte – Token Offerings und dezentrale Handelsplätze, 2nd ed. 2020, p. 67 et seq.

12 See Competition Bureau Canada, Technology-led Innovation in the Canadian Financial Services Sector – A Market Study, pp. 8, 20 (December 2017, available at https://www.competitionbureau.gc.ca/eic/site/cb-bc.nsf/eng/04322.html)., and the Spanish Comisión Nacional de los Mercados y la Competencia (CNMC), Study on the Impact on Competition of Technological Innovation in the Financial Sector (FinTech) (Madrid 13 September 2018, E/CNMC/001/18),, p. 21 et seq. (available https://www.cnmc.es/sites/default/files/2218346_1.pdf).

13 CNMC (fn. 12), p. 80.

14 *Christopher P. Buttigieg et al.*, A Critical Analysis of the Rationale for Financial Regulation Part II: Objectives of Financial Regulation, ECFR 2020, 437, 464 et seq.

15 See on the allocative effects of the regulatory commitment to promote innovation: *Saule T. Omarova*, Technology v. Technocracy: FinTech as a Regulatory Challenge, 6 J. Fin. Reg. 75, 109 (2020).

16 See on the interface between financial regulation and private law: *Olha O. Cherednychenko*, Two Sides of the Same Coin: The EU Regulation and Private Law, 22 (1) EBOR 147, 151 et seq. (2021).

17 *Omarova* (fn. 15), p. 6 J. Fin. Reg. 75, 109 (2020).

and systemic risks, if applied as a normative imperative[18]. Instead, "public accommodation" should provide a framework for "privately created risks and liabilities"[19]. It is difficult to see, however, how the macro-economic effects of a purely transactional approach towards regulation can be ascertained without analysing the private law framework for FinTech transactions[20]. Innovation in finance critically depends on the evolutionary potential of private law[21], as regulators find it difficult to produce standards which demonstrate both understanding and anticipation how machine learning produces (undesired) outcomes[22]. This suggests that EU Financial Regulation might also operate under the tacit assumption that private law will be capable of supplying workable solutions where statutory financial law remains silent[23]. Thus, a polycentric approach is apposite which combines rule-making by governmental actors[24] with efficient rules for private contracts and digital assets.

---

18 *Omarova* (fn. 15), 6 J. Fin. Reg. 75, 109 et seq. (2020).

19 *Saule T. Omarova*, New Tech v. New Deal: FinTech as a Systemic Phenomenon, 36 Yale J. Reg. 735, 756 (2019).

20 See *Randall E. Duran/Paul Griffin*, Smart contracts: will Fintech be the catalyst for the next global financial crisis, 29 (1) J. Fin. Reg. & Compliance 104–122 (118) (2021), on devising best practice guidelines mandatory settlement requirements for certain types of smart contracts.

21 See *Cherednychenko* (fn. 16), p. 147, 163

22 See Financial Times online 6 August 2019, *Imogen Tew*, Full robo-advice' impossible to regulate' (available at https://www.ftadviser.com/your-industry/2019/08/06/full-robo-advice-impos sible-to-regulate/). *Christopher Woolard* (FCA), The future of regulation: AI for consumer good, Speech London 16 July 2019 (available at https://www.fca.org.uk/news/speeches/future-regu lation-ai-consumer-good), Financial Times online 16 July 2019, *Imogen Tew*, FCA concerned about firms not tackling tech risk (available at https://www.ftadviser.com/regulation/2019/07/ 16/fca-concerned-about-firms-not-tackling-tech-risk/). See also regulators' uncertainty due to asymmetric information on digitised processes: FinTech Working Group of the United Nations Secretary-General' Advocate for Inclusive Finance (UNSGSA)/Monetary Authority of Singapore/ University of Cambridge, Early Lessons on Regulatory Innovations to Enable Inclusive FinTech: Innovation Offices, Regulatory Sandboxes, and RegTech, p. 23 et seq., on frequent exchanges between the industry and regulators (2019, available at https://www.jbs.cam.ac.uk/fileadmin/ user_upload/research/centres/alternative-finance/downloads/2019-summary_ear lylessonsregulatoryinnovations.pdf), passim ESMA/EBA/EIOPA, FinTech: Regulatory sandboxes and innovation hubs – Report p. 8 et seq. (JC 2018 74) (available at https://www.esma.europa.eu/ sites/default/files/library/jc_2018_74_joint_report_on_regulatory_sandboxes_and_innovation_ hubs.pdf), p. 6 et seq. Cf. *Douglas Arner/Janos N. Barberis/Ross P.Buckley*, FinTech, RegTech, and the Reconceptualization of Financial Regulation, 37 (3) Nw. J. Int'l. L. & Bus. 371, 403 et seq., (2017) on the challenges for regulators.

23 Cf. *Cherednychenko* (fn. 16), p. 147, 163 et seq.

24 See *Yane Svetiev*, in: Liber Amicorum Micklitz (fn. 4), 153–177 (p. 157 et seq)., invoking normative and institutional pluralism and a fragmented legal landscape as arguments supporting a

1.2 Outline of the Paper

Financial services are credence goods[25] which depend on consumer confidence[26], trust and the enforceability of public and private law rules[27]. This paper takes a private law perspective on FinTech. It explores the underlying assumption of the EU Commission's digital finance strategy[28] that the law for FinTech and private law rules interact. The – tacit – appeal to Member States to play the evolutionary private law part of FinTech operates to trigger competition between their respective private legal orders[29]. This, however, assumes that the EU's FinTech law 'asks' the right questions. Therefore, prominent FinTech business models will be tested on their capacity to stimulate evolution of national private law orders, but also to aggravate deficiencies from an exclusive reliance on private law solutions.

This paper identifies payment services, outsourcing business models, crowdlending, robo-advice and aspects of blockchain applications as test cases where the interface between the EU's financial market regulation and private law is most acutely felt. Especially in blockchain law, the EU faces competition from non-Member State legal orders. The EU's regulatory approach, as reinforced by

---

plea for European Regulatory Private Law. See generally on the notion of a European Regulatory Private Law: Guido Comparato/Hans-W. Micklitz/Yane Svetiev (eds.), European Private Regulatory Private Law – Autonomy, Competition and Regulation in European Private Law (European University Law Institute Working Paper LAW 2016/00).

25 See *Iris H-Y Chiu*, FinRech and Disruptive Business Models in Financial Products, Intermediation and Markets – Policy Implications for Financial Regulators, 21 J. Tech. L. & Pol'y 55–112 (74) (2016), cf. *Hillary J. Allen*, Regulatory Sandboxes, 87 (3) Geo. Wash. L. Rev. 579, 587 (2019).

26 See on (limited) consumer acceptance of automated enforcement through smart contracts: *Danielle D'Onfro*, Smart Contracts and the Illusion of Automated Enforcement, 61 Wash. U. J.L. & Pol'y 173, 183 et seq. (2020).

27 The debate on the private law effects of conduct of business rules under the Directive 2014/65/EU of 15 May 2014 on markets in financial instruments, O.J. L 173/349 of 12 June 2014 (MiFID II) demonstrates the crucial importance of the interface between supervisory law and private law rules. For a detailed analysis see: *Federico Della Negra*, MiFID II and Private Law – Enforcing EU Conduct of Business Rules, Oxford 2019, p. 27 et seq., and *Marnix W. Wallinga*, EU investor protection regulation and private law (PhD thesis Groningen, 2018), p. 60 et seq. Passim on the interface between supervisory capital market and private laws: *Florian Möslein/Christopher Rennig*, in: *Marco Cian/Claudia Sandei, M. Cian/C. Sandei* (eds.), Diritto del FinTech, Milan 2020, p. 471, 472.

28 See EU Commission, Communication on Digital Finance Strategy for the EU (Brussels 24 September 2020 (COM(2020) 591 final) at # 4.2. (available at https://eur-lex.europa.eu/legal-content/EN/TXT/PDF/?uri=CELEX:52020DC0591&from=EN).

29 See the country studies in: *Cian/ Sandei* (fn. 27), p. 439 et seq.

the digital finance package of September 2020[30], is understood as an incentive to fill – deliberate – gaps by private laws and their evolutionary potential or, private contracting. Shortcomings of this approach will be highlighted which may ultimately trigger the enactment of European regulatory private law instruments. This applies particularly to incoherent liability concepts and the complicated relationship between digital finance and data protection law.

The analysis of current FinTech business models will be supplemented by a survey over regulatory sandboxes. Regulatory sandboxes have been so devised as to test innovative digital business models under the auspices of financial market authorities. Businesses are afforded an opportunity to scrutinize the viability of their digital concepts. Financial market authorities collect empirical data and assess the viability of a principle-based approach to regulatory action. Most sandbox models attempt to avert negative externalities by imposing transparency and insurance requirements. Sandbox models may operate as early-warning mechanisms, indicating where future regulatory action might be necessary. A final section sums up the findings on the state of interaction between financial law and private law.

2 FinTech Activities and the Evolving Law of Decentralised Finance

2.1 Payment Services – Basics

The amended Payment Services Directive (PSD II)[31] has opened up traditional banking. Peer-to-Peer (P2P) and peer-to-Business (P2B) payments are widely accepted[32], including transactions from mobile wallets[33]. Real-time payment sys-

---

30 See EU Commission, Press Release, Digital Finance Package: Commission sets out new, ambitious approach to encourage responsible innovation to benefit consumers and business (Press Release, Brussels 24 September 2020, available at https://ec.europa.eu/commission/presscorner/detail/en/IP_20_1684).

31 Directive (EU) 2015/2366 of 25 November 2015 on payment services in the internal market amending Directives 2002/65/EC, 2009/110/EC and 2013/36/EU and Regulation (EU) No 1093/2010, and repealing Directive 2007/64/EC, O.J. L 337/35 of 23 December 2015.

32 See Schweizerische Eidgenossenschaft, Eidgenössisches Finanzdepartement, Änderung des Bankengesetzes und der Bankenverordnung (FinTech), Erläuternder Bericht zur Vernehmlassungsvorlage, p. 9 et seq.) (1 February 2017, available at https://www.admin.ch/ch/d/gg/pc/documents/2834/Fintech_Erl.-Bericht_de.pdf).

tems operate on the basis of platforms, frequently surveyed by the ECB or national banks[34]. End-users can observe any delay and disruptions[35], creating reputational risks for the payment services provider[36]. Due to stricter regulatory requirements[37] customer online identification is embracing tokenisation of payment processes, supplemented by artificial intelligence devices to verify customer transactions on the basis of past payment patterns[38]. Once tokenised payments are integrated into distributed ledger technology, such a token may operate as the private key allowing access to value stored on a blockchain[39]. The private law classification of tokens and keys will then determine whether

---

33 ING Bank Blog, The impact of real times payments on consumers and their businesses (available at https://www.ingwb.com/insights/articles/the-impact-of-real-time-payments-on-consumers-and-their-businesses); Banking Hub Payments eine Branche im Umbruch – Mit welchen strategischen Veränderungen sind Banken und Zahlungsdienstleister heute und in der Zukunft konfrontiert? (Blog 2 April 2020, available at https://bankinghub.de/innovation-digital/payments).

34 See European Commission, Communication on a Retail Payments Strategy (fn. 4), sub # III. (Brussels 24 September 2020 (COM(2020) 592 final, available at https://eur-lex.europa.eu/legal-content/EN/TXT/PDF/?uri=CELEX:52020DC0592&from=EN); European Central Bank, MIP Online, The new TARGET instant payment settlement (TIPSservice (June 2017, available at https://www.ecb.europa.eu/paym/intro/mip-online/2017/html/201706_article_tips.en.html), *Harsh Sinha*, PayThink The Fed has a key role to play in real-time payments (Blog 18 December 2019, available at https://www.paymentssource.com/opinion/the-fed-has-a-key-role-to-play-in-real-time-payments).

35 See on near real-time delays prior to the modernisation of the system: *Zhiling Guo et al.*, Near Real-Time Retail Payment and Settlement Systems Mechanism Design, p. 5 et seq. (Swift Institute Working Paper No. 2014–004, 8 September 2015) (available at https://www.swiftinstitute.org/wp-content/uploads/2015/11/WP-No-2014-004-1.pdf).

36 See *González-Páramo*, Revista de Estabilidad Financiera, Núm. 32 (May 2017), 11–37 (p. 17 et seq.), European Banking Authority (EBA), ℙ 33 Final report on EBA guidelines on outsourcing arrangement (GL/2019/0225, 25 February 2019, available at https://eba.europa.eu/sites/default/documents/files/documents/10180/2551996/38c80601-f5d7–4855–8ba3–702423665479/EBA%20revised%20Guidelines%20on%20outsourcing%20arrangements.pdf).

37 See also FINMA's insistence on algorithms designed to scrutinise a client's power to dispose of an external wallet: FINMA; FINMA-Aufsichtsmitteilung 02/2019, Zahlungsverkehr auf der Blockchain (26 August 2019, available at https://www.finma.ch/de/news/2019/08/20190826-mm-kryptogwg/).

38 *Michael Lynch*, PayThink Real-time payments breaks security 'rules' (Blog 11 December 2019, available at https://www.paymentssource.com/opinion/real-time-payments-breaks-security-rules).

39 Cf. ibid., p. 170. For a blockchain payment project based on a tokenised fiat currency see Singapore's Project Ubin: Deloitte/Singapore Exchange/Monetary Authority of Singapore, Delivery versus Payment on Distributed Technologies (2018, available at https://www.mas.gov.sg/-/media/MAS/ProjectUbin/Project-Ubin-DvP-on-Distributed-Ledger-Technologies.pdf).

a payment service provider has separated customer accounts properly (with values stored on a blockchain), insolvency-proof from third-party attachment[40]. Ultimately, the success of electronic storage and verifications schemes hinges on their compatibility with data protection law[41].

Digitisation pushes contract law analysis towards exploring specific duties of loyalty and care, once payment services are offered in the context of outsourcing arrangements[42] or distributed networks[43]. Payment service providers delegate the actual transfer of monies to comprehensive algorithms without ever getting hold of the transferred values[44]. Cloud computing supplies an infrastructure for banks and start-ups, allowing for offshore data processing to save cost[45]. It is for the national legal orders to decide whether designing a payment system or a distributed network also means liability for malfunctions[46].

2.2 Outsourcing

Under both statutory law and supervisory practice, outsourcing is conditioned on risk management mechanisms[47], assuming that the enforcement threat remains credible. Standard contracts may offer a pragmatic approach to facilitate digital transactions, but it is obvious that the bargaining power of those adhering to a digital network may vary: Banks may lose their autonomy as FinTechs seize some of the added value[48]. A 2013 data protection case from Sweden reveals that data processors may be in a stronger position than the data control-

---

40 See infra sub 2.5.1.

41 Cf. Clifford Chance Talking Tech Blog 18 October 2019, PSD2-innovation and GDPR-protection: a fintech balancing act – Part One (available at https://talkingtech.cliffordchance.com/en/data-cyber/data/psd2-innovation-and-gdpr-protection–a-fintech-balancing-act.html).

42 See infra sub 2.2.

43 See Expert Group on Regulatory Obstacles to Financial Innovation (fn. 5), p. 50.

44 See *Florian Glatz*, in: Möslein/Omlor, FinTech (fn. 2), § 8 ¶ 53. If payment services are outsourced to a blockchain-based intermediary, the latter does not have to issue guaranties for monies 'stored' in the system, because blockchain technology allows for real-time payments: *Glatz*, ibid., § 6 ¶ 56.

45 See European Commission, Digital Finance Strategy (fn. 28), at # 4.2. and *Xenofon Kontargyris*, IT Laws in the Era of Cloud Computing, 2018, p. 42 et seq., p. 216 et seq.

46 Expert Group on Regulatory Obstacles to Financial Innovation (fn. 5), p. 48 et seq.

47 See the analysis in Expert Group on Regulatory Obstacles to Financial Innovation (fn. 5), p. 24 et seq.

48 *Dorfleitner/Hornuf* (fn. 1), p. 85 et seq.

lers[49]: The Swedish Data Protection Agency criticised that the controller was not afforded sufficient control and insight into the data processing chain for storing information in the cloud[50].

From a consumer perspective, legal uncertainty is magnified once payment service providers operate in a network of interrelated contracts with organizational features[51], sometimes difficult to trace back to a jurisdiction[52]. Moreover, diverging proprietary standards and protocols jeopardise cross-border business[53]. Art. 4 of the Commission's Draft Regulation on digital operational resilience for the financial sector[54] builds on professional standards for financial service providers, their contractors and sub-contractors. Art. 4 of the Draft Regulation prescribes internal governance mechanisms and control frameworks to manage the risks: The financial services provider who plans to outsource remains responsible for the safe storage of personal financial data. Thus, contractual arrangements with third-party providers and potential subcontractors are to

---

49 See on the bargaining power of artificial intelligence-equipped platforms in finance: Financial Times online 19 November 2020, G. Tett, Artificial intelligence is reshaping finance (available at https://www.ft.com/content/c7d9a81c-e6a3-4f37-bbfd-71dcefda3739).

50 *Jenna Lindqvist*, New challenges to personal data processing agreements: is the GDPR fit to deal with contract, accountability and liability in a world of the Internet of Things?, 26 Int'l. J. L. & Techn. 45, 54 (2018).

51 See Expert Group on Regulatory Obstacles to Financial Innovation (fn. 5), p. 48 et seq. on distributed financial network, *Mark Beer*, in: Marc Schmitz/Patrick Gielen (eds)., Avoirs Dématérialisés et Exécution Forcé, 2019, 153, 159. On nanopayment systems: *Sebastian Omlor*, Nanopayments – Monetisierung des Cyberspace?, MMR 2018, 428–433, p. 432.

52 Cf. on the operational risks if FinTech activities are outsourced to third parties not subject to the existing regulatory framework: European Investment Bank, Blockchain, FinTechs and the relevance for international financial institutions, Economics Working Papers 2019/01, p. 31 (available at https://www.eib.org/attachments/efs/economics_working_paper_2019_01_en.pdf), Basel Committee on Banking Supervision, Sound Practices of FinTech developments for banks and bank supervisors (Bank for International Settlements, February 2018), p. 32 et seq. (available at https://www.bis.org/bcbs/publ/d431.pdf).

53 European Banking Authority (EBA), Discussion Paper on the EBA's approach to financial technology (FinTech) (4 August 2017), p. 45 et seq. (EBA/DP/2017/02, available at https://www.eba.europa.eu/sites/default/documents/files/documents/10180/1919160/7a1b9cda-10ad-4315-91ce-d798230ebd84/EBA%20Discussion%20Paper%20on%20Fintech%20%28EBA-DP-2017-02%29.pdf?retry=1); Bank of Canada/Bank of England/Monetary Authority of Singapore, Cross-Border Interbank Payments and Settlement – Emerging opportunities for digital transformation (November 2018), p. 10 (available at https://www.mas.gov.sg/-/media/MAS/ProjectUbin/Cross-Border-Interbank-Payments-and-Settlements.pdf).

54 European Commission, Proposal for a Regulation on digital operational resilience for the financial sector (Brussels 24 September 2020, COM(2020) 595 final (available at https://ec.europa.eu/transparency/regdoc/rep/1/2020/EN/COM-2020-595-F1-EN-MAIN-PART-1.PDF).

replicate the safety standards to be observed by the outsourcing financial enti-ty[55]. However, the Financial Stability Board (FSB) has cautioned against too much optimism that such safeguards will be passed along the chain of contracts with fourth or fifth parties or beyond[56]. Both, the European Banking Authority (EBA)[57] and the Board of the International Organization of Securities Commis-sions (IOSCO)[58] have promulgated detailed sets of governance rules which seek to reduce the risk that original safeguards will be watered down the line of sub-contracts[59]. The Expert Group on Regulatory Obstacles to Financial Inno-vation (ROFIEG) envisages a certification or licensing scheme to ensure observ-ance of minimum standards[60].

The Draft Regulation on digital resilience remains silent on liability stand-ards with respect to third-party storage of electronic assets and values[61]. Under art. 10 (1) (a) PSD II safe storage of tokenised funds on permissioned blockchain can be guaranteed only if such tokens are insolvency-proof. Strict observance of art. 20 (2) PSD II would indicate no-fault liability if digital assets stored in net-works are misappropriated. Under art. 24 of Directive 2009/65/EU (UCITS), as amended[62], the depositary may escape liability if a loss has arisen due to an ex-ternal event beyond its reasonable control with unavoidable consequences[63].

---

55 Art. 44 of the Draft Regulation provides for administrative sanctions if the statutory profes-sional duties are disregarded.
56 Financial Stability Board (FSB), Regulatory and Supervisory Issues Relating to Outsourcing and Third-Party Relationships – Discussion Paper (9 November 2020), p. 6 et seq. (available at https://www.fsb.org/wp-content/uploads/P091120.pdf).
57 EBA, Final Report on EBA Guidelines on outsourcing arrangements (25 February 2019), p. 44 et seq. (on the contractual phase) (available at https://www.eba.europa.eu/sites/default/docu ments/files/documents/10180/2551996/38c80601-f5d7-4855-8ba3-702423665479/EBA%20revised %20Guidelines%20on%20outsourcing%20arrangements.pdf?retry=1)
58 OICV-IOSCO, Principles on Outsourcing – Consultation Report (May 2020), p. 20 et seq. (CR01/2020, available at https://www.iosco.org/library/pubdocs/pdf/IOSCOPD654.pdf).
59 On the legal force of these standards see infra 2.4.
60 Expert Group on Regulatory Obstacles to Financial Innovation (fn. 5), p. 44 et seq.
61 See the assessment of regulatory policy choices in: European Commission, Commission Staff Working Document, Impact Assessment Report – Proposal for a Regulation on digital operation-al resilience for the financial sector (Brussels 24 September 2020 (SWD(2020) 198 final, available at https://eur-lex.europa.eu/LexUriServ/LexUriServ.do?uri=SWD:2020:0198:FIN:EN:PDF), with-out analysing in detail the interface between digital resilience and data protection requirements.
62 Consolidated text available at https://eur-lex.europa.eu/legal-content/EN/TXT/?uri=CELEX %3A02009L0065-20200107.
63 See also § 36 (4) of the German Kapitalanlagegesetzbuch (KAGB) on liability in an outsourc-ing scenario.

Art. 82 (2) of the General Data Protection Regulation[64] allows for an escape from liability if the data controller or processor can establish that they are not responsible for damages sustained by the data subject. As a corollary, a data controller can escape liability if a contractor or sub-contractor dictate the rules of an outsourcing scheme[65]. The Draft Regulation on digital resilience does not decide whether the use of artificial intelligence would be tantamount to imposing no-fault liability on those who stand to benefit from it[66]. Competition between the national private law systems will determine whether joint or vicarious liability is the solution for buttressing digital resilience. On the other hand, the quest for a single digital market may require legislative action on the EU level to eliminate differences between national liability concepts.

2.3 Crowdlending

Crowdlending and crowdfunding platforms owe their existence to a shortage of finance for community projects, small businesses and start-ups[67]. Platform-based credit schemes connect project proponents with investors[68]. In Europe, crowdlending essentially takes two forms: In a direct peer-to-peer lending sce-

---

64 Regulation (EU) 2016/679 of 27 April 2016 on the protection of natural persons with regard to the processing of personal data and on the free movement of such data, and repealing Directive 95/46/EC, O.J. L 119/1 of 4 May 2016.

65 Cf. Christopher Docksey, in: Christopher Kuner/Lee A. Bygrave/Christopher Docksey (eds.), The General Data Protection Regulation (GDPR) – A Commentary, 2020)), p. 566, commenting on a safe-harbour approach in the context of art. 24 GDPR.

66 For a survey over third-party risks in the context of employing digital technologies for outsourcing financial services: European Commission, Commission Staff Working Document, Impact Assessment Report, Proposal for a Regulation on digital operational resilience for the financial sector, sub ℙ 2.1.4. (Brussels 24 September 2020 (SWD(2020) 198 final, available at https://eur-lex.europa.eu/legal-content/EN/TXT/PDF/?uri=CELEX:52020SC0198&from=EN).

67 See the analysis undertaken in this issue by *Eugenia Macchiavello/Antonella Sciarrone Alibrandi*, Marketplace Lending as a New Form of Capital Raising in the Internal Market: True Disintermediation or Re-intermediation, ECFR (2021). For surveys see: OICV-IOSCO, Crowd-funding: An Infant Industry Growing Fast, Staff Working Paper of the IOSCO Research Department, p. 21 et seq. ([SWPP3/2014], available at https://www.iosco.org/research/pdf/swp/Crowd-funding-An-Infant-Industry-Growing-Fast.pdf); *Olha Havrylchyk*, Regulatory Framework for the Loan-Bases Crowdfunding Platforms (OECD Economic Department Working Paper No. 1513, 13 November 2018), p. 10 et seq. (available at http://www.oecd.org/officialdocuments/publicdisplaydoc umentpdf/?cote=ECO/WKP(2018)61&docLanguage=En).

68 See *Havrylchyk* (fn. 67), p. 11 et seq. For a country-wise survey over the regulatory approaches: OICV-IOSCO, Crowd-funding (fn. 67), p. 52 et seq.

nario, the crowdlending platform acts as the agent of both, the investor-lender and the borrower and establishes a direct loan contract between the parties[69]. Indirect peer-to-peer lending takes place when the platform cooperates with the banks which receives monies from the investor and channels them to the borrower[70]. The new Crowdfunding Regulation of the European Union conditions the establishment of a digital platform on obtaining a license from national authorities[71]. Recital 20 to the Crowdfunding Regulation introduces an analogy with respect to auto-investing: investment decisions triggered by pre-determined algorithms and smart contracts without any direct human intervention will be classified as individualised portfolio management.

From a private contracting perspective, the direct crowdlending model is quite straight forward[72]. The platform provides a digital meeting area where the borrower and the lender-investor conclude a loan contract or an investment contract (in the case of equity-based lending)[73]. The lender acquires the right to use financial information listed on the platform on the basis with an agreement with the platform[74]. The borrower applies to the platform by submitting information on the project to the platform which assesses the quality of the application and eventually lists the project[75]. The platform refrains from making an investment recommendation[76]. However, under the new Crowdfunding Regulation extensive behavioural rules are to be observed, including the risk management and assessment of the of the projects offered to the public via the platform[77].

P2P-lending schemes have suffered from a disconnect between the lender's freedom of contract to conclude a loan agreement and the crucial role of the plat-

---

69 *Lea Maria Siering*, in: *Möslein/Omlor*, FinTech, fn. 2, § 24 ¶ 5 et seq.

70 *Moritz Renner*, in: *Möslein/Omlor*, FinTech, fn. 2, § 23 ¶ 6 et seq.

71 Regulation (EU) 2020/1503 of 7 October 2020 on European crowdfunding service providers for business, O.J. L 347/1 of 20 October 2020.

72 See *Mark Cummins et al.*, in: *Theo Lynn/John G. Mooney et al.* (eds.), Disrupting Finance – FinTech and Strategy in the 21st Century, 2019, 15, 17; *Ajay Byanjankar et al.*, Predicting Credit Risk in Peer-to-Peer Lending: A Neural Network Approach, 2015 IEEE Symposium on Computational Intelligence 719–725 (p. 720) (available at https://ieeexplore.ieee.org/stamp/stamp.jsp?tp=&arnumber=7376683).

73 See *Manuel Stutz*, Anlegerschutz und FinTech – unter besonderer Berücksichtigung von Zahlungssystemen, Crowdfunding, Tokens und Robo-Advice (Dissertation No. 4923, Universität Sankt Gallen, 2019), p. 192 et seq., see also recitals 10, 11 of Regulation (EU) 2020/1503 of 7 October 2020 on crowdfunding service providers for business, O.J. L 347/1 of 20 October 2020.

74 See e. g. the Loan Management Service Agreement used by the Landbay P2P Platform (available at https://landbay.co.uk/terms-and-conditions).

75 *Siering*, in: Möslein/Omlor (fn. 2), § 24 ¶ 1 et seq.

76 This does not avert problems of adverse selection: *Havrylchyk* (fn. 67), p. 22 et seq.

77 See art. 3 et seq. of the Crowdfunding Regulation.

form in assessing the creditworthiness of the borrower and the quality of the investment project submitted[78]. P2P-platforms operate digital scoring mechanisms, classifying the borrower and his project within certain risk categories[79]. Art. 5 et seq. of the Crowdfunding Regulation impose rules of sound business administration on the platform managers and addresses conflict of interest. This is intended to stave off situations of asymmetric information between the platform and the investor-lender because the latter bases an investment decision on the information received from the platform, which, in turn, has a business interest in brokering the loan contract. Under the new Regulation financial service providers are under organizational requirements and a duty to disclose the algorithms and smart contracts they are using for obtaining credit-rating scores[80].

As soon as the platform undertakes to manage loans[81], platform services overlap with elements of robo-based asset management. Based on the investor's risk preferences, the platform will re-allocate loans, diversify the portfolio and arrange for collateral[82]. Blockchain technology can be employed to manage client accounts and to match borrowers' requests for finance, based on 'intelligent' smart contracts and algorithms[83]. Art. 11 of the new Crowdfunding Regulation addresses the risk of loss for those investors who place funds with the platform. Platforms shall observe prudential requirements. They must have a minimum capital of 25,000 € and funds to cover operational risks or, alternatively insurance and/or own funds (CET 1). Platform activities may be outsourced but the platform cannot escape liability under the Regulation by way of contractual stipulation with a third-party service provider. Moreover, funds held must be placed with a depositary, unless national law allows for the storage in a separate account administered by the platform.

The new Crowdfunding Regulation has the potential of fleshing out duties which are owed under the contracts normally concluded in the context of plat-

---

78 Cf. *Deidre Ahern*, Regulatory Arbitrage in a FinTech world: devising an optimal regulatory response to crowdlending, 2018 J. Bus. L. 193, 196 et seq. See on lender risks in crowdlending settings on the basis of empirical data: *Henri Palomäki*, European Crowdlending Platforms: Evaluating Risks and Comparing Platforms from Investors' Perspective (Oulu Business School 2019) (available at http://jultika.oulu.fi/files/nbnfioulu-201905081654.pdf).

79 See *Byanjankar* (fn. 72), p. 721 et seq., for a credit scoring model relying on artificial intelligence to classify default and non-default loans.

80 *Ahern* (fn. 78) p. 198.

81 See e.g. the Loan Management Service Agreement used by the Landbay P2P Platform (available at https://landbay.co.uk/terms-and-conditions

82 Ibid.

83 Eidgenössisches Finanzdepartement (fn. 32), annotation to Art. 7 paras. 1/2 of the Bankenverordnung.

form-engineered contracts. But its success crucially depends on the ability of national contract laws to expand the scope of duties of care and loyalty under a contract which also rests on the observance of organizational duties[84].

2.4 Robo-advice

Robo-advisory schemes reinforce the question whether private law systems are capable of balancing the interests of investors against those of financial institutions relying on artificial intelligence. Robo-advisers operate with a variety of business models, depending on the degree of human interaction and intervention when collecting and processing information to generate a recommendation for a specific investment[85]. Fully digitalised robo-advisory systems process market information and restructure customer portfolios. Algorithms invest and rebalance the account in accordance with customer risk preferences[86]. At the outset, robo-advisory services are based on a service contract between the customer and the financial service provider[87], backed up by a contract with the cooperating bank of the financial service provider[88]. Risks under automated financial advice schemes may be magnified if automated services are provided by a network of firms with an unclear allocation of liabilities between the financial institution and an outsource provider[89].

Robo-advice has been observed to be prone to home biases[90], behavioural biases[91] and undisclosed conflicts of interest. Deficient software and design of

---

84 Cf. *Florian Möslein/Arne Lordt*, Rechtsfragen des Robo-Advice, ZIP 2017, 293, 702.

85 U.S. Securities and Exchange Commission, Division of Investment Management – Guidance Update, Robo-Advisers (No. 2017–02, February 2017) (available at https://www.sec.gov/invest ment/im-guidance-2017-02.pdf). See art. 54 (1) of the Delegated Regulation (EU) 2017/565 (O.J. L 87/1 of 31 March 2017) on the suitability assessment when investment advice is provided through ab automated system.

86 *Christoph Kumpan*, in: Möslein/Omlor (fn. 2), § 29 ¶ 6 et seq., cf. *Wolf-Georg Ringe/Christopher Ruof*, A Regulatory Sandbox for Robo Advice (European Banking Institute Working Paper No. 26 May 2018, available at https://papers.ssrn.com/sol3/papers.cfm?abstract_id= 3188828&download=yes). See also U.S. SEC, Guidance, fn. 85, p. 3.

87 *Alexis Darányi*, in: Möslein/Omlor (fn. 2), § 30 ¶47.

88 *Möslein/Lordt* (fn. 84), ZIP 2017, 293, 798.

89 ESMA/EBA/EIOPA (fn. 22), p. 28 et seq.

90 Risksave.com News 12 March 2018, Home-country bias in Robo-Advice (available at https:// risksave.com/news/2018/3/13/home-country-bias-in-robo-advice).

91 Cf. on "honesty of the algorithms": *Baker/Dellaert*, 103 Iowa L. Rev. 713, 736 (2018), see also: *Kumpan*, in: Möslein/Omlor (fn. 2), § 29 ¶12.

(matching) algorithms have the potential of translating into customer losses[92]. Regulators have reacted by requiring automated investment services firms to improve the governance and risk management structures, supervise and update algorithms and inform potential customers on the underlying assumptions, limitations and risks of the algorithms[93]. Singapore's Monetary Authority places the responsibility for oversight and governance of client-facing tools with the board and senior management of the robo-advisory firm; EU law takes a similar approach[94]. It remains to be seen whether this combination of oversight and disclosure duties supplements the concept of offering proper investment advice under the service contract[95].

In the US, the scope of duties owed under the service contract has sparked a debate on how robo-advice can be reconciled with statutory duties under investment law, informed by portfolio theory[96]. The US FINRA has noted that financial service providers relying exclusively on robot-generated advice do not meet the

---

92 Cf. FCA, Automated investment services – our expectations (21 May 2018, available at https://www.fca.org.uk/publications/multi-firm-reviews/automated-investment-services-our-ex pectations), (Monetary Authority of Singapore, Guidelines on Provision of Digital Advisory Services (Guidelines No. CMG-G02, 8 October 2018), ¶ 28 et seq. (available at https://www.mas.gov. sg/-/media/MAS/Regulations-and-Financial-Stability/Regulations-Guidance-and-Licensing/Se curities-Futures-and-Fund-Management/Guidelines-on-Provision-of-Digital-Advisory-Services-CMGG02.pdf), *Möslein/Lordt* (fn. 84), ZIP 2017, 793–803 (p. 801 et seq.).
93 MAS, Guidelines on Digital Advisory Services (fn. 92), ¶ 26 et seq., 31, FCA, Automated Investment Services.
94 Ibid., ¶ 28 and Art. 54 (1) of the Commission Delegated Regulation (EU) 2017/65 of 25 April 2016 supplementing Directive 2014/65/EU as regards organizational requirements and operating conditions for investment firms and defined terms for the purposes of that Directive, O.J. L 87/1 of 31 March 2017.
95 See the FCA's concerns about suitability of advice for (vulnerable) customers: FCA Automated Investment Services (fn. 92), Moneymarketing 21 May 2018; *Stephen Little*, Robos under fire over suitability and disclosure failings (available at https://www.moneymarketing.co.uk/news/ robos-fire-suitability-disclosure-failings/), cf. *Möslein/Lordt* (fn. 84), ZIP 2017, 793, 801, on the delicate interface between the law of contracts and the financial market regulation during the execution of a service contract for robo-advice.
96 *Melanie L. Fein*, FINRA's Report on Robo-Advisors: Fiduciary Implications (April 2016) (available at https://pdfs.semanticscholar.org/fd40/34cf0fa3654ce05fd0401c4f97675e27427a.pdf); *Megan Ji*, Are Robots Good Fiduciaries? Regulating Robo-Advisors under the Investment Advisers Act of 1940, 117 Colum. L. Rev. 1543, 1563 et seq. (2017); *Jill E. Fisch/Marion Labouré/John A. Turner*, The Emergence of the Robo-advisor, Wharton Pension Research Council Working Paper No. 10 (1 December 2018, available at https://pensionresearchcouncil.wharton.upenn.edu/wp-content/up loads/2018/12/WP-2018–12-Fisch-et-al.pdf), *Demo Clarke*, Robo-Advisors – Market Impact and Fiduciary Duty of Care to Retail Investors (University of Maryland 13 February 2020) (available at https:// papers.ssrn.com/sol3/papers.cfm?abstract_id=3539122&download=yes).

standards of fiduciary care owed when advising clients[97]. As a consequence, financial advisory companies have established hybrid concepts where robot-generated advice is counter-checked by human beings before being applied to customer risk parameters[98]. The Bank of England and the FCA point to specific risk management mechanisms when financial service employ machine learning applications: Prior to execution, machine learning activates an alert mechanism which calls for human approval[99]. In testing robo-advice schemes under its regulatory sandbox scheme, the FCA insists on involving a qualified financial adviser to assess the quality of the underlying algorithms[100]. Algorithms have to be amended in accordance with the advisor's assessment[101]. The US FINRA has proposed a similar approach[102].

In the EU, art. 25 (1) of MiFID II and art. 54 (1) of the MiFID II Delegated Regulation[103] require investment firms to undertake a suitability assessment before giving advice to invest. If investment advice or portfolio management is provided through an automated or semi-automated system, the ultimate responsibility for an appropriate suitability assessment lies nonetheless with the investment firm and shall not be delegated to algorithms[104]. The European Securities and Markets Authority (ESMA) has promulgated organizational standards for investment firms assessing suitability with algorithms[105]: These include *inter alia* policies to review and update algorithms to reflect market changes or legislative developments. Moreover, internal procedures should operate to detect error within the algorithms which might generate inappropriate advice or disregard relevant

---

97 Financial Industry Regulatory Authority (FINRA), Report on Digital Investment Advice (March 2016) (available at https://www.finra.org/sites/default/files/digital-investment-advice-re port.pdf).

98 See *passim B. Ferguson* (FCA), Robo Advice: an FCA perspective, Speech London 11 October 2017 (available at https://www.fca.org.uk/news/speeches/robo-advice-fca-perspective).

99 Bank of England/FCA, Machine learning in UK financial services, p. 27 (October 2019, available at https://www.bankofengland.co.uk/-/media/boe/files/report/2019/machine-learning-in-uk-finan cial-services.pdf?la=en&hash=F8CA6EE7A5A9E0CB182F5D568E033F0EB2D21246).

100 FCA, Regulatory sandbox lessons learned report (2017, available at https://www.fca.org.uk/ publication/research-and-data/regulatory-sandbox-lessons-learned-report.pdf), at para. 4.40., and infra sub 3.1.

101 Ibid., at para. 4.41.

102 FINRA, Report (fn. 97).

103 Delegated Regulation (EU) 2017/65 (fn. 94).

104 Art. 54 (2) of the MiFID II Delegated Regulation.

105 ESMA, Guidelines on certain aspects of the MiFID II suitability requirement, at ₽82 et seq. (06/11/2018/ESMA, available at https://www.esma.europa.eu/sites/default/files/library/esma35-43-1163_guidelines_on_certain_aspects_of_mifid_ii_suitability_requirements_0.pdf).

law[106]. Although ESMA's guidelines constitute the EU's soft law on finance, they enjoy a high degree of compliance[107]. Standard interpretation techniques will have little difficulty in transforming codes of conduct into specific (algorithm-related) duties of care and loyalty[108] under innovative FinTech contracts[109].While it has been suggested that investment firms should not contract out of their liability under the suitability rule[110], the exact legal implications of art. 25 MiFID and the MiFID II Delegated Regulation for national contracts laws remain unclear. The evolutionary potential of contract law, however, still faces its test when it comes to determining what specific rights parties have when they sue an investment firm for breach of contract[111].

2.5 Distributed Ledger Technology – FinTech and Private Law at a Juncture

2.5.1 Blockchain Law – The Status Quo

Distributed ledger technology and crypto-assets[112] owe their existence to private contracting. Digital tokens on a ledger stand for the commodification of any bundle of rights and obligations for token holders[113]. The contractual origin of digital tokens has also contributed to one of their major weaknesses: The degree of pro-

---

106 Ibid.
107 *Niamh Moloney*, The Age of ESMA – Governing EU Financial Markets, Oxford 2018, p. 145 et seq.
108 Cf. *Möslein/Lordt*, ZIP 2017, 793, 702, on ‚algorithmic organization duties'.
109 For an extensive analysis see *Della Negra* (fn. 27), pp. 84 et seq., 177 et seq. This is also the position of Swiss law: *Rolf H. Weber/Rainer Baisch*, Regulierung von Robo-Advice, AJP/PJA 8/ 2016, 1065, 1071.
110 *Della Negra* (fn. 27), p. 86.
111 See the survey in: *Della Negra* (fn. 27), p. 186 et seq.
112 According to art. 3 (1) (2) of the Draft Regulation on crypto-assets (Proposal for a Regulation on Markets in Crypto-assets, European Commission (Brussels 24 September 2020 (COM(2020) 593 final, available at https://ec.europa.eu/transparency/regdoc/rep/1/2020/EN/COM-2020-593-F1-EN-MAIN-PART-1.PDF)) "'crypto-asset' means a digital representation of value or rights which may be transferred and stored electronically, suing distributed ledger technology or similar technology...".
113 See *Javier Wenceslao Ibáñez Jiménez*, Derecho de Blockchain y la tecnología de registros distribuidos, 2018, p. 215 et seq.; *Philipp Hacker/Chris Thomale*, Crypto-Securities Regulation: ICO's, Token Sales and Cryptocurrencies under EU Financial Law, ECFR 2018, 645 – 696 (651). On potential benefits of asset tokenisation: OECD, The Tokenisation of Assets and Potential Implications for Financial Markets (2020), p. 38 et seq.

tection afforded to tokens depends on the willingness of a national legal order to confer property-like status with erga-omnes effects on crypto-assets. Failure to attain this status is to magnify financial risks from investing and trading with crypto-assets. In this, distributed ledger technology and crypto-assets are a model case for demonstrating that the success of a market for FinTech products is conditioned on an efficient interface between the evolutionary potential of private law, FinTech regulation[114] and data protection law[115]. In the following, the evolution of blockchain law will be assessed from its private law beginnings to legislative intervention by national legislators and the European Union.

Legal aspects of distributed ledger technology and tokenisation first reached the courts when cybersecurity was ineffectual and large amounts of bitcoins had disappeared from customer accounts, held with virtual currency exchanges[116]. The owners of bitcoins filed claims for damages, arguing that the loss of bitcoins was caused by a breach of duty the exchange owed to its customers[117]. Although investors in bitcoins entrust value to the operator of an exchange or a currency-platform courts are reluctant to impose a fiduciary duty: Significant control over the platform and customer accounts does not establish a custodianship, triggering a fiduciary duty to protect digital value held[118]. Investors suffering losses of bitcoins have a chance of obtaining a judgment for damages only if the operator of the currency platform or exchange had positive knowledge of the risk of impending hacks, but failed to take protective action or to warn customers[119]. In a recent New Zealand case, the High Court accepted a breach of trust claim after cryptocurrencies had disappeared in a computer hack[120]. In a 2019 Singapore case, the court had to assess the repercussions of a computer malfunction which had occurred in a blockchain-based exchange[121]. The court was receptive to causation analysis, but did not impose a fiduciary duty on the developer of the

---

114 See *Philipp Paech*, The Governance of Blockchain Financial Network, 80 (6) M.L.R. 1073, p. 1097 et seq. (2017), on third-party effects of blockchain-held assets, regulation and the interface with private law.
115 See also in this volume the contributions by *Paolo Giudici/Guido Ferrarini* and *Heikki Marjosola*.
116 See *Peter Susman*, Virtual money in the virtual bank: legal remedies for loss, (2016) Butterworth's J. Int'l Banking & L. 150−152.
117 See Carmel v. Mizuho Bank, Ltd., 2018 WL 6982840 (C.D. Cal., 2018).
118 Fabian v. Lemahieu, 2019 WL 4918431 (D. Md., 2019).
119 Asa v. Verizon Communications, Inc., 20127 WL 5894543 (E.D. Tenn., 2017).
120 Ruscoe v. Cryptopia Ltd., [2020] NZHC 728, accord: *Ken Moon*. New Zealand: Are Cryptocurrencies Property?, CRi 5/2020, 135, 138.
121 B2C2 v. Quoine Pte. Ltd., [2019] SGHC (I) 03.

software with respect to those who store digital assets on a blockchain[122]. The Singapore case sheds light on the core problem of FinTech networks where elements of services are frequently outsourced. Uncertainty about the scope of liability in the context of blockchain-based storage of digital value and smart contracts just reflects the current uncertainty on how to accommodate artificial intelligence in traditional concepts of the law of contracts and torts[123]. It is equally uncertain whether courts would go as far as stretching traditional concepts without legislative intervention[124].

The current state of liability rules for assets stored in a blockchain has forced investors to emphasise property aspects of digital value stored on a distributed ledger[125]. Unrestrained by the civil law concept of *numerus-clausus* of property law[126], common law jurisdictions have found it less difficult to integrate digital value into law[127]. In 2019, the UK Jurisdiction Taskforce of the LawTech Delivery Panel recognised crypto-assets as property, inter alia, for the purposes of common law and insolvency law[128]. The panel relied on Lord Wilberforce's test in *National Provinvial Bank v. Ainsworth*[129]: To qualify as a property right, it has to be "definable, identifiable by third parties, capable in its nature of assumption by third parties, and have some degree of permanence or stability"[130]. The panel

---

122 Ibid. See, however, the plea for placing the responsibility on the firms which develop algorithms: *Kirsten Martin*, Ethical Implications and Accountability of Algorithms, 160 J. Bus. Ethics 835–860 (p. 844 et seq.) (2019).

123 See *Gerhard Wagner*, Verantwortlichkeit im Zeichen digitaler Techniken, VersR 2020, 717, 724 et seq.

124 See *Raina S. Haque et al.*, Blockchain Development and Fiduciary Duty,2 Stanf. J. Blockchain Law & Pol'y 139, 179 et seq. (2019), arguing against a fiduciary duty owed by the operator of the blockchain.

125 Cf. *Charles Draper*, Unlocking Value In An Insolvent Estate: An Update on Cryptocurrencies (2020) (available at https://www.restructuring-globalview.com/2020/02/unlocking-value-in-an-insolvent-estate-an-update-on-cryptocurrencies/).

126 *Kelvin FK Low/Eliza Mik*, Pause the Blockchain Revolution, 69 (1) I.C.L.Q. 136, 149 et seq. (2020).

127 See the US and Canadian cases on recognising digital assets: Fortified Holistic v. Lucic, 71 N.Y.S. 3d 922 (S. Ct. N.Y., 2017) ('intangible property'); Ajemian v. Yahoo!, Inc., 84 N.E. 3d 766 (768 et seq.) (Mass., 2017); Audet v. Fraser, 332 F.R.D. 53 (65 et seq.) (D. Conn., 2019) (Owners of digital assets also qualify as members of a class for the purposes of class action under securities law.); Copytrack v. Wall, 2018 BCSC 1709; Shair.Com Global Digital Services Ltd., 2018 BCSC 1512.

128 The LawTech Delivery Panel Legal Statement on crypto-assets and smart contracts (UK Jurisdiction Taskforce) (November 2019) (available at https://35z8e83m1ih83drye28o9d1-wpen gine.netdna-ssl.com/wp-content/uploads/2019/11/6.6056_JO_Cryptocurrencies_Statement_FINAL_WEB_111119–1.pdf).

129 National Provincial Bank v Ainsworth [1965] 1 AC 1175 at 1248.

130 Legal Statement (fn. 128), sub ¶ 39.

then proceeded to reiterating the criteria enounced in *Fairstar Heavy Transport NV v. Adkins*[131]: Property rights are characterised by "certainty, exclusivity, control and assignability"[132]. The panel clarifies the notion of exclusivity with respect to the keys which allow for access to the blockchain: Multiple keys for a cryptoasset indicate shared ownership or separated ownership of different functions of the key[133]. However, a key as such is information, but not property[134]. This reflects the position of English law that pure information does not constitute a proprietary interest[135]. Although the panel's statement is not binding on the courts, it has been treated subsequently as an authoritative statement of English law[136]. In *Ruscoe v. Cryptopia Ltd.*, the New Zealand High Court recognised the property quality of digital assets on a blockchain, based on Lord Wilberforce's criteria[137]. The High Court then analysed the nature of the public and private keys. The private key, the court noted, is "like a PIN", protecting the owner from involuntary transfer of his funds[138], but also provides for the tradability of the digital assets[139]. In Australia, cryptocurrency is accepted as security for costs[140].

With the exception of Italy[141], private keys for access to blockchain-stored digital values present a major obstacle to civil law jurisdictions recognising dig-

---

131 [2013] EWCA Civ. 886.
132 Legal Statement (fn. 128), sub ¶ 39.
133 Ibid., sub ¶ 43 (b).
134 Ibid., sub ¶ 85 (e).
135 *Leigh Sagar*, The Digital Estate.,2018, at ¶4 – 01 et seq.
136 AA v. Persons Unknown, [2019] EWHC 3556 (Comm). See also the 2018 case Vorotnytseva v. Money-4 Ltd. (t/a Nebeus.com), 2018 WL 09909285 (Ch., 2018). It should be noted, though, that the notion of 'property' in an insolvency context might be broader than in a law-of-contracts scenario: cf. *Sagar* (fn. 135), at ¶ 4 – 03 et seq.
137 [2020] NZHC 728, sub ¶ 112, for an analysis see *Moon* (fn. 120), CRi 5/2020, 135, 137, and *Paolo Giudici*, Insolvenza di un "custodial marketplace" di valute virtuali e tutela dei clienti, Le Società 5/2020, 588, 591.
138 See [2020] NZHC 728, sub ¶ 111.
139 *Paul Babie et al.*, Case Note – Cryptocurrencies as Property: *Ruscoe and Moore v. Cryptopia Ltd. (in Liquidation)* [2020] NZHC 728 (2020) (University of Adelaide Research Paper No. 2020 – 33, available at https://papers.ssrn.com/sol3/papers.cfm?abstract_id=3578264& download=yes).
140 Hague v. Gardiner (No. 2), [2020] NSWDC 23.
141 Art. 8-ter of the Italian law no. 12/19 of 11 January 2019 (Gazzetta Ufficiale della Repubblica Italiana of 12 February 2019 (anno 160 – Numero 36) recognises the legal enforceability of time stamps on a distributed ledger by establishing an analogy with time stamps within the meaning of art. 41 of Regulation (EU) no. 910/2014 of 23 July 2014, O.J. L 157/73 of 28 August 2014, see also the judgment of 19 December 2018 (Sent. 18/2019) of the Tribunale di Firenze – Sezione Fallimen-

ital values as property and pledging them as collateral[142]. A key stands for the right to exclude others[143]; the 'possession' of the access code demonstrates control over the crypto-asset[144]. A Tokyo District Court declined to confer property status on bitcoins, since the co-existence of several digital items on a blockchain excluded exclusivity required by Japanese property law[145]. The Japanese legislator has since amended the law[146]. In proposing a rudimentary blockchain law the Swiss government observed that private and public keys as well as multi-signature scenarios exclude that digital assets can constitute an insolvency asset[147]. The Swiss legislator has bypassed this obstacle by conferring property status with erga-omnes effect on tokenised rights once they are registered[148]. Thus, under the amended Swiss insolvency law crypto-assets can now be retrieved from the insolvency estate if the insolvent company administered tokenised assets[149]. Liechtenstein's new blockchain law has chosen a similar approach[150]:

---

tare (available at https://www.coinlex.it/wp-content/uploads/2019/01/Sentenza_Fallimento_ Bitgrail.pdf); *Giudici* (fn. 137), Le Società 5/2020, 588, 591.

142 Cf. *Geoffrey Peck*, Practical Law – Security Interests: Bitcoins and Other Cryptocurrency Assets (24 April 2019, available at https://uk.practicallaw.thomsonreuters.com/w-017-6122?origi nationContext=knowHow&transitionType=KnowHowItem&contextData=(sc.Default)&firstPage= true).

143 Under art. 5 (2) of Liechtenstein's new blockchain law (fn. 11), ownership of the key to the blockchain system constitutes a rebuttable presumption that the owner is also entitled to conclude transactions over the token. See also on the 'right to exclude' and the 'right to use' in a blockchain, context: *Philipp Paech*, Securities, Intermediation, and the Blockchain – An Inevitable Choice between Liquidity and Legal Certainty, 21 (4) Uniform L. Rev. 612, 628 (2016).

144 See commentary on art. 11 of the UNCITRAL Model Law on Electronic Transferable Records, Explanatory Note on the Model Law (13 July 2017). (available at http://www.uncitral.org/un citral/en/uncitral_texts/electronic_commerce/2017model.html).

145 District Court, Tokyo, 5 August 2015, (2014 (Wa) 33320) (Japan), Reference number 25541521 (English translation commissioned by the Digital Assets Project Harris Manchester College, Oxford (available at https://www.law.ox.ac.uk/sites/files/oxlaw/mtgox_judgment final.pdf).

146 *Ken Kawai/Takeshi Nagase*, The Virtual Currency Regulation Review – Edition 2: Japan (September 2019), The Law Reviews online: The Law Reviews https://thelawreviews.co.uk/edi tion/the-virtual-currency-regulation-review-edition-2/1197588/japan.

147 Schweizerische Eidgenossenschaft, Eidgenössisches Finanzdepartment, Bundesgesetz zur Anpassung des Bundesrechts an Anpassungen an Entwicklungen der Technik verteilter elektronischer Register – Erläuternder Bericht zur Vernehmlassungsvorlage (22 March 2019), at ¶ 3.2.1.2. et seq. (available at https://www.newsd.admin.ch/newsd/message/attachments/56192.pdf).

148 Ibid., at ¶ 3.2.2.

149 In June 2021, Germany promulgated a new law (Gesetz zur Einführung von elektronischen Wertpapieren, BGBl. 2021 I 1423 [Federal Gazette]), providing for electronic securities (*Wertpapiere*) to be registered in an electronic register. Crypto securities (*Kryptowertpapiere*) may be stored in a decentralised register. In what looks like an overly cautious attempt to catch up with to-

A token is basically a crypto-value with erga-omnes effects and goes well beyond the limitations of utility or security tokens[151]. Liechtenstein's law also refers to (trustee-like) standards of duty and care for those who administer the tokens and hence, the digital assets stored. Luxembourg law classifies security tokens as intermediated securities[152]. French law confers property status on some securities[153]. The new San Marino *Decreto Delegato* on blockchain technology allows for erga-omnes effects of blockchain-stored investment tokens, but treats utility tokens as mere creatures of contract valid only between the issuer and the holder[154]. Common law countries have legislated for recognising financial tokens as assets[155].

---

kenisation rules under Swiss law, German law will confer property law status on these electronic securities by classifying them as a 'thing' under the Civil Code. It should be noted that this law project does not introduce a general recognition of crypto-assets or digital shares. See Gesetzentwurf der Bundesregierung, Entwurf eines Gesetzes zur Einführung von elektronischen Wertpapieren (14 December 2020, available at https://www.bmjv.de/SharedDocs/Gesetzge bungsverfahren/Dokumente/RegE_Einfuehrung_elektr_Wertpapiere.pdf;jsessionid=DE28652C C1EB52BA58814BB62453EBB2.1_cid289?__blob=publicationFile&v=3), and *Elena Dubovitskaya*, Gesetzentwurf zur Einführung von elektronischen Wertpapieren; ein zaghafter Schritt nach vorn, 41 Zeitschrift für Wirtschaftsrecht 2551–2561 (2020), Matthias Casper, in: Möslein/Omlor, fn. 2, § 28.

150 Cf. *Bergt* (fn. 11), p. 86 et seq.

151 Ibid., pp. 67, 177 et seq.

152 Art 18bis of the Loi modifiée du 1er août 2001 concernant la circulation des titres, and the report for the Luxembourg parliament: Luxembourg Chambre de Députés, Session ordinaire 2017–2018, Projet de loi no. 7363 (6 November 2018) (available at https://www.chd.lu/wps/ PA_RoleDesAffaires/FTSByteServingServletImpl?path=C9D0C9CB5AC1682F8AD1DC36175252 FF26530FBAB20F896BDEC2D74A3FBAB31A3C2CAC62A625123D0A0B697273B03BC6$7517CFC69 E1CF4D4FAD36945BC69A3E3)

153 Cf. Ordonnance n° 2016–520 du 28 avril 2016 relative aux bons de caisse (JORF n°0101 of 29 April 2016, mini-bonds), Ordonnance n° 2017–1674 of 8 December 2017 relative à l'utilisation d'un dispositif d'enregistrement électronique partagé pour la représentation et la transmission de titres financiers (JORF n°0287 of 9 December) 2017 (blockchain-based register for financial instruments)

154 Artt. 8, 9 of the Decreto Delegato no. 86 of 23 May 2019 of the Repubblica di San Marino (available at https://www.consigliograndeegenerale.sm/on-line/home/archivio-leggi-decreti-e-regolamenti/scheda17163166.html).

155 See the survey in: The Library of Congress, Regulatory Approaches to Crypto-assets in Selected Jurisdictions (April 2019, available at https://www.loc.gov/law/help/crypto-assets/cryp toasset-regulation.pdf).

2.5.2 The EU's Regulatory Strategy

The EU Commission's regulatory strategy towards distributed ledger technology is twofold: The Draft Regulation on a pilot regime for market infrastructures based on distributed ledger technology (DLT) aims at establishing efficient secondary markets for security tokens, as the primary market does not develop significantly[156]. The Draft Regulation on markets in crypto-assets is intended to supply harmonised rules for certain types of crypto-assets and related activities and services[157].

The Draft Regulation on a pilot regime for DLT market infrastructures does not purport to replace existing market infrastructures[158]. Instead, it seeks to open up securities settlement processes and central securities depositories for distributed ledger technology[159]. This will also include crypto-assets which can be classified as financial instruments[160]. Both, multilateral trading facilities and central securities depositories operating a securities settlement system may settle payments by accepting *inter alia* commercial bank money in a token-based form or e-money tokens[161]. In prescribing a catalogue of duties to be observed by operators of distributed ledger technology market infrastructures, art. 6 of the Draft Regulation attempts to flesh out the interface between private law and FinTech regulation. It also highlights where national laws will have to evolve to supply an appropriate framework for cross-border DLT market infrastructures. The Draft Regulation assumes that the participants in digitised market infrastructures can freely stipulate the scope of liabilities of the operator and the applicable law. It remains to be seen whether courts will accept such a choice of law clause when a tort law claim will be litigated. Moreover, art. 6 of the Draft Regulation does not address the private law implications of accepting crypto-assets as tradable securities. Member State law still applies for ascertain-

---

156 European Commission, Commission Staff Working Document, Impact Assessment Proposal for a Regulation on a pilot regime for market infrastructures based on distributed ledger technology (Brussels 24 September 2020 SWD(2020) 201final). According to art. 2 (2) of the Draft Regulation a digital ledger technology structure consists of a multilateral trading facility or a securities settlement system.

157 Recital 5 of the Proposal for a Regulation on Markets in Crypto-assets (fn. 112). See *Dirk A. Zetzsche et al.*, The Markets in Crypto-Assets Regulation (MICA) and the EU Digital Finance Strategy, University of Luxembourg Law Working Paper 2020 – 018 (available at https://papers.ssrn.com/sol3/papers.cfm?abstract_id=3725395#).

158 Recital 6 of the Draft Regulation on a pilot regime (fn. 156).

159 See recital 2 and artt. 2 (2), 5 (1) of the Draft Regulation on pilot regime (fn. 156).

160 Recital 4 of the Draft Regulation on a pilot regime (fn. 156).

161 Art. 4 (3) lit. f, 5 (5) of the Draft Regulation (fn. 156).

ing the scope of legal protection afforded to a crypto-asset, thus triggering uncertainty and regulatory arbitrage. Art. 5 (2) lit a. of the Draft Regulation may dispense with the requirement to maintain securities accounts within the meaning of art. 2 (28) of Regulation 909/2014[162]. But this does not solve the problem of whether crypto-assets are insolvency-proof or whether settlements involving crypto-assets generate erga-omnes effects with respect to third parties.

The Draft Regulation on a pilot regime expects operators of a DLT market infrastructure to provide appropriate cyber arrangements and to ensure the safekeeping of clients' funds, collateral and crypto-assets[163]. This emphasises a need to determine liability standards owed under private law. If smart contracts produce undesired results, the operator might be tempted to escape liability by pointing to the developer of the software. Moreover, once artificial intelligence malfunctions dramatically[164], the operator could attempt to exonerate himself by arguing that a knowledgeable businessman should be expected not to benefit from obvious problems of the digitised infrastructure[165]. As an aside, the Draft Regulation on a pilot regime may also call for an amendment of national rules of civil procedure so that electronic evidence of digitised settlement processes can be admitted.

The Draft Regulation on markets in crypto-assets takes a functional approach without interfering with the property law systems of the Member States. It focuses on uniform rules for transparency and disclosure requirements for issuing and trading crypto-assets, the oversight over service providers for crypto-assets and issuers of asset-referenced tokens and electronic money tokens, and for consumer protection[166]. It is specifically designed for assets which have not been covered by existing EU rules on financial instruments, and e-money tokens[167]. The Draft Regulation imposes behavioural duties and governance standards on those who issue and store digital assets. A combination is introduced between data protection principles under the GDPR and traditional principal-agent relationships in private law. Whereas the Draft Regulation on crypto-assets replicates the no-fault liability standard of the Draft Regulation on digital operation-

---

162 Regulation (EU) 909/2014 of 23 July 2014 on improving securities settlement in the European Union and on central securities depositories, O.J. L 257/1 of 28.8.2014.
163 Art. 6 (4), (5) of the Draft Regulation (fn. 112).
164 See the factual setting in B2C2 v. Quoine Pte. Ltd., [2019] SGHC (I) 03.
165 See the dissenting opinion of *Lord Mance* in the appellate judgment of the Singapore Court of Appeal: *Quoine Pte Ltd v. B2C2 Ltd*, [2020] SGCA(I) 02.
166 Art. 1 of the Draft Regulation.
167 Ibid.

al resilience for outsourcing schemes[168], traditional fault standards remain applicable when selecting third-party providers for administering the reserve of assets for asset-referenced tokens[169]. Similar rules apply if asset-referenced tokens are held in custody by different crypto-asset service providers[170]. Recital 58 and art. 63 (1) of the Draft Regulation refer to the "ownership rights" of clients who have stored crypto-assets with a crypto-service provider, and admonishes service providers to safeguard them in the case of an insolvency scenario. This assumes that 'ownership rights' are creditor-proof in insolvency proceedings[171], relegating owners, service providers and creditors to the respective national order to ascertain the scope of rights enjoyed by the holder of crypto-assets[172].

The viability of DLT business models critically depends on their compatibility with data protection law. The EU's General Data Protection Regulation (GDPR)[173] conditions the lawful, fair and transparent processing of data *inter alia* on the data subject's consent or the data controller's duty to comply with a legal obligation[174]. Art. 17 (1) GDPR confers the 'right to be forgotten' on the data subject unless the establishment, exercise or defence of legal claims is predicated on processing (and storing) of data (art. 17 (3) (e) GDPR). In order to strike a balance between data protection and FinTech's interest in blockchain-based transactions it has been suggested that efficient encryption should qualify as a method of erasing data[175]. However, once crypto-assets attain legal status as

---

168 See art. 66 of the Draft Regulation.

169 See art, 30 (5) of the Draft Regulation.

170 Art. 41 (1) of the Draft Regulation.

171 This appears to be in accord with the approach by *Aurelia Gurrea-Martínez/Nydia Remolina León*, in: *Chris Brummer* (ed.), Crypto-assets – Legal, Regulatory, and Monetary Perspectives, 2019, 117, 119 et seq., when they discuss initial coin offerings.

172 In this respect, crypto-assets are different from intermediated securities where no uncertainty about the legal foundations exists. Legal certainty about the scope of enforceable rights emanating from securities is a blockchain context appears to be tacitly assumed by *Eva Micheler/Luc von der Heyde*, Holding, clearing and settling securities through blockchain/distributed ledger technology: creating an efficient system by empowering investors, (2016) Butterworth's J. Int'l Banking & L. 652–656, and *Eva. Micheler*, Custody Chains and Asset Values: Why Contemplating Crypto-Securities Are Worth Contemplating, 74 (3) Cambridge L.J. 505–533 (p. 528 et seq.) (2015) (on liability for the loss of financial instruments).

173 Regulation (EU) 2016/679 of 27 April 2016 on the protection of natural persons with regard to the processing of personal data and on the free movement of such data, and repealing Directive 95/46/EC (Data Protection Regulation), O.J. L 119/1 of 4 May 2016.

174 Art. 5 (1) (a), 6 (a), (c) GDPR.

175 Expert Group on Regulatory Obstacles to Financial Innovation (fn. 5), p. 85 (Recommendation 25), Study for the European Parliament, Blockchain and the General Data Protection Regulation – Can distributed ledgers be squared with European data protection law?, p. 76 et seq.

property with erga-omnes effects, it could be argued that the controller of the blockchain is under a duty to protect the integrity of the data storage device[176], and hence, the right to erasure does not apply (including insolvency scenarios). Art. 13 (3) GDPR imposes a duty on the data controller to inform the data subject once the solicited data shall be used for another purpose than originally agreed. Although this does not seem to apply to a mere change in the investment strategies in a robo-advice situation, the duty to inform would be triggered if the data controller plans to outsource data processing to a country with uncertain cybersecurity standards[177]. As a corollary, an information duty would arise if a hybrid robo-advice model is replaced by complete machine-based decision-making processes[178]. Art. 82 (1) GDPR provides for compensation from material or non-material damages if the Regulation has been infringed. The courts will have to flesh out which of the obligations under the Regulation are intended to operate as protective devices for the data subjects[179]. Outsourcing models may affect the allocation of responsibilities: If the processing of data is transferred completely to a third party (e. g. a cloud provider), the latter assumes the status (and liabilities) of a data controller[180]. If not, the parties may act as joint controllers (art. 26 GDPR)[181]. Nonetheless, if banks or financial service providers decide to rely on a given (external) infrastructure with distributed ledger technology, they will be classified as data controllers as they determined the specific purpose for processing data[182]. Art. 5 (4) of the Draft Regulation on a pilot regime for DLT market infrastructures[183] demonstrates that the relationship between data protection law and blockchain may have to be recalibrated: It envisages cyber arrangements which combine the integrity and confidentiality of the data stored with their availability and accessibility. It is for such a scenario that the expert group on

---

(July 2019, available at https://www.europarl.europa.eu/RegData/etudes/STUD/2019/634445/EPRS_STU(2019)634445_EN.pdf).

176 See *Paul Voigt/Axel v.d. Bussche*, The EU General Data Protection Regulations (GDPR) – A Practical Guide, 2017, p. 113.

177 Cf. *Lorenz Franck*, in: *Peter Gola* (ed.)., DS-GVO (Datenschutz-Grundverordnung VO (EU) 2016/679 – Kommentar (2nd ed. Munich 2018), Art. 13 ¶ 35.

178 Cf. *Franck*, in: Gola (fn. 177), Art. 13 ¶ 35.

179 For a broad interpretation of the concept of damage in the context of the GDPR: *Voigt/Bussche* (fn. 176), p. 205.

180 Ibid., p. 239. See also the concern of the European Commission, Digital Finance Strategy (fn. 28), at # 4.4., about risks arising from techno-financial conglomerates and groups.

181 This would require a common plan, allocating responsibilities between the parties: cf. Recital 79 of the GDPR and *Carlo Piltz*, in: Gola (fn. 177), Art. 26 ¶ 3.

182 European Parliament, Blockchain and the General Data Protection Regulation, p. 49.

183 Fn. 112.

regulatory obstacles to financial innovation calls for rules facilitating data sharing.[184]

2.5.3 Cross-Border Aspects

FinTech regulation and private law systems are jurisdiction-bound. Once digital business transcends national borders (or those of the European Union), diverging regulatory standards and private law differences in accommodating network services and artificial intelligence-based solution cause friction. In *Ruscoe v. Cryptopia Ltd.*, the defendant had operated a cryptocurrency exchange from New Zealand, but stored some of the customers' digital currency online on servers, physically located in Phoenix/Arizona (and perhaps also in the Netherlands)[185]. In recognising a property right under New Zealand law, the High Court appears to have assumed that the place of the register for blockchain-recorded transactions (New Zealand) determined the applicable law. However, as soon as the register is distributed across nodes in various jurisdictions it is unclear on which criteria to base a conflict of laws analysis[186].

From a practical perspective, the International Swaps and Derivatives Association (ISDA) has stepped up its efforts to develop a manageable set of rules for digitising trade in derivatives[187]. ISDA's standards for digitised trading with smart contracts and distributed ledger technology reflect an effort to overcome jurisdictional obstacles by private agreement. Due to the complexity of FinTech transactions it would seem that most distributed ledger systems will be permissioned blockchains where access is conditioned about acceptance of the terms of the platform. Thus, choice-of-law clauses do not appear to present a problem even if the servers are not located at the platform's place of business and mandatory laws are observed[188]. Nonetheless, problems of enforcement through

---

184 See Recommendation 28 – Data Sharing (fn. 5).
185 See Ruscoe v. Cryptopia (fn. 120), at ¶ 22 (c) (ii).
186 ISDA/Linklaters, Whitepaper – Smart Contracts and Distributed Ledger – A Legal Perspective, p. 9 (August 2017, available at https://www.isda.org/a/6EKDE/smart-contracts-and-distributed-ledger-a-legal-perspective.pdf).
187 See *Christopher D. Clark/Ciaran McGonagle*, Smart Derivatives Contracts: the ISDA Master Agreement and the automation of payments and deliveries (April 2019) (available at https://arxiv.org/pdf/1904.01461.pdf.)
188 See the private international law analysis by ISDA et al., Private International Law Aspects of Smart Derivatives Utilizing Distributed Ledger Technology, at pp. 9 et seq., 26 et seq. (January 2020, available at https://www.isda.org/2020/01/13/private-international-law-aspects-of-smart-derivatives-contracts-utilizing-distributed-ledger-technology/).

courts are likely to remain. Moreover, tokenisation is likely to cause considerable problems, especially as civil law jurisdictions may find it difficult to accept the property law reasoning adopted by courts of common law countries. Swiss and Liechtenstein laws seem to assume that the place of the electronic register for tokens is controlling, and hence the respective domestic law would apply. The attractiveness of non-EU jurisdictions and Brexit ensure that private international law problems persist. Nonetheless, the EU Commission should strive for private international law rules within the Union[189].

3 Sandboxes – A Regulatory Try and Error Mechanism

In FinTech, regulatory sandboxes are commended as innovative solutions for triggering regulatory learning processes[190], sometimes subject to regulatory capture[191] and an absence of transparency[192]. Current practice appears to confirm the criticism that proponents of regulatory sandboxes are suffering from a micro-transactional bias towards assessing FinTech business models[193]. Closer inspection suggests that sandboxes – however unsystematically they are employed – are likely to offer important insights into the interface between FinTech regulation and private law systems. If properly applied, sandboxes might operate as early warning mechanisms where the balance between financial regulation, the commodification of data and private needs to be recalibrated. The following survey focuses on a typology of regulatory sandboxes[194] to explore potential externalities and private law repercussions[195].

---

189 See Recommendation 8 on the commercial law for crypto-assets of the Expert Group on Regulatory Obstacles to Financial Innovation (fn. 5).

190 Cf. on the positive external effects of regulatory sandboxes: *Dirk A. Zetzsche et al.*, Regulating a Revolution: From Regulatory Sandboxes to Smart Regulation, 23 Fordham J. Corp. & Fin. L. 31–103 (78) (2017), *Ringe/Ruof*, Regulating Fintech in the EU: The Case for a Guided Sandbox, 11 European J, Risk Reg. 604, p. 607 et seq. (2020).

191 *Christopher P. Buttigieg et al.* (fn. 14), p. 464 et seq.

192 *Zetzsche et al.* (fn. 190), p. 80.

193 See *Omarova* (fn. 15), p. 110 et seq.

194 For a global overview: *Robinson et al.*, 9 (1) Comp. & Risk 10–14 (2020); Baker/McKenzie, International Guide to Regulatory FinTech Sandboxes (2018, available at https://www.ba kermckenzie.com/en/-/media/files/insight/publications/2018/12/guide_in tlguideregulatorysandboxes_dec2018.pdf).

195 Some Member States of the European Union (EU) argue for a level playing field in order to escape the negative consequences of regulatory competition in FinTech: See on the competitive

3.1 The UK Approach – The FCA's Sandbox[196]

The FCA's regulatory sandbox does not dispense with licensing requirements or authorisation processes to gain access to regulated markets[197]. Rather, it provides for a graduation procedure with admitted cohorts of (innovative) firms on their way to the regulated market[198]. After successful application, cohorts of firms are tested in two six-months-periods per year[199]. The FCA's admission procedure is highly selective[200]. In cohort 4, 40 percent of the participants were testing applications of distributed ledger technology[201] (including crypto-assets, cryptoasset-backed securities, tokenised debt and initial coin offerings)[202]. Cohort 5 included decentralised digital platforms using machine learning identity verification and blockchain-based key management, and facilitating securitisation of debt (by

---

concerns among Member States of the European Union if diverging approaches to innovation exist: ESMA/EBA/EIOPA (fn. 22).

196 The FCA studies the establishment of a cross-sector sandbox in order to provide a mechanism for innovative business models which come under the remit of several UK regulators: FCA, Call for Input: Cross-Sector Sandbox (May 2019, available at https://www.fca.org.uk/publication/call-for-input/call-for-input-cross-sector-sandbox.pdf).

197 FCA, Regulatory Sandbox (November 2015, available at https://www.fca.org.uk/publication/research/regulatory-sandbox.pdf), para.1.1.For a survey of the FCA's practice: *Michael Huertas*, The UK's FCA's regulatory 'sandbox': any lessons for the EU?, 33 (2) B.L.R. 50, 51 (2018).

198 This applies also to firms which would be subject to dual regulation (i. e. capital market law and prudential law requirements). FCA will consult with prudential authorities to obtain a restriction or a rule waiver so that the innovation can be tested properly: FCA, Sandbox (fn. 197), sub para. 3.2, FCA, Regulatory sandbox lessons learned report, at para. 2.1. (2017, available at https://www.fca.org.uk/publication/research-and-data/regulatory-sandbox-lessons-learned-report.pdf).

199 To be admitted, the applicant company has to demonstrate that it complies with the FCA's eligibility criteria: "carrying out or supporting financial services business in the UK, ...[a]genuinely innovative [project with] ...identifiable consumer benefit, ... the need for sandbox testing ... [and the readiness] ... to test" (FCA, Regulatory Lessons learned (fn. 100), at para. 5.11). The FCA will look for special FinTech competence and financial viability of the applicant firm in the interest of business integrity and customer protection (FCA, ibid.).

200 For cohort 5, the FCA selected 29 businesses out of 99 applicants (FCA Update 20 May 2019, Regulatory sandbox – cohort 5 (https://www.fca.org.uk/firms/regulatory-sandbox/cohort-5). For cohort 4, the FCA had admitted 29 businesses out of 69 applications (FCA Update 20 February 2019, Regulatory sandbox cohort 4, (available at https://www.fca.org.uk/firms/regulatory-sandbox/regulatory-sandbox-cohort-4-businesses).

201 FCA Press Release 3 July 2018, FCA reveals the fourth round of successful firms in its regulatory sandbox (available at https://www.fca.org.uk/news/press-releases/fca-reveals-fourth-round-successful-firms-its-regulatory-sandbox). On earlier cohorts see *Huertas* (fn. 197), 33 (2) B.L.R. 50, p. 53 et seq. (2018).

202 FCA, cohort 4 (fn. 201).

connecting loan issuance to the underlying financial data with the help of distributed ledger technology and artificial intelligence)[203]. The FCA's first review of sandbox activities noted that some of the start-up firms having successfully passed the sandbox test had entered into partnerships with larger financial institutions (including banks and insurance companies)[204].

The FCA's scrutiny focuses on bilateral relationships, although it acknowledges the specific risks of outsourcing activities to third parties[205]. With respect to negative externalities of sandbox projects, the FCA rejects all-inclusive liability for participating businesses[206]: Admission to the sandbox will not be conditioned on an undertaking that any customer loss will be compensated (including investment losses), and the showing that the applicant business had sufficient funds to finance potential compensation payments. The FCA does not think it appropriate to provide for the same degree of legal protection enjoyed by customers who contract with authorised firms. Instead, the FCA's approach is risk-informed, relying on transparency and disclosure: During the sandbox testing phase firms have to develop arrangements for customer protection while the FCA assesses the suitability of such safeguards in view of disclosure to customers and compensation requirements[207]. The FCA's insistence on compensation arrangements is informed by the insights into the economics of deposit insurance which generate ambiguous welfare effects[208]. Insurance schemes at fair rates will increase competition between financial institutions, but financial institutions may still assume too much risk if they compete for customer money in the face of non-internalised social cost of failure[209]. The FCA's policy aims at cost internalisation[210], but it also acknowledges implicitly that English law does not welcome pre-contractual duties of disclosure or specific warning duties flowing

---

203 FCA, cohort 5 (fn. 201).

204 FCA, Regulatory lessons learned (fn. 198), para. 5.7. et seq.

205 See FCA, Finalised Guidance (FG 16/5), Guidance for firms outsourcing to the 'cloud' and other third-party IT services, p. 5 et seq. (July 2016 (updated September 2019, available at https://www.fca.org.uk/publication/finalised-guidance/fg16-5.pdf).

206 See Appendix 4 (Customer protection approaches) to FCA, Sandbox (fn. 197).

207 Ibid.

208 See *Xavier Vives*, Competition and Stability Banking – The Role of Regulation and Stability in Banking, 2016, p. 107.

209 Ibid., p. 127.

210 See FCA, Regulatory lessons learned (fn. 198), p. 4 et seq., where the FCA notes that sandbox testing may facilitate access to finance for innovators while consumer protection safeguards are implemented.

from a general duty of good faith[211]. Under the sandbox scheme, customers are offered speedy relief. The have to use the Financial Services Compensation Scheme (FSCS)[212].

3.2 FinTech Regulatory Sandboxes under the Monetary Authority of Singapore

Singapore's 2016 "FinTech Regulatory Sandbox Guidelines"[213] support a principle-based approach for the benefit of "experimentation of a wide range of financial services"[214]. Once admitted to the sandbox, firms will be subject to a risk-based approach which regards externalities of a project as a trade-off for temporary exemptions from statutory requirements[215]. For admission, the applicant firm has to demonstrate that it plans to apply a different technology, or apply the same technology differently. The applicant has to show due diligence, including an assessment that the proposed financial service is commercially viable in Singapore[216]. The evaluation of a sandbox application is conditioned on welfare

---

211 See *Stathis Banakas*, Liability for Contractual Negotiations in English Law: Looking for the Litmus Test, 1 InDret 1–21 (2009); for a comparative approach: *Pierre Legrand*, Pre-Contractual Disclosure and Information: English and French Law Compared, 6 (3) Oxf. J. Leg. Stud. 322–352 (1986). This may have pushed the FCA into enquiring whether a statutory duty of care should be introduced: see FCA, A duty of care and potential alternative approaches: summary of responses and next steps (Feedback Statement FS 19/2 (April 2019, available at https://fca.org.uk/pub lication/feedback/fs19–02.pdf), *Christopher Woolard* (FCA), Regulation in a changing world, Speech 21 October 2019 (available at https://www.fca.org.uk/news/speeches/regulation-chang ing-world).

212 *W.-G. Ringe/C. Ruof*, "Regulating Fintech in the EU: the Case for a Guided Sandbox" 11 European J. Risk Reg. (2020), p. 604; FCA, cohort 5 (fn. 201).

213 Monetary Authority of Singapore, FinTech Regulatory Sandbox Guidelines (November 2016, available at https://www.mas.gov.sg/-/media/MAS/Smart-Financial-Centre/Sandbox/FinTech-Regulatory-Sandbox-Guidelines-19Feb2018.pdf?la=en&hash= B1D36C055AA641F580058339009448CC19A014F7).

214 Monetary Authority of Singapore, Response to feedback received – FinTech Regulatory Sandbox Guidelines, at para. 2.4. et seq. (November 2016, available at https://www.mas.gov.sg/-/media/MAS/Smart-Financial-Centre/Sandbox/Response-to-Feedback-Received.pdf?la=en&hash= 3F35F4C5F1CF0C7EE85D22E62C4C0B28114BF97E). MAS will move from testing to regulation if the risk of new technology becomes material and regulation is proportionate to the new risk: *Pei Sai Fan*, in: *David Lee Kuo Chen/Robert H. Deng (eds.)*, Handbook of Blockchain, Digital Finance, and Inclusion, Vol. 1, 2018), 347, p. 351.

215 See MAS, Guidelines (fn. 213), paras. 2.1, 5.1. et seq. and Annex A.

216 Ibid., para. 6.2.

criteria[217]. The proposed financial service should focus on innovation, measured by an enquiry of whether 'comparable offerings' are available on the Singapore market[218]. If preliminary testing reveals risk, a mitigation proposal has to be submitted[219]. Although the MAS undertakes a cost-benefit analysis with respect to risks for customers and the financial system and potential benefits, the guidelines fall short of providing for compensation arrangements. The Guidelines refrain from prescribing behavioural standards which might translate into specific contractual undertakings for the applicant firms. Instead, the MAS favours information over compensation. The applicant firm, the 'sandbox entity' shall inform customers of the sandbox nature of its financial service and emerging risks. The 'sandbox entity' has to demonstrate that customers are aware of these risks[220]. It is unclear whether a failure to seek customer awareness automatically triggers damages or whether it will terminate 'only' the sandbox experiment.

After nine months, the applicant firm will either 'graduate' or lose its temporary authorisation to do business[221]. Contrary to the FCA, the number of positive 'graduation' cases concluded by the MAS is relatively small, but includes several blockchain projects[222]. In its policy statement, the MAS appears to be at much greater ease in granting ease exemptions from specific legal and regulatory requirements than the FCA: "Possible to Relax" requirements include, inter alia, cash balances, fund solvency and capital adequacy, minimum liquid assets and minimum paid-up capital[223]. MAS has released guidelines for robo-advice[224], but maintains that no exemption from its general sandbox approach is intend-

---

217 Cf. *Yaru Chia*, Regulating the algorithms of tomorrow's advice in Singapore, 2020 J.B.L. 40, p. 45.

218 Consumer and industry research may be adduced to establish the problem-solving nature or the benefits of the new product or service: ibid., at para 6.2 (a), (b).

219 Ibid., at para 6.2 (f).

220 Ibid., at para. 8.2 (e). In this context, it is unclear whether the MAS is guided by a notion of sophisticated customer-investors, or whether the MAS also envisages consumer-investors in a contractual relationship with the applicant firm.

221 For a practical example: Blockchain News 9 November 2019, *Daniel Phillips*, Singapore Sandbox Program Adds Third Blockchain Project) (available at https://beincrypto.com/singa pore-sandbox-express-program-adds-second-blockchain-project/).

222 Ibid.

223 MAS Guidelines (fn. 213), Annex A ("Examples of Flexibility around Regulatory Requirements and Expectations for the Sandbox").

224 MAS Guidelines on Provision of Digital Advisory Services (October 2018) (available at https://www.mas.gov.sg/-/media/MAS/Regulations-and-Financial-Stability/Regulations-Guid ance-and-Licensing/Securities-Futures-and-Fund-Management/Guidelines-on-Provision-of-Digi tal-Advisory-Services-CMGG02.pdf).

ed[225]. In 2017 MAS initiated a project for studying the use of distributed ledger technology for interbank payments[226].

3.3 Testing FinTech Products in Australia

The Australian Securities and Investments Commission (ASIC) relies on statutory exemptions from licensing requirements and adds flexibility in interpreting statutes[227]. Its sandbox policy focuses on four FinTech business models: digital advice, marketplace lending platforms, payment products and digital currency wallets[228]. A FinTech licensing exemption acknowledges the interface between regulation and potential private law claims raised by customer-consumers. Exemptions are conditioned upon appropriate consumer information[229], and caps on the volume of the total business or a maximum value per individual (consumer) transaction[230]. Systemic risk concerns have led ASIC to introduce a limit on total exposure for testing activities per individual project (including wholesale and sophisticated clients)[231].

In order to "reduce the risk of poor consumer outcomes"[232], FinTech companies must disclose to their clients that they are operating without a licence under the licensing exemption scheme, and that normal protections may not necessarily apply[233]. ASIC requires 'adequate compensation arrangements'[234], but at-

---

225 *Chia* (fn. 217), p. 45 et seq.
226 Deloitte/MAS, The future is here – Project Ubin: SGD on Distributed Ledger (2017, available at https://www2.deloitte.com/content/dam/Deloitte/sg/Documents/financial-services/sg-fsi-project-ubin-report.pdf).
227 See *N. Selvadurai*, 25 (5) C.T.L.R. 141–148 (2019).
228 Digital currencies are not regulated by the ASIC. Nor does the licensing exemption apply to certain complex financial products.
229 Retail clients are to be supplied with basic information on the service provider which is reminiscent of a rudimentary prospectus (RG 257.89).
230 FinTech companies may only test their business project with respect to a limited number of retail clients. The individual exposure of a retail client may only relate to certain (safer) financial products and may not exceed AUS $ 10,000. With respect to testing services for insurance contracts, the sum insured shall not exceed AUS $ 50,000: See RG 257.83 (a): Deposit products, simple managed investment schemes, securities, government bonds and payment products (ASIC Regulatory Guide 257, Testing fintech products and services without holding an AFS or credit licence (August 2017, available at https://download.asic.gov.au/media/4420907/rg257-published-23-august-2017.pdf).
231 RG 257.84.
232 RG 257.79.
233 RG 257.88.

tempts to strike a balance between innovation without barriers and consumer protection against negative externalities. 'Adequate compensation arrangements' are not intended to introduce all-inclusive insurance or a deposit insurance scheme for the testing phase. ASIC favours a professional indemnity insurance[235], which does not extend to product failures, losses from investment or unsatisfactory returns[236]. Instead, professional indemnity insurance operates to supply coverage for financial losses resulting from poor-quality services and misconduct[237]. Disputes are to be settled in specific resolution procedures[238]. Contrary to Singapore's MAS, ASIC does not determine whether the envisaged innovation will advance Australia's competitiveness or generate consumer benefits. ASIC confines itself to "address[ing] the issues faced by new, innovative businesses"[239]. It would seem that ASIC's scrutiny also addresses the applicant's potential for cyber risk management if services are to be outsourced or cloud-based[240]. The applicant firm and the market will have to decide whether the financial service or product is commercially viable[241].

3.4 The Swiss Experience

The Swiss sandbox model favours an institutionalist approach over regulating specific business activities[242]. It does not envisage a graduation mechanism.

---

234 See RG 257.96. This reflects compensation requirements under RG 126.6 (ASIC Regulatory Guide 126, Compensation and insurance arrangements for AFS licensees (August 2017, available at https://download.asic.gov.au/media/4425351/rg126-published-29-august-2017.pdf).
235 See RG 257.97 et seq.
236 RG 257.99.
237 ASIC insists on minimum coverage requirements per individual claim, and for aggregated claims, and a ‚run-off cover' for 12 months: RG 257.100 et seq.
238 See RG 165 (Regulatory Guidance 165, Licensing: Internal and external dispute resolution, (May 2018, available at https://download.asic.gov.au/media/4772056/rg165-published-18-june-2018.pdf).
239 RG 257.55.
240 See ASIC, Cyber resilience good practices (last update 30 May 2019, available at https://asic.gov.au/regulatory-resources/digital-transformation/cyber-resilience/cyber-resilience-good-practices/).
241 See, however, the list of financial services benefitting from the exemption from statutory licensing requirements during the sandbox testing phase.
242 See Schweizerische Eidgenossenschaft – Eidgenössisches Finanzdepartement, Revision der Bankenverordnung (BankV) "FinTech-Bewilligung" – Erläuterungen, paras. 1.3.3, 3.2.1.1. et seq. (30 November 2016, available at https://www.newsd.admin.ch/newsd/message/attachments/54881.pdf).

The Swiss Financial Market Authority (FINMA) issues FinTech licenses to non-bank institutions[243] soliciting deposits from the general public which may not exceed the total of 100 m Swiss Francs[244]. Non-bank financial services include alternative finance (e. g. crowdfunding), money transfer and storage facilities on the basis of blockchain technology, and (algorithm-based) investment advice and asset management[245]. An application for FINMA's licence has to be supported by documentation on the envisaged business model, governance structures, risks management and compliance mechanisms[246].

The FinTech license scheme supplements private law duties of care with statutory disclosure duties[247]: Under art. 7 (a) of the amended Banking Regulation, the non-bank financial service provider has to inform its customers on its business model, the services to be rendered and the risks potentially arising from the underlying technologies. If the business model implies the holding of customer funds, the non-bank financial service provider must hold them separately and safely[248]. Customers have to be alerted that a deposit insurance scheme does not exist. The information has to be conveyed to the customer timely to allow them to make an informed judgment. Since the introduction of the FinTech licence in 2019 FINMA has noticed an increasing demand for information on the regulators' attitude towards business models with distributed ledger technologies and tokenised securities[249]. From a regulatory perspective, transparency and disclosure duties have to compensate for the fact that FINMA does not assess the merits of the business model submitted by the non-bank financial service provider[250]. Nonetheless, FINMA scrutinises crypto-related risks and insists

---

243 See FINMA Press Release 15 March 2019, Fintech licence and sandbox: adjustments to FINMA circular (available at https://www.finma.ch/de/news/2019/03/20190315-mm-fintech/).
244 Art. 1b of the Swiss Banking Law.
245 Eidgenössisches Finanzdepartment (fn. 32), para. 1.1.
246 See the list of criteria for assessing the applicant's business standing: FINMA, Mindestgliederung für den Prüfbericht betreffend das Bewilligungsgesuch für ein um Bewilligung ersuchendes Institut – Berichtsvorlage (April 2019).
247 Crowdlending now comes within the ambit of the law on consumer credits. See artt. 2 and 4 of the Federal on Consumer Credit (Bundesgesetz über den Konsumkredit).
248 In this context, the Swiss approach towards non-bank FinTech companies taking in customer monies appears to reiterate legislative choices under the E-Money Directive of the European Union.
249 FINMA, Jahresbericht 2019 (2020), p. 16 et seq. (available at https://www.finma.ch/de/news/2020/04/20200402-mm-finma-gb-2019/). In 2018, FINMA's advice was frequently sought with respect to initial coin offerings and payment tokens: FINMA, Jahresbericht 2018 (2019), p. 30 et seq. (available at https://www.finma.ch/de/news/2019/04/20190404-mm-jmk2019/).
250 See the explanations on art. 7 (a) of the Banking Regulation by the Eidgenössisches Finanzdepartement (fn. 147), at para. 2.1 (art. 7a).

on governance structures assuring the safe storage of tokens. This scrutiny includes risks (including cyber risks) resulting from outsourcing transactions to third parties[251]. The courts will have to develop standards for allocating risk in such a scenario, including risk warnings which may allow non-bank financial service providers to contain liability.

3.5 More Room for Innovation in the Netherlands

The Dutch capital markets authority (AFM) and country's national bank (DNB) focus on innovation in the sandbox industry without announcing an outright departure from existing law or a rule-based approach[252]. Their regulatory sandbox is primarily an instrument for facilitating the exchange of know-how and accommodating innovative practices within the existing framework of rules. Admission to the sandbox is conditioned on corporate governance processes which the applicant financial service company has implemented to protect, inter alia, customer and stakeholder interests[253]. During the testing phase, a financial product will be assessed on its real-world viability. Innovative projects should be advanced by invoking traditional techniques of continental interpretation of statutes, going beyond the very language and exploring the policy thrust of a specific norm[254]. In approaching blockchains, supervisors should resist a "strict application of the law"[255]. With respect to innovative asset management, AFM/ DNB are prepared to relax the traditional scrutiny of the initial intake process, if the investment company is "scrupulously observing its duty of care"[256]. This policy tacitly assumes that interpretation of statutes will be able to accommodate the most sophisticated forms of FinTech where artificial intelligence triggers investment processes which are difficult to trace back to human intervention.

---

251 FINMA, Jahresbericht 2019 (fn. 249), p. 18.

252 See the title of the policy statement: AFM/De Nederlandsche Bank (DNB), More room for innovation in the financial sector (December 2016, available at https://www.dnb.nl/en/bi naries/More-room-for-innovation-in-the-financial%20sector_tcm47-361364.pdf?2020070217.

253 Ibid. Dutch law provides for opt-in authorisation mechanisms into financial supervision where a financial service company receives and holds repayable funds, grants credits or invests monies without qualifying as a bank. In the age of financial disruption, the AFM/DNB feel that such financial service companies should prefer the regulatory sandbox mechanism over opt-in authorisation schemes.

254 See ibid., p. 7.

255 Ibid.

256 Ibid., p. 4.

Financial service companies are eligible to the Dutch sandbox scheme if their innovation project supports an objective of the country's financial supervision laws[257]. This includes companies which are encountering legal barriers although their project conforms to the underlying legislative policy[258]. Sandbox supervisors may impose constraints or requests for modifications which may take the shape of a tailored arrangement, a partial authorisation or an exemption from statutory requirements if the law so allows[259]. Moreover, the applicant company may be restricted to offering its services to professional clients only[260].

4 Conclusion

FinTech cannot do without private law and private contracting. The success of the EU's Digital Finance Strategy is conditioned on an efficient interface between financial regulation and the evolutionary potential of private law in the face of a principle-based approach of regulators. It is the intention of the EU to enhance global competitiveness in FinTech while maintaining a high degree of investor protection. In asserting its role as a rule-maker, the EU proceeds on two assumptions with respect to competition. As mandatory rules and soft law codes of conduct are promulgated, they are motivated by the belief that this is sufficient to unleash innovation and frictionless private ordering. Conversely, it is tacitly assumed that externalities flowing from this policy choice will be absorbed by private law. This, in turn, will unleash regulatory competition for the best set of private law rules under the legal system of the Member States. Regulatory sandbox models demonstrate that private contracting frequently is ahead of a formal regulatory framework for FinTech. They also favour ex-ante transparency over ex-post liability for innovation.

This article has assessed both the need and potential for a meaningful interface between financial regulation and private law in prominent fields of FinTech. With respect to payment services, outsourcing models, crowdlending, robo advice and blockchain applications, the EU proceeds with varying degrees of (legislative) intensity. Nonetheless, national private law systems will have to evolve as the enforceability of claims becomes increasingly important: There is a need for re-interpreting contractual duties of care and loyalty in view of the specificities of soft law codes of conduct, algorithmic business models and the digital

---

257 AFM/DNB (fn. 252), p. 4.
258 Ibid.
259 Ibid., p. 6 et seq.
260 Ibid.

division of labour in service chains. Any attempt to establish ground rules for the infrastructure of digital markets is predicated on adequate liability rules. The business models surveyed above are exposed to incoherent degrees of liability under finance law and data protection law (including the intricacies of data sharing). This is partly due to practitioners' and legislators' uncertainty about how to incorporate algorithms and artificial intelligence into established concepts of liability. Moreover, the current practice under regulatory sandbox models to combine transparency for customers with insurance requirements strangely focuses on bilateral business relationships. This ignores a more fundamental liability problem which needs to be resolved especially in the context of long outsourcing chains and digital networks. The courts or perhaps, legislators will have to decide whether those who design the organizational structure of a network should also shoulder liability for its malfunctions. This will also require a re-assessment of current burden-of-proof rules.

The EU's Digital Finance Strategy side-steps the private law classification of crypto-assets. The comparison with non-EU jurisdictions demonstrates that crypto-assets need to be afforded erga-omnes status with respect to third-party interventions. This is especially relevant to service chains for digital payments, outsourcing to clouds, DLT-facilitated settlement processes and insolvency scenarios. The dynamic of FinTech has it that the EU's regulatory instruments and Member State private laws are still in a state of flux. This is not due to deliberate regulatory design or legislative bias. But once private law systems will steadily accommodate the impact of practitioners' creativity and regulators' principle-based approach, shortcomings might be expected to emerge with greater clarity: Where Member State diversity becomes a liability, the EU should move to adopting fine-tuned private law rules for digital finance. Private international law rules for FinTech transactions, and the interface between digital finance law and the GDPR merit priority on a future legislative agenda.

Heikki Marjosola

Security Tokens and the Future of EU Securities Law: Rethinking the Harmonisation Project

Abstract: This article investigates the missing legal dimension in European Commission's digital finance strategy; namely, rules for holding, transferring, and collateralising digital financial assets known as security tokens, as well as their treatment in insolvency. The lack of EU rules would expose future token holders to a patchwork of unpredictable and inconsistent Member State laws and further fragment the private law underpinnings of EU capital markets. The article argues that digital transformation presents an opportunity for securities law harmonisation that the EU should not miss. At the same time, the EU needs to rethink its prevailing approach to harmonisation, which has ignored transparent holding systems. Three key issues for future EU securities law will be discussed: first, disintermediation fits poorly with the current conflict of laws *acquis* based on the so-called Place of the Relevant Intermediary (PRIMA) approach. The article nevertheless argues for preserving a modified PRIMA rule rule as an option in order to support market integration and competition. Second, future holding systems must be able to accommodate different market needs, including those of the securities financing market where liquidity is valued over control. This underlines the continuing relevance of intermediated securities law. Finally, as a first step towards more comprehensive harmonisation of substantive rights, the article presents a modest proposal for protecting the rights of token holders in insolvencies.

Keywords: Security tokens, blockchain, EU law, harmonisation, securities law

Table of Contents

Heikki Marjosola, Associate Professor of Financial Law, Faculty of Law, University of Helsinki.
Email: heikki.marjosola@helsinki.fi. I would like to thank Emilios Avgouleas, Eva Micheler
and Rainer Kulms for helpful comments and suggestions.

∂ OpenAccess. © 2022 Heikki Marjosola, published by De Gruyter. (cc) BY-NC-ND This work is licensed under
the Creative Commons Attribution-NonCommercial-NoDerivatives 4.0 International License.
https://doi.org/10.1515/9783110749472-009

1 Introduction

Although the hubris around blockchains, smart contracts and other FinTech buzzwords has given way to reality checks, the number of new digital financial assets, as well as platforms, brokers, custodians and other intermediaries trading and safekeeping those assets, has continued to grow.[1] The expansion of the new digital financial space might be quick and unpredictable, especially in payments.[2] The boundary between the token economy and the traditional financial system is also blurring; institutional interest and adoption of digital assets is growing[3] and more crypto firms and infrastructures are being licensed to offer financial services through regulatory sandboxes and FinTech Hubs.[4]

However, digital disruption has gained less momentum in capital markets. Despite significant interest in using distributed ledger technology (DLT) to issue securities (Security Token Offerings, STOs)[5] or to tokenise existing (book

---

1 See, e. g., *PWC*, 6thICO / STO Report, A Strategic Perspective, Spring 2020 edition (*PWC* Report).

2 *Tobias Adrian/Tommaso M. Griffoli*, The Rise of Digital Money, FinTech Notes No. 19/001, IMF 2019.

3 According to a recent report, more than a third of institutional investors surveyed invest in digital assets. See *Fidelity Digital Assets*, The institutional investors digital asset survey, 2020 Review (by Ria Bhutoria), June 2020.

4 See *A. Blandin et al*, 3rd Global Cryptoasset Benchmarking Study, University of Cambridge, Judge Business School, the Cambridge Centre for Alternative Finance (CCAF), September 2020 (3rd Global Cryptoasset Benchmarking Study). See also *Kulms* in this volume.

5 A distinction is sometimes drawn between DLT-native security tokens and tokenised securities that also exist outside DLT. See *OECD*, The Tokenisation of Assets and Potential Implications for Financial Markets, OECD Blockchain Policy Series, 2020 available at www.oecd.org/finance/The-Tokenisation-of-Assets-and-Potential-Implications-for-Financial-Markets.htm accessed 4 March 2021 (*OECD* report), p. 15. A similar distinction has been drawn between off-platform asset tokens and on-platform asset tokens. See *Financial Market Law Committee (FMLC)*, Distributed Ledger Technology and Governing Law: Issues of Legal Uncertainty, March 2018, available at www.fmlc.org accessed 4 March 2021 (*FMLC* report), p. 8.

entry or physical) securities[6] the market has remained marginal, especially in Europe.[7] The technology itself faces challenges regarding e. g. scalability and interoperability[8] but the primary hurdle is legal: unlike many other crypto-assets that have benefited from regulatory lags and gaps, security tokens qualify *prima facie* as transferable investment securities. This means that they must comply with the plethora of regulation concerning securities issuance, trading, post-trading, and investor protection. Indeed, STOs are primarily designed to be securities law-compliant and marketed as such.[9]

Digital finance plays a key role in the European Union's (EU) new industrial strategy.[10] There has been no shortage of official documents highlighting legal obstacles to tokenisation in Europe and calling for path-clearing legislative action.[11] Finally, in September 2020, the European Commission released a Digital Finance Package including a new digital finance strategy and a set of legislative proposals aiming to embrace the transformative potential of digital finance.[12] A

---

6 A recent *OECD* report identifies tokenisation of securities "as the sector with the most imminent potential for growth." OECD report (*ibid.*), p. 13.

7 Commission Staff Working Document, Impact Assessment accompanying the document Proposal for a Regulation of the European Parliament and of the Council on Markets in Crypto-assets and amending Directive (EU) 2019/1937, 24 September 2020, SWD(2020) 380 final 24, p. 29 (MiCA Impact assessment, 24). See also *PWC* Report (fn. 1), which shows that USA, Singapore, Hong Kong and UK dominate the global market for token offerings.

8 *OECD* report (fn. 5), p. 19.

9 *OECD* report (fn. 5), p. 13. In contrast, Initial Coin Offerings (ICOs) have been typically structured to avoid securities regulations. See *Clifford Chance*, Security Token Offerings – A European Perspective on Regulation. October 2020, 5, available at https://www.cliffordchance.com/content/dam/cliffordchance/briefings/2020/10/security-token-offerings-a-european-perspective-on-regulation.pdf accessed 4 March 2021.

10 Communication from the Commission, A New Industrial Strategy for Europe COM/2020/102 final.

11 See, e. g., *European Parliament*, Report on FinTech: the influence of technology on the future of the financial sector, Committee on Economic and Monetary Affairs, Rapporteur: *Cora van Nieuwenhuizen* (2016/2243(INI), 28 April 2017.; EUCO 14/17, CO EUR 17, CONCL 5, 19 October 2017); *European Commission*, FinTech Action Plan: for a more competitive and innovative European financial sector, 8 March 2018, COM(2018) 109 final. See also two expert group reports charting venues for regulatory intervention: Final Report of the High Level Forum on the Capital Markets Union, A new Vision for Europe's capital markets, June 2020, p. 74 – 76 and *Expert Group on Regulatory Obstacles to Financial Innovation (ROFIEG)*, 30 Recommendations on Regulation, Innovation and Finance – Final Report to the European Commission, December 2019.

12 Communication from the Commission on a Digital Finance Strategy for EU, 24 September 2020, COM(2020) 591. On balance, the package also addresses risks such as fraud, market manipulation, and money laundering, which have been salient features of the new digital markets. See *European Securities and Markets Authority (ESMA)*, The Distributed Ledger Technology Ap-

proposal for a Regulation for Markets in Crypto-assets (MiCA) would introduce common rules for the thus far unregulated part of the crypto-asset market[13] while another proposal for a Regulation on a pilot regime for market infrastructures based on distributed ledger technology ("DLT Pilot regime")[14] is designed specifically for crypto-assets that qualify as financial instruments under the MiFID II framework.[15] The DLT Pilot regime would in effect establish an EU sandbox – the first of its kind[16] – for experimenting in and facilitating the development of DLT-based infrastructures for capital markets.

Adoption of the Digital Finance Package would support the creation of markets for security tokens. The proposed rules would enhance legal certainty by explicitly extending the scope of regulation to securities issued in token form, whereas the DLT Pilot Regime would enable offsetting and adjusting the rules nationally where necessary. By allowing Member States to tailor their regulatory frameworks for individual DLT market infrastructures, the pilot regime would support local financial innovation and enhance the competitiveness of EU capital markets. The package would also promote cross-border marketability of security tokens by introducing a Union-wide passport system, thus expanding funding opportunities for European SMEs.

However, the Digital Finance Package does not address the legal uncertainties concerning the rights of security token holders. It includes no initiatives with

---

plied to Securities Markets, February 2017; *ESMA*, Report with advice on Initial Coin Offerings and Crypto-Assets, ESMA50–157–1391, 9 January 2019 (*ESMA Advice*); *European Banking Authority*, Report with Advice for the European Commission on Crypto-assets, January 2019; *European Parliament*, Report with recommendations to the Commission on Digital Finance: emerging risks in crypto-assets – regulatory and supervisory challenges in the area of financial services, institutions and markets (2020/2034(INL).

13 Proposal for a Regulation of the European Parliament and of the Council on Markets in Crypto-assets, and amending Directive (EU) 2019/1937, 24 September 2020, COM(2020) 593 final (MiCA proposal).

14 Proposal for a Regulation of the European Parliament and of the Council on a pilot regime for market infrastructures based on distributed ledger technology, 24 September 2020, COM/2020/594 final. In addition, the package includes a proposal for digital operational resilience (Proposal for a Regulation of the European Parliament and of the Council on digital operational resilience for the financial sector.

15 More specifically, financial instruments qualifying as transferable securities admitted to trading or traded on a trading venue, as defined in Article 4(1)(44) of MiFID II. Directive 2014/65/EU of the European Parliament and of the Council of 15 May 2014 on markets in financial instruments and amending Directive 2002/92/EC and Directive 2011/61/EU.

16 *Wolf-Georg Ringe/Christoph Ruof*, The DLT Pilot Regime: An EU Sandbox, at Last! Oxford Business Law Blog, 19 November 2020, available at https://www.law.ox.ac.uk/business-law-blog/blog/2020/11/dlt-pilot-regime-eu-sandbox-last accessed 4 March 2021.

regard to holding, transferring, safekeeping, and collateralising security tokens or their treatment in insolvencies. Moreover, neither the EU legislation in force nor the proposed Union legislation help determine with certainty which national law governs such proprietary aspects of security tokens. Leaving these issues for Member States (while introducing a passport to operate freely within the single market) seems surprising given the numerous examples of failed crypto custodians and outdated national legal regimes failing to provide even basic legal protection for clients of bankrupt crypto custodians.[17] The omission is more understandable, however, if viewed against the historical travails of harmonising general securities law in the EU, an exercise of notorious complexity and political sensitivity. Even as long as twenty years ago, the absence of a common legal framework for holding, acquiring and disposing of securities, and the uneven application of national conflict-of-laws rules regarding securities, were identified as significant legal barriers to integration of EU capital markets.[18] In 2015, the Commission's Capital Market Union (CMU) strategy restated yet again the need for securities law harmonisation.[19] However, little progress has been achieved and no legislative initiatives are currently in the pipeline. Existing EU securities law therefore remains restricted in scope, piecemeal, and inconsistent in substance.[20] Core conceptual issues, such as the legal nature of a security (or a securities account), and the legally recognised techniques of possession and dispossession of a security, remain matters to be determined by Member State law.

One might therefore excuse the EU legislator for leaving these contentious policy issues out of the Digital Finance Package – a controversial initiative in its own right.[21] This article nevertheless argues that digital transformation pres-

---

[17] For a discussion of nascent case law, see *Kulms* in this issue; *Matthias Haentjens/Tycho de Graaf/Ilya Kokorin*, "The Failed Hopes of Disintermediation: Crypto-Custodian Insolvency, Legal Risks and How to Avoid Them". Singapore Journal of Legal Studies (2020), p. 526. From the perspective of Bitcoin case law, see *Janis Sarral/Louise Gullifer QC (Hon)*, "Crypto-claimants and bitcoin bankruptcy: Challenges for recognition and realization", Int'l Insolvency Rev. 28 (2019), p. 233.

[18] *The Giovannini Group*, Cross-border Clearing and Settlement Arrangements in the European Union, November 2001.

[19] Commission Communication, Action Plan on Building a Capital Markets Union, 30 September 2015, COM(2015) 468 final, and Commission Communication on the Mid-Term Review of the Capital Markets Union Action Plan, 8 June 2017, COM(2017) 292 final.

[20] A recent comprehensive review, in the footsteps of the Giovannini Group, appears in *European Post Trade Forum* Report, 15th May 2017 (*EPTF report*), available at https://ec.europa.eu/info/publications/170515-eptf-report_en accessed 4 March 2021.

[21] For a brief discussion on reasons why legislative action in this area is unlikely, see *Philipp Paech*, "Securities, intermediation and the blockchain: an inevitable choice between liquidity and legal certainty?" Uniform Law Review 21 (2016), p. 612, p. 612–613.

ents a novel opportunity for private law harmonisation that the EU should not miss. First, many of the reasons that have complicated securities law harmonisation so far are either idiosyncratic to intermediated securities or not (yet) present in the case of security tokens.[22] Second, failing to act would add a further layer of legal complexity and uncertainty to the colourful patchwork of European securities laws. Indeed, DLT-based securities holding systems and tokenisation have already prompted uncoordinated legal action in several Member States.[23] Finally, DLT-facilitated disintermediation of securities holding systems presents novel problems in terms of legal certainty that require rethinking the philosophy of harmonisation projects for intermediated securities – particularly their difficult relationship with so-called transparent holding systems.

The article is structured as follows: the next section briefly discusses distributed ledger technology and its central promise of eliminating intermediaries and making the financial system more transparent. The third section identifies the missing private law dimension of the Digital Finance Package and makes the case for further harmonisation. The fourth section discusses three key concerns for future EU securities law: the need to update the existing conflict of laws *acquis* regarding intermediated securities; the continuing relevance of intermediated securities law and the need for future holding systems to accommodate different market needs; and finally the need to protect the rights of token holders in insolvencies as a first step towards more comprehensive substantive harmonisation. The fifth section concludes.

2 Disintermediation of Securities Holding Systems

2.1 The Promise of Distributed Ledger Technology

In modern, intermediated, securities holding systems one or more intermediaries (i.e., firms offering safekeeping, administration and other securities services) disconnect issuers from investors. In most holding systems risk-bearing investors

---

22 Apart from the EU, two international securities conventions have been completed: The 2009 UNIDROIT Convention on Substantive Rules for Intermediated Securities (Geneva securities convention) and the 2006 Hague Convention on the Law Applicable to Certain Rights in Respect of Securities held with an Intermediary. Neither of the conventions has entered into force. The Hague convention has been ratified by three countries (The United States, Mauritius and Switzerland) and the Geneva securities convention by one country (Bangladesh).

23 See *Kulms* in this volume; MiCA Impact Assessment (fn. 7); Clifford Chance report (fn. 9).

are not identified at Central Securities Depositories (CSD), where CSD participants acting as nominees hold client securities in a pooled form on so-called omnibus CSD accounts.[24] The intermediated holding structure has evolved to facilitate post-trade clearing and settlement of securities transactions and it provides specific efficiency gains, e.g. by minimising the number of accounts and transactions at the topmost tiers of the holding chain (thus allowing net settlement).[25] However, the intermediated system also imposes diverse legal risks and costs on market participants. Although modern securities laws generally provide investors with proprietary or quasi-proprietary rights that enjoy priority in the event of a custodian's bankruptcy, the substance of these rights varies among jurisdictions and their effectiveness may be compromised, especially in cross-border situations.[26] Additionally, to exercise their personal rights related to securities, investors must act through their account-providing intermediary, who may, in turn, have to rely on the relevant intermediary next up the custody chain, and so on. This "no-look-through" principle, whereby each party in the custody chain has rights against their own counterparty but not beyond, remains a cornerstone of – especially Anglo-American – securities law.[27] Whilst the principle brings several efficiency benefits, it also complicates enforcement of investor rights and corporate governance.[28]

---

24 Identification of investors at the level of CSD is internationally exceptional, but in some countries it is possible while in some others, as in Finland, mandatory. Such systems are sometimes called transparent because the client's ownership is identifiable on the level of CSD. See section 4.1 below.

25 Clearing and settlement comprise post-trade processes which together ensure the conclusion of a securities transaction, i.e., executing transfer or delivery of securities against payment (delivery and payment together constituting the settlement phase). See, e.g., *Charles W. Mooney Jr*, "Beyond Intermediation: A New (FinTech) Model for Securities Holding Infrastructures." University of Pennsylvania Journal of Business Law 22 (2019), p. 386, p. 399–401.

26 See e.g. *Mooney, ibid*, p. 404; *Eva Micheler*, "Custody chains and asset values: why cryptosecurities are worth contemplating." The Cambridge Law Journal, 2015, p. 505–533; *Eva Micheler*, Transfer of Intermediated Securities and Legal Certainty, in: Thomas Keijser (ed.), Transnational securities law, 2014; *Luc Thévenoz*, "Intermediated Securities, Legal Risk, and the International Harmonization of Commercial Law", Stanford Journal of Law, Business and Finance 13 (2008), p. 384.

27 *Joanna Benjamin/Louise Gullifer*, Stewardship and Collateral: The Advantages and Disadvantages of the No Look-Through System, in: Louise Gullifer/Jennifer Payne (eds.), Intermediation and Beyond, 2019, p. 223; *The Law Commission*, Intermediated securities: who owns your shares? A Scoping Paper, 11 November 2020, p. 83.

28 For a recent review from the perspective of the United Kingdom, see the Law Commission, *ibid*. For a discussion on recent British case law documenting the (sometimes tragic) consequences of intermediation, see *Eva Micheler*, Intermediated Securities from the Perspective of Invest-

The onset of DLT has introduced a new dimension to the holding system debate. The technology promises to solve some, if not all, of the problems of intermediated holding without compromising much of its benefits. Blockchains and other DLTs combine existing and new database technology and cryptography to facilitate value transfers over a distributed database, maintained and operated by a network of computers. Running code-based consensus algorithms, DLT systems enable transaction validation without a single designated authority, thus replacing centralised intermediaries, such as banks, as a source of trust. To the same effect, some DLT systems allow integration of smart contracts, i.e., pieces of code that run on DLT that automate contract execution and other transactional processes.[29] Smart contracts could automate several administrative intermediary functions in relation, e. g., to corporate actions, tax handling and collateralization. Given that DLT-based databases are also exceptionally difficult to tamper with, it is no surprise that some expect the technology to reform our centralized, exclusionary and antiquated financial market systems, which are based on "a kludge of industrial technologies and paper-based processes dressed up in a digital wrapper."[30]

Many have already charted the potential of DLT to overcome the problems and risks inherent in today's intermediated securities holding systems,[31] the fragmented and opaque securities markets[32] and even the fragilities of the modern financial system more generally.[33] From the perspective of the securities holding system debate, the central promise of DLT is that it will reconnect investors with issuers, thus enabling transparent and direct ownership.[34] Market participants

---

ors: Problems, Quick Fixes and Long-term Solutions, in: Gullifer/Payne (*ibid*) and *Richard Salter QC*, Enforcing Debt Securities, in: Gullifer/Payne (*ibid*).

29 On blockchains and DLT, See *Primavera De Fillppl/Aaron Wright*, Blockchain and the law: The rule of code, 2018, p. 33 – 57.

30 *Alex Tapscott/Don Tapscott*, "How blockchain is changing finance" Harvard Business Review 19 (2017), p, 2, 3.

31 *Mooney*, Beyond Intermediation (fn. 25); *Micheler*, Custody Chains and Asset Values (fn. 26); *Sarah Green/Ferdisha Snagg*, Intermediated Securities and Distributed Ledger Technology, in: Gullifer/Payne (fn. 27).

32 *David C. Donald/Mahdi H. Miraz*, "Multilateral Transparency for Securities Markets through DLT", Fordham Journal of Corporate & Financial Law 25 (2019), p. 97.

33 *Emilos Avgouleas/Aggelos Kiayias*, "The promise of blockchain technology for global securities and derivatives markets: the new financial ecosystem and the 'holy grail' of systemic risk containment", European Business Organization Law Review 20.1 (2019), p. 81.

34 *OECD report* (fn. 5), p. 16.

have recognised the efficiency-increasing potential of DLT.[35] The technology could therefore transform the infrastructure underlying securities transactions, which currently depends on the services of several intermediaries (brokers, clearing members, custodians) and infrastructure providers (trading venues, central counterparties, CSDs). According to the most optimistic predictions, DLT could merge trading, clearing, and settlement into one seamless and uniform global infrastructure.[36]

The emerging token economy is yet to fulfil the visions of borderless peer-to-peer networks heralded by the original blockchain protocols.[37] Re-intermediation rather than disintermediation has been the predominant trend. Participation in DLT systems has been outsourced to wallet providers and other crypto custodians.[38] Moreover, most crypto-asset exchanges or trading platforms remain centrally operated and controlled and only a few offer direct on-chain integration.[39]

In the EU, several projects have been launched to create DLT-based securities holding systems or post-trade infrastructures. However, regulatory constraints continue to limit the scope and level of ambition of these projects.[40] The Commission's digital finance package seeks to address some of these constraints.

---

35 Commission Staff Working Document, Impact Assessment accompanying the document Proposal for a Regulation of the European Parliament and of the Council on a pilot regime for market infrastructures based on distributed ledger technology, 24 September 2020, SWD(2020) 201 final (DLT Impact assessment), p. 21, noting that these benefits in terms of efficiency were expected by almost 4 out of 5 respondents to the public consultation.

36 *De Filippi/Wright* (fn. 29), p. 94. For a more detailed view of DLT's potential from the perspective of European post-trade infrastructures, see *European Central Bank*, The potential impact of DLTs on securities post-trading harmonisation and on the wider EU financial market integration. Advisory Group on Market Infrastructures for Securities and Collateral, September 2017 (*ECB* Report).

37 *Randy Priem*, "Distributed ledger technology for securities clearing and settlement: benefits, risks, and regulatory implications." Financial Innovation 6.1 (2020), p. 1, 13. On intermediation and re-intermediation in the digital finance space, see also *Iris H-Y Chiu*, Fintech and Disruptive Business Models in Financial Products, Intermediation and Markets – Policy Implications for Financial Regulators. Journal of Technology Law & Policy 21(2016), p. 55.

38 DLT impact assessment (fn. 35), 8; *Louise Gullifer/Henry Chong/Hin Liu*, Client-Intermediary Relations in the Crypto-Asset World, 23 September 2020 available at http://dx.doi.org/10.2139/ ssrn.3697946 accessed 4 March 2021, p. 1.

39 *OECD* report (fn. 5), p. 16, p. 30 (also reporting that many exchanges are "contemplating for applying for broker-dealer licence").

40 MiCA Impact Assessment (fn. 7), p. 21.

2.2 The Digital Finance Package and "DLT Market Infrastructures"

The Digital Finance Package introduces two separate Union regimes for crypto-assets. The MiCA proposal would set up a tailored regime for crypto-assets that currently fall outside the scope of EU financial services legislation, including all crypto-assets that do not qualify as financial instruments, deposits or structured deposits under that same legislation.[41] The proposal would impose disclosure rules for issuers of crypto assets and numerous requirements for crypto-service providers such as exchanges, custodians, brokers and advisers.[42] A full harmonisation instrument, MiCA would replace all existing national regimes and establish an EU passport for all crypto issuers and service providers.[43]

The MiCA proposal also confirms that all crypto-assets qualifying as MiFID II financial instruments[44] remain regulated under existing Union financial legislation "regardless of the technology used for their issuance or their transfer".[45] To the same end, the definition of a 'financial instrument' in MiFID II would be amended "to clarify beyond any legal doubt that [financial] instruments can be issued on a distributed ledger technology."[46] Without alleviating measures, this would set an insurmountable obstacle for security token issuers and service providers. For instance, the CSD Regulation segregates post-trading functions by requiring that all securities traded on trading venues must be issued and recorded in book entry form in a CSD.[47] Many rules also impose mandatory intermediation, thus preserving the market's multi-tiered and hierarchical structure. For instance, MiFID II requires all members or participants of multilateral trading facilities (MTFs) to be investment firms, credit institutions or other persons meet-

---

41 MiCA proposal, p. 10.
42 MiCA proposal, recital 12, p. 18.
43 MiCA proposal, p. 7.
44 Defined in Article 4(1)(15) and Annex I C of Directive 2014/65/EU of the European Parliament and of the Council of 15 May 2014 on markets in financial instruments and amending Directive 2002/92/EC and Directive 2011/61/EU, p. 349.
45 MiCA proposal, recital 6, p. 16.
46 Proposal to amend MiFID II and other directives, p. 5.
47 Article 3 of Regulation No 909/2014 of the European Parliament and of the Council on improving securities settlement in the European Union and on central securities depositories and amending Directives 98/26/EC and 2014/65/EU and Regulation (EU) No 236/2012, p. 1–72 (CSD Regulation).

ing strict competence, resource and organisational arrangements.[48] A similar requirement applies to securities settlement systems (operated by CSDs), which may only admit certain institutional counterparties as participants.[49] The latter rules would prevent DLT networks or crypto trading platforms from accepting individuals as members.[50]

To overcome these and other structural obstacles, the DLT Pilot Regime would create a specific environment for experimenting with DLT. In effect, the regime would allow certain targeted and temporary exemptions from regulatory rules which refer to notions such as "security account" or "book-entry form".[51] Possible exemptions, detailed under articles 4 and 5 of the DLT Pilot Regime proposal, as well as in the proposed MiFID II amendment,[52] would be granted on application by national competent authorities and the permission would be valid throughout the Union.[53] The new licensing regime would therefore operate on a decentralised basis with limited oversight from ESMA.[54]

The decentralised sandbox approach of the DLT Pilot Regime is a necessary first step towards more comprehensive reform. It would be difficult if not impossible to foresee the shape and architecture of evolving technological arrangements for holding and disposing of securities.[55] Even as a first step, however, the proposed regime is notably conservative. Only CSDs authorised under the CSD Regulation, or investment firms and market operators authorised under MiFID II, would be entitled to apply for permission to operate a new "DLT market infrastructure" – either a "DLT MTF" (in the case of a MiFID II firm) or a "DLT Settlement System" (in the case of a CSD). The proposed regime also only recog-

---

48 Article 19 of Regulation (EU) No 600/2014 of the European Parliament and of the Council on markets in financial instruments and amending Regulation (EU) No 648/2012, p. 84–148 (MiFID II).
49 Article 2(f) of Directive 98/26/EC of the European Parliament and of the Council of 19 May 1998 on settlement finality in payment and securities settlement systems, p. 45–50 (the Settlement Finality Directive).
50 For an early review of compatibility issues, see *ESMA* Advice (fn. 12 above).
51 DLT Pilot Regime proposal, recital 20 (recognising that "double-entry (or multiple-entry) book keeping of securities accounts may not always exist in a DLT system.").
52 See the proposed amendment to article 19 of MiFID II under the proposal amending MiFID II and other directives. As the proposal explains (recital 8) "DLT multilateral trading facility should be allowed to request a derogation from such an obligation so that is can provide retail investors with easy access to the trading venue, provided that adequate safeguards are in place in terms of investor protection."
53 DLT Pilot Regime proposal, p. 8. For DLT MTFs, see Article 7(5) of the DLT Pilot Regime proposal.
54 See articles 7(3) and 8(3) of the DLT Pilot regime proposal.
55 See recital 4 of the DLT Pilot Regime proposal.

nises *restricted or permissioned* DLT networks. Unlike the MiCA proposal, the DLT Pilot Regime proposal does not allow building tokenisation solutions on open and permissionless DLTs such as Ethereum – so far the dominant platform for STOs.[56] The proposal clarifies that the new DLT market infrastructures "should establish the rules on the functioning of the *proprietary DLT they operate*, including the rules to access and admission on the DLT[...]."[57] DTL infrastructures would therefore be designed, owned, operated and governed by licensed firms. As a moderate sign of a more disruptive approach, a DLT MTF could be licensed to perform certain important functions now reserved for CSDs, such as taking care of the initial recording of securities (the notary function) and settlement of transactions.[58]

The Pilot Regime would also have a limited material scope. The proposed regime would apply to transferable securities that are negotiable on the capital market and exclude, e.g., private placements of unlisted SMEs.[59] To safeguard financial stability, the regime would also be limited to *illiquid* securities that do not exceed a specified market value: the maximum market capitalisation for issuers of shares would be EUR 200 million. For public bonds other than sovereign bonds (which would be excluded) the maximum issue size would be EUR 500 million. To control the size of the new infrastructures, the proposal limits the

---

56 See *French Digital Asset Association (FD2 A) et al.*, Report on "security tokens" or "financial tokens similar to financial instruments.", p. 1, available at https://www.afg.asso.fr/wp-content/uploads/2019/05/report-on-security-tokens-may-2019 – 1.pdf accessed 4 March 2021 (finding that a vast majority of players involved with issuing or servicing security tokens opt for a public blockchain). For one example, see, e.g., *OECD* report (fn. 5), p. 47 describing how Swiss company Mt Pelerin Group SA tokenised all of its issued (and uncertificated) shares on the Ethereum blockchain (a combination of public offering and private placement). Société Générale, a French bank, has completed two covered bond issues using the Ethereum blockchain. See *FitchRatings*, SG Covered Bonds Issued and Settled with Blockchain Technology, 21 May 2020, available at https://www.fitchratings.com/research/banks/sg-covered-bonds-issued-settled-with-blockchain-technology-21 – 05 – 2020 accessed 4 March 2021.
57 DLT Pilot Regime proposal, recital 28. Compare recital 5 of the MiCA proposal which notes that "a Union framework on markets in crypto-assets should not regulate the underlying technology and should allow for the use of both permissionless and permission-based distributed ledgers.".
58 DLT Pilot Regime proposal, recital 9.
59 As defined under MiFID II Article 4(1)(44), i.e., securities such as shares or bonds or other forms of securitised debt (incl. depository receipts in respect of shares or debt securities). See DLT Pilot Regime proposal, recital 11 ("DLT transferable securities should be crypto-assets that qualify as 'transferable securities' within the meaning of [MiFID II] and that are issued, transferred and stored on a distributed ledger.").

total market value of securities recorded on either of the new DLT market infrastructures to EUR 2.5 billion.

To conclude, the Digital Finance Package facilitates disintermediation by enabling disapplication of certain mandatory EU financial services rules that, e. g., centralise the recording of securities within CSDs and disqualify all but certain professional financial firms from participating in trading platforms and securities settlement systems. At the same time, users would access security token markets through established and licensed gateway service providers, which would also remain the central points of responsibility for regulatory and supervisory purposes. The proposal's main purpose therefore seems to be eradication of regulatory barriers to investment in digital infrastructure by existing market players, which are struggling to match increasing competition from their peers outside the EU.[60]

3 The Case and Opportunity for Private Law Harmonisation

3.1 Legal Uncertainty on Substantive Rights and Applicable Law

Levelling the regulatory playing field for DLT market infrastructures does not alone make the arrangements legally sound.[61] Even a perfectly transparent "single golden record"[62] of transactions and security ownership would fail to provide legal certainty in a cross-border context unless all the jurisdictions involved treated the recorded rights and interests (replicated in identical form throughout the cross-border network) in a legally compatible way. Such private law issues are ignored in the Commission's Digital Finance Package, which includes no initiatives as to rights of token holders vis-à-vis the operators of DLT market infrastructures, their participants, or creditors of both. The case for such harmonisa-

---

60 A good example of the type of DLT infrastructure envisaged by the DLT Pilot Regime is the SDX project by SIX, a company that owns and manages Switzerland's stock exchange. SDX would host a fully integrated infrastructure for trading, settlement and custody of digital assets. See SIX, https://sdx.com/ accessed 4 March 2021.
61 *BIS Committee on Payments and Market Infrastructures (CPMI)*, Distributed ledger technology in payment, clearing and settlement. An analytical framework, February 2017, 16 ("DLT can increase legal risks if there is ambiguity or lack of certainty about an arrangement's legal basis.")
62 See MiCA Impact Assessment (fn. 7), p. 22.

tion is clear. For instance, the revised CMU strategy acknowledges that a key to encouraging cross-border investment is ensuring that investors may rely on adequate and effective legal protection in other Member States.[63] This applies to the DLT market infrastructures and their legal underpinnings as well.

However, there is nothing new in such legal uncertainty with regard to end investors' ownership rights. On the contrary, it has been a permanent feature of European markets for intermediated securities. As the 2017 European Post-Trade Forum Report explains:

> Across the EU, Member States have developed legal mechanisms which are intended to ensure that an end investor enjoys in rem "ownership" of securities, notwithstanding that a chain of intermediaries may separate the end investor from the issuer. These mechanisms work reasonably well within each Member State. But the mechanisms differ from each other, and can come into conflict if the chain of intermediaries crosses borders.[64]

In the case of intermediated securities, it has therefore been assumed that the legal position of account holders is relatively secure as long as the chain of custodians does not involve intermediaries from other jurisdictions (with possibly conflicting laws). A similar assumption could not be made in the case of security tokens. EU jurisdictions are already split on how they apply their securities laws to security tokens: some Member States have enacted (or are in the process of enacting) laws that characterise security tokens as securities while in other Member States the issue would be resolved via unpredictable rules governing intangible property.[65] Many national legal systems are yet to adapt to the requirements of DLTs, security tokens and other crypto assets.[66] Lack of common or compatible rules would further fragment the private law underpinnings of EU capital markets and expose future token holders to a patchwork of unpredictable and inconsistent Member State laws.

---

63 Communication from the Commission, A Capital Markets Union for people and businesses – new action plan COM/2020/590 final, p. 14.
64 *EPTF* Report (fn. 20), p. 85.
65 See *Clifford Chance* report (fn. 9 above); *Kulms* in this volume; *Matthias Lehmann*, "National Blockchain Laws as a Threat to Capital Markets Integration." Uniform Law Review 26 (2021), p. 148.
66 As a good example of such modernisation, in December Germany initiated a law project the purpose of which is to allow recording of securities in crypto securities registers. See the proposal and press release of the *Federal Ministry of Justice*, Gesetz zur Einführung von elektronischen Wertpapieren, available at https://www.bmjv.de/SharedDocs/Gesetzgebungsverfahren/DE/Einfuehrung_elektr_Wertpapiere.html accessed 4 March 2021. Compare the reforms of France and Luxembourg as, e. g., described in the report by the *French Digital Asset Association (FD2 A) et al.* (fn. 58), p. 2–3.

This legal uncertainty is amplified by unclear rules of private international law. It is unclear how the EU's existing conflict-of-laws rules applicable to inter-mediated securities would apply – if they were to apply at all – to security tokens held within DLT market infrastructures. Without uniform conflict rules, any harmonisation of substantive law (short of absolute unification of relevant property, insolvency and corporate law) would fail to resolve the legal risks attaching to security tokens. Leaving the issue to be resolved by each Member State would lead to inconsistent and incompatible outcomes, particularly considering the large menu of alternative conflict rules available.[67] Therefore, just as in the case of intermediated securities, harmonisation of conflict-of-law rules should be considered a priority.[68]

3.2 The Opportunity for Private Law Harmonisation

For good reason, securities law is considered one of the most challenging areas of private law to harmonise.[69] In addition to the topic's general complexity and technicality, negotiators must cope with a diversity of national legal approaches and technical arrangements.[70] The onset of security tokens and DLT market infrastructures will complicate the mix of laws and technologies even further. One might reasonably expect that this will also diminish the chances of success of (currently stagnant) harmonisation projects. This section argues the contrary:

---

67 For review and discussion, see the *FMLC* report (fn. 5).

68 *Matthias Haentjens*, European Harmonisation of Intermediated Securities Law: Dispossession and Segregation in Regulatory and Private Law, in: Gullifer/Payne (fn. 28 above), 259– 287, p. 261; *FMLC* report (fn. 5), p. 5–6. See also Recommendation 8 of the *Expert Group on Regulatory Obstacles to Financial Innovation* (fn. 11).

69 *Luc Thévenoz*, The Geneva Securities Convention: objectives, history, and guiding principles, in *Conac/Segna/Thévenoz*, Intermediated Securities: The Impact of the Geneva Securities Convention and the Future European Legislation. (New York: Cambridge University Press, 2013), p. 16–17.

70 *Thévenoz, ibid.*, p. 16–17. For instance, in 2005 *Goode et al.* listed the following established legal constructs to characterise the account holder's legal position: "Regular deposit; special deposit; co-property rights in an identifiable pool of securities; some other form of property right traceable to individual securities; irregular deposit; general deposit; some other form of purely personal (contractual) right against the intermediary to the delivery or transfer of a given type and number of securities; interest of a beneficiary under a trust; a statutory fiduciary interest; *Gutschrift in Wertpapierrechnung*; co-property rights in a fungible, notional or book-entry pool of securities; security entitlements; some other bundle of property, contractual or other rights." *Roy Goode/Hideki Kanda/Karl Kreutzer* (with the assistance of *Cristophe Bernasconi*), Hague Securities Convention, Explanatory Report, 2005.

that digitisation of finance has created a window of opportunity for private law harmonisation that should not be missed.

First, the versatile legal problems of digital financial assets are new to all jurisdictions, which means that divisive doctrinal tradition would less likely defeat harmonisation attempts. Compare this situation to the happenstance mix of laws and systems of intermediated securities that has evolved over decades as each country has aligned its laws with its own needs, traditions, markets and infrastructures.[71] Some countries have adapted the law to market practice while others have done the exact opposite; still others have done either nothing at all or have adopted hybrid approaches, flexing existing legal concepts and institutions to confusing limits.[72] These legal-cultural differences have complicated the EU securities law legislation project, which has failed to produce a legislative proposal.[73] The onset of digital financial assets is forcing legislators, courts, and legal scholars to ask similar questions: whether to adapt the law to the market, or *vice versa*; whether existing doctrines of property are fit to deal with digitized assets and DLT infrastructures, and so on. In response, several countries have already enacted private law reforms. However, the outcomes are hardly as entrenched as in the case of intermediated securities, nor are they as wrapped up in anachronistic doctrines of property. By adopting a proactive minimum harmonisation approach early on and as a first-step measure, the EU would ensure a minimum level of protection for token holders while mitigating the risk of replicating the fragmented legal system for intermediated securities.[74]

Second, the DLT Pilot Regime would be an ideal opportunity for private law harmonisation because of its limited scope. In addition to legal and cultural obstacles, legal reform of the intermediated system has been subdued by conflicting market demands. The modern financial system hosts two classes of investors whose interests and priorities do not align. The first class represents investors who hold securities as medium-term or long-term investments and who value effective governance and enforcement rights in addition to protection against third-party claims; the second class of investors operates mainly on the short-

---

71 *Thévenoz* (fn. 69), p. 18. As the Giovannini report of 2001 noted, "laws about what securities are and how they may be owned form a basic and intimate part of the legal systems of Member States, and to change them will have many ramifications." *Giovannini* report 2001 (fn. 18), p. 54.
72 *Philipp Paech*, Conflict of Laws and Relational Rights, in: Gullifer/Payne (fn. 28 above), p. 290–291.
73 See e. g. *Madeleine Yates/Gerald Montagu*, The law of global custody: legal risk management in securities investment and collateral, 4th ed., 2013, p. 201–202.
74 See also *Paech*, Securities, intermediation and the blockchain (fn. 21), p. 614; Lehmann (fn. 65).

term securities financing market and prioritises liquidity, cheap credit and effective collateralisation.[75] According to Benjamin and Gullifer, the commercial pressures of the growing securities financing market are partially responsible for the ongoing structural separation of investors from their entitlements.[76] Lack of consensus has also obstructed legal reform.[77] DLT-based holding systems are not immune to these conflicting market demands, at least in the long term. However, the interests and priorities of the securities financing market need not affect the design of the first generation of European DLT infrastructures, which – as the proposed DLT Pilot Regime suggests – could only be used for illiquid securities of limited value. Such systems could therefore be designed to respond to the needs of medium-term and long-term investors without the corresponding trade-offs for, or opposition from, the securities financing market.

3.3 Disintermediated Systems and Securities Law Harmonisation

A possible hindrance for the creation of "EU security tokens law" is that the legal systems of most Member States are relatively unfamiliar with transparent securities holding systems or their specific legal needs. Various categories of transparent holding systems exist but they all recognise the ultimate account holder's interest at the CSD level.[78] Such "end-investor segregation" is possible and popular in some Member States such as the Nordic countries,[79] but most Member States subscribe to the intermediated model.[80]

---

75 See *Benjamin/Gullifer* (fn. 27); *Gullifer/Payne*, Conclusions, in: Gullifer/Payne (fn. 27), p. 391, p. 393 and 396. Such divisions are visible even within single financial institutions. See *Paech*, Market Needs as Paradigm: Breaking Up the Thinking on EU Securities Law, in *Conac/Segna/Thévenoz* (fn. 69), p. 25.

76 *Benjamin/Gullifer* (fn. 27), p. 215.

77 Ibid., p. 231, p. 234.

78 *Unidroit*, Report of the Transparent Systems Working Group, Study LXXVIII – Doc. 88, May 2007, 2. See also *ECSDA*, Account segregation practices at European CSDs, 13 October 2015, available at http://ecsda.eu/wp-content/uploads/2015_10_13_ECSDA_Segregation_Report.pdf accessed 4 March 2021, p. 2–3. Such systems have also been called transparent. However, see *Mooney*, Beyond intermediation (fn. 25), p. 398–399 (noting that the term is misleading since "this does not necessarily mean that the investor's identity is disclosed to any particular person, much less made available to the public generally").

79 See *Lars Afrell/Karin Wallin-Norman*, "Direct or Indirect Holdings-A Nordic Perspective." Uniform Law Review 10 (2005), p. 277, 283. For the features of the "end-investor segregation model" as opposed to "individual client segregation" (where the client can also be an intermediary act-

In international harmonisation projects, transparent holding systems have mainly represented distracting deviations from mainstream intermediated holding models, which have provided the blueprint for harmonisation. The Geneva Securities Convention, completed in 2009, struggled to accommodate the specific features of transparent holding systems. Compatibility problems related, for example, to the special operational and administrative role of CSD participants in controlling CSD accounts directly, technical integration of intermediaries' systems with those of the CSD, and the general problem of whether and when CSD participants could qualify as "intermediaries".[81] Permissioned DLT systems, directly accessible by individuals (including foreign), will probably introduce similar issues. The participants or nodes of DLT systems, acting as points of entry to the DLT infrastructure, might not qualify as intermediaries, at least in the traditional sense – unless they acted as custodians and used their own *separate systems* for the purposes of recording their clients' security tokens.

The marginal status of transparent holding systems has been mainly due to their negligible international importance. It has been assumed that transparent systems simply do not work for cross-border holding of securities.[82] Indeed, most transparent systems (including those hosted by the Nordic countries) are mixed systems where a significant proportion of the holding chain is non-transparent (intermediated) in order to facilitate international access and cross-border securities trade.[83]

DLT-powered disintermediation means that transparent holding systems might be much less marginal in the future. After all, the entire point of DLT is to enable disintermediation in a cross-border environment. The explicit objective of the DLT Pilot Regime is to promote direct access for retail investors to new DLT infrastructures,[84] which could operate freely in the single market with a Union-wide passport. In building the legal foundations for such systems, much could

---

ing on end-investors behalf) and "omnibus client segregation" (where client securities are pooled or commingled at the CSD level) models, see *ECSDA* 2015 *(ibid)* p. 8 and *Delphine Nougayrède*, "Towards a Global Financial Register? The Case for End Investor Transparency in Central Securities Depositories", Journal of Financial Regulation 4.2 (2018), p. 276, p. 286–288.

80 See *ECSDA* 2015 (fn. 78) p. 11.

81 *Unidroit* report (fn. 78).

82 *Victoria Dixon*, The Legal Nature of Intermediated Securities: An Insurmountable Obstacle to Legal Certainty?, in: Gullifer/Payne (fn. 27), p. 47–83, p. 62.

83 *Unidroit* Report (fn. 78) (noting that "Individual client or end investor account segregation typically does not apply in cross-border scenarios").

84 As recital 22 of the proposed regulation clarifies, one purpose of the pilot regime is to eradicate regulatory obstacles "to the development of alternative models of settlement based on a DLT that allow direct access by retail clients.".

be learned from legal systems hosting transparent and mixed holding systems. For instance, since the 1990s the Nordic countries have had in place special legislation clearly defining the ownership rights of end-investors at their national CSDs.[85] However, these systems are equally unprepared for the demands and intricate technical details of DLT-based systems. Definitional confusion about accounts, records, ledgers and their possible legal differences will hardly be avoided.[86]

4 Elements of EU Security Tokens Law

4.1 Which Conflict of Laws Rule for Security Tokens and Direct Holding Systems?

The absence of consistent rules for establishing the applicable law for issues of ownership rights and other proprietary interests in intermediated securities remains an important legal barrier for the development of the EU single financial market.[87] In the case of intermediated book entry securities, the problem is not the lack of EU-level rules so much as their diversity and limited scope. The existing rules, representing variations of the so-called Place of the Relevant Intermediary Approach (PRIMA),[88] refer as a connecting factor to (a) the country where the relevant register, account or centralised deposit system recording the security is *located* (Settlement Finality Directive (SFD));[89] (b) the country where the register, account or system is *held or located* (the Winding-up Directive (WUD))[90]; and

---

85 *Afrell/Wallin-Norman* (fn. 79), p. 277. Most Nordic CSDs also act as formal registrars under corporate law and operate national settlement systems. See *ECSDA* 2015 (fn. 68) p. 8 and *Nougayréde* (fn. 79) p. 285.

86 *Priem* (fn. 37), p. 18.

87 The *EPTF* Report (fn. 20), p. 71. The barrier was originally identified in the Giovannini Reports of 2001 and 2003. See the *Giovannini* 2001 report (fn. 18 above) and *The Giovannini Group*, Second Report on EU Clearing and Settlement Arrangements, April 2003. See also *Legal Certainty Group*, Second Advice of the Legal Certainty Group: Solutions to Legal Barriers Related to Post-trading within the EU, August 2008; and *European Commission*, Securities Law Legislation: 7th Meeting of the Member States Working Group: Non-paper, 15 May 2013.

88 The PRIMA approach was developed during negotiations for The Hague Convention of 5 July 2006 on the Law Applicable to Certain Rights in Respect of Securities (effective as of 1 April 2017).

89 Article 9(2) of the Directive 98/26/EC of the European Parliament and of the Council of 19 May 1998 on settlement finality in payment and securities settlement systems, p. 45.

90 Article 24 of the Directive 2001/24/EC of the European Parliament and of the Council of 4 April 2001 on the reorganisation and winding up of credit institutions, p. 15.

(c) the country where the *relevant account is maintained* (the Financial Collateral Directive (FCD))[91]. The Commission recently assessed the compatibility of these approaches and the diversity of their national interpretations, if only to conclude that they all "appear to be valid" and that there was no need for legislative action.[92]

It would be difficult to predict how the existing conflict rules designed for intermediated securities and account-based structures would be applied in a DLT context – if they were to apply at all considering their limited substantive and personal scope. On the one hand, in a pure DLT environment the PRIMA rule based on the location of the account or register, or the location of the entity in charge of maintaining the account or register, would not work for the simple reason that there are neither accounts nor intermediaries in the traditional sense.[93] Indeed, the main feature of distributed registers – shared and replicated across a transnational network of nodes – is that tokens exist at the same time everywhere and nowhere in particular.[94] On the other hand, in the case of permissioned or proprietary DLT holding systems it would not be clear whether the notion, e.g., of "maintaining" a register or system would be interpreted as referring to the licensed entity responsible for the entire system (the provider of the "DLT market infrastructure") or the entity (e.g., node, member, participant) that makes the entries in the system based on a mandate or agreement.[95]

To design the most appropriate conflict-of-laws rules for DLT systems requires a balancing of multiple policy and legal issues as well as market needs. For disintermediated holding systems, the most logical conflict-of-laws rule would be *the law governing the DLT system*. In fact, such a rule has already

---

91 Art. 9(1) of the Directive 2002/47/EC of the European Parliament and of the Council of 6 June 2002 on financial collateral arrangements, p. 43, as amended by Directive 2009/44/EC of the European Parliament and of the Council of 6 May 2009 amending, p. 37.

92 Communication from the Commission to the European Parliament, the Council, the European Economic and Social Committee and Committee of the Regions on the applicable law to the proprietary effects of transactions in securities, 12 March 2018COM(2018) 89 final, p. 5–6.

93 *Green/Snagg* (fn. 31), p. 354; *Thomas Keijser/Charles W. Mooney Jr*, Intermediated Securities Holding Systems Revisited: A View Through the Prism of Transparency, in: Gullifer/Payne (fn. 27), p. 325. See also the *FMLC* report (fn, 5), p. 6 and *Kulms* in this volume (discussing the case *Ruscoe v. Cryptopia Ltd.*, [2020] NZHC 728).

94 *ESMA* Advice (fn. 12), para. 72 (In a DLT environment, it might be less clear where the securities and their records are located); *FMLC* report (fn. 5), p. 11.

95 These problems are not alien to intermediated securities either because to speak of a "location" of a securities account is also a simplification. See the *EPTF* report (fn. 20), p. 76. See also *Unidroit* report (fn. 78), p. 11–13 discussing the problem of defining the "relevant intermediary" in so-called transparent systems.

been identified and discussed; a rule termed "PROPA" would look to the "Place of the Relevant OPerating Authority/Administrator" of the DLT system.[96] This type of rule would fit well with the approach adopted in the proposed DLT pilot regime because it only works if the relevant holding system is permissioned and centrally operated and administered.[97] In the DLT Pilot Regime context, the governing law would therefore be linked to the location of the licensed DLT Market Infrastructure provider.[98]

The PROPA rule, however, involves important trade-offs. The "law of the system" approach would mean that an investor holding security tokens issued through different DLT systems (applying different laws) would have to ascertain the certainty of their legal title to, and other interests in, security tokens in each jurisdiction.[99] An investor wishing to buy security tokens on margin, for instance, would find it cumbersome to use the portfolio, and its changing content, as collateral. Indeed, the oft-cited benefit of the above-discussed PRIMA rule and the "no-look-through" principle is that they facilitate diversification and efficient portfolio financing. They allow a single law to apply to a securities account, and to all the securities credited on that account, regardless of their origin.[100]

The same drawback concerns another possible conflict-of-laws approach which has been called *elective situs*. According to this rule, the proprietary effects of transactions would be governed by the law "*chosen by the network participants for the DLT system*."[101] All tokens and transactions within the system would be governed by a single legal framework and all system participants would agree to the applicable law by way of a contract when connecting to the DLT system.[102] Like the PROPA rule, elective situs might not facilitate collateralisation and market integration. Moreover, political consensus for such a party autonomy-based approach would be difficult to achieve. The Hague Securities Convention was rejected by many EU Member States precisely because the contractual PRIMA rule ultimately adopted would have allowed displacing national property and insolvency laws with a foreign law (e.g. English or New

---

96 *FMLC* report (fn. 5).

97 *FMLC* report (fn. 5), p. 18.

98 *FMLC* report (fn. 5), p. 18. Such "*lex systematis*" is also discussed – and tentatively supported – in *Paech*, Securities, intermediation and the blockchain (fn. 21), p. 636.

99 *Yates/Montagu* (fn. 84), p. 101 and *Paech* (fn. 72)

100 *Paech* (fn. 72), p. 294; *Keijser/Mooney* (fn. 93), p. 324. According to Gullifer and Payne, this is "probably the most significant advantage of the intermediated system, and the one most difficult to replicate in other ways". See *Gullifer/Payne*, (fn. 75) p. 362.

101 *FMLC* report (fn. 5), p. 15.

102 Again, this would be a workable option especially for proprietary permissioned systems. *FMLC* report (fn. 5), p. 16.

York law) as long as the relevant intermediary had a branch in that foreign jurisdiction when entering into the contract.[103] The party autonomy approach has nevertheless received support in the crypto asset context.[104]

The drawbacks of the PROPA or the *elective situs* rules in terms of cross-border investments or portfolio financing would naturally depend on the number of relevant infrastructure providers and the number of laws applying to them. The higher the number of infrastructures and therefore of applicable national laws, the higher the attendant transaction costs. The transaction cost problem could therefore be mitigated by market consolidation driven by economies of scale. But this might also support an oligopoly of centrally controlled holding systems, which would hardly be the best way to support efficient and competitive digital capital markets, especially in terms of trading cost and the cost of using and accessing the new cross-border financial market utilities.[105] Of course, legal diversity within Europe could also be mitigated via a radical substantive harmonisation agenda.

A third conflict-of-laws solution would be to preserve the PRIMA approach as an alternative. As the market for security tokens evolves, investors are likely to access security tokens held in a variety of DLT infrastructures through "global crypto custodians" or other gateway services.[106] These arrangements could be facilitated by a modified PRIMA rule (contractual or factual) which would look at the place of the relevant *participant in the DLT system*. Such a conflict rule (which could be called PREPA) would support both market integration as well as competition and efficiency by allowing, just as the PRIMA rule, the investor to hold a portfolio of securities "in one account [or address] with one intermediary in one jurisdiction."[107] A rule of this kind would contribute to the shortening of custody chains as it would only cover direct participants of the holding systems.[108]Alongside this conflict rule, the above-discussed PROPA rule (or *elective*

---

103 *Paech*, Conflict of Laws and Relational Rights (fn. 83) p. 293; *FMLC* report (fn. 5), p. 15 – 16.
104 *FMLC* report (fn. 5); *Haentjens/de Graaf/Kokorin* (fn. 17), 27 (arguing "that the Hague Securities Convention approach is the most appropriate approach for proprietary claims of customers against their crypto-custodians.").
105 Indeed, crypto-economy is not alien to oligopolistic pressures. See *Avgouleas/Seretakis* in this issue. A recent article by Priem explains how investor segregation at CSD level affects settlement costs and inter-CSD competition. *Randy Priem* Asset Segregation at CSDs: Protecting Investors with a Level Playing Field. European Business Law Review 31.5 (2020).
106 Beyond security tokens, some wallet producers (custodians) already support multiple crypto-assets and DLT systems. See Pilot regime IA, p. 8.
107 *Gullifer/Payne* (fn. 75), p. 366.
108 Nowadays direct participation in national CSDs requires costly legal, technical and operational arrangements, which is why many intermediaries choose to access foreign CSDs indirectly,

situs) could apply to direct relationships between a participant (token holder or an intermediary acting on its behalf) and the DLT market infrastructure. This discussion is tangential to the bigger issue of market structure and intermediation, which will be briefly discussed in the next section.

4.2 Intermediated Access to DLT Market Infrastructures

The DLT Pilot Regime proposal is (perhaps deliberately) silent on intermediated access to the envisaged DLT market infrastructures. However, the proposal does indicate that the business plan of a DLT market infrastructure may involve safekeeping of clients' funds, such as security tokens, or the means of access to them *"including in the form of cryptographic keys"*.[109] Operators of a piloted DLT system could therefore act as custodians and administer the client's tokens on their behalf and even under their own name. Nothing in the Digital Finance Package indicates that participants or members of DLT market infrastructures could not perform such intermediary functions. The DLT Pilot is equally silent on use of omnibus accounts (or addresses) for pooling investor's tokens.[110] However, participants in DLT Settlement Systems could be exempted from the present obligation to offer their clients *both* omnibus client segregation *and* individual client segregation.[111] In other words, national authorities could grant a licence to a national CSD to operate a DLT Settlement System that does not offer omnibus segregation.

Such flexibility should be welcomed. DLT infrastructures need not ban intermediation or disqualify nominee or omnibus structures to mitigate the legal risks of intermediated securities or to increase the efficiency, reliability and transparency of their record-keeping.[112] Reconciliation, i.e., matching of internal records across the custody holding chain, is currently particularly time-consuming and

---

usually via global custodians or international CSDs. *Christopher Twemlow*, Why are Securities Held in Intermediated Form?, in: Gullifer/Payne (fn. 27), p. 94–95. See also *Mooney*, Beyond intermediation (fn. 25): "involving only one intermediary [a global custodian] would avoid the exacerbated custody-chain risk of holding through a chain of intermediaries across borders."

109 DLT Pilot regime proposal, p. 16–17. In public-private key cryptography the private key functions as an instrument of authentication and encryption, while the public key and the shorter public address are publicly known and used for identification.

110 It is not uncommon that crypto custodians pool their clients' cryptocurrencies on omnibus addresses. As *Haentjens/de Graaf/Kokorin* (fn. 17) show, this increases legal risks.

111 This obligation is currently laid down by article 38 of the CSD Regulation, which is among the exemptible rules listed under art. 5(2) of the DLT Pilot Regime proposal.

112 *Keijser/Mooney* (fn. 93), p. 321.

labour-intensive.[113] Successfully standardised and implemented, DLT could eliminate data discrepancies and facilitate quicker or near instantaneous reconciliation of information, shared throughout the network of market participants in a common format.[114] The possible use of omnibus addresses would nevertheless mean that part of the records might be kept in the intermediaries' own disparate systems. This underlines the continuing relevance of intermediated securities law.

Flexibility would also be needed if the DLT market infrastructures (and the legal frameworks underpinning them) were in the future to provide a credible alternative to present intermediated systems.[115] As already discussed, modern securities markets host a diversity of market participants with diverse needs (see section 3.3. above). In a similar vein, Mooney has observed that one of the main challenges of any future direct holding model is the need "to preserve the flexibility of existing intermediated systems that accommodate transactional patterns of financing, collateralization, and securities lending."[116] The proposal by Benjamin and Gullifer of a bifurcated system where intermediated securities would be replaced by depositary receipts deserves closer scrutiny, also in the context of tokenisation of securities.[117] Interestingly, at least one non-custodial liquidity solution for token lending is already functioning and quickly expanding in decentralised finance (DeFI) space.[118]

The real challenge lies in combining a regime based on investor choice with rules and incentives that help make direct holding ("end-investor segregation") an affordable and attractive alternative. Some countries such as Sweden have succeeded in this, while in other countries, such as the UK, direct holding has become prohibitively costly and unpopular despite being legally possible.[119]

---

113 As an ECB study explains: "Each entity involved in the processing of financial transactions currently keeps an independent central record of its clients' asset holdings and needs to reconcile this record with data kept in other centrally managed databases at different levels of the post trading value chain." *ECB* report (fn. 36 above), 8. See also *CPMI* 2017 (fn. 63), 13.

114 *CPMI* 2017 (fn. 61), 13.

115 The case for complete tokenisation of public equities in developed markets is far from straightforward. See *OECD* report (fn. 5), p. 29.

116 *Mooney*, Beyond intermediation (fn. 25), 401.

117 *Benjamin/Gullifer*, Stewardship and Collateral (fn. 28).

118 See the Aave open source DeFi protocol available at https://aave.com/, accessed 4 March 2021. Within the protocol, interest bearing tokens are minted upon deposit and burned when redeemed.

119 See *Gullifer/Payne* (fn. 28)

4.3 A Modest Proposal for Substantive Harmonisation

The DLT Pilot Regime Proposal seeks to ensure that clients of new DLT market infrastructures could retrieve their funds in the event of default, resolution or insolvency of the infrastructure provider. To achieve that goal, the proposal effectively replicates the EU's existing client asset regime.[120] Infrastructure providers are prevented from using client assets on their own account and without clients' express consent.[121] The operator (whether an investment firm or market operator or a CSD) should also maintain safe, accurate, reliable and retrievable records of client assets and segregate the assets from its own assets as well as from its other clients' assets. In addition, operators should ensure that assets are protected from hacking, theft and other unauthorised access.[122] The DLT pilot regime would also require that DLT market infrastructures preserve the integrity of security token issues and ensure effective asset segregation regardless of, and as a precondition for, any exemption from applicable law granted by national authorities (see section 2.2 above).[123]

Consistent with the existing regime, the proposed rules on client assets are purely operational and as such do not guarantee the effectiveness of investors' rights. Whether the investor qualifies as the "owner" of the asset in question depends on national provisions on property, insolvency and company law, none of which have been harmonised at EU level.[124] Introducing yet another regulatory framework for client asset segregation, the proposed regulation also adds to the general inconsistency and diversity of this area of EU financial services law.[125]

The operational approach is partly justifiable given the maturity of the market structure and the incomplete understanding of its drivers. Even if the necessary political consensus existed, EU-wide harmonisation, let alone comprehensive unification of substantive laws regarding security tokens, would be

---

120 The EU's existing financial services law ensures the availability and identifiability of client assets in such stress situations mainly through MiFID II (articles 16(8) and 16(9) and various sectoral legislations, which all require operational segregation of client securities and prohibit their use without clients' express consent. For a succinct review and discussion of existing EU legislation, see *Haentjens* (fn. 68), p. 272–277. See also *EPTF* report (fn. 20), p. 46–49.
121 Article 6(5) of the DLT Pilot Regime proposal (safekeeping including the safekeeping of "the means of access" to such assets, "including in the form of cryptographic keys").
122 Article 6(5)(2)-(4).
123 See Articles 4 (for DLT MTF) and 5 (for DLT Settlement Systems) of the DLT Pilot Regime proposal.
124 *Haentjens* (fn. 68 above).
125 *EPTF* report (fn. 20), p. 49.

premature. Such fundamental issues as the exact moment when legal title to security token passes or the moment when a transaction becomes final and irrevocable would be difficult to define at the current experimental stage.[126] Imperfect knowledge, however, does not preclude less interventionist measures exemplified by the *functional approach* of previous international and European securities law projects. The approach entailed drafting rules using language as neutral as possible and by reference to facts and results instead of legal notions and concepts.[127] The functional approach has so far served as an instrument to steer clear from conceptual and cultural disagreement, but it could also work as a more future-oriented harmonisation tool. For instance, using Article 22(8) of UCITS V[128] as a model, the DLT Pilot Regime could include the following simple rule:

> Member States shall ensure that in the event of insolvency of the operator of a DLT market infrastructure, the funds, collateral and DLT transferable securities of the members, participants, issuers or clients using the DLT market infrastructure are unavailable for distribution among, or realisation for the benefit of, creditors of the DLT market infrastructure.

Such a result-oriented rule would not address all insolvency-related risks (e. g., of possible intermediaries) let alone harmonise proprietary issues relating to legal transfer, priority, and security perfection. On the contrary, it would only address the most fundamental custody risk especially as regards novel holding systems operated by MiFID investment firms or market operators. In the functionalist spirit, however, it would accommodate a variety of national approaches and infrastructures with varying technical detail, leaving room for learning and incremental harmonisation in the future. The proposed rule would also be compat-

---

126 *Bank for International Settlements*, Distributed ledger technology in payment, clearing and settlement: An analytical framework, 2017, available at https://www.bis.org/cpmi/publ/d157.pdf accessed 4 March 2021 (noting that "fixing the point in time when the settlement can be considered as final will be very burdensome in a DLT environment as it might not be a clear moment in time". See also *CPMI* 2017 (fn. 61), p. 16. It should be noted that the DLT Pilot Regime would not require that the new DLT market infrastructures are notified as securities settlement systems under the Settlement Finality Directive.
127 *The UNIDROIT Study Group on Harmonised Substantive Rules Regarding Indirectly Held Securities*, Position Paper, UNIDROIT 2003 – Study LXXVIIII – Doc. 8, August 2003, p. 5 – 6, available at www.unidroit.org accessed 4 March 2021.
128 Directive 2014/91/EU of the European Parliament and of the Council of 23 July 2014 amending Directive 2009/65/EC on the coordination of laws, regulations and administrative provisions relating to undertakings for collective investment in transferable securities (UCITS) as regards depositary functions, remuneration policies and sanctions, p. 186 – 213.

ible with the client asset rules as currently included in the DLT Pilot Regime proposal.

The minimum harmonisation approach might also prompt beneficial forms of regulatory competition as transactions and holding systems gravitated to Member States with the most solid, flexible and predictable laws. Indeed, compatibility of legal systems does not necessarily require total substantive harmonisation; gentler approaches are available and diversity may even be instrumental for advancing objectives such as market integration.[129]

5 Conclusions

The Digital Finance Package will provide much needed legal certainty for markets in crypto assets. The innovative EU sandbox approach for DLT market infrastructures and security tokens also enables a degree of experimentalism, even within its somewhat confined and conservative scope. However, by disqualifying the use of permissionless DLT networks for issuing and holding security tokens, the EU relies heavily on CSDs and investment firms to develop their own proprietary platforms. A complete exclusion would also cast an inconvenient shadow of legal uncertainty on to STOs completed via public blockchains. Testament to the fast evolutionary pace of the new digital marketplace, the Digital Finance Package hardly recognises predominant trends within Decentralised Finance space.[130]

This article has aimed to show that the evolution of DLT systems has not outdated the fundamental objectives of securities law harmonisation, i.e., ensuring effective protection of investor rights, preserving the integrity of the holding system, and ensuring mutual compatibility of legal systems.[131] Failing to act would risk magnifying the unresolved legal risks of intermediated securities and further fragmenting the private law underpinnings of EU capital markets. As a first step, the EU should exploit the opportunity to adopt a common approach, at least to protect security token holders in the insolvency of a DLT market infrastructure provider (or a participant). However, a functional minimum harmonisation approach would not work for conflict-of-laws rules where uniformity and predicta-

---

129 For an excellent discussion on alternative convergence strategies in the context of secured credit laws, see *Teemu Juutilainen*, Secured credit in Europe: from conflicts to compatibility, 2018.

130 *Emilios Avgouleas/Aggelos Kiayias*, "The Architecture of Decentralised Finance Platforms: A New Open Finance Paradigm", Edinburgh School of Law Research Paper No. 2020/16, available at: http://dx.doi.org/10.2139/ssrn.3666029 accessed 4 March 2021.

131 *Thévenoz* (fn. 80), intro, p. 17.

bility are needed. To choose the right rule, policy-makers must assess various trade-offs in terms of legal certainty, market integration, competition, and efficiency. To support market integration and internationalisation, the article suggested maintaining a PRIMA-type of rule as an alternative.

Going further, DLT-powered securities holding systems are likely to offer wider participation rights and more convenient (and hopefully cheaper) investor segregation for all market participants, retail and institutional alike. Nevertheless, the intermediated securities holding system continues to offer benefits – with respect, e. g., to legal risk management, securities financing, diversification and portfolio collateralisation – which will be hard to replicate in a pure direct holding system. In developing a legal framework for holding systems that integrate investor choice and flexibility with end-investor transparency, useful lessons could be drawn from the mixed holding systems currently hosted by the Nordic countries.